Living Out Loud

TOYAH WILLCOX

Living Out Loud

Hodder & Stoughton
LONDON SYDNEY AUCKLAND

To Mum and Dad and Robert
I love you very much.

First published in Great Britain in 2000
This paperback edition first published 2001

10 9 8 7 6 5 4 3 2 1

British Library Cataloguing in Publication Data
A record for this book is available from the British Library

ISBN 0 340 74631 9

Typeset by Avon Dataset Ltd, Bidford-on-Avon, Warks

Printed and bound in Great Britain by
Clays Ltd, St Ives plc

Hodder and Stoughton
A division of Hodder Headline Ltd
338 Euston Road
London NW1 3BH

Chapter 1

My great, great, great, great grandfather was hanged in Lincoln prison for forgery. He was a lawyer. Well, that's what my father told me and what his father in turn had told him. And I rather like to believe it. When my father Beric was nine years old his father, a wealthy Lancashire construction engineer who died before I was born, walked Dad up the steep steps of Lincoln Castle to the final resting place of all those hanged within the prison walls. There, beneath a shady tree, stood a plain gravestone marked 'J. W.' (John Willcox, a lawyer with light fingers).

On a cold October day in 1998, while on tour in *The Live Bed Show* with Joe McGann, I climbed those very steps to find my ancestral blood. Dialling my father on the mobile, I told him I was standing where he had stood seventy years before. In the bitter autumn wind I traced his every step, in and out of the gravestones dodging the many tourists, telling my father every detail and reliving his childhood steps with him, and at the end of this exhilarating phone conversation my father said that Grandpa had been pulling his leg. Thus lie bare the bones of my relationship with my father and the world.

We both fully realised that the bigger the lie, the further the adventure of life spread. The story of my wayward ancestor *is* true. My father, in a desperate attempt to get me off the phone, lied himself because he wanted to get back to the telly and watch *Ironside*.

But there is further truth in my grandfather's story. We are all forgers and we are all selective in what we believe. My father could have conned me into climbing Mount Everest in search of a good story only to find it was yet another of his jests, and I would still love and believe him as I always have.

My forgery comes out of my mouth too. I spent the first twenty years of my life committing verbal forgery, because the truth was too tedious, the next ten clearing up the mess of those lies, and then my thirties sifting and searching for my truth. The odd thing is, the truth I found wasn't that far from the lies. In most cases.

At the excruciatingly young age of five I was already desperate for independence, especially from the pink, cuddly, ever-so-nice little girls I had to spend desperately tedious schooldays with. In my desire for an adrenalin rush I told a boggle-eyed classmate that my mother was a dolphin and I had spent my first year in the sea. This really impressed Little Miss Pink, and I was the centre of attention – until she told the teacher. Then I was the centre of attention for all the wrong reasons. Well, at least I experienced how to make an audience laugh at such a numerically tender age.

My very earliest memories are both bizarre and exceptionally ordinary. Silly little things, such as the way as soon as my mother placed me in the crib my sinuses would block up. Then came layer upon layer of bedding and I was close to suffocating. So I started the tactic of crying as soon as I saw that crib and I'd cry till I could hear *Bootsie and Snudge* start on the TV downstairs. So that was a good four hours of vocal exercise.

The safety pins back then seemed to be enormous. As I lay on my back, my mother changing my nappy, tickling my round hard tummy, powdering my nether regions and smiling brightly in my face, she wrapped my lower half in this huge towelling triangle – and then came the giant safety pin. Sharp and glinting and big enough to secure ten nappies at any one time. It was at this moment that I'd smile and push and push and push, till I was red in the face and there was a kaleidoscope effect dancing before my eyes and Mum would know I had poo-pooed. Now that made me laugh. I wonder if Mum boiled my nappies in the same aluminium pan that she cooked the hams in. I will have to ask her that.

My mother was a good mother. I was a bad child. Mum never gave me much information about herself, other than that when she was a child, she was so light she didn't leave footprints in the snow. (This was said rather pointedly towards the fact that I was a podgy child at the time.) For the first forty years of my life (and let's face it I hope there will be another forty) I thought my mother was an orphan. Full stop! No history! It was taboo even to mention her past. Then on 20 December 1998 I told her over the phone I was to dine out that night with Helen David of English Eccentrics at Cliveden. Mum said, 'Oh, how lovely. My father was the ground-keeper at Cliveden. We lived opposite the entrance, and my brother and I used to play in the gardens.'

Why had it taken forty years to receive this precious moment? I had known as a child that her mother had been a dresser at Pinewood for Jessie Matthews. My mother, whose maiden name was Barbara Joy Rollinson, went to stage school at twelve and by fourteen was a professional dancer. Her stage name was Joy Courtland and she danced with a troupe of six girls who went under various names, from the Six Junior Misses to the Rhapsody Girls in 1947. When my father met her she was seventeen and already orphaned. We think her parents were hit by a car after going to see her on stage in Weston-super-Mare. No more was ever said. But I always imagined that my mother visited some secret hell in her sleep. All through my childhood nights at the family home my mother would scream in her sleep – not screams of passion, but more like a desperate anxiety, which would take me years to work out of my own character. I inherited two things from Mum, a quick-fire temper and enough anxiety to keep my bed-sheets in sweat for a lifetime.

My father was born into a wealthy family in Kings Heath, Birmingham. Beric was the youngest of seven. By the time he arrived, Grandma – again whom I never knew – had already had two children who had died, as a result of TB and appendicitis. And Dad had a brother who unfortunately, during a piggy-back ride, hit his head on the mantle of the pigsty and within days passed away from septicaemia. Beric shared his bedroom with sister Olive who was considerably older than him. Olive had TB. My father desperately loved and looked up to her. Olive was fourteen when she died. In a desperate attempt to save her, the family moved briefly to a house with a veranda, so that Olive could sleep in the open air, believing this would cure her. You'd have thought her death would have made Dad an angry child, but he always – still – has a knack of talking about the dead as if they are in the room with him, breathing next to him, but invisible. Dad had two sisters left, Mary and Marge.

My grandpa built the family home when Beric was three. Grandpa built most of Kings Heath. Each remaining child was given not one but at least three houses to live in or manage as landlord. In 1920, when Dad was born, Kings Heath was mostly country. Our home – I say 'our' because three generations lived in it – was a grand, free-standing family house surrounded by fields. Grandpa built the front porch out of reclaimed stained glass from the rubble of the demolished Lincoln Cathedral, and the Jacobean staircase in the hall was from Lady Godiva's house in Banbury. So the house was a storyteller in itself and full of character and colour.

At nineteen, my father joyfully went off to war. My poor grandmother must have been devastated. He was aboard a ship that travelled down the west coast of Africa, past Marrakesh, Agadir, the Ivory Coast, round the Cape of Good Hope and back up the east coast and stationed itself in the Red Sea, cushioned between Egypt and Israel and Saudi Arabia. By all accounts my father had a ripe old time. As part of my sex education in my teens he recounted stories of prostitutes whose vaginal muscles were so strong they'd keep a vice-like grip upon your tender parts until money had been exchanged. When the ship docked after exercises and patrols, the sailors were set free for the night, and they'd all have their fill of the local women – leaving Dad on watch back at the ship. My father claimed that at this point in his life he feared women; he probably feared what could be caught off 'women of the night' more. The sailors would return to ship, blind drunk, all strip off and fight totally naked till only one man was left standing. Dad being a studious man, would try to work at his desk, and would occasionally get accidentally punched by a wayward fist. The fight would stop, the offender would apologise and then the fisticuffs could resume in good faith. Apart from sex and punch-ups, my father also did his bit for the war effort.

The war over, when my father, who was twenty-six and hadn't seen his family for six years, walked up the street to his house, Grandma thought she was seeing his ghost.

The war taught Dad how to live. He could fly; he owned a Tiger Moth. Unfortunately he couldn't navigate, but road signs were quite readable ten feet above the ground. He had fast cars – they did at least 60 m.p.h., although they were a little shaky at that velocity. And by the time he saw my mother for the first time on stage in Weston-super-Mare, he was already engaged to five women and on a dirty weekend with one of them. Then, it was love at first sight. To meet my mother, he had to write to her chaperon and request permission to have tea with her. This took six months, by which time my father had followed Mum's touring show around the country. At the tea, Dad was lost for words; Mum was by far the most beautiful woman he'd ever met. They married when she was nineteen. The matron of honour was Nan Kenway, and the best man Douglas Young – the pianist-and-comedian duo known as Kenway and Young. The honeymoon was in Weston-super-Mare, as Mum was still appearing on stage. She was part of a dance troupe who supported Max Wall and Flanagan and Allen. On one occasion during the honeymoon, the chaperon (now promoted to dresser), who was in fact my mother's aunt, got so drunk with my father that they forgot to see the show and crashed in legless for the finale. My mother didn't talk to them for days.

Mum, Barbara, left the stage. My grandpa gave my parents a temporary house in Kings Heath, before they moved into the family abode. Within nine months and seven days, my sister Nicola was born, on Wednesday 12 July 1950.

By all accounts Mum found married life frustrating. When she cooked her first leg of lamb for my father's supper, it got so burnt that Dad couldn't help laughing. Mum skewered it and threw it through the window (it wasn't open at the time).

My brother Kim was born three years after my sister, and another five years later, on Sunday 18th May 1958, while preparing Sunday lunch, Mum went into labour again. She called the midwife, went upstairs, gave birth to me and was down again in a few hours. Dad was so overjoyed he ran into the garden and hung a rubber sheet on the washing line to tell the angels and the neighbours that I had arrived safely. Unlike my brother, I didn't resemble a young gorilla when I was born, but my spine was twisted, my feet were clawed and my left side was underdeveloped. I was put straight into a plaster cast, which held me rigid for the first six months of my life.

Having read the name 'Toyah' in a book about ballerinas, my

mother decided that this was the name for me. Barbara's taste was always exotic and one step ahead of fashions. My sister, Nicola, and my brother, Kim, both had unusual names for the time, but when my father added 'Pepita Boodelle' to the 'Toyah', the Registrar of Births said no. My birth name had to be predominantly British – so it was Toyah Ann Willcox who officially existed as of 30 May 1958. I was entry number 34 for the month; evidently not much sex happened in Birmingham in those days. Perhaps August '57 was just too hot for nookie.

One coincidence about my name that my mother denies any knowledge of – and it's highly unlikely she could have found this out from any average map of America, she'd have needed the US equivalent of an Ordnance Survey map – is that Toyah was the name of a Red Indian tribe in Arizona, Toyah meaning 'water sustainer of life'. The tribe had their own lake, called Toyah. Toyah Lake stood in the shadow of the Willcox mountain. The sheriff of Willcox wrote to me in 1983 to say I was welcome any time; now fans on their treks across the USA kindly have their postcards stamped by the Toyah postmistress and then the Willcox postmistress, side by side, before they post me their holiday memories.

The first four years of my life were blissful – that's probably why I have so little memory of them. I lived under my mother's skirts, naïve, unaware, and with no conceptual thoughts of the future at all. Conversations about school would pop up and I thought my parents were talking about something that happened to others or, if this bizarre 'happening' was going to happen to me, it would only be for one day.

My father ran three factories in the Birmingham area, as a construction engineer, that supplied wood and contracted out workmen. He was away most of the day and on his return I would wrap myself around his leg like a koala bear and he would carry me around the house, until I fell off, bored or exhausted. I spent my days watching Mum cook, dipping my fingers in jars of Virol or bowls of cake mixture. We got on. I did fear her temper. Mum had a short fuse. Motherhood had taken her independence away. In my earliest memories, she didn't seem to get on with my sister Nicola, who was headstrong and inseparable from Aunt Mary. So every summer we used to drop Nicola at Birmingham station and she would go off and spend long happy holidays helping Mary run her guesthouse in Penzance.

Fear has left me with vivid memories. Yes, I was a happy child, but my soul was sleeping and every now and then it would give a kick as it stirred inside me, trying to awake from a deep slumber. It was music that disturbed its rest; it was as if musical notes were the code to revive it from centuries of sleep. As soon as I heard the theme music from *Fireball XL5*, a popular children's TV puppet show, I was thrown into a state of high anxiety and I would be haunted by memories of dinosaurs and monsters for the rest of the night. My crib had pink and blue bunny transfers on either side and these would distort into fearsome ghouls as I lay in the semi-darkness.

But the real problem started later, with the *Dr Who* theme music. *Dr Who* scared me witless. My brother and I would hide behind the sofa every Saturday afternoon. The theme music also played on the radio regularly and triggered an image I could not understand which deeply disturbed me, so much so that just hearing the music had me in uncontrollable tears. The image was sophisticated, bearing in mind that I had not mastered a sentence yet, but what I felt was an archetypal fear of losing life and loved ones. As soon as the intro started, I was standing as a child with Mum, Dad, Kim and Nicola in front of two large green arched doors; there were other families behind us and others had gone through the doors before us. The green doors opened and a smell of boiled meat exuded. A hand came out, thick and muscled and covered in blood, and it took my father, and this is where the fear and panic started. Inside were many butcher's blocks; we were to be dismembered and disembowelled for food. At this point the image became positively psychedelic as my consciousness transferred to my kidneys which were being prepared for consumption. After the music on the radio had finished, I would be transfixed in a state of anxiety for hours, and my confused mother couldn't do anything to get me out of it.

I did eventually manage to tell my mother of this; it really, really upset her. Barbara has an impassioned fear of what happened to the Jews in the concentration camps, so much so that when my sister started to study Hebrew in order to convert to Judaism, to marry a fine man who escaped Germany with his family at the age of four, my mother exclaimed, 'You'll be persecuted for the rest of your life!'

I think that as I formed in my mother's belly, taking nutrients from her flesh, I also sipped at her fears. Barbara told the midwife at my birth that I was different, but as the years progressed and my behaviour became more erratic, she started to deny I was her daughter at all. I think it would be true to say that Mum found me so weird she was frightened of me. Sadly child psychiatry wasn't in common practice then. My mind has always been hyperactive and visual images had the power to possess me. I have never been good with intrusive and invasive images. Today I have learned never to watch certain films or TV programmes. Certain scenes, once I have seen them, never leave my mind – scenes of violence and abuse, and especially some from horror films. I love to watch these films in the main, but I couldn't even sit through the titles of some of them – like *The Exorcist* or *The Haunting* or any old '50s black and white horror movie.

As I grew, language freed me; I attacked it with gusto, I burbled, blurted and chewed upon it. Sadly, the language I knew didn't relate to the language of those around me, and my efforts at self-expression were all too often met with laughter and ridicule, as I was a proper mini Miss Malaprop. Then there was all that infuriating condescension: 'No, you don't pronounce the *k* in knock or knit' and 'No, you don't say "I won't" or "You liar", you say "I cannot" or "You fibber" ' and the real insult to any free spirit – 'No, you don't mean that, that's not what you mean, so don't say it.' I developed an intolerance to negativity at a very early age. As soon as I started talking and discovered this free-form gift of self-expression, which filled me with complete joy and released me as an individual into the outside world, people were immediately using it as a means to change me. My defences went up, and if the expression 'f*** you' had been common among three-year-olds in the 1960s I would have been the first to adopt it.

Language gave me access to The Lie. I loved to lie; it was supremely creative and it empowered me and gave me revenge. It seemed the bigger the lie, the more I got away with. When Mum and I went to tea with a friend of hers, and the friend said to me, 'Why are you late?' I innocently replied, out of Mum's earshot, 'Because Dad tried to murder Mum,' which put a whole new slant on what would otherwise have been a very boring afternoon. My lies made me grow in stature and left me with an exquisite guilt.

I was a happy child. I laughed a lot and if I couldn't find anything else to make me laugh, then I myself and a mirror would do – I could amuse myself for hours by pulling faces. Or, equally amusing, I could play sitting on Mum's lap and farting, then running away. Once she'd cooled down, the fun was in persuading her to let me sit on her lap again. I'd always win. Then I'd repeat the offence.

Christmases were magical. The tree, laden with decorations, smelt divine. I would sit under it for hours, hidden, looking out across the lounge as if I was in Narnia. Mum and Dad would creep around the house at 2 a.m. on Christmas morning hanging our stockings. After they'd returned to bed, I'd creep into my brother's bed and we'd play with our new toys and eat all the creme-filled bears we could find stuffed into the toes of Dad's old socks. I had no concept of the outside world. And then I started school. Mum said my laughter stopped, dead.

Chapter 2

I wasn't aware I had any disability until I went to school. OK, up till then people had laughed at what I said, but now they laughed at how I sounded. I was not aware of how bad my speech impediment was and certainly not aware of my limp, but other children were.

Edgbaston Church of England College for Girls consisted of two Georgian mansions, one for brats aged four and a half to six and the other for the big girls. As Mum's cyclamen-pink Triumph convertible with fake-leopardskin seats drove me to the front door, I thought we were just visiting. It didn't occur to me that I was going it alone inside this bedlam for fourteen years.

The front door was green, just like my recurring vision of Belsen, which really didn't help. Mum escorted me in with a fixed, 'I really am happy about this' look on her face that exuded doubt and fear and disturbed me. Inside, to the left of that green door was a cube-shaped room full of coat hangers and compartments for shoes. It was also full of noisy little girls all dressed in brown. 'Look, Mummy, we're all dressed the same,' I exclaimed. Mum pretended this was the best thing in the world and my suspicion grew. Looking round fervently I tried to grasp something familiar, something to understand, but it was overwhelming. Everyone seemed to be frenetically buzzing and clucking with a noisy happiness that felt fake and that I just didn't feel a part of. A girl walked up to Mum and me. She was big, at least ten years old, with a huge smile on her face, and she tried to take me from my mother – and worst of all my mother let her. All my animal instincts kicked in at once. The tears were uncontrollable. I cried and cried and clawed at my mother, gripped by incredible fear of her leaving, and leaving me with all these people who were telling me this is what I wanted. To hell with them all.

Eventually, exhausted, I calmed down and my mother left me with the giant ten-year-old, who did a brilliant job of surrogacy, and I ventured into Miss Lucas's class.

The rooms of this school were big, grand, antique; they had once known prosperity – grand balls, the élite. Now it catered for the private education of MPs', vicars', lawyers' and structural engineers' daughters. In a room chock-a-block with tiny desks and tables we sat respectfully and listened to an austere Miss Lucas – well, the others sat respectfully; I was just rigid with fear. The room smelt of boiled meat and cabbage, or was it the child next to me?

For the rest of the day we were lulled into a false sense of hope that our remaining days in this institution were going to be filled with play, painting, music and laughter. All day I kept running to the window, thinking Mum would be outside; I really missed her. The only respite from the gloom was a brief visit to the toilets in the basement. White-tiled and smelling of excrement and bleach, they offered no privacy: once you sat on a wet wooden seat, the saloon-style doors only shaded your face from embarrassment and exposed your private parts to the two boys in kindergarten, Robert and John. This pair were already showing a keen interest in voyeurism: every time you tried to pee with dignity, they would stick their heads under the door and blatantly have a good look. At 4 p.m., Mum's pink Triumph pulling up to the front door was akin to the arrival of a chariot full of angels. Full of joy at this conclusion to the day, I thanked everyone, said how nice it had been to meet them and that I hoped we'd meet again one day, then I got the hell out of there. Mother wanted to know all about the day, and whether I'd made any friends, which I thought was irrelevant, as I was simply happy that school was over and I could now get on with my life. 'But you go back tomorrow!' Mum said. I experienced for the first time that sinking feeling – one minute your heart is in your chest and the next it has sunk so low it is exploring Australia. We sat in silence for the rest of the journey home.

Robert and John were great fun. They liked guns. We'd take it

11

in turns secretly to shoot certain members of the class. Miss Lucas got shot every hour and I wasn't the slightest bit disturbed. When John, at the age of four and a half, told me his fantasy was to be pooed on, the only reason I didn't oblige was because I'd taken to not going to the toilet at all while at school, so that by the time Mum came to fetch me home I would be bulging out all over and very, very constipated.

At this stage in my life a strange, persistent game of push me, pull you was going on between me and the adult world. I hated being a girl. I was being forced to be a girl. Not a real girl, but one who must do ballet, point her toes, wear pink, smile, be demure, have perfect diction and clean underpants, and above all hold her knife and fork the middle-class way, grasped firmly in the palms of one's hands, not resting in the crook of thumb and forefinger. Oh no, that was far too common for a nice girl. Really, where does society get these opinions from?

When I was asked what I would like to do when I grew up, top of my list was to be a muscleman, then an astronaut, and if that all failed I'd settle for being a nun, as long as I could still get into fights like Joan of Arc. As a child I loved religion; it was both glorious and rebellious. It was never pompous – how could it be; outlining every miracle was a war of one type or another. Joan of Arc was my true heroine.

The ideals of being feminine passed me by. No one seemed to realise that having a club foot, with claws for toes, and one leg two inches longer than the other didn't make you feel feminine. Didn't make you feel human. My mother would have to buy me two pairs of shoes at any one time. First we'd get a large size to accommodate my right foot, which not only was large, wide – well round, actually – but also had an index toe that was the length of a finger. Comical or what? This would be followed by a smaller pair of shoes to fit my perfectly pretty left foot. On one occasion the sales assistant shuddered when she saw my right foot. She turned to Mum and said, 'Well, that will have to go, won't it.' Mum said, 'Yes, they'll cut it all off when she's older.'

Then we would have to take the shoes along with us to the Orthopaedic Hospital on Broad Street in Birmingham, where twice a year I was measured and examined for growth abnormalities. This would take a whole day. My left shoe would be built up to make my left leg the same length as my right. Then there would be a quick course in physiotherapy, which was mainly to teach my mum how to minister to my physical needs every day. I really enjoyed this part. The physiotherapists had so much light and spirit. They exuded a zest for life that was infectious and they genuinely loved the challenge of dealing with and healing me. It also made the task that followed for Mum much easier, because every night when she started physio on me we both suddenly engaged in the memory of the nurses' inner light.

The exercises had me in fits and giggles. All I had to do was to use my feet as hands. I painted pictures. These weren't conceptual masterpieces, but, by God, it was more fun than using my hands. I could tie complex knots and bows with pieces of rope using my feet. The trickier bit was to do with my posture and walk. My spine was still deeply bowed, but not enough to warrant more time in plaster. I was to straighten it myself, using my own discipline and movement skill. In retrospect, this technique was very basic, but all that was needed was for my awareness to be in my spine, so that I could physically hold it straight. So every minute of the day that my concentration lapsed, Mum would remind me to straighten up and I would use my abdominal muscles to pull my pelvis straight and walk as if a piece of string were attached to my head and it was pulling me skyward. It took a few years, but eventually we got there and I could walk normally, apart from a small limp which I soon learned to disguise if it attracted attention, either from adults constantly asking 'Have you hurt yourself?', or from the steely eyes of the bullies, who used any defect they could find to tease you about. 'Hop-along' was my first school nickname.

To begin with, I found learning a joy, but I never grasped it as a means to an end. I thought it was all play. Our first attempt at maths was to use small rectangular wooden blocks of different sizes and colours, each block representing a number. With these we would do basic additions. This was not a problem, even though I was more interested in how the blocks were made than in what they represented, but it really frustrated me that once I grasped a concept we moved on, so I never arrived, and eventually the boat of learning left me so far behind that all I could see of it was a speck on the horizon.

I was a strange paradox of hero and wimp. In the school playground there were three parallel climbing bars, about four feet off the ground, used for gym lessons. These beckoned to me. They were so high, towering above my head, they were to me the high wire in the Big Top, the trapeze, a rope across the Niagara Falls. I used to draw breath from an assembled crowd of five-year-olds as I walked across the bars and back again, fearless. Then one day, attempting this after a burst of rain, I slipped and landed on the rocky ground, face first, putting my front teeth through my upper lip. There was so much blood. Robert and John wanted to play with my wound, the girls ran away. The teachers brought a bowl to catch my blood; why they did still baffles me today – perhaps they wanted to make black pudding out of it. I was allowed the rest of the day off. What a perfect day.

In infants we used to have Friday afternoons off. Sometimes Dad would come to get me, wearing his huge camel coat, and we'd go off to a transport café in Kings Heath and eat ice-cream. I always had strawberry, vanilla and chocolate in huge bricks, while around us sat truckers, tucking into mounds of bacon, ham and chips. Then we'd trundle off to Cannon Hill Park to feed the ducks. Those afternoons were heaven. If I really stretched my right arm up high, I could just about hold his hand.

My father has a powerful spirituality and he too is a myriad of contradictions. He is an old soul capable of talking knowledgeably about Buddhism, Hinduism and Christianity, but at the same time he exudes a childlike fear of death. It's not that he believes in death as an end, he's more like a child who doesn't want to give up his favourite toy and move on. For all his trials and tribulations, Beric loves life.

Once, walking alone across a field at night, the sky bright with stars and the dark made iridescent by the moonlight, my father and I stopped to look at the Milky Way. I was about four and a half. Dad said, 'They are millions of miles away and uncountable; the stars go on for ever – they are infinite – and we are just a speck of dust in comparison. They are eternal and we are not.' The realisation of what he was saying was an icy shock that grasped my body like two enormous hands, as if to shake my soul awake. My heart sped up and adrenalin flowed into my system. My body experienced its first fight-or-flight response, as the notion of death entered my consciousness and my inner being opened up wide, and the fact that time is a very short gift in this world was brought to my knowledge. God protect those who waste mine, I thought, at the age of four and a half. I knew that no matter how long I had to live, until I was five or until I was 105, there wouldn't be enough time. I'd always want more. I spent the rest of the evening in a state that made me keep to myself; those around me put it down to moodiness, but fear makes you think about the future. If you can do it in a positive and constructive way, that can be one step towards making your future work for you.

In the corner of the classroom stood a Wendy House. All the girls used to gather inside, while John, Robert and I entertained ourselves with wax crayons outside. There was a pecking order in this Wendy House which was run by a pair of spiteful spoilt brats called Sarah and Nicola. They would call me in and I'd enter through the door to a conspiratorial silence. Nicola would have removed one of her shoelaces, they'd get me to sit down and Nicola would proceed to strangle me with the lace, first till I went blue and then till I cried, which filled the whole Wendy House with laughter. This became a regular occurrence until I discovered it wasn't actually normal behaviour, but the only way to stop it was to move up a year and eventually to a classroom that didn't have a damned Wendy House.

The idea that a human being could hurt another either physically or emotionally hadn't reached me yet, so I suffered this act with good grace, assuming that it was for a very good reason. Given a few more years, I would have decked Sarah and Nicola and used their plaits for shoelaces.

Whether for psychological reasons or because the food at school was terrible, or simply because I'd put my fingers in my mouth after touching either Robert or John, I used to suffer the most appalling stomach upsets at school. The teachers could see it happening, for me the room would start spinning, and this was the cue to call Mum to pick me up, *quick*, because they'd have about ten minutes before the classroom would be sprayed with the contents of my stomach. Mum would arrive with a bucket ready in the car and I'd vomit all the way home. And here's the mystery. I'd be put to bed, and the doctor called, on a Friday and I wouldn't come round till Monday. So, darn it, I'd miss a whole weekend.

These upsets were common because I developed severe anaemia. Not even the thick green liquid from the doctor, three times a day, and a home diet of spinach and Mackeson ale could get my red cells up. I enjoyed the Mackeson, though. My teeth were rotting in my gums from the sweet, iron-rich medication. The anaemia caused boils so painful it felt as if nails were being driven into my flesh. Up my nose, on my bum, on my legs. The family would gather round and just stare at them in awe. By far the worst was one on the right knee. It crippled me. My knee was the size of a football. Mother, fearing I could lose my leg, because the boil was in the knee joint, one evening boiled up bread poultices and, with the family gathered round like a team of seventeenth-century physicians, she took a vegetable knife from the drawer, held it in a flame and stabbed my knee. You couldn't tell which was bread, which was pus. But my knee was saved.

Another reason for my mother's fear was that on many occasions my surgeon said, in passing, that my leg could always be removed from below the knee. Not only would this eliminate the problem of my foot, but it would then not be necessary for me to undergo constructive surgery on my hips when I'd stopped growing. Mum and I, never knowing if this was idle conversation or a threat designed to make us conspire with other solutions, became furiously protective of all my extremities, just in case the NHS went for the cheap option and my right leg was for the chop.

By my second year at school, Robert and John had left for grammar school and I was on my own with all these girls. I never felt so alone. I so missed John's bottle-bottom glasses and smutty demeanour and Robert's swashbuckling style, rather like a five-year-old Hugh Hefner. Instead I was left behind to be educated in a prefab, post-war classroom which was about as exciting as looking at a Janet and John book on a rainy day with your index finger firmly lodged up your left nostril. But what were desks for, other than to rehouse those enormous bogeys one used to get at that age?

Miss Nelson was short, squat and rather like a troll I had on

16

top of my wardrobe at home. Her hair was so tightly permed it looked frigid and virginal, and when she announced she was engaged to be married, even her class of six-year-olds gasped in amazement. But she was a saint and my saviour. Miss Nelson used to observe me staring blankly at my Janet and John book – required reading in 1964, by order of an education authority council who obviously hated children. Janet and John was to reading what Chairman Mao was to free thought. Two boring children who did absolutely F.A. But that was not the root of my problem. My problem was that I just could not see words in a sentence. What I could see, very clearly, were strips of pattern that offered me no logic of communication from the page. But Miss Nelson looked upon me kindly, and out of school hours she ordered special books, talked to my parents and calmly led me away from the frustrations of being dyslexic.

Dyslexia, while being extremely frustrating during formal education, is also a gift. It gives you a different sense of yourself, of time, of reality. It gives you perceptions that intellectuals would die for. Dyslexics can absorb abstract and complex patterns. Our memories are frighteningly detailed and encyclopaedic. While people are always thinking you are thick, dyslexia is in fact giving you a head start. Their greatest mistake is to underestimate a child with dyslexia, and not to realise that maths and music offer infinite possibilities of pattern, shape and expression, and it's all there in 3D in our minds. Thirty-five years ago the education system didn't realise this, or if they did they were keeping it secret.

Miss Nelson presented me with books that had Greek-style characters in the lettering, joined-up letters, some back to front, and I could read it immediately. This presented a problem: would I require this type of lettering all through my education? It seemed I was to be given only twelve months to be cured of dyslexia. The school hoped that these special books would guide me out of the darkness of illiteracy and into the light of normal perceptions. It doesn't work that way. Once born dyslexic, you stay dyslexic. But you learn to trick people into thinking you are normal. You learn to recognise words for their patterns, never really understanding their spelling or form, but you can convince those around you that there is no problem and that takes time. Unfortunately, I had Miss Nelson's guidance for only twelve months – and an even bigger misfortune was that the Dyslexic Society printed Janet and John books in phonetic form.

My sister joined my school, the C. of E., around this time, in the mid-sixties. It was a time of the Beatles dominating the music scene, TV and radio. Britain was waking up, throwing off the fifties, fashion was becoming youth-orientated and ready to wear, people's daily diet was becoming more adventurous and a man was about to walk on the moon.

Unbeknownst to me, my sister was being stalked. This isn't something your parents tell you. The headlines of the day were often about child abduction, social abuse, murder and bringing back hanging. My sister, Nicola, had reported a man in a red sports car, an MG, who kerb-crawled past her as she walked home from school. He would try to encourage her into the car. For some time the police followed my sister in the hope of catching this man. I don't know if they ever did. But one evening after school, I had to wait for my sister in the big girls' section of the school, while she finished a drama class after hours. I waited and waited. Finally, after two hours, my sister emerged. I was desperate for the toilet, but was still refusing to go while at school. We caught the bus in Birmingham's rush hour, it was a slow journey home and just as the bus topped the hill at the bottom of our road, I couldn't wait any longer and I wet myself. It wouldn't have been so bad if I had been sitting next to Nicola, but I was next to a little old lady who just stared at me in disbelief. As we got off the bus my sister tried to pretend she had no connection with me, but we stepped off to a commotion of police cars and a very worried father. Our parents, thinking we'd been abducted, had called the police who had started an immediate search. Mum was at the police station. This gave my sister and father a chance to get me home and put me in the bath fully clothed – and to dispose of all evidence that I had disgraced the Willcox family on a Birmingham City Council bus.

The bullying stopped while I was in Miss Nelson's class. I excelled in maths, art and English. The system wasn't going to allow me to write in the style of alphabet I could read, so I was pulled in two directions: while in reading I was ahead of my class, in writing I'd revert to prehistoric status, having to trace on tracing paper whole pages of 'proper' writing. The only

18

effect this had on me was a desire for individuality, so that once free of rigid mimicry I created my own phonetic writing style.

I was taken completely by surprise one day, when I was led down one of the many underlit plain beige corridors to a room I'd never seen before. The school had many secret rooms. Waiting inside was an extraordinary-looking woman. Foot-high bouffant hair, blonde, pink two-piece suit. She looked exactly like Lady Penelope in *Thunderbirds*. Next to her was a reel-to-reel tape recorder. I'd never seen one of these and my eyes examined it hungrily, I so wanted to play with it and press its over-large, self-important buttons.

This was to be the first of many elocution lessons. It started with wonderful tongue exercises, as if I was a cow chewing the cud, exercises that particularly suited my physicality – it hadn't escaped me that my tongue was by far the longest in the class. These were followed by exercises in how to contain my tongue in my mouth. It appeared to me that it must have spent a lot of time 'hanging out'. Slowly it dawned that I must have been perceived as a dribbling moron by my fellow human beings, rather like Quasimodo's distant cousin. Miss Lady Penelope used to tape-record my speech and play it back to me, with little impact on me at all. I was slightly disappointed that I sounded so girlie, but that was about it.

'You have a lisp, Toyah,' she said. I had absolutely no idea what she meant. I could understand what I was saying, and that was all that mattered to me. 'Your tongue is too long and the roof of your mouth is too high. You cannot form your words properly.' Miss Lady Penelope used to wear long knotted beads that caught the only available light in the room, and as she tried to convey the terrible importance of speech to me, those beads dangled in her tea. I used to get so thirsty, I'd just want to hoick them out and suck them. Why, as children, were we never given water between meals?

Miss Lady Penelope's method of teaching was almost Dickensian. She was surrounded by mirrors, large printed letters, pictures of animals known for the sounds that they make, and all of this was there in the hope that my tongue would achieve a purchase on my teeth rather than somewhere, some-what sibilantly, in between. It was known as multi-sensory teaching. I'd sit in front of a mirror, with little printed letter cards placed before me, which helped me to recognise letters, but mainly it was an exercise in feeling and seeing sound. I became aware of my face, my tongue and the co-ordination of both.

I used to leave her room chewing on syllables and spitting out nouns, so that all the saliva that used to end up on my regulation school shirt now firmly found its place in other people's faces. For years I had to exaggerate every little utterance. Rather like Derek Nimmo with putty stuck to his teeth.

Within the routine of the three Rs and being force-fed an ideal of femininity, there was divine intervention in the way of sound. Miss Nelson would bustle into the room, under her arm a disc of vinyl that had the potential to bridge the gap between teacher and pupils. With an excitement she could hardly contain, Miss Nelson would place Holst's *Planets* upon the Dansette and command us to close our eyes, and we'd be transported into a world of different dimensions and colours never seen before. This is the world of music. Actually, I'd be transported into a world of spaceships, fire, warriors and aliens. My fellow pupils were probably dreaming about party dresses and Miss Nelson was eloping with Holst. But all the same, music allowed you to daydream, and there's no better way to shape the future and entice it to reach for you.

On a good day, perhaps when Miss Nelson didn't have a headache, we cleared the desks to the side of the room and danced and danced. The idea was to explore the crescendos, but I found myself caught up in some sort of trance-like state, like a shaman trying to banish spirits into the night. As the others would rest after their exertions, I'd still be going. Miss Nelson must have wondered what she'd started.

With music, I found a love, not fear – Holst was a long way from the theme to *Dr Who*. I loved dots, staves, bass clefs. Also the fact that you could pluck something from the air, an idea, and give it validation, give it a place in the physical world by drawing inky dots on lined paper. In turn these bland little specks were the key to an infinite world, the proof of eternity, a dialogue with God, no, the language of God, which is in constant flow, and every now and then one lucky person who has access to the spheres reaches up and plucks an idea from the ether and brings it into our consciousness – like Beethoven, Mozart, Bowie, Blur. Well, they are the exceptions. Mrs Mills's honky-tonk piano was plucked from the chip fat after a night down the bingo in Skegness.

My brother, Kim, definitely benefited from being the only boy in the family. He was pampered like a prize swine – in the kindest sense of the word. Kim would be given steak for tea, while we all had oxtail, and if I didn't eat mine quick enough he'd swipe it from my plate and push it down his gullet. Many an evening was spent with me in tears because he had finished off my supper while I was still eating it. Then at breakfast, as soon as Mum turned her back, he'd come as close as he could to my soft-boiled egg and burp in it. No wonder I wet the bed till I was eleven. But when I bought my first white rabbit, Snowy, Kim lived in fear. Snowy was ferocious. Snowy could leap three feet into the air without warning and sink his teeth into Kim's tummy. Snowy was my best defence – but Kim and I loved each other really.

I think Kim wished I was a brother. I certainly acted like one. One tremendously hot summer day he and I were playing with a hose in the garden, in just our white grass-stained underpants, when Kim had the brilliant idea of propelling me into the air from a position of my sitting on his feet while he lay on his back, his legs pulled into his chest. This was fun, I'd go up and up and land either on my feet or on my Spacehopper, but it became more out of control as Kim became stronger and over-confident. One last fling into the air, I was tired, and I landed on my left side, with my left arm tucked under me. The pain was bad, I couldn't move and I cried. Kim ran and hid at the bottom of the garden. Mum, thinking I was just being a crybaby, made me get up. The bone in my forearm protruded under the skin. Poor Mum almost passed out. The doctor was called and I hobbled inside, and suddenly a panic seized Mum. My underpants were dirty. With a broken arm and fractured elbow I had to change my underwear before the doctor arrived. I cannot describe the pain. But the ambulance ride was fantastic.

Being middle class had its benefits. Every weekend on Friday night, Mum would put my brother and me into sleeping-bags on the back seat of her pink Triumph and drive us through the darkness, listening to Radio Caroline, twenty-three miles out of Birmingham to a caravan my parents kept in the grounds of a huge water-mill. Surrounded by the watery silence of the River Avon, this truly was an island escape. My father had his boat, a thirty-foot river cruiser, and a dinghy that I could escape on, which I would row till I was exhausted. My real friends were all here and we played late into the night, elaborate games of hide-and-seek, sardines and tig. Once Sunday evening arrived, my heart would sink with the sun as we drove back to Birmingham with 'Sing something simple' droning on the radio accompanied by Dad's baritone voice. I knew it was school in the morning.

Mum and Dad had two cars. Mum had her Triumph, and Dad a Princess Rolls which smelt like a tannery and guzzled petrol. At weekends we drove the Princess Rolls. Dad got through more cars than Mum. When I was seven, Dad told me that a brother or sister would be joining the family soon. Sex was never, ever talked about in those days. Even evidence of Mum's pregnancy was hidden beneath billowing smocks. I had no idea whatsoever that the new arrival was concealed in her belly. Once, in my excitement, I shouted to the people in the caravan next to ours that I was going to have a little sister. Mum and Dad both cringed with embarrassment and told me, 'We don't say such things, it's not right.'

One calm balmy evening, under the weeping willows that lined the river banks, Mum announced that she didn't feel well. The sun was still high and it was hot. Dad quickly bundled my brother Kim, sister Nicola and me into the back of the Princess. Its leather seats smelt from the heat of the sun and made me feel nauseous, but I didn't say anything as Mum was very quiet and ashen-faced. Dad was silent too as we made our way through the country lanes towards the M5 and home. Every now and then Mum would give out a cry. This frightened me. On being asked what was the matter she'd say, 'Just look out of the window, Toyah, look at the clouds, they're beautiful.' There weren't any clouds. I'd turn to my sister and ask what was going on, but her face was pressed against the window and tears were running down her face. Kim, sandwiched between us, just stared ahead with a stunned look on his face. Either he'd just remembered something terrible, or there was something extremely sharp on the seat beneath him.

Mum was really noisy now, and all of a sudden my feet were wet from a fluid dripping through the front seat. It was blood. 'Mummy, Mummy, there's blood on the floor,' I shouted. Mum couldn't reply. Dad was in a deep, trance-like panic. 'Nicky, why is Mummy bleeding?' I asked. 'She's dying,' came Nicky's reply. All Kim could say, while staring right in front with fixed eyes, was 'This is disgusting.'

Mum tried desperately to be silent, but I started crying. 'Are you dying, Mum?' 'No, sweetheart, just look out of the window.' So I did. The smell of the leather seats was intolerable, and now it was mixed with sweat, blood and fear.

We did not head for Birmingham – it was obviously too far to go, so Dad drove to Worcester, where we began the nightmarish task of trying to find the hospital in a town with no signs. Every traffic light was against us. The queues of cars seemed to be miles long and we had to wait patiently in line till they eventually moved. This went on for about an hour, by which time Mum's contractions were so regular that she had to put her feet against the dashboard and push.

In desperation, with no clues as to where the nearest hospital was, Dad pulled over to ask a pedestrian. It didn't seem to occur to Dad that it would be Mum's window closest to the pavement. Mum calmly wound the window down and, still sitting in a pool of blood, about eight minutes away from giving birth, she asked the nice man the way to the hospital. He politely pretended not to notice her condition, or the fact that we were all crying in the back.

Finally we pulled in through the gates of the hospital. It was a typical soot-covered granite building with large iron gates. Dad ran in and emerged with a surprised team of nurses. They took one look at Mum and ushered the rest of us out – not outside the car, but outside the gates, where we stood alone for the next two hours. The nurses screened off the car, so we couldn't see what was happening, and we didn't see Mum again for three weeks. Dad was devastated. Mum gave birth to a little girl; they called her Fleur. She was severely underdeveloped and showed much worse signs of the condition I was born with. Fleur didn't survive. It was never talked about, but Nicola, Kim and I think that she did survive for a few days because of Mum's absence. Every year after her birth, Dad always informed us it was Fleur's birthday and we must wish her well and remember her. He still does to this day.

Chapter 3

It seemed by the mid-sixties that life was speeding up and no one had time for individual needs, ironically in a period in history where it was individualism that made its mark. In moving away from Miss Nelson's protecting influence, I stepped into a class run by a piranha. The year after Miss Nelson was so disastrous by comparison that I cannot even remember the name of my class teacher. She was a tall, raven-haired beauty who poured scorn and resentment over the children she was supposed to cultivate. She created a pecking order by over-praising the bright and quick to learn, to the detriment of the others. She left me with the feeling that in some stuffy staff meeting, on being told I had special needs, she had replied, 'We'll see.' My dyslexia was her excuse for mockery and my condition gave her plenty of ammunition.

Very simple things were completely out of my realm of concept. Why is there an *h* in when? Who needs the *k* in knit? And why can't 'clean' be spelt 'cleen'? This woman would spend half the lesson with my exercise book in her hand laughing at my spelling, using it as a form of entertainment to be shared between her and the bright girls via a demonstration on the blackboard.

One of the sixties' vilest inventions in the run-up to a processed-food and off-the-peg society was Sandwich Mix. As loathsome as this so-called food was, it presented me with a great way of getting out of the Queen Bitch's lessons. Concealed between two pieces of bread and carefully inserted into the mouth without others noticing, this Sandwich Mix, which consisted of chopped peppers, carrots and onion bits in a bile-like mayonnaise, could be chewed into a vomit-like consistency. Then, picking your moment carefully, preferably waiting for the old witch to be in an inspired flight of spite, you would 'chuck up' the Sandwich Mix next to her feet and run out of the class. Thus you would never have to see her again that day and could amuse yourself for the rest of school hours – at the expense of your father paying for your private education – in the toilets, vandalising the sanitary-towel machines and blocking up the loos with Dr White's.

This was the year that anger grew upon me without my invitation. It crept up like a slow flood across a plain – before you know it you're consumed. I would describe myself as an angry person. I carry anger, it motivates me. Now I am lost without it; I cradle it silently and disguise it with a smile.

There were many moments of joy in my childhood. Isn't it strange that these are the moments you have to dig deepest to find? My mother infused the world of fantasy into me, and its importance. Barbara took me to see the ballet, classical and modern, and in the context of being in the audience I could understand its form and power, which eluded me in dance class at school as we all bounced around like elephants and ostriches in our pink tutus.

I remember vividly the heightened joy of walking back to the car after seeing the Royal Ballet at the Birmingham Rep, Mum and I chattering excitedly. We passed a bag lady, who shouted at Mum, who was wearing a flowing cloak she'd made herself, 'Who do you think you are, Florence Nightingale?' Mum ignored her, I ignored her, but I wanted to punch her face in for insulting the woman who tried so hard to form her children. Mum and I struggled to have a relationship. We are polar opposites, but I learned very early that I would fight the world to protect my family, and I needed to channel all this aggression in me into a more creative force.

It's hard writing this, because I have to plug in to a person who is still within me and very volatile. The next ten years of my life were frighteningly aggressive. I was fighting not only for my self-preservation, but for my sanity. I adopted the attitude of meeting aggression full-on with ten times more anger than any aggressor could wish to meet.

Mother also took me to see *The Sound of Music*. This was the hit movie of my childhood. We'd had *Mary Poppins* (I think), *Bambi, Fantasia* and many dreadful Disney films about domestic animals fighting for survival in the American wilderness, but at last here was a film that had no cruelty, no suffering, no pain and a happy ending. Well that's what I thought. I hadn't yet heard of the Holocaust.

So my mother and I trundled up the steps to the Gaumont Cinema on Corporation Street. We'd had a good browse around John Lewis and Rackhams. The night was cold and it was exciting to be out in the dark with the lights of the cars flashing by. The light drizzle was kissing my skin and under my arm I held a spun-sugar Easter egg that I couldn't wait to tuck into. Inside the velvet womb of that art-deco cinema, my emotional state changed. As soon as the cascade of underlit red curtains pulled magically to the wings, the music started, and we saw Julie Andrews running up the mountainside, not a sign of breathlessness, and she burst into song, observed from above by some godlike eye that could swoop around her, cut to a close-up, zoom away. I knew I no longer wanted to be a muscle-man. I wanted to be Julie, a woman who ran up mountains, who sang in the face of adversity, who made dresses out of curtains and danced disrespectfully along very old stone monuments, and who above all had all her actions observed by a captivated audience. Mum and I saw *The Sound of Music* seven times; then Birmingham City Council knocked the Gaumont Cinema down.

Like most children, I spent hours wishing I could fly. I'd jump off anything in a hope that God would scoop me up and let me glide, even if it were only for twenty feet. This of course never happened. Instead, my body gained a substantial library of bruises and scars, each with a tale to tell. The closest I ever came to actual flight was ice-skating. In the winter months of my early childhood, we'd forsake the boat for the warmth of the fire at home. I'd escape the laborious chore of washing-up after meals by pretending to be inebriated on wine left over from Mum and Dad's glasses, and making the whole family laugh with my drunken routine. Then I'd curl up into a ball by the fire and pretend to be asleep while the washing-up was done. But every Saturday morning the family would trek to Solihull ice rink, past the Rover car works and into a world of steaming breath, cool air, organ music in a constant waltz and very sore bums. Gradually the family would dwindle away from the ice until eventually only Kim and I would be left, Kim endlessly skating around and around like a traumatised dog chasing its tail at high speed, me trying to copy the élite group of teenagers in the centre of the ice who obviously knew what they were doing.

My endeavours were spotted by Vie Thomas, who had just got Britain's pair skaters through the Olympics. Vie suggested to Mum that I should be formally trained, so Saturday mornings turned into a more formal affair. That, in turn, being addictive, led to my training after school as well. I'd decided skating was my future. It hadn't come to Vie's attention that I had one leg longer than the other, and the discrepancy in my shoe size was hidden by the restriction of the boots. It didn't hurt. For the sake of fashion I was learning that the only way to look 'hip' was to cram my right foot into a smaller shoe size. The occasional cramp was the only problem, especially on the double salchow, but I'd race off to the side of the rink, throw my boot off and bend my toes back to ease the pain.

There was a boy at evening classes who was obviously Vie Thomas's star pupil. I'd done ice shows with him and he was by far the most accomplished skater I'd ever seen. John Curry was young, radiant and beautiful. Vie would divide the ice up into 8 ft by 10 ft rectangles; my rectangle was next to John's, and for two hours on a Monday night I would perfect my figure of eight in a state of utmost bliss, alongside John. We never talked, never made eye contact even, but I held him on a pedestal and dreamt I could have his grace. He was balletic at a time when most men would have feared to show femininity, and it was this quality, as well as phenomenal strength, that won him the Olympics twelve years later.

By now I was growing – not much, I was by far the smallest in class. I was growing in all the wrong places, especially concerning my right foot. Just after Christmas 1968, on one of my twice-yearly visits to hospital to see my orthopaedic doctor, Mr Cotterell, he showed concern that not only was my right leg growing faster than my left, but the foot was, too. By now my index toe was so long it was on a par with my forefingers. Surgery was recommended. Only minor to begin with – Mr Cotterell would remove half the toe, the middle section, and stop its growth. Because I was born with pelvic dysplasia it would also be necessary, once I'd shown signs of having stopped growing, either to shorten my right leg or to lengthen my left. Both involved techniques that were not 100 per cent foolproof back then. This really put a strain on Mum. She knew I hated the hospital visits and that they disturbed me, but she agreed to the simple operation to correct my toe.

Before I was due in hospital I had to sit my eleven-plus. This was to be my first official exam. By this time my father's life had taken an unexpected turn for the worse: he had lost his factories as a result of a shares slump. Overnight he was reduced to being penniless, his only disposable assets being the factories. Rather than sit it out in the hope that share prices would recover, my father took the advice of an accountant and sold the business that he and his father had spent a lifetime developing. This broke my father's heart. It wasn't a means to an end. He still had escalating debts. Even though I grew used to falling asleep at night to the sound of my father's tears in the next room, and occasionally Mum's too, I never really realised how bad things were until I was twelve.

I certainly didn't realise the importance of my passing the eleven-plus. It would have meant a scholarship to the best school in Birmingham. That's the school I was already at, believe it or not. The ritual of the exam took me totally by surprise. It was stern, cosmetic. The teachers who would normally at least make eye contact with you averted their eyes as we sat at our desks staring at the exam papers. The atmosphere was positively hostile, and you could taste the competition in the air. I sat frightened and confused, unable to unravel my thoughts and decipher the language of the questions. I failed miserably, and so presented my father with yet another financial problem.

My parents decided, openly, that neither our education nor quality of life should ever be compromised, so ignoring my pleas to be taken away from the C. of E. and placed in a comprehensive down the road, my father decided I was to stay as a paying student. He opened an antique shop on Broad Street, Birmingham, with the wife of Jack Johnston, who at that time was the equivalent of managing director of BBC Pebble Mill. Jack always kept his eye on me, gently persuading a reluctant Mum and Dad that I did have a future in showbiz.

For a while Beric found happiness at the shop. His many customers were almost exclusively from the ITV studios and the Birmingham Repertory Theatre, both neighbours of his emporium of treasures.

Just after my eleventh birthday I was due to go into hospital in Selly Oak for two weeks to have my toe corrected. It was an adventure. There was no problem with Mum leaving me there. The children's ward was big and bright, full of toys, colour and fascinating predicaments. Jane, in the neighbouring bed, had been born with a twisted spine; she was beautiful and always laughing. Her head was shaved and a metal halo was screwed to her skull. Pins went straight through her calves, allowing weights to be added to a pulley system daily. Jane was being stretched straight by some monstrous torture contraption. With all this she was a joy to be with. All the other girls in my ward escaped Jane's fate, but weren't much better off: instead of the metal halo, they were all encased in huge body plasters. So a game of billiards was out of the question, but we had as much fun as one could with a horizontal gang of team-mates on wheels.

My op was straightforward, but when I looked under the bedclothes and saw the blood-soaked plaster I burst into tears. Also, it is very painful to have bone cut. The pain kept me awake for nights. If you've ever had a part of your body in plaster you'll know what it's like when you want to move the injured limb all the time. I never cared about my foot until it was in plaster, and now it was twitching and itching and clicking all over the place. The latter I could not understand until eight weeks later when I returned to the hospital: the staff nurse cut the plaster off, and sticking right out of the top of my shortened toe was a thick piece of wire. 'How deep does that go?' I enquired. 'Half-way down your foot,' came the answer. 'How does it come out?' I asked. 'We pull it out,' came the reply. They had to sit on my chest. I screamed the place down. It didn't hurt so much as make me nauseous as the wire racked along my bone, like a stick against iron railings. My toe looked as if it had been bitten off and stuck back on, but my shoes fitted better. Mum vowed there would be no more operations and no more visits to the hospital. I agreed and chose to live with the consequences of pelvic dysplasia.

I returned to ice-skating as quickly as possible, but it was too painful. The restrictive boots felt as if they were breaking my bones. I gave up, and in doing so I gave up my first real dream. This confused me for a long time. But I'm sure if I'd really wanted to skate I'd have hung on to that dream. It was more likely that my hormones kicked in, as my periods started when I was eleven. I had only just learned what a period was; it really scared me. I felt I was being condemned to a life of hell. It took me days to tell Mum – what if she wanted proof? Suddenly my body was my private sanctuary and I didn't want to share it with anyone. Also, all too suddenly, I was set apart from my father and brother by a gender role I refused to play. A kind of guilt accompanied me on this journey into womanhood, probably caused by the hushed tones the teacher used to break the news to us and which my mother now used so as not to embarrass the men in the house. All in all, I was being made to feel unclean. In those days you had to wear a sanitary belt and attach the sanitary towel to it. It was so hideous you knew men could spot one a mile away by the way you walked, or more likely waddled. But I soon learned to treat the event as my secret: a powerful occasion witnessed only by myself, the sun and the moon. Eventually, once a month, I began to feel special, blessed. How menstruation came to be called the curse is perverse. It is a blessing of pain. Not all blessings have to be material. As soon as the girls in my class found out that I was the first to 'come on', they all bundled me into a toilet and I had to show them everything. The towel, the belt, the blood. They watched, knowing they'd be next.

Chapter 4

Nineteen seventy was born to be a paradox. The air was filled with anticlimax after the swinging sixties and everyone did their darndest to announce that the seventies could never live up to its predecessor. Not even the Monkees, the Bay City Rollers or the Osmonds could lull the world into feeling that the future was 'cool, man'.

But I didn't care, the world evolved around me, my consciousness was the world, the world was me, oh yes, my hormones had kicked in. There were too many boys, too little time and as for every teenager the catchword was me, me, me. There was a bright futuristic world to be discovered and that couldn't be done while at school or in a uniform. All I could think about was the future and I spent every day wishing the present away.

My sister had boyfriends, my brother had girlfriends; they were positively adult and I wanted into that world too.

Slowly, the carnation wallpaper in my bedroom disappeared drowning under a sea of short-lived idols, numerous posters, ever changing, going from supercool to lukewarm in my favours in the space of a month.

The first bra was a mammoth, or should I say a mammary occasion. It was tiny, like two flowery handkerchiefs sewn together, and very flat. But in the space of one year my chest size grew from 32 to 42B. Mum was terrified, it meant a new bra every month – each to be modelled in front of the family at teatime. Even worse, a twelve-year-old in a school uniform with a 42B bust practically caused pile-ups at the bus stop each day. I was never short of anyone to talk to, even if they were all male and over twenty-five.

All through school I had tolerated and experienced extreme anxiety from a kind of bullying that was too subtle to prove. It was a psychological bullying. I was not a quick-thinking child or a great conversationalist. Words and responses had to be considered. Never would I have a quick retort, especially not a catty one. Instead, lying in bed at night I'd suddenly sit up and think, Why didn't I say that? There was one girl alone responsible for the mockery and ridicule that had gone on for at least five years. She was pretty, much liked and very spoilt and always had her own way. As soon as I'd strike up a friendship with a girl, Rosemary would do her utmost to destroy that alliance. She'd invite my new friend to tea, to ride her pony or to stay the night for midnight feasts, and before I knew it my friend was no more. Then later, in recreation, there would be a gaggle of gossips and I would be excluded as I was the subject of their laughter – especially my lisp. Now most girls would ignore this, but it was as if I was being stalked. Wherever I went for solace, she'd follow, with her flunkey, Angela, who would threaten physical abuse if Rosemary's intellectual rebukes failed. It was no good trying to ignore them because they made sure they were in my line of vision constantly, staring, gossiping, giggling, and if I fought back, Angela was there, threatening fists. This caused me many sleepless nights. They were getting a kick out of intimidating me and watching how I dealt with it. As I arrived at school my heart would sink and I literally went into a cold sweat of distraction.

I hit Angela many a time; Mum even had to break us up once in the school car-park. But what she and Rosemary did was turn me into a bully. Because words and strength of mind escaped me, I used the next best thing I had, and that was physical strength – and an ability to scare the wits out of people.

One class year Rosemary was separated from Angela. She adopted a new flunkey, Alison. Alison just didn't have the background Angela had, and for all her mimicry, Alison was laughable. This meant Rosemary's power was slipping. After one night of particularly memorable mental angst caused by Rosemary, because I'd declined to do a class project with her – purely because even when she was sweet, she had the quality of a vampire sucking the life-force out of your body – I walked into the classroom, picked up my chair and swung it at both Rosemary and Alison. They ducked. I pinned Rosemary to the wall and told her, 'If you so much as fucking look at me again, I will kill you.' Alison was terrified. Rosemary burst into tears. I prepared for war at lunch with Angela but I stared her out, and as much as she tried to laugh it off I think she knew – she'd educated me to become a mightier bitch than her. Neither ever bothered me again.

In this way I became overnight the terror of the school. Out of school I was having quite an adult life. At weekends down at the mill in Pershore, my best friend Trish and I were dallying with boys, fighting with the girls and growing up fast. Faster than the mamby-pambies I went to school with. One great friend at school was Vicky. Vicky hung out with Rubery Hell's Angels and I tagged along too. The Angels took an immediate liking to me; they thought I was mad and fearless. I'd provoke the most feared of them, but unbeknownst to them I was as scared as I ever was. I just didn't want to end up a victim in their eyes. So when their leader Nick got out of prison for knifing five people and turned up at the Lickey Hills Youth Club disco, I danced with him all night. And when this huge smelly man made a pass at me through his drugged-up delirium, I stared him in the eyes and told him I'd kill him if he touched me. Thus I won his respect.

These Hell's Angels were all soft at heart. OK, they peed, shat and vomited on their own clothes as a mark of initiation, but they accepted me for myself and this was my first experience of that.

Back at home I would lie in my bed at night, staring at the moon through the window, and I'd pray so hard that my ears would start to ring. I'd pray to get out of family life, out of school, out of Birmingham, and to be something that would prove all the cynics wrong.

Home life was pretty dismal. Dad was struggling financially. Kim was about to leave for the Air Force and my sister was a student nurse. Everything and everyone was in transition, it felt, except me. I was stuck in the glue of home life. So it came as no surprise on the morning of my twelfth birthday that Mum was nowhere to be found. There were no presents because there was no money. Mum usually drove me to school in the morning –

this being once of only twice that she didn't in the whole of my school life, because if she didn't, I wouldn't go. Grumpily and full of self-pity, I caught the bus to school. And what really piled the pity on was everyone asked me what I got for my birthday, even Miss Williams, my class teacher. My reply: 'Nothing.' I felt pleased with myself about this, because by now I was modelling my school life on James Dean in *Rebel without a Cause*, and today put my dream well on course.

Just before lunch I was called to the headmistress's office. This wasn't a rare occurrence. Miss Joyce dished out detentions from behind her oak-veneer desk, with a Van Gogh print on the wall behind her to remind us all how close to insanity we were in our everyday lives.

Today, though, rather than doing a very accurate impersonation of Cruella de Vil, Miss Joyce showed a more tender side as she sat me down and proceeded to inform me, to the tenderest of her ability – which still had an icy edge to it – that Mum had been found under my brother's bed. She had hidden there till we'd left the house because she was in so much pain. Then she called for Dad, who on finding her realised it was very serious and called an ambulance and that day the doctors removed two gallstones from her, each the size of a large marble. The worrying factor was that her gall-bladder had burst, leaving her severely poisoned. The headmistress's job was to warn me that Mum might not pull through.

Receiving this news, I left the room numb. Not fully realising Mum's condition, I was still in a mammoth pre-teenage sulk over the lack of birthday presents. Miss Nelson summoned me to the staffroom. As I stood in the doorway, the teachers fell quiet and looked at me. Miss Nelson, who had the ability to forgive me all my monstrous acts, had bought me a box of sweets. Meltis Jelly Fruits to be precise. This completely took the wind out of my sails. The one thing I hadn't learned to respond to was a blatant act of kindness. I was embarrassed. Then Miss Nelson produced a huge handmade card, which the girls had made for me that morning, and a large ball of blotting paper resembling a jellyfish out of water, with the words 'You'll have to pretend this is your cake, Love Vicky'. This for some reason, in its comic absurdity, triggered my tears. This blotting-paper cake and the sweets were the most moving gifts I'd ever had, and it's not that I was ever starved of gifts, not at all. Birthdays and Christmas were the best, but today the timing, the place and the intention had me running down the corridor looking for a place to cry unobserved.

When I got home that evening Dad wasn't there. He'd stayed at the hospital all day with Mum, who unbeknownst to me was dying. Mum had always been physically strong and a real fighter. This had all happened so suddenly. Beric was drained when he finally returned. We had a fight over £12 I wanted to buy a pair of platform shoes with. Dad didn't have £12 to his name. I ridiculed this poor man for not giving me a present on my birthday. I didn't really care about my birthday. The emergence of platform shoes made me look tall, attractive and ahead in the fashion stakes. Forget home life. I only had boys on my mind.

The next day I asked if I could go with Dad to visit Mum. The air had cooled and the fracas of yesterday was already forgotten. Dad said he'd already asked the hospital if I could go and they'd said no. Nicola did see Mum; she said Mum was in intensive care, with wires and tubes attached all over, and really it was better that I didn't see her.

Mum was in hospital for a month, during which time the rest of us buckled down, cooked, cleaned and had very little fun. In fact no fun whatsoever. In that time we realised that Mum cooked, cleaned, shopped, did the washing and got us from A to B. Strange that it never occurred to us before then. I was desperate for Mum to come home because I was fed up of Nicola bossing me around.

A month after Mum's disappearance, I returned home from school and Dad said there was someone here to see me. When Mum stepped round the corner, I longed to run up to her and hug her, but I'd changed so much in that month. I'd really hardened and a steely determination never to fall victim to my emotions had set like rock inside me, so I subdued my tears, said, 'Hello, I'm glad you're home,' and walked upstairs. Mum was half the size I remembered her being and her clothes hung off her. It made her look waif-like and years younger. She stood there, obviously still weak, and from this moment we never touched again, as mother and daughter, for the rest of our lives. A rule was silently made and an invisible wall secretly built between us. For the next few years our relationship was downhill from there.

In fact everything was downhill from there. I'd given up on education. I'd just idle the time away in class, much to the annoyance of pupils and staff, but by now I'd made sure everyone feared me. I was by no means the worst girl in the school, either. Interestingly enough, I'd say at least four of the brightest, most original thinkers – and from the most respected backgrounds – were by far the worst girls in the school. I will not name names, but alcohol, marijuana and sex were top of the list of extra-curricular activities.

They set standards that not even I could aspire to. Drugs scared me. Full stop. Boys, even though I was obsessed with them, luckily were not so with me. I had a kind of neanderthal look about me, which in retrospect was a saving grace. I'd become so determined to be 'someone', to be a star of stage, screen and music, that deep down I knew that my ability to show dog-like devotion to another person would be the downfall of that dream. So I dallied with boys and if one showed too keen an interest, such as suggesting a follow-up date, I dumped him.

Why the school never expelled the lot of us baffled me. Expulsion was often talked about, especially after I hit Miss Threadgold, my English teacher, but cynically I presumed that our fathers' money for termly fees was more important than our social behaviour. The truth is that the school, knowing that we were all particularly bright, saw us as a challenge. But one of the reprobates took the challenge too far when she stood drunk in morning assembly and screamed across the hall for Miss Joyce to go f*** herself. The father of the inebriate, a vicar no less, collected her unconscious on the pavement outside the school perimeter and we never saw her again. The rest of the bad clan subsequently behaved for about a week, then reverted to our normal bad behaviour.

After this particular girl had been banished from the kingdom of a single-sex school run by women with the minds of patriarchs, it appeared that I became public enemy number one. Rather generously, I feel, I was now seen as not only the naughtiest girl in the school, but also the ringleader of all the dark deeds that were conspired in those lightless corridors.

It takes one telling incident in your life to give you the information you can never glean on your own: how others perceive you. It never occurred to me how highly unregarded I was until the day I was summoned from class to the main cloakroom. On my way down, thoughts ran through my mind as to what I was about to be in trouble for – theft, graffiti or supergluing plimsolls to walls. As I walked down the corridor, before me in the cloakroom I could discern a gaggle of teachers, cleaners and the one male caretaker (who by the way was rumoured to be having an affair with a girl in a class one year above mine). All stood in a circle, looking inwards and down at their feet. I had no idea what event had composed this comical arrangement. They looked like hens feeding.

As they heard my steps – I was not a light child – they all turned towards me with accusatory scorn, flames in their eyes. Miss Joyce asked without hesitation, 'Miss Willcox, are you responsible for this?' I'm not saying Miss Joyce was unattractive, but she did look as if she was compiled from Michael Jackson's offcuts. She pointed to the floor. There lay an immaculate and enormous human turd – slightly dessicated as a result of the school's policy of overheating every room. I was shocked. I thought, How could this be mine? It's enormous. I would have had to stand on a chair, or otherwise be lifted off my feet in the action of such an excretion. Couldn't these bureaucratic bimbos see that I was all of four feet five inches? This monster came from an eight-foot man. I just stared at it, trying to suppress my laughter. Then I looked up and said, 'Not me, not possible,' and walked off as quickly as my little legs could carry me, before they could make me clear it up.

I think Miss Joyce was the culprit, out of spite for me. In the silence of class time I think she snuck to the cloakroom, coopied down, giggling to herself, and took her revenge.

Chapter 5

Rebellion and insolence were not enough to quench the insatiable hunger I had to be different. I knew I did not feel or experience life in the same way as my fellow pupils, but I just could not approach endless years of schooling with insouciance in the hope that time would pass quickly, because it wasn't passing quickly so far. Every morning on arriving at school I'd run to the same window and face the eastern sun and pray, with so much effort that my body was rigid with conviction, 'Please God, get me the hell out of here, let me find at least one like-minded soul.'

From about the age of fourteen, or, more accurately, from the first time I saw David Bowie perform 'Starman' on *Lift Off with Ayshea*, I knew I was an alien abandoned on earth – at least that thought kept me sane and kept me apart from all the others.

The importance of gender roles really grated on me, like teeth on silver foil or fingernails down the blackboard. I felt irritated by all those around me who accentuated their femininity by protruding their little finger, exiling it from the rest of their hand, or chewing their food as if some invisible hand had pulled their lips from their face and tied string around the mouth, so the mouth resembled an anus; and by the greatest crime to mankind – the unwritten patriarchal law that women wear skirts and men wear trousers. We are who we are, not what we wear.

At the time I was born to exist in, trousers were a big no-no for women. Why? Because men said it was vulgar. Was it a woman's fault if men found vulgarity in a garment that hugged the crutch? I so loathed my gender because of all the stupid

39

restrictions that went with it. So out of school, I only wore trousers and I only wore black and I developed a tendency to hit any man who questioned this, no matter how politely.

On reading Ray Bradbury's *I Sing the Body Electric*, I found in the title alone the words that conveyed how my body felt within this universe. I can only think that because school was so like a concentration camp designed to commit genocide on all my senses and abilities, as night fell in my bedroom, my mind, body and consciousness expanded beyond suburbia. To a psychologist, this was simply growing pains, but to me the energy of the universe was beaming down on me, as if my prayers, or should I say pleas, were being answered. Some nights I felt as if I was going to explode with the force, and I continued to invite all these forces into my body for many years.

In my lonely, unaided and unguided search for a deeper more magical and gnostic spirituality than the misogynistic religious lessons I was receiving at school – from an unhappy bitter closet queen who threw the blackboard rubber at my head every time I asked him if he was gay – I discovered books on witchcraft. First, there were books on the history of witchcraft, which disturbed me greatly, because it appeared women were condemned for being different and their spells were so silly and harmless. All the accounts I read were of men with needles who went around the country piercing the many layers of women's garments, and if they didn't scream, it was hell-fire for them. The history of the witch hunts sickened me and fuelled my distrust of dogmatic teachers who believed they were right because they received a teacher's diploma many years ago. A good teacher learns with you and realises that everything shifts and changes. Each generation brings new perceptions that radically change history, present and future. I felt that all my teachers, bar two, were firmly fixed in the past.

Regrettably, following the books on historic witchcraft came the books on Satanism. Not a wise choice for someone who'd naturally grasped the power of prayer and visualisation. I was undoubtedly a powerful child, but sadly an impressionable one to boot. Allowing these books and their rather obscure knowledge into my life was a huge mistake.

Words I never forgot were spoken by a psychic, who fought

through crowds to meet me at the beginning of my fame in 1979. This woman, dressed in a kaftan and beads, was a throwback to the sixties who'd probably spent most of her life hitching around Morocco. Looking completely out of place amongst the punks waiting to get an autograph, she grasped me and said, 'We all have one major choice in our lives, either to choose the path of goodness, or to choose evil. You, Toyah stand firmly between the two; you cannot stay there for ever. Make your choice or be lost.' At this point she thrust a huge wooden crucifix into my hand and asked me if I wanted any marijuana or cocaine. But she was right, a choice had to be made. At the age of fourteen I suppose I tripped into rather than chose the dark side. Until my fingers got burned.

My dabbling was far from sophisticated. I never ventured into Crowley and group sex. To be honest, neither ever appealed to me. My journey was that of a teenager, not allowed out at night – locked in my bedroom, by my own choice, listening to Black Sabbath on the record player with a few books for company. The books were general ritual books, unsophisticated, but they seemed to unlock something in my subconscious. In my desire to become the person I dreamed of being – strong, independent, imaginative and attractive – I managed to turn the family house upside down. It wasn't that I was practising these rituals with all the paraphernalia or ceremonial daggers, crystal balls or potions; I was visualising them. Being quite a lazy child, I concluded that if I *thought* the spells then they would be just as effective, and I have no idea if my wishing materialised, but what did was my fear – my fear of archetypal demons. Once I started all this – the spells, mind expansion, visualisation – there was a presence, as if invited into my room, a presence I really didn't like, and it would not go away. It was a dark, paranoid shadow that felt like an angry abusive man ready to explode and invade my soul if I let my guard down.

It started like a slow flood. I'd spent the evening in my room, drawing futuristic landscapes and their inhabitants, perhaps penning a poem, as this seemed a cathartic way of dealing with all my frustration. I'd then looked through a spell book for a spell that could possibly take some of the mundanity out of my life, such as the spell for creativity or charisma, attraction or even slimness. Turning off the bedroom lights, opening the curtains to allow the moonlight in, I'd lain in bed and prayed to the moon for a free future, visualising everything I wished to be, until sleep had taken me by surprise.

Rising from sleep, I could hear my mother downstairs, cleaning. It must have been around midnight. The landing light bled under my door. The handle was turning, the small round wooden ball was rattling in its socket. 'Dad?' I enquired, jumping up and opening the door. No one there – and no siblings at home to wind me up. My brother had joined the RAF and my sister was a trainee nurse. Back to bed, eyes closed. The door handle started to turn. I watched it in the darkness. This time the door opened – not wide, but wide enough for a human to enter, except of course no human did – and then it shut, leaving me in silence, well, as silent as one can be when one's mind is trying to rationalise an unusual event. My eyes darted round the room, searching the darkness for a shadow. Nothing.

In the morning I deliberated whether to tell Mum and Dad, knowing that Mum's view of me was, with due cause, of a strange and rather frightening individual, and being aware of Dad's ability to dismiss problems. But I'm not one to keep things to myself, so over breakfast I told them, and waited for the ridicule. They took the information rather well and instead of the immediate derision that I was expecting, both digested what I had said. Mum fell quiet and said very little. Twenty years later, during a conversation about the following months' events, Mum admitted to me that she was so afraid to be alone in my bedroom that she wouldn't even contemplate going in after dark. That is why she fell silent: best not to stir this hornet's nest; her instincts had already informed her that something wasn't right.

My father has always talked about death as a great spiritual mystery and adventure – even though feared, definitely never believed to be the end. I suggested that since, many years earlier, his father and mother had both died in my bedroom, this could possibly be a visitation. Dad said, 'I can always contact my parents by just remembering them, and when I do think of them something slightly unusual happens such as an ornament falls off the mantelpiece or if I'm in the car the wipers will spring to life.' But Father didn't believe that anything as obvious and vague as the door opening and closing could be anything other than the wind or a dream. I chose to believe it was a dream.

The next night I went to bed full of trepidation and expectation, partly willing the event to repeat itself and partly wishing it not to. Realising a need to silence my mind, I lay there refusing to let even the thought of a supernatural event play itself in my head. I willed silence and peace – so much so that the noise from the blood in my ears became industrially loud. Then the door opened, paused and closed again. Being so afraid made me angry, and under my breath I cursed the energy responsible for this disturbance with promises of a fight in this world and the next. Then sleep again took me by surprise, as it did every night of my life.

Over breakfast I casually said that the event had happened again. This time no explanations were offered, not because my parents were bewildered, rather they'd become dismissive in the space of twenty-four hours.

At school I achieved a far more satisfactory reaction. I'd tell my story to boggle-eyed scaredy-cats, knowing they'd go home and lie awake at night waiting for the same to happen to them. I just loved telling stories; it was the only time people listened to me, and the thought that I could repay my fellow pupils' ridicule with fear was just too good to resist.

In 1995 a fellow classmate, whom I don't remember being directly horrible to at school, became a national heroine when she sailed round the world single-handed. Lisa Clayton was being surprised for *This is Your Life* and I was one of the surprise guests. I felt guilty as I walked on stage to greet her; a year earlier she'd asked me for money towards the project and I just hadn't had any to give, but when she saw me she simply exclaimed, 'My God, you were awful at school, you were so bad.' There lies my defence. She was right, but the extent to which I affected those around me I never knew; all I can remember is how they affected me. I'm glad to say that, given twenty-odd years' life experience, all that youthful selfishness eventually falls away.

Anyway, back to the paralysis of home life. I'm sure I would have been a mentally more stable girl if I had been allowed out at night, but all I had to occupy me on weekdays was homework or TV. So I spent many an unhealthy hour in my room daydreaming, reading horror, witchcraft, poetry and science fiction, drawing aliens and listening to rock.

The door opening had become such a regular event that all I did now was say, 'Hello, you're welcome,' before turning over and going to sleep. Then one night I heard the sound of footsteps entering the room and continuing around the bed. I could see clearly in my moonlit room that no one was there. My bed was to the right of the door. The door opened as it usually did and then footsteps circled the bed and stopped on my right side. I listened in the silence. Nothing. Suddenly an almighty force grasped me round the neck, pushing me so hard into the bed that as well as choking I could feel the bed-springs pushing a resistance against my ears, and a voice close to my face, sounding like a man with throat cancer, said, with undiluted anger and hatred, 'You fucking bitch. I'm gonna fuck you.' The grip released, I shot into the air as if on the rebound from a trampoline. Finding my feet, I put the light on and stared in disbelief at the empty room. It was cold, very cold, and I was shaking with shock. I was too frightened to go downstairs and be alone in the kitchen or the lounge. The house was quiet, Mum was asleep in her room and Dad in his. I just didn't want to be alone, and perhaps company would keep this thing at bay.

I crept across the landing and harshly whispered through Mum's door, 'Mum are you awake?' On trying the handle I found it was locked from the inside. 'Mum, I'm scared, there's something in my room.' No reply, I couldn't wake her, so I curled up on the landing outside her door and tried to sleep.

Mum was visibly terrified when I told her what happened. Terrified and helpless. What organisation can you turn to when some violation such as this happens? Father was quick to defend his ancestors: absolutely no way would they have harmed a soul, in life or after. I was left truly shocked by the hatred and the language of this drama. It was 1972; nowhere had I heard words like it, not on TV, not on film, not even in the Andy Warhol films my brother used to sneak me into at midnight in Worcester on a Saturday, not even in jest on the playing fields. I was too young to understand the concept of rape or sexual violence, but somehow my psyche had experienced it.

And things got worse.

At the same time as the development of events in my bedroom, my sister, Nicola, was a trainee nurse at Dudley Road Hospital in Birmingham. Nicola had a staff flat at the hospital but often came home when she needed home comforts. Trainee nurses are put through hell, mainly to harden them, but mostly because the illnesses, afflictions and accidents they have to deal with are hellish. My sister's first testing experience was to be put on the cancer wards for about seventy-two hours a week. Her job was to ease the last days of the terminally ill, changing soiled clothes and bedding, feeding those who no longer had the strength to do so themselves, dealing with irate relatives and cajoling those dying in fear and confusion from the administered drugs into a belief that everything would be all right tomorrow.

Often my sister would return home in tears of disbelief at what she'd just seen. Death is not an easy companion when it comes. It comes not only with grief but with an awful smell and distortion of the flesh, which Nicola could not shake off.

One night she returned unexpectedly in uncontrollable tears. An old lady Nicola had grown particularly fond of, and who had no relatives, had passed away that day after a long, painful fight against cancer. My sister sobbed at the injustice and loneliness of the woman's end; it seemed the ward Nicola had been put on to harden her was having the opposite effect. After a stiff whisky she went to bed.

My sister's bed lay lengthways against the wall. On the other side of her bedroom wall my father's bed lay as if mirroring hers. That night my father was awoken by his sheets being pulled off with great force. Thinking nothing much of it, he got up and replaced the sheets. They were pulled off again. My father lay awake contemplating my previous experiences, and became more than a little worried.

In the morning Nicola came downstairs elated, a completely different person to the one she'd been the night before. It was hard to believe that sleep could be that refreshing. It transpired that in the night, at the same time as Father's, her duvet had been pulled off her with great force. Nicola had got up and replaced the duvet and got back into bed. Then she'd felt a tugging at the duvet, an attention-seeking energetic tugging, with an urgency to it. On becoming more conscious my sister saw her little old lady standing by the bed, with a huge beaming

45

smile. The lady thanked Nicola for caring for her and said she was so happy, it was beautiful where she was now and she was safe. Then she was gone.

Because of the increased intensity in my own life situation, Mum, Dad and Nicola didn't tell me of this occasion for some time. Why? Because they believed I was the cause of it all, either through a powerful imagination, or as a result of some pubescent telekinetic energy. Whatever it was, they just didn't want to encourage my beliefs about my experiences to disrupt my life any more than they were already.

But there was a definable connection between me and my sister at this time. When I was in the house with just my parents, the extra spiritual activity was contained in my room, but when my sister came home all hell would break loose over the entire house, as if my sister was being followed home by lonely souls of the dead. Doors slammed, ornaments moved, items would completely disappear without trace. I believed, and still do to this day, that it was a telekinetic energy exclusively linked to women going through puberty; once puberty was complete, the activities would stop as quickly as they had started.

Unfortunately I still had a few years of puberty to go. When I awoke one morning to find all the wallpaper, posters and paintings stripped off my bedroom walls, lying neatly con-certinaed around the edges of the room, the walls dripping wet, my mother decided enough was enough. She contacted the Samaritans.

Mum had firmly made up her mind that I was not the daughter she had given birth to. I was either a doppelgänger or a changeling or I was possessed – the latter being the most favoured and obvious choice. At last, having someone passive to speak to, Barbara gained a kind of strength to fight me back, and I didn't like it. The whole idea of dealing with a problem by suppressing it was turning me into a time bomb. The breakdown of mutual respect and any form of obedience between us was making us two companions you would not want to be in the same room as.

One way this was resolved was quite simple: we would never ever in any circumstances occupy the same room at any one time. Mum still drove me to school, but the journey was endured in complete silence from both of us. We'd eat at separate times, never cross on the stairs and if Mum came into the lounge while I was watching telly I'd leave to go to my room. And sulk, basically. And spend most of the time dreading sleep.

If we did speak, no matter how deliberately politely, I would purposely find something she said to pick a fight from. And I mean a fight. My poor father pulled us apart many a time. Once I punched Mum after she hit me; this visibly shocked her, but it was the last taboo for Dad. In no uncertain terms he communicated to me that this was one thing he would never allow to happen to his wife.

It was Mum who brought up the suggestion of exorcism, in the kitchen with Dad present. Partly out of desperation for peace in the family home, partly out of goading me into spiritual combat and one-third out of guilt for the fact that I was the only child in the family who had never been christened.

Mum said christening was out of fashion when I was born, but she always worried that she might have denied my soul divine protection and guidance, and by all accounts her maternal neurosis was correct. The suggestion of exorcism woke me out of my isolation. At last, contact from those I depended upon – my parents. I gave it a lot of thought and came up with the conclusion that I'd find it excruciatingly embarrassing; also, I myself didn't want yet another external force changing me – or trying to – and I felt that the only way to deal with the dark shadow hanging over the family home was for me to make the changes. I had to change in order to banish the uninvited or to suppress the part of me that was making things happen. So I opted for being christened.

My God, if I could show you the Scripture teacher's face when I announced I wanted to be christened at the age of fourteen. Here was a man who loathed all that was feminine, who regularly threw blackboard rubbers at me when I asked if he was gay. He searched my face for truth, for a glimpse of a practical joke. But by the time I had my first private meeting of prayer and guidance with the Reverend at St George's Church in Edgbaston, my Scripture teacher – somewhat confused – knew I meant it.

Twice a wek for three weeks I met in the vault of St George's with the Rev, constantly wondering how women figured in his life and his teachings, but I absorbed the stories, the lessons, the irrepressible arcane power of it all and his acceptance of what he must have had a knowledge of – that I was the worst girl in the C. of E. and possessed to boot. Slowly, I felt the violent negativity, the living energy harbouring hatred at every level, leave my body. I was right: I had to change, because whatever was going wrong, I was the cause. It was as if every tense muscle, ready to hit out, simply relaxed.

I was christened in St George's Church in Colmore Row, Birmingham. A row at home preceded the event. The week before, I discovered no one was prepared to be godparent to me, which presented a slight hiccup. The teachers at school, admittedly bemused by events, always wanted to be posted on developments and events surrounding my surprise conversion. On hearing of the dire lack of godparenting, Mrs Beard, my long-suffering but ever-accepting history teacher, called me to an empty classroom and volunteered to be godmother. As I'd hardly ever bothered to attend any of her (mandatory) lessons, I thought this was exceptionally decent of her.

This put pressure on for the dress code. Not only church. Not only my teenage christening, but a representative from school. The row that preceded the event was about dress. No way was I going to be parted from my beloved platform shoes; anyway, they meant I could reach the font. So I walked into the church with Mum and Dad, very suitably attired – wearing six-inch platforms and a Biba-copy maroon smock coat with little velvet collar. From a distance I probably looked pregnant.

At the font, apart from Mrs Beard I had another godmother waiting, which was a surprise. She was Gee Nelmes, my mother's Samaritan ears. Gee was wonderful, kind and focused only on the good within people. It was an intimate affair: Mum, Dad, me, Gee and Mrs Beard (I never learned her first name) and their spouses. I did feel a right twit as the vicar put holy water to my forehead, but afterwards a calm sense of security fell upon the house.

Six weeks later I was confirmed in the same church by the Archbishop of Canterbury, and six weeks and one day later I was back to creating havoc in the classrooms.

Even though calm fell on the house – which slightly disappointed me, as I missed the uninvited interruptions – my parents, while not exactly showing a renewed respect for me, seemed to realise they could not predict my behaviour or afford to have preconceptions about me. I was still driven inside not to be a part of the greater picture of domesticity and acceptance of one's lot.

Not long after my confirmation, like an absolute idiot, I snuck into a cinema on New Street to see Saturday's 6 p.m. showing of the shock horror film *The Exorcist*. As the lights went down the whole cinema went into a mock scream of terror. In the darkness I could make out hordes of skinheads, many underage viewers and the odd responsible-looking Brummie. I was with Billie, my hold-hands, snog-once-a-week boyfriend from the youth club, and Karen Tredwell from school and her entourage of boy-friends. There had been so much publicity about this film – stories of suicides, reels of film mysteriously catching fire, members of the crew dying in car crashes and members of the public going mad after seeing it – that the cinema was charged with fear and hysteria by the time the title was up.

I made myself watch, and no way was I going to let myself bury my head in Billie's armpit. Thirty minutes in, one of the skinheads in front of us had already vomited in the aisle from fear, and forty minutes in they all got up and ran screaming for the exit.

As for me, I sat in horror, transfixed – because as soon as Linda Blair's possessed voice sounded out, I recognised the voice that had confronted me in my bedroom months earlier. Partly absorbed by a huge sense of relief that someone some-where in Hollywood must have had the same experience, and partly not wishing to hear that kind of naked hatred in a voice ever again, I stared at the screen and was thankful I'd never shot bile at my mother.

As Mike Oldfield hit the first chilling note of *Tubular Bells*, I realised I was glued to my seat in fearful anticipation of returning home. My mind was racing. I shouldn't have seen this film. It opened all the doors of my mind that allowed irration-ality in.

My parents were away for the weekend. I had the house to myself. I returned home alone, determined not to go to bed. I played David Bowie's *Diamond Dogs* over and over again until the sun came up. Nothing unusual happened, the house was silent and I slept till midday Sunday. By now I was bored stiff. I missed the friction from Mum and Dad's presence. All my albums had gone on strike from being played too much and all that was left for this surly teenager to do was eat (no drink, that was hidden away) and watch afternoon telly. *Alias Smith and Jones*, probably. My nose was running, I needed a tissue, or perhaps I just wanted to finish reading another chapter of *Lord of the Rings* – anyway, at about 3 p.m. I walked up the stairs, with the brilliant sunlight hitting the stair carpet through the window, and into my bedroom. As loud as if I was standing next to a drunk at a party, from just outside my door suddenly came the most maniacal genderless laughter I had ever heard; it was moving away from my room into my brother's, and then it stopped.

I stood very still. Listening. Waiting for anything. Proof of my brother's return home, the floorboards creaking, a door hinge, a garden party next door. Anything. Nothing. Just silence. I crept around the corridor to my brother's room, pushed the door slowly open. It was empty.

I should never have seen that film. The disappointment I felt at the thought that all this rubbish could start again was breathtaking. From that day on, I set myself the task never to digest images that might awaken a certain part of me that is just that little bit too real to be merely imagination.

Things still went bump in the night, but it seemed that, by virtue of the mere fact that I and the rest of the family treated this as a normal occurrence, such events slowly faded away as if being drawn into a past they couldn't escape.

Meanwhile I had my eyes firmly on the future. The present was too dull, so I bided my time, knowing that one day, even today, could be transcended by tomorrow and like that old cliché become yesterday.

My choice of reading material changed dramatically. The books on witchcraft were never to be touched again, but that doesn't mean I leapt on the Scriptures or Enid Blyton; my reality was too normal. Science fiction offered the travel my mind craved. So goodbye Crowley, hello Bradbury. One book I came across purely by accident was *The Link* by Matthew Manning. Matthew is a very talented telekinetic. His childhood was plagued by poltergeists, objects shifting and ancient objects appearing in his house from nowhere. Whereas Matthew had a gift, when I felt an energy touch my shoulder I refused to play ball with it. Matthew Manning is now a highly regarded healer in Bury St Edmunds; one day I will meet him.

Reading Matthew's story partly made me envious, because his family positively encouraged his phenomena, but it also convinced me that we all, as a race, are telekinetic. But it needs to be tapped to be honed.

Shortly after this, possibly the nicest thing I have experienced in the whole of my life started.

All my life my dreams have been ordeals, sometimes journeys, sometimes leaps into the future, sometimes catastrophic. So vivid is my dream life that I respect it, and in my conscious existence I dowse the dreams from the previous night. I dreamed about the National Theatre four years before I was employed there; the dream informed me how the building was perceived by the world and how I would be perceived by those who worked within it. That dream was prophetic. Genocide, sadly, used to be a regular dream, which would leave me emotionally exhausted, but by far the worst of my dreams is the most Freudian: I'm on a beach in a storm, and my mother is in a car on the cliff top above, waiting for me; she doesn't know where I am. She thinks I'm not coming and she can't hear me shout in the storm. She starts the car and heads for the cliff edge. I wake in tears.

One day, just before I was fifteen, I woke from a dream that made the present tolerable. No matter how successful I've been or how miserably I've failed, the experience of this dream is alive and vivid in my heart even today; it was a dream that indicated that my soul is just passing through.

The experience is still so vivid it is as if I was fully awake throughout it. As I slept in my bed, a hand pressed my right shoulder. I awoke to see by my side a man who must have been all of seven feet tall; he was very thin, like a Masai warrior, but his skin was silver, his long hair was silver and the short small growth around his jaw line was silver. He wasn't so much wearing clothes, rather he was draped in an effervescent flowing gown. His presence was lovely. He smiled and extended his very long fingers towards me, took my right hand and said, 'Come with me.'

I rose from the bed like the slow trajectory of a rocket firing up its engines and pushing against gravity. We passed through the ceiling and through the roof and shot past the stars as if we'd taken the M6 bypass. Away from Birmingham and into the next galaxy. As the stars blurred into streaks of light, I observed my silver man: a breeze permanently ruffled and softly folded his gown and hair. I felt very, very ecstatic. We stopped abruptly and floated in silence and stars. 'This is time travel,' he said, and we were off again. More stars, more streaks of light. Again we stopped abruptly. 'Time shifts,' he said. 'The time you experience in your body is only temporary. Once you're free of your body you will be able to alter the speed of time.' And we were off again. It was as if I was test-driving a Lamborghini; the service was great and the experience exhilarating.

We shot further and further into the cosmos. How do I know? Well, at this point only instinct could tell me. Approaching a gas cloud, which was in our sight for longer than any of the stars we'd seen so far, we slowed and I realised I was approaching a population, a community, a mass consciousness: From a distance the gas cloud was enormous, the size of a small galaxy, and as we approached, it mapped out into different provinces of colour – beautiful, oxygen-rich, vibrant, pulsing colours of an intensity I have never been able to find since in my waking life.

As my silver man and I pushed into this bubble I became aware of a vast populace. All around us, as if stepping the path of a suggestion of a street, with non-physical squares and meeting-places, voluminous bubbles about five feet in circumference moved, each one a unique, intense, individual colour. These bubbles passed through one another, and as they did so they sang out a note and created in their brief union a totally new colour. I realised I'd witnessed their form of communication. All over this spectral city rang notes from a random choir. It was chillingly beautiful. I think these were souls.

I must have been swimming towards wakefulness, or willing it. One last sentence passed through my man's lips. 'Vibration, we are all vibration, we are all music.' I woke.

I woke in a state of utter bliss, as if every endorphin my brain could produce had been released and was partying in my veins. I felt as if I'd travelled a million miles and witnessed a million lives. I told no one of the dream. I wanted it all to myself.

On my travels I have met at least three other people across the world who have met the same man in their dream state and received lessons from him. Human consciousness is a wondrous thing. I am sure we are all potentially one mind.

Whether dream, whether reality, this experience changed me and that is real enough. You cannot live your life through fear. My fears dissipated and I knew I could break the mould of safe, pre-conceived, 'dead' ideals.

Sadly for me, I have only met this enigmatic man twice since. He seems miraculously to appear when I'm in crisis or about to be. Once, when I was twenty-five and fame was weighing heavily on me, I flew from my bed with him to have a lesson, suspended among the spheres, on equations of Einsteinian proportions. Being number blind, I wondered on waking if he'd accidentally picked up the wrong person. I woke none the wiser, but happier to have seen him – and at least I knew the equation for time.

The last time I saw him in a dream, I was thirty-two. He bent over my sleeping body and whispered, 'Be strong.' I hope I haven't disappointed him. I pray I haven't failed him. But I suspect that the next time I see him, he'll be lifting my soul from a silent body and cutting the umbilical cord between my soul and earth.

Chapter 6

'Have you heard?' said Hazel turning away from her desk. She had a blasé tone indicating that what was to follow was trivial. 'Nick died yesterday.' I stared at her in horror. Miss Smart was desperately trying to teach maths. She had lost her fiancé to World War II, and the shock had left her permanently twitching like a dormouse, as if her heart beat twice as fast as any other human's. I used to taunt her about her engagement ring. 'Are you engaged, Miss Smart?' I'd say, intimating that she was really a racy old fish. One day she burst into tears and told a stunned class full of bitchy fifteen-year-olds how her one and only love was gunned down on the beach at Dunkirk. I never mentioned her engagement ring again.

Today it was my turn to cry. Nick Bowes was my first love and my first introduction to death. I stole him off my best friend Trisha, who had dated him since she was twelve. We all used to spend weekends at the old mill in our boats and caravans. One day I decided I was fed up of waiting outside Nick's caravan on balmy Saturday nights while he and Trisha snogged inside. I was fed up of following them down the country lanes like a frustrated chaperon. He was only Trisha's plaything; what I felt was love – spiky, appetite-suppressing, heart-rending love. Plucking up considerable courage, I phoned him and invited him to be my male companion at Vicky Richardson's teenage party.

We never kissed that night, but he tentatively put his arm around my shoulder and we danced. My heart raced so much I thought I'd pass out. The next day after school, I waited and waited for the phone to ring. It didn't. No food passed my lips for five days. The pangs of love were excruciatingly painful, yet I'd never felt so brilliantly alive.

As far back as the age of seven I was having blinding crushes on people, anyone, anything. Slowly over the years the crushes became oriented towards males, and they were always unrequited.

At last the weekend arrived and at the mill Nick and I, as if darned by an invisible thread from the heavens, became an item. The real thing. We held hands. Talked an awful lot. And kissed as if that was enough to make babies. Both of us were so completely innocent that no other progression ever crossed our minds. It was bliss.

Nick taught me to sail. Every Saturday and Sunday afternoon we'd sail the stretch of the River Avon from Wyre Mill to Pershore, racing at great speed, daydreaming at leisure, crashing conveniently into reedbeds and waiting to be rescued. We'd capsize and resuscitate each other in the chill autumn air. Nick was a gentleman. Once his father sailed past us in his own boat, almost hitting us in a sudden gust of wind, and exclaimed, 'Whoops, I dropped a gooly there.' A simple phrase that had Nick and me hyperventilating with laughter for hours. We won cups – well, Nick won cups, I won spoons for crewing.

Nick became devoted to me, and eventually I pushed a resistance against him. It was all becoming too intense. I'd fail to return his phone calls, and one Christmas, when he walked over to my house to give me the customary bottle of the Brut aftershave I always wore, I didn't invite him in. We were over.

Now, a year and a half later, to the resonating notes of Hazel's casual utterance, 'Have you heard? Nick died yesterday,' I sat imploding with guilt.

Not knowing how to react, I returned home and told Mum. She went ballistic and ran into the garden screaming. Her catharsis was my lead, and I cried for months. In retrospect I think I had a breakdown. I cried myself hollow thinking of Nick's perfect family: two loving sisters and two very in-love parents. Over the months his sisters fell ill with depression and the parents faded from bright lights into grey.

Nick, he of such a brilliant mind, about to study to become a doctor, was killed by an oncoming car as he returned home from a date on his motor bike. That's all I knew. It was enough.

Miss Joyce didn't allow me to attend the funeral. I caught my father coming out of her office the day before it was due to take place. Both had decided I would overreact in the presence of his coffin and I suppose they were right. Even today, hardened by many fellows' funerals, I cannot bear the evidence of vitality, love and laughter being swallowed up by earth or fire.

Nick graced me with the greatest lessons about life. First, never be cruel in or behind the face of love; secondly, always be awake, aware and ready for other people's errors – no matter how intelligent, how skilled you are, it takes but a moment of another's lapsed concentration to wipe you, and consequently your family, out.

I believe 'remembering' is part of people's immortality. I send Nick good thoughts as often as my forgetful brain reminds me. That's quite often, but not so often that it can explain something that happened in the autumn of 1990. I hadn't, I admit, thought about Nick for quite a while. My head was wrapped around the concept of a new band I had formed with my husband, Robert Fripp. It was autumn, the nights were black and the leaves were falling like rain. In the countryside where we lived there were no street lights, so when I say the nights were black, it means black.

Part of my home life has always been the preserve of a large white rabbit. At this time my large white companion was Cecil, a four-year-old New Zealand white, the size of a small dog and white teeth as sharp as cut-throat razors. Cecil lived in a porch at the back of the kitchen and on this particular night, around 8 p.m., I'd called him in from the stable yard to feed him and bed him down for the night. The prospect of a juicy apricot always enticed him in, prising his nostrils away from the seductive smells of grass, dandelions and wild bunnies of the female variety.

Once Cecil was in, he usually settled right down on top of his hutch. This night a madness took him. It was a blustery night, so my hair kept whiplashing my eyes, which irritated and distracted me, but the elements were certainly not responsible for the distress this gentle bundle of white fur started to show. Cecil kept running against the far wall, crashing sickeningly into it, as if to get away from the outer door he'd just dozily walked through. At first I thought he'd picked up the scent of a fox, so

I tried to calm him with my voice and then touch him. He repeatedly rammed the far wall with his head. As I bent to touch him, aware that he could sink his teeth into me in this state, I realised I was the cause of his fear. Stepping back to close the door, I turned to see, outside, above the steps the rabbit had just descended, hovering, full size, the age he was when I last saw him, encased in a halo of light, with autumn leaves blowing through him like memories, Nick smiling down at me, his hands outstretched in a welcoming gesture.

I just stared, wondering what trick this was. Thoughts of Nick had left my mind recently and instead my head was full of record deals, management and accounts – the usual concerns of a recording artist.

Nick hovered in a serene silence and eventually spoke. 'Everything is all right and will be all right. I am safe.'

I said nothing. The thought that this was a mind trick was being heavily investigated in my head.

But the rabbit was still terribly distressed. Closing the door, I called for Robert who was in the kitchen. When he came I asked if he could see anything in the yard. 'No,' came an honest reply. But the aura was still there. Nick had begun to fade; the autumn leaves blew and bustled and roamed through him. It was as if Nick was forgetting us. For two days the rabbit circumnavigated the spot where Nick had appeared.

Chapter 7

After six months of solid iron grief holding me below the surface of life, I emerged determined not to waste a minute on all I found trivial and irrelevant to my future. The pain of loss put me in a cocoon that allowed me to think deep, deep into my consciousness, and I emerged knowing myself better than anyone could imagine. (Self-pity may have been in the equation at the beginning of my grief; now only life mattered.) Letting the handbrake off my vehicle of experience for the next decade, I freewheeled over hill, over dell – very occasionally having to get out and push – and ended up experiencing the kind of motional momentum that a meteor must feel for most of its journey.

What was trivial in my opinion? School, home life, domesticity, periods and babies. Well, that was 99.9 per cent of my world that needed to go.

By the time I was fifteen, all school chit-chat was about boys, university or careers. The only conviction in my life that held a rock-solid continuity with me was that I wanted to act and sing. And nothing was going to budge it. One morning at school we were informed that an obligatory visit from the careers officer was pending. Great, I thought, at last, contact with the outside world. Predictably, as I entered the room for my session with the officer, a pudgy, bland woman who obviously hated her job, she looked up and took an instant dislike to me. Why do people do this? You know, those bad days we all get when we've been touched by the ugly stick and even a priest reacts badly to you. Well, at the age of fifteen, I found that people who neither knew me nor had ever seen me before would jump to conclusions about me that inspired me to fulfil their worst nightmares. Was it my face, my colour, my posture, my lisp? Who cares. I seized the careers officer's weakness by the throat and turned it into my strength.

'And, Toyah, interesting name that, what are your ambitions?' She talked as if dragging a verbal leg behind her.

'I'm going to be an actress.'

Silence. Long pause in fact. 'Have you thought about nursing?'

'No.'

'How about university?'

'I'm going to be an actress. When I leave school I will go straight to drama school. Can you help?'

'Drama isn't a career. There's lots of unemployment; you need something solid. So many people fail at acting.'

At this point she piled my hands full of leaflets on nursing, social work, being a librarian, dental nursing, caring, making cakes for the WI. Basically she passed the buck on to bureaucracy, which is the best thing she could have done for me, because God help me, if she had found me a drama school it would have been in a garage in Moss Side.

Just before leaving, I performed a cliché that was just too good to miss. 'My name is Toyah Willcox, you may want to remember it.' And as I left her I thought, If I don't find fame acting, I'll find infamy by robbing banks, preferably hers.

Miraculously, my teachers felt I was capable of taking ten O levels. How they came to this conclusion still baffles me today. An English teacher I almost got expelled for punching; a maths teacher who never saw me in class; a history teacher who only saw me for detention and at my christening; an art teacher who campaigned not to have me banned from her class, as punishment for my behaviour, and a music teacher who recognised my love of singing; oh and a geography teacher whose very physical presence so repulsed me that I set fire to all my geography books rather than spend one minute in her class; a religious teacher who so repulsed me, I turned him from a saint into a murderous demon; a PE teacher who simply fancied me (she obviously liked a bit of rough); a biology teacher whom I adored, except that we fell out when I found dead laboratory rats in her office; and a physics teacher who allowed me to carve 'love and death' into my desk and on one momentous occasion forgave me when I dropped magnesium into her coffee.

To this day I'm convinced that they made me sit all those exams to make up for all the hours I didn't sit in their classes.

There were things I excelled at, but, being of phenomenal arrogance, I knew I could excel, therefore I didn't bother. I could always catch up later in life. Let this be a lesson – I'm still trying to catch up.

Around 1972 our school was a favourite target for bombers – I think exclusively IRA, but we as children were never told. Across the road from the main buildings of the school was a news agency. That was the real target, but miscalculations on the gelignite front meant that we got the blast too.

On one rare occasion I attended a maths class on the first floor of the school overlooking the main road. We'd heard a rumour that a bomb was being defused on the corner by a lone soldier. Owing to a profusion of leafy trees, nothing could be seen, but when the blast came I experienced how flexible glass can be.

The blast itself caught all our attention and we turned to look outside; then came the force, the displacement of air. Astonished, we watched the large Edwardian windows bulge in towards us; the glass seemed to curve inwards over our heads and bounce back. If it had gone, shattered, about fifteen girls would have needed plastic surgery. By this time the Birmingham pub bombings had already happened. They were bad enough, and this blast threw a young soldier to his death, twenty feet across the main road. He left a wife and child.

I don't know whose daughters were at my school but security was stepped up a hundredfold. Along with the front doors being locked during school hours, there were extra personnel watching all areas like Big Brother. Twenty of us were selected by the school to have a meeting with the Birmingham Fire Brigade. I suspect I was the only one chosen and the others came along to watch, as a rather jovial fire officer taught me not only how to recognise and smell high explosive, but also the workings of your average bomb – mainly how to defuse it. At last the school had found a use for me. Absolutely loving every moment of this experience, I set about for the next few weeks earnestly trying to find items to defuse, but alas, nothing was to be found, so I set about making my own explosive moments, metaphorically speaking.

The then Minister of Education was Margaret Thatcher and she was coming to visit the school. Funnily enough, none of my friends nor I had the faintest idea who she was, but knowing that all parents would be present in the school hall and encouraged by the sudden appearance of sniffer dogs and armed police, I set about making my mark. Also knowing that I would be placed as far away from the stage as physically possible, so that no verbal or anal raspberries could be heard from my quarters, I was aware that I had to act quickly if I was to get a laugh out of this.

I gathered my brother's, my father's and my sister's alarm clocks into my satchel, and on arriving at school scurried below the stage in the vast assembly hall and synchronised and set them for 3.10 p.m. By that time Margaret Thatcher should be at least five minutes into her speech in the hall. As I left the hall after setting the clocks, the sniffer dogs were already at work outside the building. Surprisingly they didn't find any dope on certain key pupils, but no doubt that wasn't what they were trained to look for. Neither were the dogs trained to detect alcohol, which was invariably on my breath by 8.40 a.m. after a swig from the gin bottle kept in the piano in the fifth-form common room.

The day was accompanied by the usual sense of drudgery with the exception of a few additional twinsets and pearls. It appeared Mrs Thatcher shopped at the same couturiers as my teachers – either that or there was serious evidence of cloning. And while I had never in the past seen my school as middle-class Conservative, on this day, with all the parents preening around in the recognition they felt the presence of their Tory minister bestowed, you could wipe the snobbery from your skin like an oil slick.

Come the afternoon, we all gathered in the hall like sheep, some wanting words of enlightenment, but most just pleased to be missing history or geometry, and the odd few in search of a good deep snooze. We all stood, somewhat bemused, as Mrs Thatcher, mayors, councillors, school governors and a smug-looking headmistress Miss Joyce entered the hall and walked up to the stage. There was rapturous applause for a group of people only one per cent knew anything about, yet alone recognised.

Miss Joyce introduced the proceedings with a speech worthy of a condemned man begging for his life. I grew increasingly twitchy as not only did Miss Joyce milk every moment but so did the school governors. It would make no sense if the alarm clocks went off during their self-appreciation monologues.

Finally, Mrs Thatcher stood to speak. Even then she had the body language of a self-proclaimed empress. As the majority of the audience sat and gawped at her, she turned our bewilderment into worship as she translated our lack of interest into amazement. Today, either I have no memory of what Mrs Thatcher spoke about or I just simply didn't understand a word she uttered, so I'm afraid I cannot communicate her speech, but I'll take a wild guess that it was about statistics and figures.

As each carefully laboured word marked the seconds 3.10 p.m. drew teasingly close. Sitting in my bottom-numbingly hard plastic chair, I felt my heart pick up pace, and my thighs started to sweat on to my regulation skirt. Anticipating the laugh was too much to bear. 3.10 came, nothing happened. I must have turned blue as I held my breath until eventually a solitary alarm clock burst into life under Mrs Thatcher's feet. It rang out with irrepressible gusto and expression but sadly lost steam as its coil wound down. Such is the problem with wind-up alarm clocks.

But then, as a chorus in response to the dying of a fellow clock, another alarm kicked in and then another. So much for synchronising, these guys kept to their own mean time.

The first ring drew a bewildered reaction and was ignored as a believable accident. Mrs Thatcher paused to consider it, but even she knew an icy glare couldn't stop an alarm in its determination, so she continued. But when the chorus of rattle started, she knew something was going on. I kept a completely straight face, as slowly, like a Mexican wave, the teachers, pupils and most parents turned to look at me. The only titter to break out was upon the very last 'dink' cried out by a dying alarm clock. Mrs Thatcher drew breath and continued without air, it seemed, for another forty-five minutes, which led me to believe that rather than being a fellow mammal, perhaps she was reptilian.

Since I'd just won the school art award for designing the

programme for the end-of-term play, *Tobias and the Angel* (which I directed as well), while being banned from art classes and consequently not taking art O level, it is very possible that Miss Joyce was suffering some minuscule pangs of guilt for suppressing – or at least attempting to suppress – the only talent I had, but I received no punishment for the alarm-clock incident. As I'd grown accustomed to seeing punishment as reward, this was a little bit of an anticlimax.

But for all the scorn I have poured upon my school, they were making huge efforts to see the world through my eyes. Upon realising that I was not just plain thick and that there was a strange justice in my ways and that it wasn't a reign of terror I was inciting, but a reign of honesty, the teachers actually began to barter with me and ask my advice.

On one occasion a young Asian girl, to whom I was very close, had run away. She was the sister of my much-loved best friend Bina. Gita was fabulous, her whole family were fabulous, but both Bina and Gita were being brought up in the tradition that Indian girls are obedient and must honour family tradition. Both Bina and Gita were beautiful beyond words. Outside school, men and women would stop in their tracks and just watch them. This wasn't always easy for me, being the one who wanted fame; in their company I was hugely overshadowed. I felt enormously protective towards them: very occasionally a shout of 'Wogs' would be flung in their faces and I would launch into World War III on an unsuspecting white male, just to make sure that words never passed his lips again with ease.

Bina and Gita were modern women, and hanging over their potentially brilliant futures was the prospect of arranged marriages. I think this was more of a disciplinary threat than a reality, but Gita was not getting on with her mum and she disappeared.

I was in history detention when Miss Joyce called me to her office and for the first time in five years we had a two-way conversation. With almost trembling trepidation Miss Joyce, it seemed, astonished herself and asked for my help. She asked me to be the mediator in getting Gita to return. The temptation to play power games with old Joycey was ignored, and I agreed not only to get Gita back but also to try and get to the centre of her troubles and see if they could be resolved. Bina, Gita and I had had our own wars, I had fought physically and psychologically with both of them in the past, but that had done nothing other than build a rock-solid respect between all three of us, and neither they nor I saw one another as any threat. So on finding Gita – which wasn't hard; she was at the home of the most beautiful man in Birmingham, Derek Goddard, our hairdresser, of course – I got her to return home and then to come back to school.

Gita's parents were doctors. I always called them Mr and Mrs Jaraij. I never knew their first names, but I felt great compassion for them as they had to learn to give their girls a greater independence than they were prepared to. How two traditionalists managed to raise two *femme fatales* who dressed in Biba and stilettos, who knew the latest fashions before *Vogue*, who had every male in Birmingham following them home, I'll never know.

Mrs Jaraij had to sit down and negotiate a future that was acceptable to both her and Gita, or else Gita would go to London and never be seen again. For a short while a compromise was met.

What Mrs Jaraij didn't bank on was that within days I would have such a huge punch-up with my mother that she would offer to take me in, while both Mum and I calmed down.

I can't even remember what the fight was about – probably fashion and hair, Derek Goddard's latest cut; I was changing so quickly beyond recognition and Mum's control – and there were so many fights, but this time I smacked Mum full on the face and Dad had to separate us. I was hysterical; if I stayed one more night under the same roof as Mum I was sure I'd take my own life. When I phoned Bina and asked if I could stay the night, Mrs Jaraij talked to my Dad and it was agreed I should live at the Jaraijs' until Mum and I could be reconciled.

Mrs Jaraij was a very honest woman. At first she'd talk in Hindi if she felt the conversation shouldn't include me, but very soon she'd voice her opinions in English straight to my face. Believing I was the bad influence in her daughters' lives, she'd repeatedly tell me not to lead them astray. It seemed pointless arguing with her that perhaps her daughters' handicap was their beauty.

For two weeks I experienced happiness and calm, though quite how amid the arguments between the Jaraij mother and daughters I do not know, but for once I was not the subject of the hostilities. Dad would telephone every day and talk to Mrs Jaraij, with me gesticulating behind her back that I was not available for comment, but a happy equilibrium was maintained by both: neither did Mrs Jaraij say that I'd turned her home into hell, nor Father that life was bliss without me.

Belonging is not a state I have ever known well. I have always felt like a visitor even in my own home, constantly waiting to move on or in a perfect world simply to transform and transcend. Change stopped me belonging.

Mealtimes at the Jaraijs were fantastic: Indian food three times a day, with Mr Jaraij threatening – well, teasing really – his daughters with arranged marriage, constantly talking about this long-lost cousin in India and that one who had shown an interest in marriage. And then there was Bina and Gita's little brother, who so loved the company of us girls. There was no promise of marriage for him. University beckoned, his education must go on and on. No time for childhood. How his little face would fall with the weight of the world placed on his shoulders.

The Jaraijs were incredibly tolerant. They could have thrown me out at any time, but never was this threatened, even when the worst happened. In Indian terms, that is.

Bina, Gita and I hung out with Derek Goddard, a star hairdresser at Rackhams in Birmingham. Our relationship with Derek was purely innocent, but wildly exciting all the same. I was Derek's hair model. Derek had tons of models, all stunningly beautiful; I was the weird one he could do anything to, and thanks to Derek I adopted a permanent space-age look.

Mrs Jaraij loathed her daughters' relationship with Derek. He wasn't Indian and it looked as if either of her girls might walk down the aisle with him, with me tagging behind broken-hearted – but that's another story.

One sunny schoolday morning, when the scent of averageness was hanging in the air, we three sisters of intent managed to persuade Mrs J that we were going to school on the bus rather than have her drive us in to Edgbaston. Somewhat reluctantly she agreed to let us go. We walked with so much normality to the corner of the street, it made our muscles ache, then we legged it into the city centre, into the nearest public loo and into our fabulously vampy Biba clothes. Well, I didn't own any, but Miss Selfridge did good cheap copies. Then, freed of our chastity-enhancing school uniform, we zapped into the coach station and caught the bus to London.

We were meeting Derek in Biba on Kensington High Street. I hadn't been to London since I was seven and in no way could Madame Tussaud's compete with Barbara Hulanicki's clothes emporium. Sheer exhilaration pumped through my veins at the thought that I was about to walk on her hallowed turf and maybe even buy a genuine article. London offered a feast for the eyes on every street corner. The atmosphere in Biba was thick with moody lights, black walls, mirrors, Roxy Music and patchouli oil. We let our hands brush over the clothes on the rails, the shoulder pads, the satin, and for one brief moment we forgot about the existence of Derek, and shopping almost claimed us as addicts.

Tearing ourselves away, we made for the main entrance of the store where we'd agreed to meet Derek. We ambled and pouted and minced through the trendy London shoppers, as if we were models off a cover of a rock album – albeit very short models, one being exceptionally dumpy and unattractive. Supercharged with confidence and attitude, exuding self-importance, we strutted to where Derek would be waiting, wearing our best wiggles on our hips, laughing and smiling – and we came face to face with Dr and Mrs Jaraij.

They were fuming. Mrs Jaraij had noticed that morning that our best clothes were missing from the wardrobe and on phoning the school had received an answer she was dreading. No, her daughters were not in school today. Then Mrs J phoned Rackhams hair salon where an innocent receptionist boasted that Derek had gone shopping in London at Biba; so an earnest phone call to Dr J's surgery was followed by what must have been a 100 m.p.h. journey down the M1 into the centre of sinful London.

The Jaraijs kept perfect steely self-control and dignity. Their offspring didn't. Ignoring Derek's gentlemanly promises that he would not molest their daughters and would have us safely back in Birmingham by 7 p.m., the Js escorted all three of us out of

Biba and into a waiting car. So much for cool. We could never show our faces in Kensington again.

The journey home was icy terrible. Gita argued all the way. The teasing about arranged marriages turned into promises; the threats of telling my mother had no effect, but the fact that the sisters were grounded for a month really hurt. Bina in retaliation threatened to sleep with Derek at the next possible chance and Mrs J convinced herself that her daughters already had. All the time this bickering was going on, we quietly passed a bag of toffees between us, munching and spitting accusations while trying to stem our hunger.

Mrs J must have breathed a huge sigh of relief the day my father came to collect me, a day that left me hollow. The one family I could live with couldn't live with me any longer. At least I left in the comfort of knowing that the Jaraij girls didn't need my presence to rebel and a reluctant Mrs J would still have the emancipation of her daughters to deal with.

I have always loathed the melancholy of returning to a silent house. It's not the rich melancholy that the view of the ocean can give you; at least the ocean speaks to you. Silence was the only way my mother and I could deal with each other. No words, no war. How I missed the Hindi language; even when it wasn't understood, it pushed a path forwards through a dense forest of misunderstanding.

When I saw the Jaraij girls at school in the week we'd act like freedom fighters in our gym slips, impersonating David Bowie at every opportunity, putting on burlesque rock shows in the assembly hall at lunchtime and then getting into an anti-racist fight by teatime.

Chapter 8

At weekends it was often a different picture. It seems I had different friends to suit my different personalities. On Friday nights, I hung out with a group of Hell's Angels in the Lickey Hills. In this beauty spot on the outskirts of Birmingham there was a landmark, a large Swiss chalet – like a cuckoo in the nest. I loved its large black beams and wooden roof placed between the food factories on one side and forest on the other. My grandfather built this chalet, so my father says; it was as out of place as me.

I'd met the Hell's Angels at a disco in a church hall. They were pursuing my friend, yet another pretty one, Karen Tredwell. Karen was tough; she outshone me. Watching her was an education in unarmed combat. Her fists had more contact with flesh than the Queen's right hand and I'm not talking about polite social etiquette here. Karen was dating a member of the gang who was reputed to be a lord. Steve was a much-loved leader, a surprisingly passive man, small in size, big in charisma, public-school educated and inheritor of the big manor in the Lickey Hills. There were about thirty Angels in the group; all wore their ceremonial trousers and leather jackets, nothing new there, except the ceremony that initiated each of them into the gang meant that the whole gang would relieve themselves and vomit on the initiate's trousers, so an interesting aroma followed them. But all in all these guys were truly nice people.

My involvement with them was simplified by the fact that none of them was interested in me. For Karen it was a different story. She had all their 'molls' to fight with, while I danced the night away. For me it was an opportunity to be near bikes, a personal symbol of freedom, especially since I'd seen *Easy Rider*. The more chrome the better. Also the juxtaposition of such bright minds in such dirty trousers thrilled me. They didn't care how the world saw them, because they'd created their own inner island within which they ruled and from which they poured scorn on neighbouring kingdoms.

To them I was just this weird outsider, who occasionally made a point of picking a fight with their largest, most unbalanced member, always male, just to show how hard I was (trying to be). To me they were the most wonderful, exotic circus that had ever come to town.

For a while life at home had been relatively peaceful, partly because I was now allowed out – and even though I always promised to be home by 10 p.m. I would creep in at 4 a.m. Both Mum and Dad were intrigued to know more about the mysterious new company I was keeping. Their conversation was carefully plotted, as to glean as much information from me as possible without my losing my temper. Keeping their fears at bay, I used Steve's title to justify all the time I was spending with the gang, plus my love of motor bikes.

I couldn't have been that successful; the smokescreen was more of a mist as both my parents insisted I invite the gang to tea, and I knew it wasn't because they were desperate to meet a lord.

Steve took this request with great enthusiasm, in fact, I'd say he was genuinely touched. So a date and time were set: 3 p.m. one Sunday in October 1974.

Mum set about making plates of neat cucumber sandwiches. Salmon sandwiches, vol-au-vents, scones and cream. All on the best plates with the best china cups and saucers. Also, as she did before all her guests arrived, Mum cleaned the house. Dad kept out of her way; instead he and I set up the billiard table, ready for a friendly bout of snooker, then he settled down for an afternoon in front of the TV.

At 3.30 precisely, half an hour late, a rumble could be heard on the distant horizon. Being unsure that I wasn't about to be stood up, I was waiting out on the pavement. The rumble was familiar; no doubt a friendly pub had waylaid my friends.

As they came into vision, the noise growing in intensity, the autumn sun caught the chrome on about thirty motor bikes. I stood waving with glee as they all poured into the front garden. The reason for the late arrival was that Pedro had had to build a new side-car out of orange boxes, because the demand for this tea party outweighed available bike and pillion capacity. Steve, the lord, bless him, wore his best suit. I think he was a lawyer by day, lawbreaker by night. He confidently strode up to my mother, kissed her, shook my father's hand and charmed the pants off both of them.

Even so, that look a rabbit has, when caught in the headlights of a car, didn't leave Mum's face for a few days. About forty Hell's Angels turned up in all. The cucumber sandwiches lasted ten seconds. Mum, between heated secret conversations with Dad, busied herself being the hostess with the mostest among the mostest with the hostess.

The gang were on their best behaviour; we played snooker all afternoon. Individually each member cornered Mum and let it be known to her that they were all highly educated, good people with a penchant for being on the outside of society. Mum couldn't answer back; it was more a case of look and learn and pray that the walls of prejudice break down.

Dad's afternoon of telly-watching wasn't interrupted, he just had about ten people join him for the John Wayne film; the occasional 'Sshh!' could be heard coming from the lounge. All in all it was a huge success. No one smoked dope. No one farted. They all left at 6 p.m. Mum and Dad never enquired about my friends again. And the neighbour's curtains eventually stopped twitching.

The thing I adored about this gang was that they were incredibly easygoing and never pushed anyone into anything. Never once did they threaten me sexually, in fact they did the opposite and often protected me from outsiders forcing themselves on me. It was as if instinctively they immediately knew how incredibly naïve I was about relationships. Also how paranoid I was about a serious relationship changing my life direction, which I fully intended to be stage, film and fame.

But friends aren't always there to protect you. One winter's afternoon in Solihull, a posh suburb of Birmingham, my friend Dawn and I were in a café frequented by a far more frightening gang of Angels. Dawn was more worldly-wise than me, having been sexually active since the age of twelve, and I think she found my self-control frustrating, if not a little irritating. Dawn and I had a very close relationship; we knew everything about each other, from our bodily functions to intimate details about boyfriends – mainly hers. We even practised our snogging techniques on each other. Now that's what a friend is for – until we could get our hands on the opposite sex.

This day we'd caught the eyes of two quite scary guys, and it soon became evident we weren't going to be able to shake them off. Dawn enjoyed male company and didn't seem disturbed by the fact that these guys were armed up to the hilt with knuckle-dusters and blades. When after the café, a pub, window-shopping down the High Street, they decided they wanted to go to the nearby park, I made one last-ditch attempt to shake them off. Walking ahead with Dawn I begged her to catch a bus with me, out of there, pretend we had to meet some other guys, anything. But Dawn said, 'Don't be such a stick in the mud [my brother's nickname for me], it'll be fun.' While Dawn disappeared into a bush with her guy, I fought mine off, with as much boring conversation as I could come up with, till Dawn emerged. It seemed it was my turn to be dragged off. Determined not to show fear, I feigned every off-putting condition in the book – disease, food poisoning, madness, fits, period pains, being gay – all in the space of five minutes. I pleaded with Dawn to get me out of this. She said, 'Go on, it's fun.' But the atmosphere changed when my man pulled a knife on me. Dawn went white, made her excuses and left.

Knowing that fear would do nothing but work against me, I decided I had to follow the process through till I had the right moment of escape. So upping the bravado, I changed tack and pulled the man into the park Gents. He was drunk. That was my strength and my opportunity. Putting his blade down to unzip his trousers he pushed me to the floor and lay on top of me. This seemed to make his intoxication worse – perhaps he was stoned as well; he momentarily became confused and lost co-ordination of his hands. I stared him in the eyes and asked him, 'Would you like to meet the Devil?' He was dumbstruck. Then with all my willpower I visualised the presence that had haunted me in my early teens. I don't know what his experience of this moment was, but as I focused as much fear and hate upon him as I could muster, without flinching a facial muscle, his erection subsided and he turned aside to vomit. Seizing the moment, I got up, expressed my disappointment with his performance and left the building.

He was a completely different man when he came out. Completely unsure of me, he walked me to the bus stop. The following week he followed me and Dawn around Solihull like a whipped puppy. I brushed him off with the lie that I had to see my heroin dealer. He was impressed. I was rid of him.

Although I've had painful crushes on men since the age of about seven, I have never trusted them with my emotions. I tend to love people intensely and resent the power they have over me. In this vulnerable state I've therefore loved many in mind and few in the flesh.

My other best friend Trisha and I hung out, at weekends, with a gang of girls in Pershore who loved many men in the flesh and none in the mind. M. was the Amazon leader of this predatory pack. She towered over Trisha and me. We admired her greatly. To a pubescent teenager she was a worldly-wise goddess, who slept with whom she chose and how many she chose and knew everything there was to know about birth control. So brazen was our leader that men slept with her in awe. One night at a party in a house on a Pershore housing estate, M.'s then boyfriend discovered that in the space of one evening she'd bedded every man at the party, which left Trish and me tackling him in unarmed combat as he tried to strangle her.

M. and the girls saw me as a sad middle-class reject. They liked me, but by their own admission they didn't understand me. We'd squabble over what we each wanted for our future. I wanted education, qualifications, a career and no family. M. wanted a baby and no man. If M. fell pregnant she'd get a flat and a single-parent income. I thought this was throwing her life away; she thought it was perfection. Each to their own.

As we supped our beers in the back-street pubs of Pershore, David Bowie's 'Life on Mars' playing on the juke-box, the boys in the back rooms were shooting heroin, while we were talking babies and stardom. As the sun poured such perfect beauty through the windows on to our flesh, I'd sit there in a deep sense of melancholy, and I soon grew accustomed to it as the spur to drive me out of dead-end habits and attitudes.

I loved the girls, but not enough to follow their dreams. Don't get me wrong – I know I'm in serious danger of sounding smug. M. truly believed my dreams were sterile. Childbirth to her was, and is, the ultimate creative gift given to man and woman. I could neither face childbirth nor, more than anything, more than any fear of failure, could I stay in the same town, the same house, look at the same view for the rest of my life, no matter how wonderful family life could be.

Often, in a state of excruciating loneliness – usually after a concert, or a row with the boyfriend, when I was so famous that a casual stroll down the street was tantamount to suicide – I would drive through the night to Pershore and just sit in the shadows of its Edwardian splendour and pine for M. and the boys. Sadly, at least half the gang have now died, either through heroin or as a result of reckless driving. But deep down inside I could sense that through motherhood M. had found an inner peace that the rest of us were incapable of discovering.

In recent days I have acquired a home in Pershore. Its main street hasn't changed for years. It bustles with market-town life and a welcoming friendliness, and funnily enough, my soul feels at rest and at home as soon as I turn off the M5 and head for this little piece of England that used to play host to a subterranean culture.

My home lies in full view of Pershore Abbey as the sun sets behind it. Now, the Abbey is to me like a Constable: perfection, held in time. Back then, at the stroke of midnight, we'd all run round it anticlockwise, thirteen times to invoke the Devil. Somehow I think the Devil has left; he no longer gets the kind of attention he craves. And ironically I have found a view that has been under my nose, or should I say above my head, for most of my life, that I could look at for the rest of my life.

Chapter 9

I'd wake in a cold sweat at 4 a.m., sit at my east window and watch the sunrise like a great Japanese symbol of good fortune, and wonder what the hell I had to do to pluck it from the sky and put it in my pocket. Revision eluded me. I'd left it too late. All I could think about was walking in a silent Japanese garden, staring into Ziggy Stardust's face. I'd grown so accustomed to seeing the sunrise that I felt David Bowie had designed it from the birthmark on his forehead. A great orange disc.

I had left my O-level revision to the eleventh hour, and horror was setting in at the thought of three weeks of sitting looking at blank pieces of paper. I was to take nine O levels, nine exams for classes I had hardly attended. Served me right.

When the day came – maths first, as my premonition had warned me – I sat for four hours writing out the lyrics of 'Life on Mars', hoping the examiner would mistake it for a highly sophisticated form of algebra. Algebra! What a waste of time. If the education system could waste my time, I wasted theirs in turn. I hope the marker was a Bowie fan. My brother Kim and sister Nicola had always swotted for exams and had always felt they'd done their best. I remember thinking, All that angst and pain for such mediocre results – when in fact the results weren't mediocre at all, it was just that no one in our house celebrated Bs and Cs, only straight As. If I remember rightly there was little celebration, so what was the point?

The same process followed for history, geography, physics, English, music theory and history, biology, Scripture and French. I could very possibly have answered at least half the written questions, but my fear of exams was too great and my loathing of the ritual of silence, mistrust and separation from all those around you completely freaked me out. I felt like a condemned criminal going to the gallows. There was no way I could construct even a sentence, let alone an essay. And then at the end of every bum-numbing marathon, all the girls would break into a dawn chorus of nervous chatter about how well they felt they'd performed and how inspired they'd been or how they'd not revised for just one of the questions, which had taken them by surprise. I'd just stay silent in a cloud of shame, pretending I didn't care, but I did. I cared that I could never fit into this way of justifying one's existence, and if I could have I would have spread my hidden wings and flown the world in search of like-minded, intelligent people who could not find a firm foothold within the system. But those wings only worked in my mind, and anyway, the last day of school for the rest of my life was looming. The day I'd prayed for, for fourteen years, was well and truly on the horizon. Who needed wings when time could get you out of a fix?

On the last day I felt hollow. I had nothing to show for it all; it was as if the whole experience had been an empty gesture from a group of disciplinarians who didn't want to see children on the streets during the day. Everyone swapped numbers, cried and lovingly packed their books. At least I learned I didn't like goodbyes. I felt nothing. I said nothing. All I was aware of was that the big old sun, which had risen into this day at 4 a.m., was above my head, and as it turned to chase the night, I was going with it.

Everyone who was leaving for good had to line up outside Miss Joyce's office to say goodbye. It was embarrassing and not even her most ardent fans wanted to be there, but she dutifully shook every hand and pretended to know every girl and wished them well.

When she got to me, she held my hand in a vice-like grip, like an enemy commander admitting defeat, and said, 'I'm so very glad you're not coming back next term.' 'So am I, Miss Joyce, so am I.' I never saw her or thought of her again. Well, not till fame allowed me my bitter public revenge through the media. As I waited at the bus stop alone, outside the silent empty school, I couldn't believe that time had released me from one race, a very slow, intolerable race, into a much faster, less tolerant one. I knew I had to be quick or I'd miss the start of my life.

My father was at home when I got there. He asked me how I felt. Not one for showing emotion, I just said, 'Great.' What I really felt was, Oh my God, I'm out here on my own. No school to blame, no uniform to rebel against, no classes to miss; I'd better become someone, something, fast or my lack of substance will render me invisible.

Now most intelligent people would have looked for a job before this day, but that kind of prudent forward thinking escaped me until I was about thirty-three. I spent the afternoon scouring the local paper for jobs, booking appointments for interviews and signing on. Because I intended to go to drama school full time, that was my one and only priority. Since the age of fourteen I had attended the Old Rep Theatre School on Station Street in Birmingham on Friday nights and Saturday mornings. The principal, Miss Richards, who must have been about ninety-two years old, truly, was going to audition me for the three-year adult course. I had to learn a piece of Shakespeare – my speech was Ophelia from *Hamlet*; a contemporary piece – I chose *Under Milk Wood*; and a poem – I went for Wilfred Owen. It was will alone that got me through the audition. Shaking with nerves I delivered Shakespeare in a way that would have had him digging his escape out of the grave to retrieve his work off me. *Under Milk Wood* must have sounded like William Hague on Mogadon, and my poem was completely freed from poetic rhythm. But Miss Richards was a kindly soul, who recognised my pure will to achieve, my sense of belonging to the theatre and the fact that not every potential drama student was flocking to her door. I got on the course. This made me deliriously happy.

But before the term started, I had to find employment for the summer and win a grant for my course.

I trudged from job interview to job interview. From jewellers to market stalls, shops to office blocks. I had the same reaction from all of them. As soon as I walked in, they'd decide on spec that they didn't like the look of me and tell me the job was not for me, or ask, 'How many O levels have you taken?'

'Nine,' I'd reply.

'Oh!' They'd be taken by surprise. Stop. Pause. Thought.

'Well, you're overqualified for us then,' and out I'd go, knowing there wasn't a hope in hell that I would have passed even one of my exams.

I think maybe my punk hair, plus black clothes and white-faced make-up, all about twelve month pre-punk explosion, may have been taken as antisocial.

In the meantime I had applied for a drama grant. I had no money in the bank and so far no hope of paying for my course. My parents, having always been honest about their financial situation, which was nil, said they could let me stay at home, but that was it; any help with upkeep would greatly be appreciated.

Mr Slade was my adjudicator for my grant. I met him in a black-painted room in the centre of Birmingham's College of Music. I wore black. As I walked in, he visibly cringed; by the time I left he was twitching. I performed exactly the same pieces as I had for Miss Richards, but this time with a sense of desperate appeal. Mr Slade made it quite obvious I was wasting his time; apart from my image I don't think the nervous shake helped. I was terrified.

'Why do you want to act?' he asked.

'Because I love theatre and performance,' I replied.

'What do you want to specialise in?' he enquired.

Specialise? Why the hell should I want to specialise? The whole world tastes good, not just one corner. 'I want to act, sing and dance,' came my reply.

'In musicals?'

'No, I loathe musicals. No, I want to act in films mainly, have a band and perhaps do a bit of choreography.' I think he thought I'd applied the final nail to the coffin of my theatrical education.

Mr Slade breathed a tired sigh of wannabe fatigue and started to write on his many forms. 'Not attractive' caught my eye. Then he looked up and said; 'You know you have a speech impediment, don't you?' I hadn't a clue what he meant. Impediment. What the hell was that?

'No,' I replied.

'You have a lisp!'

'So?'

'You'll need to do something about it; you cannot act with a lisp.' He was bored of me.

I left the room knowing I had done my best. It may not have been an Oscar-winning performance, but it gave me bravado and confidence in a way I had never experienced before. I was starting to find my feet in this world.

Be yourself, no one can be that for you. Be forceful, push back others' walls of resistance! Don't absorb their shit; reflect it back and earn respect.

While I waited for my grant results I was given a job interview I didn't expect. Legal & General were looking for recruits in office management. I'd only talked to a secretary on the phone when applying for an interview, but either my plummy public-school voice or the fact I went to Edgbaston C. of E. College placed my feet firmly through the doors of this huge corporation just off New Street.

For the interview I made sure I looked immaculate. Immaculate to me in those days was tight black pencil skirt, French black sailor's top, black bolero jacket, stilettos and seamed stockings, with my jet-black and blue hair sleeked down smooth, pointed fringe snipped off into a straight bang. This was my immaculate. I think in the eyes of the Legal & General personnel officer I was his dream dominatrix. As I walked into the building heads turned, not a titter; my appearance obviously pleased the eyes of this concrete block of bureaucracy. My Cecil Gee-suited interviewer stared at me non-stop and was possibly the first person I'd ever met who treated me like an intellectual. I knew I could be a good actress in the right environment. By the following week I was in the boss's office being offered the top job irrespective of the results of my nine O levels, which I described to the boss as Einstein doing the *Sunday Sport* crossword. If I'd failed any of the exams *that* would be the miracle.

The boss was a lovely man, in no way salacious. I think he genuinely liked my individuality; he may even have had hopes that I would pep the office up a bit. On my first day at work he sat me in his office and told me that the company were looking forward to having me there for life. Promotion would be a reality within six months. I didn't have the heart to tell him that within six months I would be happily ensconced in drama school.

The summer drifted by. The Legal & General weighed round

my neck. The predictability of the paper work. The endless repetitive sums. I never quite arrived on the same planet as the office girls who had dreams of Hoovers, duvets and babies. At lunch I'd sneak off to find Bina in Rackhams for a touch of life and sanity.

I shared an office with six other desks. The sun never reached our windows, possibly because the neighbouring building was thoughtfully placed eight feet away. If I craned my neck I could see the sun's rays pass us by in Union Square. Steve sat opposite me. His complexion was pallid, grey – unfortunately the same colour as his suit. Steve lived with his sick mother. His spirit was so repressed that I could find no identifying marks in his personality. His characteristic imprints were so smooth it was like looking at and talking to a canvas that held no paint. I resisted being cruel to him; I think he'd had enough of that from life. I tried to tease him out of himself, but sadly the effort on his part was too much. I started to feel guilt that I was about to leave him behind, because if no one made the effort, the next time those offices were to be decorated, someone might paper over him.

My performance as a mathematician was letting the boss down dreadfully. It was not that I made mistakes, more that I didn't excel, and really I didn't bother to excel. My wage was very good: already within a month I could afford my first year at drama school – but my wage was not for that use. I wanted the money for independence. A flat, clothes, possibly a car. After all, I was waiting for my grant. My boss was ever suspicious, waiting for my O-level results.

One Friday night when I returned from the office, Dad handed me the rough brown envelope from the City Council. I was terrified. I opened it with Dad beside me leaning on the ironing-board in the kitchen, Mum at the cooker making supper. It was a cooker she had had all her married life, old and unreliable, and it frustrated her.

Tears flooded down my face as I read the words: 'You have not been accepted for a drama grant as we believe you are not a suitable applicant. You may try again in six months.'

Trying to hide my disappointment from Mum and Dad, I quietly went to my room and cried. Dad was brilliant; in her way so was Mum. Money was talked about in this household with great honesty. There was none – but worse than that, for me, is to go on and on about it. I loathe people who moan and take no action, so in this moment I was grateful that neither of my parents got overly upset on my behalf.

After I had calmed down, I went downstairs to Dad's leaky old study. It needed a new roof. I called Mary Richards at the Theatre School. Remarkably she was still there.

'Hello, ducky!' came the paper-thin voice.

'Oh hello, Miss Richards, I've had some bad news and I don't know what to do. I hope I don't have to give my place up at the school, but my grant has been refused.' I tried desperately to sound strong.

'Oh typical, ducky, typical.'

'There is one thing. I've earned enough for the first term, September till December. Please could I come for that?'

'Of course, ducky, of course. Don't worry, we'll find you some work, we'll get you through the course. Oh and ducky, you must reapply for the grant in the following term, you never know.'

I did reapply and I never got it, leaving me the only paying pupil in the entire school without a grant and today the only one still in the business, bar two, Donna Croll and Phil Grady. Thank you, Mr Slade, you inadvertently gave me a will of iron. And thank you, Miss Mary Richards, who lived alone with her ten cats and passed away the night before her hundredth birthday. She never charged me a penny after that first term and she found me work.

When I handed in my notice at the Legal & General they were devastated; they'd truly hoped I would be there for life. When people believe in you the guilt is twofold, but the truth is my life wouldn't have been very long if I'd stayed there. There was just too much paper, too many suits and ties, too many stilettos and just a tad too much control. As I walked out of the overheated building for the last time, I took an intake of breath so deep you'd have thought I could have held my breath for a month.

As I left Legal & General my exam results fell on the doormat of 119 Grove Road. There really was no point in opening them. They'd all be Ds. I'm surprised my mum bothered to harbour any hopes over them. But there, buried on the list that told my parents they'd wasted fourteen years of school fees on me, was a B in music theory. That B sat on the kitchen table, laughing like a little angel, coaxing me into the future. Mum and Dad didn't see the funny side.

Chapter 10

Every day when I stepped through the stage door my heart would rush with excitement. The smell of this theatre was unique; the dust was possibly the very same that scurried and swirled around Sybil Thorndike's feet or Laurence Olivier's. Even Richard Burton, Peggy Ashcroft, Errol Flynn or Vivien Leigh. Inhaling the smell of that dust was like breathing gold. It had a bouquet of talent. I've never known a building like it; it was a bell-jar of ghosts.

I already knew the Birmingham Old Repertory Theatre well. I knew the area. I'd been attending the Theatre School there for the past four years every Friday evening and Saturday. The rumble of the trains bringing strangers to and from New Street station. The porn cinema right next to the cartoon cinema, right next to the greatest sweetshop in town, right next to the greatest theatre in the world, which now lay dormant except for the love of amateurs and students.

The very first day I walked into the school on the top floor as a fully-fledged full-time student, a titter ran among the new arrivals – perhaps it was my Dr Spock haircut, black and pink today, or the fact that I was dressed like Cruella de Vil – but I didn't care. The most important thing was that I was noticed, and if I was going to get anywhere in this business, that was the first step. Tip number one. Don't blend in with the crowd.

A lot of my fellow students proved to be very, very good. So good, in fact, that it made me want to give up on quite a few occasions. The school wasn't rigid or technical enough to get me through my own obstacle course of lisp, dyslexia and limp. It wasn't even able to recognise that those three qualities were both a problem and a gift. Anthony Sher has to act them. I have them.

There was one girl, Nicky, who had a truly serene, angelic quality; she could recite a poem, a sonnet, a psalm, graffiti from the toilet wall and make it liquid, effervescent with music and lust. Then I would follow her on to the stage, and murder Keats by tying boulders around the words and drowning them in public. I think I've cried more having had to follow Nicky on to the stage than over anything else in my life.

What the school did provide for me was a home. I'd stay late and sit in the dark and the silence, daydreaming, or should I say night dreaming, creating a matrix of desires and wishes. Still today I feel strongly that those quality moments of daydreaming helped my future shape itself. I'd arrive early in the morning so I could centre and ground myself, absorbing the building.

Most activity happened upstairs in the eaves of the building. There were just two rooms and Miss Richards's office. It was modest beyond belief, very Birmingham at that time. All natural light from the four windows this space shared was diffused by grime from inner-city trains. This was permanently a twilight world, hidden from the hubbub of city life. It was unfailingly sexy in its drabness, purely because it was a harbour for dreams which collected in every corner like froth.

In the main room was a stage, a very modest stage – the room itself was only 30 feet by 14 feet. The stage was just 6 feet deep and 6 inches high, but it had drawstring curtains and that was stage enough for me.

There were two permanent teachers. Bless them, they had to do everything, but at least they did it as badly as the rest of us, so we were all in the same boat.

Margaret was an angel in disguise. Six feet tall, she must have been in her mid-fifties. Having been a Bluebell Girl in Paris for most of her working life, she was not only a teacher but a natural counsellor for overstressed 'luvvies'. We'd all have rather heard her stories of Paris than be directed through J. B. Priestley by her, but we loved her and by some miracle there would be an end-of-term production. Then there was Mr Webb, probably in his late fifties. Mr Webb did the serious work and sadly almost never chose me for his productions, because I was too 'distinctive'. Mr Webb would have made a wonderful Hobbit.

He was challenged when it came to height, had a wonderfully shiny head that fought shy of hair and was always immaculately dressed. He was possibly the most qualified person in the school.

Miss Richards would direct a play per term, but as you can guess we played merry hell with her. Her hearing and eyesight were so bad that she'd direct our messing around, mistaking it for the play, and then she'd lose her temper and go ballistic when we finally organised ourselves and started to act.

There was one man who struck terror in us all. He was the Theatre School governor and manager of the Alexandra Theatre next door: Mr Gordon Price, Nicky's father. No one messed around in his chain-smoking presence. If the air wasn't blue with his smoke, it was blue with his language, and we all respected him because he had one foot in our world and the other firmly in the world of professional drama. And apart from that, he might employ us one day.

Gordon Price knew I was in dire straits, and beneath his nicotine and beige tweed jacket beat a heart of gold. One just had to prospect by showing determination and hard work to find it. Luckily I did. Gordon arranged for me to meet the wardrobe mistresses at not only the Alexandra Theatre but also the Hippodrome Theatre on Hurst Street.

There were two scourges of the drama student at this time, September 1974. One was the necessity of getting an Equity card – the one guaranteed path was to be a Butlins redcoat for forty weeks, a hell I managed to escape. The other was cash, or lack of it, just like for any other student. But a sure-fire way of getting your hungry hand on some readies was to be a dresser at your nearest theatre. In the hallowed rooms of the drama school, fellow pupils talked with dread and disgust at the thought, but that was all right for them, they had grants. Dressing was below them. How could they 'dress' a fellow artist? It was menial and demeaning.

So I walked through the stage door of the Alexandra Theatre feeling like a skivvy. Walking into the wardrobe department in the basement I was immediately hit by the heat, sweat and steam. Among piles and piles of bustles, skirts, corsets and touring cases slaved one woman who had to wash, iron and deliver to the dressing room by 6.30 p.m. all the costumes for the entire company of this week's touring show. She was desperate. So my work and my education started right there and then. It's a very scary prospect knowing you are responsible for the artist being on stage in the right costume at the right time; also, on top of that you have to make sure they are fed and watered and in a fit mental state to perform – so psychiatry comes in handy if you're going to be a truly excellent dresser.

All that and you never get to see the show. All the information you receive on the Monday is a handwritten list of which costumes are needed, for which scene, which are quick changes and how many sugars the artists like in their tea during the interval. Then you're on your own.

My very first dressing experience was to be with Sylvia Syms and Simon Williams. As one of my all-time favourite films is *Woman in a Dressing Gown*, I could hardly speak in Sylvia Syms's company. As I knocked on her door, my heart was in my mouth.

'Come,' came her very theatrical command.

'Hello, Miss Syms, I'm your dresser for the week.'

'Hello, darling, do come in.' She managed to size me up in the space of five words and didn't visibly flinch at my appearance. Miss Syms was wonderful. She didn't walk to the stage, she flourished and performed all the way to it. She even performed in the dressing room. I started to feel guilty that she felt she had to entertain me, so I'd do my bit and creep out, in case I became the cause of the leading lady's possible exhaustion.

Sylvia was starring in an Oscar Wilde, which one escapes me, but she had to wear the most fantastic clothes. I loved dressing her in them. Her main outfit was black and white taffeta with corset and bustle. The ritual before the show – and I soon learned that every artist has specific rituals, and God help you if you bugger them up – was first a cup of tea, general niceties about the day, perhaps I would need to go and get her a sandwich, then our very own private performance of putting on layer upon layer of Edwardian clothes, and slowly but surely Sylvia became the part.

Sylvia would put on her white silk stockings and tiny leather ankle-boots. Then came the white cotton bloomers, followed by a camisole. All this baggy free-flowing simplicity was then encased in an implement of torture, a corset. And in those days the corsets were real. You'd place it around the front and lace it up at the back, and depending on your leading lady's 'slimness' or 'vanity' you'd either pull it in modestly or all the blood-stopping way. Sylvia being both slim and self-possessed went all the way. With my foot placed firmly in the small of her back I'd pull on the laces till the sides of the corset touched, and my leading lady would stay that way until the last curtain call, at which point I'd race to the stage entrance and loosen the lace, to an enormous sigh of relief from Miss Syms.

I loved watching her from the wings. She was by far the most dignified and controlled actress I'd ever seen. With a flash of an eyelid or a swift turn of the head she could encourage the audience with subtle innuendo and they'd follow her every thought. I wouldn't say that we became buddies that week, but our relationship was one of reliable teamwork and mutual respect. So when Sylvia took her third or fourth curtain call I was immensely proud to be part of her life.

And as for Simon Williams, well it was just as well I only had to take him the occasional tea, because every time he asked me, 'Is Sylvia OK today?' I'd just have to pick myself up off the floor, dust myself down, wipe the dribble from the sides of my mouth and run off giggling.

The week went quickly. By the end of the first week's dressing I felt totally satisfied. Every day at drama school I held court with those who thought dressing was below them, and told all the wonderful details of how Miss Syms liked her tea, how she applied her make-up and all the hidden jokes she played upstage, so none other than Simon Williams and those standing in the wings could see. Every day at drama school I took a little of her magic with me and sprinkled it around the room for the others to share, or choose to be dismissive of. At last I had something to talk about other than vowels, bowels and Shakespeare.

After the last show on the Saturday, the stars pack their belongings with the speed of small tornadoes and scram back to London or wherever home is. A whole new team inhabit the theatre from that moment on. At 11 p.m. the building is filled with ants, worker ants, who skilfully take the set apart and load it on to lorries which will carry it overnight to the next theatre for reassembling on Sunday.

I, as a dresser, had to stay behind and carry all the costumes from the dressing rooms and load them into wardrobe crates for travelling. This would take until about 1 a.m. Then I'd stay and help the wardrobe mistress set up for the new week. Usually I'd leave the theatre at about 2 a.m. for the night bus back to Kings Heath.

What I loved about this moment is a strange and often painful thing that I think an awful lot of performers become addicted to: in the silence of Birmingham's back streets, walking on the wet cobbles, through the pools of light thrown by the odd street lamp, I realised I would never see any of those people again – except maybe if our paths crossed through work; everything was left up in the air, no time for long goodbyes, no room for sentiment, and I loved it. Often I'd forget about the night bus and walk home, reliving every moment of the week. Then I'd spend all day Sunday in bed.

Soon I was dressing at both the Alex and the Hippodrome. Word of my willingness to please and placate artists must have spread like wildfire. I absolutely loved being in the theatres, and it meant I could pay Mum some rent as well as my drama-school fees. I was earning £21 a week, enough in those days to live on, and I occasionally topped it up by being a shop assistant in Lewis's on Saturday morning or a waitress in a café-bar between school and theatre. I'd never been so happy.

Drama school was going fine, though I didn't feel I was actually going anywhere and inevitably frustration was starting to set in. I didn't feel I was developing, and also there was no room or opportunity to develop. And at the same time – well, for the entire time I was at drama school – I had this god-awful crush on a boy called Simon Ward. No, not the famous actor, but a Saxon blond with an infectious laugh and carefree attitude that just made one want to tie him down with rope and marriage vows. He was by far the prettiest boy in the school, and no doubt completely uninterested in the ugliest girl in the place.

This crush hung round my neck like a millstone, it invaded my thoughts and followed me home. I hated it. What made it twice as painful was the fact my best friend Liz Malone managed to pull him, so I had to sit over lunch, tea and evening telephone gossip listening to every detail. I just buried myself in more work and tried to forget him.

It still amazes me today that from the age of fourteen till my twentieth birthday I had no intimate contact, by that I mean any form of physical touch, with the opposite sex whatsoever. Boy, I must have been ugly.

Another friend, Donna Croll, with her exotic green eyes and coffee-coloured skin, was occasionally fitting classes in around her social life. The fact that she'd miss the odd day here and there didn't really matter, because her talent far outweighed the rest of ours put together. I used to love hiding in the costume store with her; she'd light up a fag under the original 1920s costumes hanging from the ceiling and tell me of her sexual exploits from the past weekend. Donna had a very colourful life. She had friends who would actually have the nerve to walk into Rackhams department store, pick up a Hoover or microwave they wanted from the shop display, claim it was going for repair and walk straight out with it. Donna was often for me a port of sanity and laughter amidst the storm of my own self-obsessed angst. She saw nothing wrong with anyone; all were part of life's rich tapestry.

There were those you could see growing at drama school. I was not one of them. But I was growing in an unexpected way. The best things always seem to come as a surprise, and it seems I was gaining a reputation in the stage and TV world of Birmingham as being unusual and reliable.

Another source of income for a drama-school student is doing walk-on parts – 'extra' work – for TV. A day's work earned you £12 and free food. It was March 1974. I had my first day's work as an extra on a '50s drama at Pebble Mill. I reported to wardrobe, where I was fitted in a '50s jive skirt, blouse and cardi. Next, to make-up for my hair to be slightly 'bouffanted' and certainly disguised from its sci-fi shape and colour – in those days natural-coloured hairspray hid a thousand sins – and false eyelashes applied. We were then herded on to a coach with the rest of the 'untouchables' of the acting world, and driven to a café, where I sat alone at a table for twelve hours, pretending to be watching a band that wasn't actually there, while a camera and crew skirted around me. Then we'd be driven back to Pebble Mill, where Mum would collect me, and we'd gas about the day all the way home.

In my mind the events of this day were filed to the back of

my cranium, instantly forgotten. Little did I know that this was the beginning of the rest of my life. Little did I know that as I sat at that café table with a numb bum, too scared to move or go to the toilet or even eat at the catering bus because I was crippled with shyness, a whisper had started on the set. Apparently I was being talked about by people who had never even talked to me.

The next day at drama school Miss Richards called me into her office. There had been a meeting between her, Margaret and Mr Webb. As usual I thought I was in trouble, but no, not this time.

'Ducky,' croaked Miss Richards. 'There's a director coming in to see you today.'

'A director? Where from?' I enquired.

'The BBC, Pebble Mill, ducky. How did he find out about you?'

'I've no idea. I don't know anyone at Pebble Mill.'

'Well' – and here Miss Richards sounded apologetic – 'we feel it's unfair that a director should come here and see only you. So we've insisted that he come and watch every class and therefore see every pupil. Isn't that so, Mr Webb?' At this point Miss Richards pointed the invisible finger of blame at the one man in the school who never took me seriously enough to include me in his classes.

Mr Webb chipped in all chipper as if I was too thick to care. 'As you know, Toyah, there's some wonderful talent in this school and it's only fair the others have a chance too.'

I didn't know how to feel as I left Miss Richards's office. All the students already knew what was going on and kept asking me what it was all about, and all I could think of was that my one and only chance was to be scuppered by this mysterious director seeing me alongside Nicky, Donna and Liz.

The rest of the day was buzzing with anxiety and paranoia. Everyone who walked into our classes that morning was treated to scenes reminiscent of *Fame* on speed, even the cleaners. The mysterious director eventually appeared during our afternoon dance class at Digbeth Hall. He tried to be invisible and also, it seemed, tried to show no particular interest in any of us. Then he was gone. That was it. Not a clue, not a goodbye, not even a name to place with the person. The day returned to normality.

At the end of the day, tired from all the adrenalin that my

body had managed to produce, I was summoned to Miss Richards's office.

'Well, ducky,' she relented, 'he still wants to see you and only you.' By the tone of her voice I could tell she thought he was mad.

The director's name was Nick Bicât. He was and still is a writer as well as a director, and his partner was his brother Tony Bicât, who was and still is a music composer. They wanted to meet me in London, at BBC Shepherd's Bush.

So the following day, at their request, I caught the train to Euston. Mum, worried about my not eating, prepared a whole plastic shopping bag full of cheese and tomato and salmon sandwiches. They weighed a ton. Travel by train was a rare thing for me, so experiencing having to share a confined space with people staring at me for an hour and a half was a lesson in tolerance and temper control.

Off the train and into a cab, down to Shepherd's Bush. My face pressed against the window all the way. London went on for ever. How could I ever get to know it?

Sitting inside the reception at Threshold House I couldn't get over how drab everything was inside. It had a similar feel to a Birmingham DHSS office. I don't know what I expected, but I did expect to see at least a hint of affluence. When Nick came to get me, he took me up in the lift Tom Baker had just taken. I wondered if it was a Tardis. We got off on the third floor, where he introduced me to Robert Banks (head of drama), who passed us in the corridor, and on we went to sit in the Bicât brothers' office and talk about the script. But soon the full story of Nick's journey unfurled.

Nick was looking for an unusual girl to play the lead in his new TV play *Glitter*. She had to look different, sound different and be able to sing. He'd searched stage schools in and around London and others in Birmingham but to no avail. What he was looking for seemed to be proving not to exist. The main problem was that all the girls were too groomed and too 'stage school'. As time was running out and the production was due to start shooting in a couple of weeks, Nick in his desperation had taken to asking passing staff at Pebble Mill if they'd come across anyone unusual on their travels. One of those people was the wardrobe mistress at the studios who had fitted me for my day's extra work. She said she hadn't actually worked with anyone but had come across this very distinctive and rather strange extra, at which point she described me and Nick rang the Theatre School – only to be discouraged from his choice and told he would not be introduced to me directly but had to guess which pupil I was among the others. Thank goodness the wardrobe mistress gave a good description. He found me. Nick Bicât knew as soon as he saw me that I fitted the bill, but he dutifully and politely spent a day pretending to look at all the other students in the school just in case he had to mollify and justify his choice to Miss Richards and Mr Webb.

My first meeting with the brothers was simply social, a preliminary, so they could hear me speak, react and respond. This didn't mean I had the job. I'd have to go back at the end of the week, to sing.

So I caught the train home to Birmingham. On the journey back a man dressed in a suit who had been sitting opposite me and staring non-stop for half an hour passed me a note: 'I will pay for you to come into First Class with me.' The train was full, so although my instinct was to kick him in the balls, I showed restraint, smiled and said, 'No thank you,' in the way any woman would if they were talking to a turd on legs. The man, humiliated, left the carriage.

Back home and at drama school I had to relive every moment for every individual. Exhausting or what?

Then the phone call came to Miss Richards's office. Wigmore Hall, Friday, 11 a.m.

On this trip to London I felt as if I'd been doing this journey all my life. I was enjoying myself.

Inside the Wigmore Hall I made my way to the rehearsal room where I was to meet Nick and Tony. Outside the room in a narrow corridor stood a boy with a familiar face; I'd seen him in a lot of children's drama: Phil Daniels. We only got to say hello before Nick came out and pulled me into the room where there were Tony, a pianist and a few other nameless people. I knew I had to sing today. Singing meant so much to me. It was a priority in all my dreams. But I didn't know any stage numbers, so I'd borrowed a song book off Liz Malone and decided to sing 'Life on Mars' by David Bowie, a song that so far had punctuated the most important stages of my life.

I sang it dreadfully, shaking from head to toe, not quite being able to follow or recognise what the pianist was playing. But I didn't get kicked out on my arse. So that was a good thing.

Instead Phil Daniels came in to join us and we read from the script of *Glitter*. Phil was like no one I'd ever met before. He was just there. He didn't stand to the side, he didn't blend with the background, he didn't wait his turn to speak. He was just there in all his confidence, beaming a smile that could have been mistaken for demonic, but was more 'come on life, challenge me'. Nothing fazed him and when he spoke, the broadness of his Cockney accent fazed me and I stood glued to the spot, fascinated. We read together, acted together, me more like a puppy dog following Phil's lead, but above all I enjoyed experiencing him. I felt like a hick from out of town, but I kept that to myself.

As I stood outside on Wigmore Street, none the wiser as to whether I'd got the job or not, waiting to hail a taxi to Euston, a workman wolf-whistled at me. I was shocked. No one had ever wolf-whistled at me in my life. OK, I was standing there in my sister's black 1966 Mary Quant cossack mini-dress with black lace skirt underneath, Chanel gold belt and ankle-boots, but usually people turned and ran, they didn't whistle. I was so flattered I gave the guy a big smile, then returned to Birmingham.

I didn't bother to go straight back to drama school that day. I was tired and didn't want to have to go over every detail of the day's events. So I went home. Mum and Dad had already gone to the boat for the weekend.

At 5 p.m. the phone rang. I picked it up in Dad's study.

'Hello, Miss Willcox, the BBC here. Good news. You've got the part.'

'Oh, that's fantastic!'

'Someone will be in touch with you on Monday about costumes and scripts; have a good weekend.'

I slammed the phone down and screamed. There was no one in the house to tell. So . . . I phoned Miss Richards, Liz Malone, Donna Croll, Vicky Richardson, Bina and Gita, Trisha, Mum and Dad at the mill, the corner shop, the library, you name it, if it was in Yellow Pages, it got a call.

Phil Daniels was to be my leading man. I couldn't have been

blessed with a more supportive and non-judgemental partner. The play *Glitter* was basically a two-hander, a boy and a girl. The girl is the bullying, driving force who encourages her friend to help her break into the *Top of the Pops* studios, whereupon they are discovered by Noel Edmonds in the empty darkness. The girl explains that it is her driving ambition to appear on *Top of the Pops*, so Noel kind of magics up a band. This band was Bilbo Baggins, who at the time were competitors to the Bay City Rollers. I was in awe of them.

Now this was my first professional acting, my first time in the studio on multi-camera. To put it politely, technique eluded me, but there was a spark there that everyone seemed to recognise and a great time was had by all.

Life was not only good at work, it was good at home. Mum and I actually managed conversations, and of course I had something I wanted to talk about for the first time in my life – work. She did overfeed me, though. I'd come home starving because I was too nervous to eat in front of anybody, and when I arrived there would be a huge pile of pancakes and syrup begging to be eaten – and their wish was granted.

Life at work was the best it had ever been. Not one for liking routine and discipline in my everyday life, I thrived on these at work, and soon I was flying. The rehearsal process is both a joy and like having your teeth pulled without anaesthetic. It's repetitive, but each repetition adds a new layer, a new dimension and if you get it right, this layer is no veneer, it's a deep rich varnish.

There were other perks too, including Noel Edmonds's haircut, sense of fun and vulnerability as an actor. We only had him for two days, so during those precious moments we stuck to him like glue, eking out as much information about the pop world as he was willing to give. Phil Daniels at the time had his own band – a fact that hugely impressed me – and he sold the idea of this band to Noel Edmonds like Frank Butcher would sell a car. With real East End zest. It was an art that Phil honed to a T.

I got a snog off Phil Daniels which wasn't in the script, which was very nice, as I'd forgotten that lips serve any function other than forming vowels and expletives. I developed a huge crush on Brian, the bass-player from Bilbo Baggins, which took my mind off Simon Ward for two weeks. The day loomed when I had to perform two songs with the band. They'd set up their equipment in an office at Pebble Mill. When Tony Bicât, the composer, walked me into the room my heart leapt with joy. They had Marshall amps, not so much stacked to the ceiling, more like hugging the floor, but enough of them to shake the dust off the desks. We had a whole afternoon to rehearse. It was my first time singing into a microphone. At first I cringed with embarrassment at the sound of my voice, but soon I got into 'sod it' mode and really went for it. The band were delightful, running through the phrasing and melody meticulously. Every now and then we'd stop to gossip about *Top of the Pops*, which they had done a few times, and about Noel Edmonds. Every time they stopped talking I'd ask a question, just to keep their Glasgow accents resonating in the air. Their voices were so beautiful.

This is definitely where my commitment to music started. All my life I had wanted to sing, but I had never done anything about it. This was it. Coaxed on by the band, the equipment, the volume, the social ambience and also the fact that Phil Daniels played three gigs a week in London and could still have a career as an actor, my mind was set. I had to put a band together or get into one. Quick.

We only had two weeks to rehearse and record this play, and returning to normality afterwards was far from smooth, emotionally. The night before the end of shooting, my stomach in a tight emotional knot at the thought of all this ending, the directors took me for my first curry in true Brummie style to a restaurant in Balsall Heath. This was an area of Birmingham hit by bombs during the war, and in 1975 most of the buildings remained bombed out. As we sat at benches on a sawdust floor in the bay window of an Indian family's sitting room, we got merry on the atmosphere and sheep's-brain curry. Using bread and fingers instead of a knife and fork, I ate a lot of this creamy mixture with zest before I enquired what it was. On finding out, I just made it home to the bathroom to reconsider and re-evaluate my dinner in the toilet bowl.

The final day came and I never wanted it to end. Tense with grief before the event, I savoured every moment. In the studio I kept looking up into the great chrome yonder of lights and thinking of all those they have shone on and will continue to shine on and wished I could be there for ever.

Our goodbyes were more civilised than the night before, this time Chinese and no brains – well, not on the dinner plates. The tension I felt was unbearable, and I mention this because I had never experienced it before. But knowing that something had to end I just wanted to kick it into oblivion and get on with the next course life would serve up, while at the same time I wanted to hold on to these people for ever. I suppose I hadn't learned to let go of a good thing with grace and trust that life can bring people back together again if it is right.

So I sat there in the lovely company of Phil, Bilbo Baggins and the Bicât brothers, just dreading the inevitable moment of goodbye.

Normality eventually found me back at drama school to finish the summer term. What was left of it. I was seen as an accidental hero, and surprisingly quickly all my self-doubt and paranoias returned to nag me.

The summer that followed was to be fun. The Ballet Rambert were in town and needed some mime artists to play old women in *Sleeping Beauty*. So I blagged my way into that for two weeks. Off stage I never so much as got a 'hello' from the company. On stage, in the stillness of a scene, as the dancers passed each other and held glances, I was amazed to find out that they all have quite matter-of-fact conversations with one another, on any subject from the weather or the price of satin to sex. I went on stage none the wiser and came off a very wise woman indeed.

After my little interlude in tights, *Dad's Army* came into town. To the Hippodrome. By now I was missing the attention of being a leading lady so much that I got Derek Goddard to dye my hair green and yellow, which certainly drew attention, if not of the quality sort. And it was back to dressing. Two weeks in the company of grumpy Arthur Lowe who shouted at me every time I laughed. 'We don't have laughing backstage, thank you!' – a strange irony in the company of so many comics. And the fabulously seductive John Le Mesurier, who would sidle off stage and chat with me in the wings whenever he didn't have lines on stage. His favourite subjects were family, wives and what colours hair could be dyed. He talked a lot about Hattie Jacques as someone who baffled and fascinated him. Then there was Clive Dunn, who'd sung 'Grandad' and was permanently mobbed at the stage door; and Ian Lavender, who was just beautiful. My job supposedly was to dress the leading ladies, but I spent most of my time with John Le Mesurier and Ian Lavender; the latter would run around backstage in only his Y-fronts, driving me wild with desire. John and Ian were the fun-lovers, and no matter how authoritarian Arthur Lowe was they would always find a discreet corner to giggle in.

Just before returning to drama school for the autumn I had a week dressing Judy Geeson at the Alexandre Theatre. Judy referred to me as her bird of paradise – because of the hair, certainly not because I was graceful. More like a young heifer with a coxcomb.

By the time the new term started in September I was simply unable to settle. My life had changed so much. Having been in the company of people I aspired to emulate wasn't the only reason. I was growing fast emotionally and I don't think I was alone; it was as if my entire generation was being called by the Pied Piper of Punk.

Chapter 11

In the eyes of my drama school I was probably becoming too hot to handle. It wasn't so much my attitude, or big-headedness, it was my independence and lust for life, which meant that the school had a student on its hands whose thirst for experience was unquenchable.

So much to do, so many things to acquire. Everything was there to experience if you were brave enough to try it.

My hair was changing colour weekly now. Derek was putting the finishing touches to my cyclamen-pink look when he asked, 'Are you going to see this new band tonight at Bogarts, the Sex Pistols?'

I'd never even heard of them. I'd never even heard of the movement they represented, so you can imagine my shock and delight as I walked to Bogarts nightclub and found myself in a room of like-minded people. I'd thought I was the only weird person in Birmingham, but from a guess, a quick head count, I wasn't alone, there were at least three hundred of us, so many that our bright hair and strange handmade clothing looked like a uniform. How come I'd never seen any of these people on the streets? Were they all in hiding? They must be laughed off the buses, as well as me.

The Sex Pistols themselves were truly awful. This was in their pre-fame days, and for me, the concept of a band walking on stage, the lead singer just staring out at the audience who were only a foot away and occasionally gobbing in our faces was alien. But the audience loved it and pogoed the night away.

It was the audience who deserved the encore, especially as the lead singer of the band, Johnny Rotten, decided to vacate

97

himself from the stage about half-way through the gig, never to return. But none of us cared and I suspect that out of all those punks there that night, only fifty per cent would still be punks in a year's time.

This became an important issue, as we learned the philosophy of punk. The definition of 'punk' is 'person in jail'. The definition of punk to all us kids on the street was 'true freedom of expression'. This meant not waiting till after office hours before spraying on false hair-colour and adorning yourself in your punk glory, and not being polite when really you were burning mad with some bigoted bore who was condescending towards you and treated you like thick scum.

Punk meant live it, be it, face it, and all its consequences, which were alienation, when not with your own kind, condemnation by those who didn't know you and general mockery by those stuck in their old ways.

This philosophy, this movement, that night at Bogarts gave me the strength to leave Birmingham. Having spent most of the evening trying to get a guy called Steve to audition me for his punk band and not geting anywhere, I decided if Brum wasn't giving me what I wanted I'd move elsewhere – and I didn't intend it to be Scunthorpe. London was in my sights.

The beauty of punk was that it preached that everyone had worth, had a place, without losing or suppressing their own unique qualities. Suddenly the world was my oyster. I could do anything. No matter how badly I did it, I now had an audience and a place.

I'd made *Glitter* at the BBC in May 1975; it was televised by November that year. As the TV announcer said, 'And now, as part of BBC2's series of half-hour plays from Birmingham, this is *Glitter*, the story of a girl's desire for fame.' I ran out of the lounge, leaving Mum and Dad to watch it on their own. I occasionally peered around the door and eventually re-entered and sat down when I got used to my voice and how I looked on screen, my heart racing with embarrassment, fear, disappointment, expectation and delight!

My first real acting wasn't truly dreadful. It was interestsing, raw, self-conscious and strange. My singing was appalling – on hearing the final number of the play, if I'd cringed any more I would have turned inside out. It was such a relief when it was all over. Mum and Dad said little, but were generally positive, and the phone rang till midnight.

The next day, entering drama school, I tried to be invisible, not wanting the true talent to look me in the eye. Miss Richards jumped out at me from her office – well as much of a jump as a ninety-year-old could muster.

'Ducky,' she squeaked, 'well done, sweet, well done, very good. Now the National Theatre have been on the phone, they want to see you today in London, for a play called *Tales from the Vienna Woods*, translated by Christopher Hampton. Maximilian Schell is directing and wants to see you at 4 o'clock.'

Cut the crap, Miss Richards, I thought. I haven't a clue who any of those people are. More importantly, how the hell am I going to get the money to get to London?

Then she added, 'Oh, and LWT want to see you for a new TV drama at 12 o'clock.'

Ahhhhhh! I had two hours to get there. Miss Richards loaned me the money and I got on the express train with my pink hair and headed for London's South Bank.

It seemed my summer of writing letters to directors had paid off. I sent two hundred letters and photos, to every theatre, TV company and film company I could find, and told them if they didn't watch *Glitter* they were missing a golden opportunity to employ a future star. No, I didn't really, yes I wrote to two hundred people but my mode of expression was more grovelling. But all the same, it paid off!

As soon as I hit Euston station, I called Doremy Vernon, the actress who played my mother in *Glitter*, and she came to meet me at LWT. My first meeting was fine, except the pink hair probably lost me the chance to play opposite Vanessa Redgrave in a war drama. Doremy then whisked me off to meet her agent, Richard Johnson. Now it's vital in many ways to have an agent; they do the dirty work while you get on and act. But from the look of Richard's office walls he did a little too much dirty work. Soft-porn stars abounded. Big-breasted women with reams of red curls pouring over their shoulders were pinned to every available space. Richard took one look at me and said, 'Yes.' He didn't have a punk on his books and I was to be his token punk. As I left, I wondered why such a fabulous woman as Doremy was with this man. But hey ho, he got us work in the end.

Doremy got me back to the National Theatre for 4 p.m. Gillian Diamond, head of casting, came to get me from the stage door and almost fainted when she saw my hair. Silently she walked me to the rehearsal room to meet Maximilian Schell. Whoever he was, I thought. As Gillian led me into the room my jaw dropped as I recognised the most famously attractive SS officer there has ever been in almost every technicolour blockbuster World War II film.

Maximilian's jaw in turn tightened as he said in his Germanic tone, 'What have you brought me here?'

'This is Toyah Willcox, Maximilian, you requested to see her after last night's TV play,' said Gillian.

'Oh!' and at once his tone softened. 'Yes, I watched you last night. Kate Nelligan, my leading lady, insisted we see you for the part of Emma. We cannot cast Emma, no one has been right. But then we saw you, and Kate and I looked at each other and said, "Yes!" Tell me, what's wrong with your hair?'

'It's the fashion,' I said.

'It's got to go,' he said earnestly.

'She will be wearing a wig,' Gillian interrupted.

Phew, I thought.

My hair, my image, was my life-blood; no way could I return to normality. It would be like scalping a Red Indian, asking the most pierced person in Britain to remove all metal objects at the airport metal-detector, the priest phoning in sick for a circumcision. Just no way could I defrock myself now; this symbolism identified my soul and broadcast it to the population. No way José, this is me, so lump it, world.

Returning to Birmingham that night I decided that theatre was not for me. I only wanted to do TV. Not having the slightest clue what the National Theatre meant to the world of acting, or even about its history, I slumbered in my cattle-class train seat and dreamed of playing Vanessa Redgrave's daughter in a war drama on TV.

But at school the next day, after I had been seriously grilled by all about the previous day's experience, I noticed a new respect from the talented élite of the school. They so obviously thought I was crap in *Glitter*, but having seen the response it had generated, they were now thinking otherwise. I was accepted back into their hallowed circle.

Miss Richards came into class. 'Ducky,' she said, furiously pointing at someone – none of us could make out who, she shook so much; she actually managed to point to all of us in the duration of one word. 'Ducky, please come on now, in my office.' Everyone looked at me.

In Miss Richards's cramped little office, stacked with scripts, bills and her hats, she sat me down. 'The National Theatre, ducky, want you to start next week.'

'But Miss Richards, I think I have this telly drama with Vanessa Redgrave,' I said.

'No, ducky, they don't want you, your hair probably lost you that one. I told you it would.' She paused to pick up a pencil. Then put it down to answer the 1930s black Dick Tracyesque phone.

I don't want to do theatre, I thought. Only TV.

'Ducky,' she jumped into my thoughts. 'The National Theatre want you for a nine-month contract. You'll have to leave the school, you know. Of course we'd always have you back, but what would be the point?'

So after a night of deliberation and some very good advice from Miss Richards about at least trying it once – put it on your CV and dine out on the experience for the rest of your life – I phoned the National and told Gillian Diamond I would be there for the start of rehearsals the following Monday.

It wasn't that saying goodbye to my friends was scary, it wasn't that I was finally leaving Birmingham, it was the fact that this was what I really wanted, now I had got it, and now I had to face it and all the change it would bring. So part of me embraced it, but an awful lot of me resisted it. I still to this day cannot believe that on that Monday morning I caught the 8.00 train with only a bag of salmon sandwiches my mother had made and thirty quid. There was no luggage and no toothbrush. For some reason. Just like my first day at school, I thought I'd be back again that night to stay. Stupid or what?

The first rehearsal day was merely a formality, a chance to meet the cast, technical crew and staff. The size of the National Theatre was a surprise – the rehearsal rooms seemed more like aircraft hangars and the corridors were endless and indecipherable; you could just as well have been in a bunker. Many years earlier I'd dreamt about this building, without knowing it. My dream was accurate, right down to the smell of the concrete.

As I wasn't used to walking into a room full of strangers, my first step into the rehearsal room, which was to be my home for the next nine weeks, was timid. But soon I was approached by a congratulating Kate Nelligan, a self-effacing Stephen Rea, a magnificent Oliver Cotton, a bombastic Warren Clarke and a divinely gentle Brenda Blethyn, with her long hair in plaits coiled like two harvest loaves on the sides of her head.

We all sat in a huge circle around Maximilian Schell, Christopher Hampton and Gillian Diamond. For the first hour Max delivered a magnificent performance about his passion for this classic Bavarian play, *Tales from the Vienna Woods*, about his life's experience in theatre and about how the Germans had a unique view of life, love and sex.

I cannot overstress how naïve I was at this time. OK, I knew Britain won World War II against the Germans. I knew Hitler was a nutter, but all I'd seen of Germany was in the film *Cabaret* – nice, entertaining, but hardly the gruesome reality. This moment, as I sat and adored Maximilian Schell's passionate and romantic rhetoric, was exactly two weeks before I bought, on Kate Nelligan's recommendation, Gitta Sereny's *Into That Darkness*, a book that taught me more about human nature than any life experience to date. Her bleak, hopeless account of the German atrocities woke me up to the responsibilities of every human being never to let this madness happen again.

So within two weeks of hitting London I was a completely different creature; it was as if someone had flipped the lighter lid and lit the flame for the first time. I'd always been capable of enlightenment and having realisations, but up until this point all spiritual growth had happened by accident. In my new awakening I discovered the simplest of truths: growth can come from one's own independent choices about one's own education. Believe me, I'd thought education stopped at the school gates.

Anyway, back to the nerd in the circle listening adoringly to Maximilian Schell talking about the works of German decadence. I'm not knocking Max, he could have been telling the whole gruesome truth; I was sitting there choosing to see a hero. In my little orbit I was counting my lucky blessings. I'd escaped Birmingham, drama school and family.

Later that day, we read through the script, laughing and marvelling at each other's embryonic performances. I nearly died with fear as I spoke my modest six lines with my fellow actor Pitt Williams. Pitt was completely bald, hairless in fact, no eyelashes or eyebrows, a wonderful man who was always kind and giving as an actor, or should I say kind and forgiving. One night many months later at 2 a.m. in the Green Room at the National, Pitt had passed out from his excesses and I borrowed one of the girl's make-up bags and proceeded to paint a face on the back of his head which remained there unnoticed throughout the Saturday matinée the following day. But that's another story. I may have been growing fast, but the old me was still very much there.

The read-through over, the day had come to an end. Thinking I would catch the train back to Birmingham, I made to leave, when a member of staff gave me my call for the next morning, 10 a.m. Well, fair enough, I could commute for the week, give myself a chance to find a bedsit, I thought. Then Brenda Blethyn approached me and asked where I was staying.

She was horrified on hearing my plan; like all actors, she regarded wasted money as a social crime, so Brenda insisted I stay with her until I found a place. This was overwhelmingly kind, but my attitude got in the way. Brenda then was just as motherly as she seems today and I couldn't quite handle the thought of leaving one domestic situation for another. This was my misjudgement and my loss. I mistook genuine kindness for a kind of emotional kidnapping, so I turned her offer down with some excuse that my mother needed me. Also, the fact that Brenda offered a sofa for me to sleep on made me think I would be in the way, or that I wouldn't be able to get out of the way, if the need arose. And, you know, being on the sofa of someone you don't know, well I just couldn't handle it.

Then Kate Nelligan, overhearing all this, jumped to life, and grabbing my arm she exclaimed, 'I have a flat in my house, it's vacant, you must have it!'

Perfect. I called Mum. 'Hi there, Mum.'

'It's "Hello", Toyah, "Hello", not "Hi there",' she said.

'Mum, I'm not coming home tonight. Instead I'm moving in

with the leading lady, Kate Nelligan.'

'Oh, and does she know about this?'

'Yes, Mum. I'll see you at the weekend. Bye.' I signed off, not to return home until a month later, at Christmas, whereupon I packed a much-needed toothbrush and a change of underwear.

So began a nine-month tenancy, an incubation period that turned me from a Brummie into a Londoner.

Kate lived alone in a massive three-storey house in Stockwell. The vacant flat was in the basement and I could see it was a blessing to her to have someone else there. She charged no rent, just asked for a contribution towards electricity and phone, and for this I had the most perfect abode. I could disappear into my room or watch telly with her upstairs. I had space, and Kate had another presence in the house.

Kate's role in *Tales from the Vienna Woods* was the biggest she had yet played. In recent months she had locked herself away in the Irish countryside to study the script and to do character notes. She had actually known for eighteen months before rehearsals began that the role was hers and I think that responsibility had slowly eaten away at her. She was immensely strong mentally, but physically frail. It didn't take long for me to realise that unless I placed food in front of her she simply wouldn't eat or drink all day.

My rehearsal hours were obviously short and undemanding, so I'd rush home ahead of Kate, shop, stock the cupboards and make sure food was waiting on the table for her return. Not every day, but enough to keep her alive. Kate would always be immersed in thought and I didn't like to break that bubble. She also had a huge capacity for laughter and girlishness, but I never wanted to be a presence who did anything other than allow her to be herself, so most of the time I crept downstairs and read *NME* and *Melody Maker* from top to bottom and front to back.

My first wage packet was a grand £60 and that arrived in a little brown envelope, which smelled of stability, promises and green ink. £60 offered so much. My first weekly kindling bought me twenty-three LPs – there was the Velvet Underground, Lou Reed, Bowie, Kraftwerk, the Tubes, the Doors, Nico and many many more. It also bought me, from Paul Howies on Long Acre in Covent Garden, my first real punk couture, a large baggy pink plastic clown suit – a must for a pudgy punk – and a silver bomber jacket. The following week I went back and bought a black cotton clown suit, a see-through plastic raincoat, with large green bug-eyed sunglasses.

I was having such a great time with my new-found freedom. Both the BBC in the summer and, now, the National Theatre had got me over my first major hurdle on the track to becoming a professional actor: they and the immense power they both wielded got me my full Equity card, which twenty-two years ago you couldn't work without. Because that worry was out of the way I had no problems to oppress me, so I did what most happy people do after years of oppression. I ran wild. Not a concern for me, but a huge concern for the National.

I was blissfully unaware that huge intellectual debates were going on within the theatre's hallowed walls as to whether a punk, or the presence of a punk, was destroying the integrity of the theatre from within. At the time I was the youngest member of the entire company, a fact I was proud of, but also I was totally unaware that there could be snobbery within such an artistic community. OK, yes, certainly there were lesser-known, older-generation actors who would never have considered looking me in the eye let alone saying hello, but apparently I was causing the royalty of the stage to 'tut'.

While I was rehearsing *Tales from the Vienna Woods*, Sir John Gielgud, Paul Scofield and Sir Ralph Richardson were all in the theatre performing in separate productions. None of them would have batted an eyelid at me, but in fact, I really was out of order on a few occasions.

Sir John Gielgud in particular brings back fond memories of measured vitriolic battles that began after I wheeled myself into his nuts outside his dressing room while in the middle of a backwards wheelchair race during a rehearsal tea break. As I steamed down the corridor with a team in hot pursuit, my wheelchair handle struck a very definite target. And as Sir John was about to go on stage, I am very grateful he remained so composed.

The theatre was not known for great administration skills at the time, so it probably didn't surprise many when I was allocated a dressing room right next door to his. Since the plays ran in rep, the likelihood of our paths crossing again was small – but they did.

I always got to the theatre at least two hours early, partly for fear of being late, which back then was a sackable offence; it just wasn't tolerated in the acting profession (an attitude probably prompted by the behaviour of some of the big stars such as Monroe, who could be as much as two days late on to a set). This gave me an hour to compose myself in the dressing room, during which time my wig and costume would be delivered. On one occasion these were all of two minutes late and I was bored, so opening the dressing-room window I shouted up to the costume department. Now the architects of this magnificent building – some would say 'block of concrete' – were very thoughtful, in that knowing how actors like to parade naked and incessantly chat, they designed the dressing rooms all to face one another in an inward-looking square, which gave everyone a great view of each other.

So communicating with wardrobe on the top floor via the window was simple. 'Oi! Where's my fucking costume?' I commenced.

'Shut up and wait, you fucking tart,' came a direct and blunt reply.

'Well get it down here soon, shithead.'

The deal was struck, at which point the phone on the wall next to me rang.

'Hello,' I shouted.

'Miss Willcox?' came a very polite voice.

'Yes,' I shouted.

'Miss Willcox, this is not a zoo, it's the National Theatre,' he continued.

This really tickled me. Looking up towards wardrobe, I tried to see if any of the guys were on the phone. No. So which one of them was winding me up? 'Look you, just get my fucking costume down here now.' I was in fits of laughter.

'Miss Willcox, this is not a laughing matter,' he persisted.

'Oh come on, dickhead, or I'll come up there and get you.' My voice started to tail off as I realised it might *not* be wardrobe on the other end.

'You are neither an ape nor an animal in a zoo, Miss Willcox, and down here in London we neither swing through trees nor go around hitting people, nor do we swear out of our dressing-room windows so may I suggest you behave like a human being.' His voice started to sound familiar.

Just as I drew in breath to start a new diatribe, a movement in the adjacent right-angle window caught my eye. Because of the nature of the light against the window I had to press my face against the pane of glass for a better view – and what a view. There was Sir John Gielgud in his dressing room on the phone, glaring at me. Dumbstruck, I squeezed the next pathetic phrase out of my black-painted mouth. 'Oh, all right then.' Slamming the phone down, I ran and hid in the corner of the dressing room. Rather like a scalded animal.

No repercussions followed from this exchange; in fact, after it, when Gielgud saw me he used to look me in the eye and laugh out loud and just walk on by.

Chapter 12

I'd been in London for eight weeks now and even though I had friends in the company, as yet I hadn't found any soulmate or friends of my generation. This concerned Kate, who felt I spent too much time alone in my room. Christmas Day had passed, for which I'd popped home to Mum and Dad and regaled them with thespian gossip. It was now New Year's Eve. The production of *Vienna Woods* was to move from the rehearsal room into the Olivier Theatre on New Year's Day, for which we would all have to be in full wigs and costume to start the technical run – and as this was to be the National's first production using the revolving stage, 'technical' was the word.

So there was tension in the air. Kate was particularly nervous and needed lots of tender loving care, but all the same she managed to set me up with a date for New Year's Eve.

Stephen Rea invited me to a party in Hampstead. I met him at his flat in Maida Vale, said hello to his beautiful girlfriend who for some reason wasn't coming, she showed me the sofa in their front room which I could kip on if I didn't make it back to Kate's and then Stephen and I caught a series of buses to Hampstead. By now I had an almighty crush on Rea. He was just sensational. So much talent, so much modesty and great company. The Stephen Rea I knew was a gentle, articulate and politically astute man. In those days the police had a 'stop and search' policy. They'd mainly stop punks and blacks on the streets, then rifle their pockets. Both Stephen and I dreaded this happening – myself, because I was a punk; Stephen, because he was Irish. His accent would immediately condemn him.

On this night no such problem occurred; we headed straight

for the party and then split into different rooms, he in search of good conversation, me in search of high jinks. I found them in the bathroom, where I stayed till Stephen took me home at 3 a.m.

Walking into the toilet in desperate need of a pee, I met Glenn and Shirley in the bath. Glenn Marks, a sixth-form student who happened to call the gatehouse at Golders Green cemetery home, had a bottle of whisky in his hands. Promptly I grabbed the whisky and filled my bladder while emptying it at the same time in the toilet. Rather like the way a good jazz musician does circular breathing, I invented the art of circular peeing.

Glenn was a wonderfully chatty chap. 'I'm Glenn. I have a punk band. This is Shirley, she's gay, a great photographer. I live in a cemetery.'

Well, what can you say to that other than 'I think I've found a soulmate'. (Shirley O'Loughlin, a schoolteacher at the time, had a great future ahead of her. She ended up managing and living with the lead singer of the Raincoats, Kurt Cobain's favourite band, a band that never lost its credibility.)

By the end of the evening I'd perfected the art of balancing in an ape-like fashion over the bar that held the shower curtain, while preserving the last precious drops of whisky in my bladder which by now was more functional as a decanter. Even though I was seriously, sickeningly pissed, when Stephen Rea came downstairs for genuine use of the bathroom he found me in the bath with Glenn and Shirley, having joined Glenn's punk band and booked a photo session. Stephen was positively joyous for me; at last the 'lion cub' had found a pride that would take her, or should I say the 'jackal' had found a pack.

I have no memory of returning home to Stephen's, only of waking in the morning with a bucket of sick next to the sofa and a wet patch where I could no longer store that precious whisky. Stephen gently and tenderly got me to the National Theatre where, on New Year's Day, I had the hellish job of getting into costume and wig at the same time as wishing I was dead. In my vain attempts to impress my new friends the night before, I had crucified myself for the tech run.

Mercifully, in the main auditorium of the Olivier, Max Schell was having major problems with the revolving stage, which kept sticking, or coming off its wheels. This gave me a little time to recover in the dressing room before I was needed.

But the moment came. I kept saying to myself, 'Act normal,' as my head spinned and my stomach churned. My grand entrance was on the revolve and we practised it and practised it till I could have sprayed the whole auditorium with sick like a scene out of *The Exorcist*. I was in hell.

Behind me on the stage was a shop front, from which I entered through a door while the stage revolved. Then I would start to seduce Pitt Williams's character as he gratuitously ate a saveloy. The stage hands, having sympathetically watched me suffer, had opened one of the windows of the shop, so they could secretly hold me up as the stage revolved and keep a grip on me throughout the scene. (This kindness didn't last long. By the time the show opened a week later, they were using this opening to tie my scarf to the set so I could not exit the scene and consequently ended up in the following scene as the stage turned.)

This hangover seemed to grow in intensity. No matter what I did I couldn't make myself feel better. When Kate found out she was both furious and determined to find out what exactly had happened the night before. I do believe she told Stephen off for letting me get in such a state.

There was one major scene in the play that could only be fully rehearsed on stage. It involved the whole cast, in the setting of a Berlin nightclub, where the male leads discover that Kate's character has become a drug addict and a prostitute. The core, the epicentre of the scene, was a series of tableaux where all the girls in the cast, about twelve of us, had to be naked, holding poses. Max had already decided that I was too young to be naked in this scene, so I lay at the women's feet in a sailor suit, smoking a pipe, minus wig, so my green and yellow hair became part of the decadent fashion of Berlin in wartime, while the girls around me waved huge ostrich-feather fans.

This very afternoon was to be the first time all the girls stripped off, including Kate. It was a well-known fact that all the actresses were dreading this moment. Originally the theatre had tried to find twelve strippers to do this scene, but it had proved too expensive and not enough strippers actually wanted to work at the National.

Nudity was all very new to me. I'd seen very little of it, and participated in none of it. Birmingham people are prone to keeping their clothes on. As soon as the girls stripped off backstage, I'd never seen so many men appear from the shadows. Stage hands actually left their tearoom to discuss the finer details of rugby, football and stage weights within inches of the shivering naked posse.

I thought all the women were brilliant. I'd have hated being in their shoes (or out of them). I'd have done it myself at a push, but inside I would have been a quivering mass. Max arranged us in a burlesque scene, then lay me at their feet. As I looked up towards a sea of boobs, I noticed one girl had drawn two faces under her breasts for my eyes only and another had written 'Hello' on the underside of her right tit. Also, today began the daily ritual whereby as soon as the revolve started to turn, most of the girls would ask me in a frantic whisper, 'Can you see my string?' So I appeared to the audience during this scene urgently peering between the girls' legs. Still, it added to the decadence. It was all surprisingly unerotic, from my point of view that is. Yet for one man, it was the centre of his life. Every Saturday matinée this stranger would sit in the same seat on the front row, in the same raincoat and with the same increasingly tatty plastic bag, for nine months. He would sleep through most of the play and then would be as alert as a lurcher for this one particular scene. The girls grew to hate him, doing anything to put him off returning the following week. They'd scowl at him, cover their bits when exiting the stage past him and occasionally mouth the words 'fuck off' when their patience was truly wearing thin. Funnily, I think it was exactly this that made him return.

After the technical rehearsal I returned to Kate's house. Like a wounded animal, vowing never to drink again. How can we be true to others when we can't even be true to ourselves? This vow was broken within forty-eight hours, but only slightly.

The show opened with no hitches. It is always a huge, almost orgasmic relief to get the very first performance over with. At least we had the luxury of a week of previews, a very necessary exercise for size and balance of performance because once the audience is in they soak up every ounce of you. Your sound, movement and thoughts are absorbed and you soon learn the need to expand on naturalism – a sort of thespian dividing of the five loaves and two fishes, making sure there's enough of you to go round.

Three nights into the previews, everything was going swimmingly well and the entire cast was floatingly happy.

I entered the backstage area for my minuscule scene with Pitt. As the stage revolved, I would skip through a shop entrance out on to a German street. I never stepped through the shop door until I could see the first half of the audience appear. On this night I skipped out and the revolve came to a grinding, scratching halt. At first, the audience didn't know anything was wrong, it just looked a little surreal. The actors from the previous scene instinctively froze to form a tableau, so Pitt and I walked to front of stage and continued our scene there, with the revolve, which was driven by manpower, coughing and spitting in its final death-twitch behind us. Slowly, titters started to be heard around the auditorium, as panicked stage hands ran on stage and tried to turn the revolve by pushing the shop front. Pitt and I continued. I think the final straw that brought the house down was one of the technicians appearing with a spanner, and then trying to take parts of the stage away. The whole house was in uproar. Pitt and I stood there, remaining in character, hoping it would all die down and go away.

It did. We started to act again. The next time there was an interruption Max Schell stood from his seat in the audience and shouted, 'Stop everyone.' He ran on to the stage. 'Ladies and gentlemen, I am Maximilian Schell, the director.' Huge applause. 'I thank my actors for bravely battling on through this problem.' Even louder applause. 'As you can see, ladies and gentlemen, we are having technical problems here. This is the first time the NT has used the revolving stage and tonight is the first time it has caused us any problems. May I suggest you take leave to the bar and we will call you back when the show is ready to resume.' More applause. How the audience love real drama.

On the return of the audience and the repair of the stage, Pitt and I made our entrance for the second time that night and by the audience reaction you'd have thought we were a reunion between Liz Taylor and Richard Burton. It's easy to see in these situations how a performer becomes addicted to audience

approval. Throughout the run of this play, so many technical
hitches occurred that we learned to improvise around a problem
quite naturally and still get a positive response from the
audience.

There was one evening that was not so frivolous. It was a
Thursday night. During my scene with Pitt, I could hear a
commotion in the audience. It was a very polite commotion. I
kept looking at Pitt to see if he could hear it too.

Basically, this very embarrassed man had stood up about six
rows back in the audience and was saying sheepishly, 'Excuse
me, there's a parcel under my seat.' Everyone, from what I
could see and hear, was ignoring him. I found myself split:
somehow my body managed to continue with the necessary
lines and movements to keep the story going, while my conscious thought was on prompt corner, which was expertly
hidden in the front rows of the audience. But she hadn't seen or
heard a bean.

As the revolve sped me off the stage, I made my exit through
the audience and ran around the back of the auditorium, to pass
a message on to whoever I could find who worked for the
theatre. There were no staff to be found; possibly knowing that
artists exited stage this way, they had kept the corridors clear.
Eventually I found someone. 'Problem in the auditorium,
something about a parcel.' I was in a panic and I ran backstage
to tell the stage manager. By now we all knew there was a
problem, but we were faced with a bigger problem – how
seriously should we take it?

Stephen Rea was on stage with Elizabeth Spriggs, when the
poor man in the audience decided the only way he was going to
be taken seriously was to shout. 'Look, I'm awfully sorry,' he
piped up, 'but there's a parcel under my seat and it's not mine.'

At last Stephen took a grip on the situation and stopped the
scene, then very calmly said, 'Ladies and gentlemen, it appears
we all have to leave the theatre; please do so calmly.'

Backstage, mayhem broke out as all three theatres within the
National Theatre complex emptied. I found myself on Waterloo
Bridge with around six hundred people, freezing in the chill
February night air. There was only one thing for it. Grabbing
the musicians, who'd all brought their violins and clarinets with
them, Oliver Cotton, Stephen Rea, Warren Clarke and I busked,

danced and entertained the audience for the hour it took the bomb squad to declare the offending parcel a false alarm. Within that sixty minutes our efforts earned us three quid.

My efforts with Glenn, the boy from Golders Green cemetery, and his seminal punk band didn't earn me much more. But money was not the aim. All my life I'd had a terror of singing in front of anyone, let alone publicly. Realising that this was a major obstacle to my ambition of world fame as a singer, I had to get my skates on quick and do something about this ridiculous phobia.

I could just about cope with rehearsals. These, in fact, were just brilliant. They took place in Glenn's bedroom, which was the top room of the gatehouse at the entrance to Golders Green cemetery. The view was inspirational for a punk band: row after row of grim, grey granite, exuding loss, exuding nothingness, being held on to by those left behind. Oh yes, this was the view for a lyricist. Glenn, being very much a control freak, was quick to point out that we were pawns in his dream, so he did all the writing, all the talking, all the dreaming, which was fine by me – I had a lot to learn and you could do a lot worse than have a Jewish megalomaniac, who genuinely knew all there was to know, as a punk music mentor. I'd sit on Glenn's bed and note every word he said. Drinking in his knowledge. I knew all too well, at this point in my life, that I couldn't pen a lyric or a song, but I also knew that all people, great or small, start at exactly the same place. So I sat, waiting and listening, every Saturday and Sunday I had free. Filling myself with a knowledge that would give me enough buoyancy to float of my own accord.

Every Sunday I'd get the tube to Golders Green. On most occasions, I'd just walk up to Glenn's house but on the one rare occasion I waited at the tube for Glenn to pick me up, an orthodox Jewish boy, no more than eleven years old, stepped up to me in broad daylight and offered me 50p if he could feel my breasts. I just stared at him and laughed. 'I'm very sorry,' I said, 'but no.' I couldn't bring myself to hit a child, but he came close.

The name of the band was When the Streets Were Dark with More Than Night, a Raymond Chandler quote. You could imagine the T-shirts – they had to be extra large. We only ever did two concerts; then Glenn decided to break the band up because he wanted to be a poet, preferably a gay poet. But Glenn had one obstacle. He was straight. He was more hetero than Sylvester Stallone. We all loved Lou Reed, as much as we loved to eat and breathe, and the word 'gay' was placed high upon a pedestal – even I, a complete asexual at the time, had the word 'Lesbian' plastered across my chest – because 'gay' meant glamour, being different, and as far as rock stars went it meant being superintelligent. So we, this bunch of posing, hetero, semi-decadent punks who in some ways were at the vanguard of the punk movement, all posed as being gay to the straight outer world. No wonder I didn't get laid till I was twenty.

Our first concert was at the Ford works in Dagenham. In a youth club within the factory. We played for twenty minutes to a stunned audience of eight fourteen-year-olds.

You'd have thought that with the experience the National Theatre had given me, stage fright would have been a thing of the past. For days before this short musical interlude in my life, I was restless with fear. My dreams were inhabited by disgruntled and angry audiences who took glee in slowly walking out of the show as I sang my heart out on a stage that was barely lit. Leaving an empty hell by the third song.

On the afternoon of the gig I rode pillion on the bass-player Tony's motor bike, through the East End of London, down the Bow Road, daydreaming all the way of rock stardom, clinging on to Tony's back in fear of the oncoming traffic and the evening's events. My daydreams have always been grandiose. By the time we arrived at the venue, I'd daydreamed myself through three nights at Madison Square Garden, an Oscar, an affair with Robert Redford and becoming the first artist to appear on the moon.

Tony and I stood in stunned silence as we faced a heavily graffitied block of concrete that was rather perversely called a 'youth club' – more like a 'trash club'. It had nothing to offer other than four walls to bang your head against. We set up our gear, which consisted of a drum kit – all of three drums – bass stack, guitar stack and two minuscule speakers for vocals. We didn't stand a chance. Neither did the audience. Not even points for effort. We were all dead on arrival. Funny how some situations are beyond saving. It was a total non-event. Glenn, bless him, strutted and preened like Lou Reed and Mick Jagger in a cockfight. I ambled on for two songs, shaking with fear, but giving off enough bravado to frighten a rugby team. Usually a show is really good, mediocre or really bad, but when a show is not even worth watching because the audience is suffering from terminal apathy and the band observing them, like a swarm of flies stuck on flypaper, unable to move, respond or object, well there is nothing but a void and a void isn't worth writing home about.

So by 10 p.m., I climbed on the back of Tony's bike and vowed never to return to Dagenham. I left with a deep sense of embarrassment and guilt. This wasn't the stuff dreams were made of. This was the stuff that the word 'change' was invented for. Things had to change. 'Things' being a collective word for 'world'. 'World' representing those who stand upon it, who possess two arms, two legs, two eyes and a brain. I left Dagenham with one concern – how to kick out the old, bring in the new and kick apathy so hard up the jacksy that it would take it a few millenniums to reach earth again. In the meantime the human race could jolly well wake up and be counted.

Glenn broke up the band. A wise move. He remained a good and loyal friend who I could always turn to for constructive advice and guidance. Apart from that he was great as a party companion. Glenn always broke the ice, the kitchen table, the bedsteads and the light fittings.

He also realised that I seriously wanted to pursue my musical dream and that to do this I had to put a band together, or at least be part of one full time. By now punk was in full swing and although I looked like and acted like a punk, I didn't quite enter the space fully. I had one half of my body and soul *in* and the other free to catch any other passing phase if it took my fancy. That sounds as if I was a trivial tourist, taking snapshots on a day trip to spiky pink-haired razor-blade town. Not so. Within punk I found my feet, my voice and my place. Ironically this gave me the strength to be free of it at will.

I wasn't fully convinced about the musical direction of punk. It was fabulous, fully abandoned and direct. But apart from a few top-of-the-tree geniuses such as the Sex Pistols, the Clash, the Banshees, Adam Ant, Penetration, Stiff Little Fingers – well actually the list is rather long and the top of the tree is stooping over with talent – it did seem that punk shot itself in the foot in that a band could only go so far. And in time only one band did go beyond punk successfully and that was the Banshees. The rest seemed to hit a wall of resistance by the early eighties, then disbanded and reformed in a different guise.

Punk placed desire above knowledge in musical terms. I desperately wanted to be a musician and to work with accomplished players, partly knowing that I had many weaknesses, one being that I wasn't a musician and another that I was a front person only, not a one-woman band.

Glenn, the punk poet, the ultimate cynic, had immense compassion. Glenn went to a grammar school in Finchley, attended solely by Jewish boys from wealthy families. He despised his school as much as I had despised mine and I could easily imagine that in no way could this gangly, scrawny, effeminate punk fit in with hundreds of orthodox Jewish boys. There was a boy in Glenn's class whom Glenn pretended to dislike, called Joel Bogen. Glenn's so-called dislike of Joel was because he played electric guitar, knew the solo of Lynyrd Skynyrd's 'Free Bird' backwards and played it all day long at a drop of a pin to an audience of admiring schoolboys and nubile schoolgirls, who would later be waiting for him at the school gate. Glenn didn't really despise him. He was quite honest about the fact that he was jealous of Joel's capabilities, as a guitarist and for scoring girls. So characteristically Glenn was dismissive of him.

Glenn suggested that I should meet Joel to explore the possibility of forming a band. In the same sentence he praised and crucified Joel: 'He's good, he can play guitar real well, but he's a shit.' So I called Joel and went to meet him, in his bedroom in the suburbs of Finchley. He wasn't a shit. He was cute. A family boy and, unlike Glenn and me, a boy with a happy disposition.

In Joel's bedroom there was a Marshall stack, an echo unit and a few guitars and Joel played 'Free Bird' for the first half-hour before graduating on to Deep Purple. We talked and improvised around a few chords. I found Joel particularly melodic, rather than thrashy, and it appealed to my ears. So we decided to give it a go and form a band. Joel had many friends in the community who could play drums, bass and keyboards, so he set about calling them with a view to Sundays being our day of creative work.

I soon learned that Joel was the Buddha of Golders Green. What I didn't know was that for the next eight years he was going to be the kingpin in my life. For the first six months of our working relationship we mainly just rehearsed, trying to pen enough songs to warrant a gig in a pub, or anywhere. We'd rehearse at friends' houses, in squats, at parties. The parties tended to be stressful. After five hours of 'Free Bird' and 'Johnny B Goode' in an upstairs bedroom, with multiple Jewish bonking going on all around you, you were not only 'somewhat' distracted, but plain bored. Also I tended to be the only punk gentile in the house, which led to many a lonely walk home. Over the months I grew to love Joel with a passion, but this was a love that sat on the sidelines and watched as Joel loved everyone else. The only really good thing we had together apart from our creative relationship was that we laughed and laughed and laughed in each other's company. Nothing was too silly for us to laugh at, cotton buds up the nose, handcuffs to railings, pissing in beer mugs. For a couple who never ended up as a couple we certainly went all the way in every other area of our lives.

Joel focused me and we began to write. For the first time in my life I had music for the lyrics I dreamt up day and night.

Sometimes my greatest fear was singing new lyrics to Joel. I felt terribly exposed. Joel and I were like chalk and cheese. Neither had ever known anyone like the other, and lyric-writing had always been my therapy, so what was gold to my ears could potentially be mud to Joel's. But we persevered with each other and finally became inseparable, though always distant. What I mean by that is we became psychic. We always knew what the other thought, whether in each other's company or apart, and we knew to ring the other if need be. And, so, eventually, my lyric composition became appropriate for Joel's music.

The one thing between us that probably alienated those around us was that Joel and I could just look at each other in a crowded room, at the shops or on the street and burst into fits of laughter. We had an equal humour that kept us together through thick and thin. But it would be many years before any form of success came our way, and then the baby we managed to make together, musically speaking, would need more than humour to keep it alive.

Chapter 13

Quite rightly for an eighteen-year-old going on nineteen, I found life was a whirl throwing out many tangents. The National Theatre was still going on strong. My new agent Richard Johnson could not encourage the National to keep me on beyond the run of *Vienna Woods*. Like most actors at the theatre at the time I was desperate for commitment, but there were no parts suitable for me in the new season other than spear-carrying, and even I agreed I had more potential than that. So *Vienna Woods* had two more months to run and after that I was on my own. In the meantime I had managed to appear as a vomiting punk rocker alongside Diana Rigg in her TV comedy series *Three Piece Suite*. This was not a critical success for anyone; that was evident in rehearsals at Acton Land, the BBC's rehearsal studios, so on the night, in front of a live studio audience at Wood Lane, I kept my head down and retched for the pay cheque. I hasten to add, the flaws in this show were not in the acting but in the writing.

The only other job my agent almost got me was a Russ Meyer movie. I had to meet Mr Meyer at a house in central London. When he walked in he looked seedy. The house was dark, with dark tapestry-style furnishings, the windows yellow with nicotine. It was a snug house, but snug for all the wrong reasons. There were too many knee indentations in the furniture. I knew I was meeting a movie legend of sorts by Glenn and Joel's reaction when I told them of the meeting. Joel's eyes popped out of his head. Anyway, Mr Meyer looked me up and down and very quickly decided I wasn't right for the second *Supervixens*. Not having seen the first *Supervixens*, I didn't realise what a great escape this was, otherwise I would probably have had to strip off there and then and screen-tested my bust, not my face.

It was no good, Mr Johnson had to go. I stopped returning Richard's phone calls, being too much of a coward to sack him.

At the National Theatre – where by now, my play was running in repertory, meaning sporadic performances – new faces were appearing. One was Ian Charleson. A beautiful man by nature and appearance. Ian held a lot of light. He literally shone in the dim corridors at the National. Always smiling, always beaming light on to others, he was a graceful man.

Ian gripped my arm one afternoon and said, 'You have to meet a friend of mine. He makes films on Super 16.' I pretended to know what Ian meant by this. 'Derek Jarman is about to make the first feature-length punk movie. I'm sure he'd be interested in meeting you. I'm going to his for tea next week; why don't you come with me?'

By now I was beyond excitement. The thought of a feature film was thrilling. Having never heard of Derek Jarman or even thought of the paradox of a feature-length punk film didn't bother me. My mind was totally on the movie. Not the content.

So the following week Ian and I caught a bus to Tregunter Road where Derek had a flat. Derek greeted us at the door. Soon I was to discover that Derek always had a ready smile on his face that broke into a laugh with ease. He grabbed Ian by the shoulders and pulled him into a tight bear hug. Then Ian introduced me. Derek took me into his huge, sparsely furnished living room, sat me on the sofa and gave me a script with some obscure name like 'Down with the Queen', explaining, 'I don't know what to call it yet so I've called it the first thing that came to mind, but it's going to be outrageous, utterly outrageous. My friend Jordan has agreed to play the lead.' I didn't know who Jordan was, but hopefully I would find out; in the meantime I did what I always did in these situations and pretended to know all and everything. Derek told me to flick through the script and pick any part other than Amyl or Chaos as they were already cast. Then he disappeared with Ian to make the tea.

I'd never been to an audition like this before. Holding the script in my hands, like a new-born pup, I could hardly conceal my excitement. The first thing I did was to flick through the pages to find the largest part available that hadn't been cast. Immediately Mad the pyromaniac caught my eye. So I quickly read all her scenes and announced to Derek, as he brought a large tray with three oversize mugs of tea on it, that I was the only person who could play Mad.

A somewhat taken-aback film director very calmly explained that, of all the characters in the film, Mad was the most superficial, because she didn't fulfil a function, at which point I jumped right back and said, 'Well, from a punk's viewpoint she's the most interesting. A true anarchist is destructive for the sake of it.'

Having quickly viewed the script, I got a flavour of all the other characters, who appeared at first glance to be twentieth-century female equivalents of Guy Fawkes, plotting against parliament, but in Derek's story it was the Royal Family who were to be disposed of. Mad simply tagged along like a passenger, setting fire to everything with her Swan Vestas.

Derek was a vivacious, effervescent and intellectually astute social butterfly. I had never, and have not since, met anyone quite like him. The milk of human kindness was cupped in his hands and the critical unforgiving wit and observation of Oscar Wilde were silently waiting to strike like a viper in his mouth. Derek could meet anyone on their level and subtly move them beyond their wildest aspirations. It may be because of this that Derek was never alone.

As Derek, Ian and I supped tea – Derek holding court and regaling us with stories, myths and legends of who did what to whom, and how, at the most extraordinary parties that London had ever seen, or heard rumour of – a succession of beautiful boys floated past the door, in the hallway. The doorbell never ceased to chime and in would float another Adonis with a face every woman would kill for.

I kept one eye on Derek and the other on the door. My view of homosexual life up until this point was a crude stereotypical vision of men with handbags, who cried at the drop of a pin. That's Birmingham for you. This was like standing at the gates of Leonardo da Vinci's heaven. Everyone who passed by was exceptionally beautiful, semi-clothed and had a lot to say. All fascinating, I might add. One particular boy, Yves, who was tall, dark and painfully beautiful – Calvin Klein would kill for him today – had a penchant for walking around sometimes in a loincloth, presumably made up hurriedly from a tea cloth (I wonder if he dried our mugs with it!), sometimes with absolutely nothing on at all. Yves's voice was as French as his name and his English as bad as the proverbial au pair's and boy! would I have liked to have one of him myself. Yves was Derek's lover at that time.

I left Derek's having learned a small dictionary's worth of who's who in London. Jordan, Little Nell, Richard O'Brien, Luciana, Duggie Fields, Adam Ant, Jenny Runacre. The list goes on and they were all to be in Derek's film. Derek took my number and said he'd be in touch; in the meantime he had to move back to his warehouse at Tower Bridge, which was where the filming was to be done.

Ian and I had performances to get to. Ian was already cast in Derek's film, and I left assuming that I was, too.

Life at Kate's was becoming complicated. Kate was hinting it was time I moved out. So Glenn was on the lookout for somewhere for me to move to, closer to him and Joel. I hadn't got a clue how to find a flat. The thought of being out on my own terrified me, and all around London all you ever saw at 5 p.m. were long queues of desperate people all trying to acquire the same bedsit. I didn't want to wait in that queue.

Kate's career in the space of three months had gone from subliminal to sublime, to coin a cliché. The girl was doing pretty damn good. She had already made *The Lady of the Camellias* for BBC2. Scripts were landing on the doormat by the hour. She was being wined and dined by the best minds in London, and for me, actually getting to spend some time with her was a rarity.

And on top of all this stress and overwork was a lot of play. Kate had many admirers. None of them was boring or forgettable; on the contrary, they were some of the biggest and best names in England. Kate did suffer a strange kind of guilt. Not because of her behaviour – she juggled her admirers admirably. My God, if you've got it, flaunt it. No, her guilt was more because of me. What Kate was anxious about was the amount of time I spent alone. She felt it was unhealthy. So one of her many concerns other than choosing parts, learning lines and dealing with difficult and obnoxious playwrights was my love life, or complete lack of it. But alas, there was no one for me, so I read a lot.

Kate was about to start filming *The Eye of the Needle* in Ireland with Donald Sutherland. All the time she was getting all this great work, she was still playing the lead in *Tales from the Vienna Woods*. But she had never been in better shape and was flourishing with all the attention and admiration.

Very soon, Donald Sutherland started to come home with her. And he was a sight to behold. Unbelievably tall, well over six feet – and great company. He'd pull up in the narrow Stockwell street in his Silver Cloud, step out, gargantuan in sheer presence and stature, in his camel-hair coat and silk scarf, hair swept back – a Canadian being an Englishman with that little bit extra good taste. He would sit with Kate and me in the kitchen and we'd laugh ourselves hoarse. There was little evidence of their being lovers in the beginning, just good friends, and they didn't seem to mind my being around.

On Donald's first visit he brought Easter eggs. On his second, he arrived with a huge gift-wrapped parcel, which Kate hurriedly tore open. It was a juicer. A complete novelty to me. We only had one apple in the house, so Donald's demonstration of this great American invention lasted all of one second. So off we all went in the Silver Cloud to Vauxhall, to a little fruit shop – there were no supermarkets in that area in those days. Donald strutted in, larger than life, housewives swooning at his feet, bought half the shopkeeper's stock and pocketed a few apples for good measure as the shopkeeper loaded his car.

We went home and juiced for our lives. It was that day I think, that Kate and Donald became an item. I wouldn't really know. Glenn picked me up and I went out with him and Shirley to Brighton.

I didn't see Donald for a few weeks. He phoned regularly but I presumed he was in Ireland, filming. Then, one Friday night after the show, I was lying in bed at midnight. Staring at the ceiling, lamenting my lack of social life, the street lamp outside illuminating the room and my thoughts. Kate came home after me. I did not see her; my boredom had taken me to my room with a copy of the *NME* for company. All was still, all was quiet. A car horn sounded outside. I hadn't heard a car pull up. But now, right outside the house, a motor was running and someone was sounding their horn. They'll bugger off in a minute, I thought as car fumes filled my basement room. The horn sounded again, but this time for about twenty seconds. Jumping out of bed I looked out of the window. There was Donald's Silver Cloud, and in the front seat, Donald, with his hand pressed against the horn. That's all right then, I thought to myself; Kate will let him in.

Silence fell. Then the car horn sounded, this time for an eternity. Well at least two minutes of blaring horn. Jumping out of bed again, I looked through the window, and this time I had a good look at Donald's face. It was terrifying. This guy was in a BAD mood. I sat on my bed and wondered what to do. Kate can't be sleeping through this, I reasoned, wondering if I should go and talk to him, let him in, make him a cup of tea.

Kate eventually appeared at my door at 12.30 a.m. 'Toyah, are you awake?'

'Yes, Kate.'

'It's Donald, he's cross,' she whispered.

'I gathered that,' I said. We were both being deafened by his car horn in the basement.

'I need you to go outside and tell him I'm not here,' she said. I thought this was sad; whatever row they'd had I hoped they'd make up, preferably tonight so I could have breakfast with Donald in the morning.

I put on my pink plastic clown suit and red plastic sandals – from the King's Road, I hasten to add – and jauntily strolled out to the Silver Cloud. 'Hi, Donald, Kate's not here,' I cheerily lied.

'She's in there,' he snapped.

'No, she had a show tonight and isn't back yet.'

'She's in there, I followed her,' he bounced back.

Brief silence. I wanted to invite him in in the hope they'd patch things up. I looked around the street, at all the bedroom curtains twitching. Flashing our peeping audience a huge smile, I asked Donald if there was anything I could do.

'Tell her I'm staying here until he leaves,' he stated.

'Who?' I was taken aback.

'That man,' he said coldly.

'Kate's in there alone; she's in bed, just trying to sleep,' I bluffed in Kate's defence.

'I'm not leaving,' was his final word – of our final conversation.

'I'll tell her, Donald. Goodnight.' Freezing to the bone I went back in and in hushed tones told Kate what he had said. 'He thinks you're with someone else, Kate, go and tell him you're not,' I insisted.

'I can't,' she insisted.

'You can,' I persisted.

'I can't, Peter Firth is upstairs, he's got nowhere else to go to and anyway Donald would go for him if he left now,' she said sheepishly.

So there was no alternative. We all went to our respective bedrooms and left Donald to stew. He was still there at 3 a.m., but by 6 a.m. he'd gone for good.

Peter was an angel who stayed for a while. For some reason he was homeless, I suspect through choice. His Fiat sat parked outside, stacked to bursting with all his wordly goods. I missed Donald.

Spring was here and it was time to move on. Thankfully Glenn found me a flat the other side of town, so I vacated Kate's wonderful house with the help of Glenn and a borrowed car, knowing I would see Kate at work; at least we didn't have to say goodbye for good.

Chapter 14

My new home was a back room above a chip shop on the Hornsey Road, Crouch End. There was traffic twenty-four hours a day. Squats to the left and to the right and a constant chorus of on-street brawling. It was just what I needed. A hint of poverty. The chance of being mugged outside my front door. No heating inside. A lecherous Greek landlord and a flasher who lived across the street. The air had so much edge, it was a dodecahedron.

I was sharing with two girls, Penny Faith, the daughter of a wealthy Hampstead property developer (Penny is now a novelist), and Lee Baumont, both drama students at Mountview Drama School in Crouch End.

This was the first time I had been with people of my own age and I suppose mentality. Kate was always cerebral; these girls were boisterous and our household was buzzing with music, boys and laughter. It was a wretched flat, stinking of chip fat from below. Broken windows, dirt-brown carpet-felt on the floor, and peeling wallpaper. But it was the right time and the right place. It had street cred.

It was only a twenty-minute bus ride to Joel's from here and we were starting to show each other commitment towards the band. By now I was getting to know his friends. A colourful and bizarre bunch of mixed-up, semi-rich Jewish kids from Golders Green, torn between the sheer Babylon of Western culture and a need to rebuild their homeland, Israel. Between smoking joints and talk of who they hadn't slept with yet would be earnest discussions of returning to the homeland and bearing as many children as possible. The majority were lovely guys. Good, strong, supportive people who genuinely loved Joel and his guitar-playing. The minority were terrifying smackheads, and I was learning fast that most people tolerated marijuana, but anyone who touched heroin was a dickhead. The few smackheads I met did nothing to disprove they were the scourge of their society.

Every Saturday Joel and I would audition his friends for the band, by turning up at their houses, throwing an impromptu party and jamming with them till dawn. If we held the interest of the drunken rabble, they were in. This is how we got our first drummer, Dave Robbins. Dave's parents had gone on holiday, so we took the house over and improvised. Jazz for most of the evening. It must have been horrendous. I could only just sing 'Free Bird' – Jazz didn't stand a chance.

And yet again as the sun rose and all the party folk poured off, I'd walk home alone. The route from Golders Green to my new flat took me across the Archway Bridge. I grew accustomed to the view from this bridge at dawn. In those days there was little traffic on the roads at 5 a.m. The bridge mesmerised me. It was known locally as 'suicide bridge'. It stood high above the Archway Road with a view across London that was enigmatic and romantic in the early hours. I could understand why many a lonely person jumped from it. It's one of those views you almost have to share with someone else or die.

I contemplated jumping every time I crossed it. Sometimes because I was drunk and bolshie. But most of the time because I was heartbroken. Up until this point I'd managed to live my life in this constant state of heartache. Still today I cannot fathom why I allow myself to love and yearn for the impossible when the possible is so much better and healthier. I'm only interested in those things that are out of my reach. Back then, loneliness and rejection were a big part of my life. Ironically, in my determination to be different, with my dress code, hairstyle and attitude, I alienated myself from ever finding a mate. This was a double irony, actually, because that fact alone left me with so much energy that I got on with my key aim in life and that was fame and fortune.

One morning, about 4.30 a.m., the sun was rising on the bridge. I'd spent the night at a succession of parties with Joel and the band, who'd all slowly disappeared into various bedrooms at various houses, leaving me with the other unattractive loners in the lounges of the rich and 'away on holiday' of Golders Green and Finchley Central. On my way home I stood watching the view from the bridge as it changed constantly in the light. It always made me cry. The thought that possibly everyone living in that view could know my name one day. Or even more, the thought that everyone wouldn't. The view as it changed light-wise also changed from being beautiful to threatening. In the space of a few thought-rambling minutes my emotional state would have travelled full circle.

This particular morning I thought to myself, Every time I'm here I keep thinking, What would it be like to jump?

So looking around to make sure the coast was clear, I climbed the extremely high railings and dared myself to jump. I do find that thoughts of suicide are constantly with me, in train stations, in cars, in tower blocks. I don't think they are there to finish me off, but rather to show me how much I want to live. As I balanced on the railings, trying to understand and contact the emotions of all those who had jumped before me, I thought of Mum and Dad, my brother and sister and how they would feel. It would destroy them. I thought of Joel and enjoyed the fact that he might just miss me. I thought of ending all possibilities and decided I didn't ever want to jump. But by now it was too late.

A hand grabbed my ankle and frightened the wits out of me. I almost fell forward.

'Don't do it. Just don't do it,' whoever was stopping the blood circulating through my feet shouted. I turned. It was a policeman. White as a sheet. The look on his face as I turned was partly horror at the state of me, all punked up and nowhere to go, and partly overwhelming pity for what he saw as a social outcast.

Where he appeared from I have no idea. There was no car, no bicycle, no footsteps. We talked for an hour – mainly me, calming him down. He was cross when he realised I was up there for kicks, but we parted friends.

The following day I clambered out of bed to call Dad from the phone box across the road. I always called home once a week to let them know how well I was and how happy and successful in London. Also, my father was ill with a heart condition, which at the time we didn't expect him to survive.

My father picked the phone up before it rang. That was a common occurrence. 'Are you all right?' he'd ask.

'Yes, I'm fine, I'm just phoning to say hello.'

'I'm worried about you – you're low; I can tell, you know,' he'd insist.

I would keep trying to say it was OK.

'Have you got money problems?' he'd continue.

'No,' I'd reply with a smile in my voice, anything to throw him off course.

But he always knew, and once we installed a phone in the flat he would ring as soon as tears were in my eyes.

Joel called at the flat the next morning, a Monday, and told me we had our first gig booked. A synagogue in Finchley this coming Saturday night. It was a paying party. The thought terrified me. Playing at house parties was all well and dandy, everyone was so drunk they never remembered you, but a paying gig, with a stage! What would I wear?!

Joel, the band and I rehearsed in the week and quickly realised we hadn't got enough original material, so it was decided we'd encore with 'Free Bird' and 'Johnny B Goode'. Dear Joel was so nervous. Not only would there be other, competitive local bands appearing, whom he desperately wanted to shame, but possibly all the 'hot totty' a Jewish boy could ever dream of would be there too.

And he was right. As we arrived to set up, the hall was filling with stunning, underdressed nubiles. I hated them. They all looked like clones of Barbie and Farrah Fawcett in leg-warmers. The band were totally distracted. Our sound-check turned into who could pull the most attention by soloing continuously. I just sat there in my pink clown suit, legs dangling over the edge of the stage, and frightened the nubiles with my evil eye, as they amazed at Joel's finger work.

It soon became apparent that every ticket sold was either to a nubile or to one of Joel's friends. Suddenly all our ethics and band policy went out of the window. That policy was: be different in every approach, from music to appearance. So much for being different, if it meant being sidelined. Another pressure I was feeling was that everyone there, including other bands, was under the impression that I looked so different and menacing because I *was*, and that I was going to be the most mind-blowing performer anyone had ever seen. There was a keen eagerness in everyone's eyes as I walked past. If they'd known how terrified I was they'd have laughed.

As we congregated in the dressing room, partly to escape the huge crowd, I was amazed at the amount of people who came in offering free drugs and sex. This was a synagogue, for goodness sake. There we were, trying to get changed, with a constant stream of smacked-out rich boys in cowboy boots and bandanas proffering us any drug we wanted and their girlfriends offering blow-jobs before the show. I was offered nothing other than suspicious glances – either that, or I couldn't recognise a pass if it was placed on a platter in front of me. One of the urban cowboys did bring a bottle of vodka which I gratefully snatched from his hand and guzzled half of on the spot.

My body by this time was shaking uncontrollably with fear. There was an air of expectation which I felt very strongly I could not live up to and there was no way out.

Bless the band, they were so excited; everything was going beyond their plans. The place was packed with loyal followers, before the followers had even heard them play a note. What made it worse for me was that dotted around the audience were a sprinkling of punks. I felt exposed as a fake, and my self-betrayal was going to be very public.

As we stepped on stage, the crowd went mad. It took me totally by surprise that they reacted to Joel as the natural leader of the band and not to me, the singer. This dented my pride and my bombastic temperament kicked in. Just to prove I was honed and serious, like Jim Morrison, and partly to impress the unimpressable punks as well, I unleashed the bottle of vodka from my pocket (very large pocket) and gulped it between verses, leering and spitting at the audience. Well I was just generally being foul. I gobbed at the pretty girls congregating at Joel's feet. Snarled at the punks – who I dare say were impressed by my guts – and shouted abuse at all the straight-looking guys waiting to hear 'Free Bird'.

Our first song was one of our first ever penned. It was called 'Jailer', about sado-masochism. I don't think the audience had a clue what I was going on about. We followed it with 'Problem Child', which speaks for itself, and then 'Israel', an ironic little number I had penned the lyrics for at 3 a.m. on a cold sleepless morning, about claiming ownership of a place thousands of miles away. Again this went completely over the heads of all those in the synagogue, but they clapped and cheered and were well away with the music fairies.

By the third number I had sung myself hoarse with the sheer effort of trying to get attention. Joel received a round of applause every time he soloed, and by now this was making me jealous.

Unfortunately I can't remember much about the rest of the gig, because I passed out. I held on to the microphone stand as I slid down it to the floor, the audience turning from faces into a multicoloured blur. The vodka got the better of me. I came round in the dressing room which was full to the brim with people. Joel was laughing in a corner and never scolded me for letting the show down, probably because the show really started after I lost consciousness. As I lay on the floor in the haze of my own fear and overindulgence I was overwhelmed with a terrible guilt and I vowed to myself that I would never, never drink at a show again. It was time to get my act together, conquer my fears, respect myself and earn respect. Ironically my brazen behaviour did earn me respect that night. But it was all too easy to behave that way. I wanted awe without the fear.

Dave Robbins, the drummer, dropped me back at my grotty flat and left me there alone, as the rest went off to party. Sitting in the darkness of Lee's bedroom, which doubled as our lounge, I cried and cried. Sometimes living with myself was like living with a partner you wish to divorce. Only part of my struggle was about trying to exert some control over outside influences; mostly it was about trying to control myself. My reflex reactions and behaviour at this age of nearly nineteen were far beyond sane reason.

Standing at the window I searched for the moon in the night sky, trying to find that childhood object of desire that grounded me when schooldays drove me insane. But no moon tonight.

For the next twenty-four hours I waited for a phone call from Joel to tell me I was out of the band. It never came. (I'm sure it was discussed.) Even though Joel and I were chalk and cheese, there was a ferocious loyalty between us.

These were unhappy times. My head was in a state of total

confusion. The National Theatre contract was coming to an end and I, like many other actors in the company, hadn't been asked to stay on. I had been there almost nine months and Peter Hall still didn't know my name. Laurence Olivier's dream of an actor's theatre had come to fruition but was becoming a treadmill. With this termination looming I was beginning to feel dislocated. This would be my first time in London without employment, and that scared me. All this and the disastrous first gig with the band was enough to make me irrational. I was starting to behave like a cornered animal. Cornered by nothing other than my own will, pride, ambition and disorientation.

At least I had Derek Jarman to fall back on. The flat I shared with Lee and Penny had no phone. Looking at the queues outside the phone boxes on Hornsey Road, I'd have said no one had a phone of their own. In recent weeks it had become a habit to phone Derek every Monday at 6.30 p.m. to get the latest news about the financing and shooting of his film *Jubilee*. Now, standing in the queue outside the phone box I was relieved that the usual gang of black girls from up the road were not around. This particular group of fourteen-year-olds had taken an extreme dislike to me and always threatened to knife me as I made my phone calls. They were nowhere to be seen.

Eventually I made it into the box and dialled Derek's number. By now he was living back at his warehouse on Butlers Wharf. A young boy answered and called Derek to the phone.

'Toyah!' My dear, I'm so glad you've phoned,' came an earnest explosion down the phone. 'I'm afraid we've had to cut the character of Mad from the film. I've had meetings all week trying to raise enough money for an extra character, but in truth there are too many in the story.'

Stunned silence.

'Toyah?'

'Yes, no, it's OK. I understand.' I laughed nervously, trying to fathom the chaos erupting in my head.

'I'm really sorry, Toyah, I so wanted you in the film.' Derek really meant it.

'Well, next time aye? We'll talk soon.' I put the phone down and ran. My front door was just across the road. I made it in and collapsed. Couldn't have *hoi polloi* of Hornsey seeing this punk reduced to rubble.

My disappointment took me by surprise, I fell on the floor gasping for air, in unstoppable tears. Our flat was on the first floor. Lee heard me from the kitchen and flew down the stairs and pulled me up into her arms begging to know what was wrong, but I couldn't talk. I'd completely lost the plot. At first Lee thought my father or mother had died. I managed to say, 'No.' So she held me till I gained some control of myself. By this time Penny and Brian, our Rastafarian lodger, were sitting on the stairs stunned. It took all three of them to get me up the stairs and into the kitchen, and when I told them I'd been dropped from *Jubilee*, they couldn't quite understand why I had reacted so badly. Yes, it was disappointing, but not *that* disappointing, they must have thought.

My world had caved in. *Jubilee* was the only thing I'd had to look forward to. Suddenly I joined the ranks of thousands of unemployed actors my father had always told me about when I was a daydreaming child. Fear had a total grip of me. Up until now, I'd had phenomenal luck: Mary Richards had got me through drama school, I'd had the lead role in a telly drama, the National Theatre and a life of passing stars with Kate Nelligan. Now here I was on the rain-swept streets of Hornsey with no guaranteed future. I was so scared I didn't know where to start.

It took a few days to sort my head out. I went very quickly from self-pity and shame to survival mode. Lee, Penny, Glenn and Joel were all fantastic. Up until that moment they'd all seen me as a hard nut, but now they knew otherwise. Joel took me to the twenty-four-hour hamburger joint in Hampstead at 2 a.m. Glenn took me to *The Rocky Horror Show* on the King's Road, and Penny and Lee cooked for me most evenings. For the first time in London, I had a secure and protective circle of friends around me.

Walking into my dressing room at the National Theatre for one of the last performances of *Tales from the Vienna Woods* – these had now become so sporadic that the company seemed like strangers when we met, and they'd all started other jobs – Ian Charleson burst into my room and pulled me from my chair. 'Call Derek, come on, you have to call Derek now,' he insisted cryptically, and frogmarched me to the nearest payphone.

I felt defiant and embarrassed. I didn't want to hear another apology. I wanted to forget.

Derek wasn't one for beating around the bush. 'Toyah, my dear, you're back in the film, we've raised the money.'

'Really? Really?! That's fantastic. Are you sure?' I was visibly shaking.

'Yes, but I can only pay you £300.' Derek started to become apologetic.

'I'll do it, I'll do it for free. Just give me my bus fares!' I meant it.

When I put the phone down I hugged Ian Charleson till all feeling left my arms.

Jubilee was to start shooting as soon as I finished at the National. Not only would I be freed, but Ian and Karl Johnson's contracts were ending too, so we could all have absolute commitment to the film. That night Lee, Penny, Glenn and I partied like it was 1999. Thus began a new emotional pattern for me, although I didn't realise it at the time: now, thanks to Derek's efforts, I was part of the great employed, and I felt worthy and connected; and as soon as that employment was over, I was to feel worthless, terrified and dejected. It was a cycle that was to become as reliable as clockwork. Full of melodrama and overreaction.

Chapter 15

Wednesday 18 May 1977 was my nineteenth birthday. It was a cold morning with a breeze blowing through the broken glass of my bedroom window. Turning the radio on I was captivated by the most astonishing record. It was almost operatic. The DJ, Dave Lee Travis, back-announced another nineteen-year-old, Kate Bush, and 'Wuthering Heights'. That day my concept of music changed. Music could be musical and dramatic, it didn't have to be just plain brash and repetitive.

Downstairs, Lee gave me the *Ladybird Book of Policemen*. I loved it. Penny and Brian gave me chocolate. And in the post arrived a box of chocolate gingers from Dad. When I opened them for my birthday breakfast I found there was a fiver inside, with a note: 'I love you sweetie pie.' I could have cried. Dear Dad, he was poorer than I was.

On New Year's Day 2000, I recounted this day to my father. He suddenly chipped in with the most surprising detail. 'Do you remember the condoms?' he said. 'No, I didn't remember any condoms – being a (reluctant) virgin at the time, I had no use for condoms – but my selective memory is far different from my father's. 'I came to visit,' he said, 'and you were mortified when I pointed out the condoms on the milk bottles keeping the milk fresh.'

Dad also reminded me that he used to bring me as many tins of food as he could muster and that I'd sit there hungrily eating straight out of the tin.

But life was on course again. Derek Jarman was becoming a constant in my life. There was so much preparation to be done for the filming of *Jubilee*. First, Derek felt I looked like a country-bumpkin punk and my hair had to go. It was too fussy and too feminine. So I was packed off to Smile in Knightsbridge, where Keith Wainwright shaved my head. I thought this was all a terrible mistake as the razor glided over my scalp. They were turning me into a skinhead. Keith left about a quarter of an inch of hair, which was then bleached and dyed orange. It was fantastic. I was a walking Belisha beacon. People on the streets avoided me, not knowing whether I was friendly or hostile, sane or mad.

The storyline of the film required me to have a band. So one of the producers, Guy Ford, picked me up in his Rolls-Royce from my flat in Hornsey and we drove in style to Dingwalls rock club in Camden to spend a conceptual evening with a newcomer called Adam Ant. Adam was already making a huge impact on the punk scene. He was charismatic, ambitious and driven. He was also to star in the film.

Inside Dingwalls we drank at the bar, my head exploding with ideas and Adam courteously writing them down on paper napkins. I'd never had someone take me seriously before, and here was Adam not only listening but responding positively too. Guy Ford, bless him, kept plying me with alcohol. The club was full of other musicians, most memorably Wilko Johnson and Lee Brilleaux from Dr Feelgood.

Adam had decided that my character should have an all-girl band call the Maneaters and he knew who they should be, so he'd put a band together. In the space of the evening we penned a very dodgy number called 'Nine to Five'. I was thrilled. I'd never written anything like this, it was so spontaneous and unselfconscious. I wanted more. Adam and I seemed to hit it off. My confidence grew as he accepted everything I suggested as a viable possibility. By the end of the evening I was prepared to leave Joel's band and hit the road with the new imaginary Maneaters. We were going to make records with Adam's help and guidance and tour the universe.

At 2 a.m. Guy, Adam and I left the club to find that someone had scratched 'FUCK OFF' down the side of Guy's yellow Rolls-Royce. Guy flipped and admitted that the car was his parents'. My initial thought was, Who could hate Guy this much? This sweet, lovely, suited and well-groomed creature. But as we drove home, somewhat silent, it dawned on me that the music world, the old music establishment, truly hated punks and their offerings. As Guy dropped me at my flat his last words were that he would have to have the Rolls resprayed by the morning.

Within days, Adam and I were in the recording studio laying down 'Nine to Five'. When I arrived, his band, the Ants, had already put down the backing track and they were all milling around enthusing about how good it all sounded. Adam was a tower of strength. He produced, kept the spirits up and enthused about everything. It was very heady. Everything I had ever dreamed of. My heart was in my throat as I did my vocal and it didn't hit me that technically my performance was verging on crap. What it was, though, was raw, truthful and packed with as much energy as a bullet from a gun. At a time when the Bee Gees and Rod Stewart dominated the charts, we all sat in the control room and cheered at the thought of a musical revolution taking the Lycra out of music.

I was having a great time – all the people around me were so driven and focused. Adam may have looked like a wild man of punk, but he didn't drink, didn't do drugs and didn't procrastinate, and that really impressed me. But I suspect that after this recording venture Adam started to doubt my capabilities as a natural singer. It would be true to say that at this time I was all mouth and mediocre delivery. That said, I was learning, and learning very fast.

The first day's shoot on *Jubilee* was not a glamorous event. More clamorous. I rose at 5 a.m. and caught the night bus across town to Tower Bridge. As I stepped off the bus a curious smell invaded my nostrils; it took me a few days to find out the source. It was hops. Derek's beautiful, majestic warehouse on Butlers Wharf sat snugly between various breweries – quite fitting for a party animal.

On the short walk to the riverfront I passed numerous night workers all going for their fry-up breakfast. This part of the city didn't have a night-time. It was tatty to the point of dereliction back in 1977, but industrious and almost untouched by time – there were even shire horses about.

Inside Derek's huge living space everyone was gathering. Derek buzzed around introducing us all. Jordan, Little Nell, Jenny Runacre, Émile, Adam Ant, Luciana. These were the principle cast. There were no hair or make-up people, we had to do our own. So Jordan and Nell were busying themselves with that. Jenny didn't bother; she was to be *naturelle*.

Adam had attached himself to Nell, and so did I. She was so fascinating. Nell could talk about anyone and anything. No taboos, no territory uncovered, and so it seemed she knew everyone in the world. Nell was a bright light that kept all our spirits up, a constant reminder that there is hope in the world. And for me it was fantastic to meet the girl with red hair from *The Rocky Horror Picture Show*. Nell had been a huge inspiration to me.

It was pretty obvious that Derek loved women. He would effervesce around us all like a permanently dissolving Alka Seltzer. Making sure we were all OK. Dealing with producers. Dealing with disgruntled set-builders who hadn't enough money in the budget. John Mapbury was the principal set-maker under the watchful eye of Christopher Hobbs, and he had Kenny, the drummer from Siouxsie and the Banshees, on hand for help. All three were great fun.

Andrew Logan lived next door to Derek, and as I'd never seen his work, Derek took me into his warehouse so I could be amazed by the life-size mirrored horses, icons, trees and flowers. I was a long way from the Hornsey Road, let alone Birmingham, mentally and physically. I was in heaven.

By 9 a.m. Derek walked us all downstairs, like his ducklings, into a vast disused space, which must once have been part of a brewery, and now was to be the principal set and home of *Jubilee*. It was teeming with film crew. They were like worker ants – appearing into the light, fiddling and then disappearing into cavernous darkness. For the first time I felt shy.

Even though Jenny Runacre was the big star in the film, for Derek, Jordan was the one on the highest pedestal. He just loved her. Jordan was extraordinary, a bizarre juxtaposition of seaside culture, punk and rare observation, which made her addictive company. Jordan had guts. She was not a natural beauty, but she created exotic personas for herself that showed no hint of cliché. I imagine she inspired Vivienne Westwood, who she worked for, when she wasn't acting, in the King's Road shop co-owned by Malcolm McLaren, called Sex.

Talking to Jordan was like having a conversation with your oldest aunt. She'd explain her love of Floris perfumes, and soaps, and her admiration for tweed and pearls – and then as if someone had flipped a coin she'd refer to bondage as if it were standard office wear. Jordan had a strength which intimated that nothing took hold of her, or could own her or harm her, yet her voice was like an infant-school teacher's, soft and nurturing.

Jordan hadn't acted in a movie before. Yes, she did catch the Hastings train every morning dressed in sex clothes. Yes, she did stand on the side of the stage at Adam Ant's concerts being a muse. But like me, she'd never been on celluloid and that bonded us.

Ian Charleson and Karl Johnson were already on the set when we arrived. Ian was always lovely company, never moody, always bright-eyed and interested. Karl was shy and almost secretive, but in an affectionate way I loved them both.

We all moved very quickly, from getting-to-know-each-other mode to filming the first scene. Time was money, after all.

The first scene to be shot happened to consist of ten pages of dialogue for me, of which eight were monologue. But my character Mad was reciting from a book. So the only problem I had to conceal was the fact that my hands were shaking like a spin-drier. Derek walked me through the shot, then we rehearsed it once and bagged it on a first take, to rapturous applause from the crew. My head was swelling by the second. Yes, I thought to myself, films is where I want to be.

My character, Mad, was a hyperactive, sci-fi punk who also had a passion for fire. She was really a sidekick character to Jordan's, but my ego kicked into hyperdrive and Mad became a scene-stealing dominatrix, who by the end of the shoot, I'm sure, everyone had grown to loathe, except me.

The second scene to be shot involved Mad jumping into the shared bed of Ian Charleson's and Karl Johnson's characters and threatening to set them on fire with a lighter. Easy-peasy. We rehearsed it a few times. My Zippo lighter played up a bit, but all went smoothly and we went for a take. The camera rolled, the clapperboard clapped and Derek shouted 'action'. I sprinted across the room, pulled the bed-sheets back and sprang into bed, between Ian and Karl, in my fisherman's waders and little overstretched leotard and I just sat there and stared, lost for words. After a few seconds I burst out laughing and Derek shouted 'cut'.

Grandma, Dad and his sister, Olive, shortly before Olive died of TB.

Mum in dance class, aged ten.

Dad, on the left, on leave with a
friend in Egypt during World War II.

Mum, left, on stage at Cheltenham. No doubt she had
a more refined singing voice than me.

Mum and Dad's wedding,
5 October 1949, Weston-super-
Mare. Nan Kenway, the pianist,
was matron of honour and Douglas
Young, the comedian, was best man.

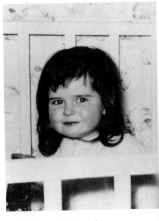

Now that's where my
love of rabbits started. In the cot,
or should I say my first experience
of feeling confined, at the age of
one and a half.

Sailing off the Isle of Wight with Dad, 1966.

The budding ice-skater at Solihull ice rink, 1968.

School mug shot. Me aged thirteen. Nice haircut!

My sister, Nicola, on the boat.

Alec and Gee Nelmes. Gee became my godmother when I was fourteen. In February 2000, Gee celebrated her 101st birthday.

My first ever photo shoot, with Shirley in Hampstead woods, 1977.

A punk always returns home to Mum's cooking. 1977.

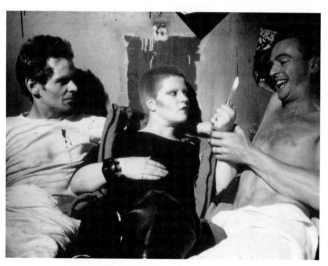

In bed with Karl Johnson and Ian Charleson on the
first day of shooting for *Jubilee*, 1977.

The band in 1978: Joel Bogen, Steve Bray, me, Charlie Francis and Pete Bush.

The Corn Is Green, with Katharine Hepburn, 1978.
Here I have just told her I'm pregnant by her star pupil.

Me as Bessie Wattie in *The Corn Is Green*.

Picnicking in Betws-y-coed with Mum, Dad and Patricia Hayes during the filming of *The Corn Is Green*. Somewhere out of shot is my white rabbit, Banacheck, nibbling on the grass.

My first recording contract signing to Safari records, 1978.
John Craig, at the back, and Tony Edwards, centre.

All greased-up and nowhere to go. On stage at the
Royal Court in *Sugar and Spice*, 1980.

Derek ran over and asked if everything was all right. Probably the fact that I'd turned bright red concerned him. I just looked at him and said, 'I've never seen a naked man before, not in the flesh, close up.' In rehearsals Karl and Ian had had clothes on. I was soon to learn that Derek preferred male nudity at every opportunity.

Derek discreetly led me aside, away from the astonished gawps of the cast and crew. He asked if I was OK with the scene, which I was, bar the fact that I couldn't stop laughing every time I saw these floppy lumps of flesh lazily lounging around Karl and Ian's groins like plucked chickens sunbathing. But this was the beginning of a very protective relationship between Derek and me. He virtually became a father figure, ready to explain any intimate detail I required knowledge of. He also kept the predators at bay.

Derek worked incredibly hard. Watching his dedication you couldn't help but fall in love with him – in a very different kind of way to how you would fall in love with anyone else. This wasn't a lust love. For me this love was an appreciation, an admiration and a kind of wishing that I could be slightly like him. He was so focused. There was no room for compromise. He could be incredibly bitchy and incredibly hurtful, but you could see that he controlled that part of himself. Derek was like a living, walking angel.

There was a side of Derek that I never really saw, the side that was exclusively homosexual; he never really opened up to me about that. The uniqueness of our relationship was probably more spiritual than anything else: he saw something in me that no one else could see, as throughout the filming of *Jubilee* I was becoming more and more big-headed and more and more out of control, as I saw the goals I'd wanted all my life coming to fruition. And Derek was forgiving of that.

As *Jubilee* progressed it was getting a lot of attention, both positive attention from the media and negative attention from the main punk bands at the time. A lot of the really credible punk bands, like Siouxsie and the Banshees, started to dissociate themselves from *Jubilee*, saying that it should never be made and that it was exploiting punk. But on the other hand there was a whole culture that wanted to know about punk, and this was where Derek was really clever. In making *Jubilee* he was giving a new generation outside of London everything they'd ever wanted.

By the time we were half-way through filming *Jubilee* we all knew that it was going to be a big film – OK, not as big as a Hollywood blockbuster, but a lot of people were going to know about it. So slowly we were all becoming stars in our own right – very much the way Andy Warhol made stars of the casts he chose for his art films. I absolutely relished the attention I was getting. I started to become addicted to the admiration of strangers – I don't mean physical admiration, but the fact that strangers would come up to me and they'd know my name, and what I'd done, and people would talk about me as if I was some kind of notorious legend. Most people get the attention they need in life from their families, but I was starting to find that nothing in my personal life could give me that kind of attention, so I was looking for it through my work and through how I behaved in the public eye. It wasn't a question of just being an actress and a singer; it was the person I was portraying as well. And I was starting to create a persona – a persona that I'd imagined and fantasised about in my childhood. It was *Jubilee* and Derek Jarman that allowed that persona to grow. I am not blaming them in any way, in fact I'm praising Derek for that, because before *Jubilee* I was actually a very timid, insecure creature, but this whole filming process was turning me into the person I needed to become to achieve my dreams. In retrospect, today, I know those dreams were wrong and misplaced. Fame back then was my object of desire. But if I hadn't made that journey of self-obsession, I wouldn't be where I am today, I suppose. (A little self-congratulatory, but I can't help thinking, I'm still alive!)

Little did I know it at the time, but I was so annoying the rest of the cast that I actually wasn't very well liked, and probably the only friend I had during the shooting of *Jubilee* was Derek; everyone else was becoming quite wary of me. When I'm happy – which isn't a lot of the time, I'm usually too thoughtful to be happy – I get hyperactive, and the happier I am the more hyperactive I am; if you can imagine a hyperactive child on amphetamines, that's how I am when I'm happy. I am completely out of control, and that was what was happening on *Jubilee*.

The rest of the filming went relatively smoothly; we all worked extremely hard and very long hours, and although there may have been ego tensions we were a tight-knit group of people and we did enjoy each other's company. I particularly loved Jordan and Nell and Jenny. They were wonderful. They were icons – they still are – and they were great role models too.

Adam had decided that I should work in a band with his wife, Eve, and he put the band together for me. This band became the Maneaters and in *Jubilee* we mime to the track Adam and I wrote together called 'Nine to Five'. The Maneaters were a very attractive group of girls. I think Adam probably had a fixation with every single member of the band except me. The fact that Eve was his wife was a secret, even though they had been separated for a while, because Adam was about to break big-time across England and didn't want it known that he'd been married. Stephanie was the bass-player, a very tall, big-busted blonde who I think Adam ardently admired.

On drums, there was Anne-Marie who was fascinating – a true feminist, and really, really hard. She was a music teacher as well. She was the first one to point out to me that the world didn't revolve around Toyah. I didn't like her saying that at the time but it was one of the greatest lessons I ever learned.

Because Adam had put the Maneaters together I started to neglect my relationship with Joel – which was fine at the time, as Joel had other things to do: he was doing exams, and his family was putting pressure on him. But it did look as though the Maneaters had a future. With the film coming out, there was the possibility of further records being made. The Maneaters track was going to be on the *Jubilee* soundtrack album, which meant we could do concerts. I was full of dreams. I was very much someone who used to tell people my dreams as if they were reality, and I can remember clearly at the end of each filming day sitting down with Adam and reeling out these dreams. We are going to play here. We are going to do this. We are going to record that. We are going to look like this. Little did I know that I was irritating the shit out of Adam by doing this. I genuinely didn't realise how selfish I was being – and Adam probably needed his own downtime anyway.

One of the very last sequences to be shot for *Jubilee* was shot in the Coleherne club, a gay club in Earls Court. On the day of shooting, Derek filled the club with his friends. It was a very colourful event. There were very few heterosexual people there and there was an awful lot of homosexual activity going on. When I arrived I was addressed by Adam, who wasn't in a particularly good mood; also he couldn't look me in the eye. He told me Eve had something to tell me. Eve took me aside into a little dark room – it must have been a cloakroom. (There was very little light anywhere, even though we were filming; the whole place seemed to share one light bulb.) And Eve said, 'I'm terribly sorry, but Adam doesn't want you in the band any more.'

At that moment the earth fell from beneath my feet. I had the sensation of falling from an aeroplane without a parachute. For a few moments I just tried to take it in. I tried to see reason in what she was saying, but I could see none. I was a very volatile person in those days; there was no possibility that I could control my reaction. I didn't say anything to Eve, I just turned and immediately went in search of Adam, and on finding him I exploded like an H-bomb. I grabbed him round the scruff and I said, 'What the fuck is going on? What do you mean I'm no longer in the band?'

Adam, confronted by this furious female, was close to giggling. Any form of confrontation made Adam giggle, in fact anything that embarrassed him at all made him giggle. There was one scene in *Jubilee* where Ian Charleson and Karl Johnson had to try and make out with him and it was virtually impossible to film because Adam couldn't stop laughing throughout the whole sequence. But this time we were in a club full of people and it was even more embarrassing for him because the whole club was silenced by my outrage and was watching us. I started to hit Adam because he was laughing at me and he just said, 'I don't want you in the band. You're not right for the band.' He probably said other things but I didn't hear them.

Derek ran over and split us up. He was absolutely astonished at what was going on, because up until then there had been absolutely no hint that Adam and I could ever have a fight. We'd been the best of friends. By this time I was in floods of tears. Over the past weeks I'd fantasised so much about the Maneaters becoming something really credible, really big, having a future, touring, being on *Top of the Pops* (as it seemed everyone else was at that time except me). I could not conceal the hurt I was feeling. After pulling me off Adam, Derek took me aside into a room and asked what was going on. When I told him he just couldn't believe it. But he didn't say anything. He didn't get involved and he didn't try to patch it up. Instead he made sure that Adam and I did not have to act in the same scene that day, so I was kept on one side of the club and Adam was kept on the other.

It was hard to think about filming that day. I was absolutely locked in the depressing thought that the Maneaters weren't going to happen, or at least they weren't going to happen for me. Eve kept away from me, obviously seeing that I was quite capable of throwing punches at anyone, but Anne-Marie the drummer dared to approach me and said that the problem was that my ego had got completely out of control and Adam didn't want to have to share the limelight; he wanted to create a band and to run it as a mentor – probably very like the way Malcolm McLaren was running the Sex Pistols. I'd become too strong a person; he didn't like my ideas and felt I was too pushy, so I had to go.

It took me a long time to get over that event. In humiliating Adam and Eve that day, I also humiliated myself. I just couldn't control my anger and in those days I always reacted before I thought about things, so I made rather a lot of enemies. It irritated me later that day to overhear Eve explain to a complete stranger that the reason for my explosion was that I had fallen in love with Adam. It was such a stupid female thing to say. I hadn't fallen in love with Adam. Adam was more of a soul partner. I admired him enormously – he had the most exquisite taste, he had great ideas, he was fabulous to be around – but there was no love there whatsoever, just respect. It goes without saying that Adam and I never talked again after that day – not even when we both appeared on the same *Top of the Pops* four years later, when Adam was a huge star and I was up and coming. We just didn't bother with each other.

For this last scene to be shot for *Jubilee*, Derek enrolled the Lindsay Kemp company. Derek and Lindsay were obviously very good friends. So the whole company had congregated in the back of the club where we were filming a short nightclub sequence. Derek had to deal not only with the fact that I was in tears all day because of the break up of the Maneaters, but also with the fact that the whole of the Lindsay Kemp company were constantly having sex all over the place. It was an absolute eye-opener. Most of the camera crew actually managed to ignore this and get on with their work, but there were things going on in the corners of the club that I'd never even imagined. I tried to divert my eyes and act cool and pretend I wasn't seeing any of it, but part of me was totally fascinated with the kind of contortions the male body could get into with another male. You'd have thought they were doing this to show off but Derek didn't actually film any of the sexual activity; he just allowed it to go on in the background as if it was off-camera entertainment. What people get up to in the Green Room when they are relaxing! But it got to the point during the day where one truly couldn't find a corner to go and be quiet or cry in because every corner, every orifice of that room was filled with men having sex.

That night when we finished filming I walked out of the Coleherne a different person. On some levels I felt as if I'd been jilted, but on many levels a huge challenge had been presented to me. *Jubilee* had gone so well and I'd felt so on course, that I was about to become this big film and rock-star – and Adam had pulled that world from under my feet. It left me with no other possibility than that I had to make it. I had to prove myself. I had to prove myself as a writer, as a performer and as a woman. The fight with Adam hurt me because he rejected me as a creative woman. My not being in his all-girl band was a challenge I had to face. To disprove him. To let him know he'd made a great mistake. So I went home and called Joel – who'd been neglected terribly throughout the filming of *Jubilee* – and I said, 'Joel, we're really really going to make a go of this.' Joel was just about to finish school, which was fantastic for us because it meant that we could write and rehearse every day, any day we wanted, any hour of the day. The timing was perfect.

Chapter 16

Joel and I put our heads together and we just wrote and wrote and wrote. We decided we weren't going to play at parties any more, we were going to get gigs, and in those days it was considered quite respectable to play in pubs. The pub circuit was the perfect way of building a following, and that's what we started to do. First, though, Glenn and his friends Paul and Jackie decided that I needed to get out of London. I hadn't got over what Adam had done to me; it was eating at me. I was lying awake in bed thinking about it, and when I did fall asleep I had nightmares about it. Then when I woke in the morning my heart sank as I realised that I was this person who'd been rejected. It was not a good time. I was depressed. So Glenn hired a cottage in Devon, picked me up, and we drove down there for a week.

The cottage was a small damp thatched affair in a beautiful Devon valley. We went to the sea one day, we ate fish and chips another day, but most days we just sat in the cottage smoking pot. Paul was particularly fond of making hash cakes. I'd never eaten hash cakes before. I sat in the kitchen with Paul, very much the way I used to sit in the kitchen with my mother as a child, and I mixed the cake mixture while Paul broke the hash into the bowl. Paul was a bit overenthusiastic with the hash. I had no idea what was a lot, what was too little, so I just went along with it and we made this whopping big cake. The smell of hash filled the whole cottage but we weren't worried; we were in the middle of nowhere, no one would be popping in. That night we ate most of the cake. I can remember passing out and coming round in the morning and still being unable to stand up.

In the morning we went shopping in the local village. I kept saying to Glenn, 'Act normal. We've got to act normal.' The dope cake had given me tunnel vision: everything appeared as if I was looking down a long tube. Glenn and I were giggling a lot. We probably bought a can of baked beans and then ran out of the shop. It was bad enough being a punk in the middle of a Devon village in 1977, but trying to act normal because we'd all overdosed on dope made it even worse. The four of us decided to go for a walk to try to get it out of our systems.

We walked along beautiful country roads, laughing and giggling and falling all over the place. After an hour we'd had enough. It had become quite warm; the sun was already quite high in the sky. I lay down in the middle of the road. When I came round it was twilight and there was a rabbit next to me. I remember waking Glenn and saying, 'Oh look, there's a little bunny rabbit.' I still had tunnel vision. We picked ourselves up, having been unconscious for at least eight hours on a country lane that no one had driven down for the whole day. We were like a small group of Rip Van Winkles. We could have been there for weeks for all we knew. We got ourselves back to the cottage, went straight to bed and didn't touch any dope for the rest of the holiday.

When I got back to Hornsey Road after this holiday, life became very very hard. *Jubilee* had finished filming. Derek wasn't really available as a friend because he was now editing, a process that took all his attention and all his time. For the first time since I'd lived in London, I was truly touched by loneliness. Penny and Lee were at drama school during the daytime, and I was left alone in the flat. I had to sign on. I have only ever signed on twice in my life; this was the second time and I absolutely loathed it. I did my utmost to write all the time and to keep myself motivated. It was hard to be motivated in Hornsey.

Up the road was a series of squats and I often walked up there because they were full of interesting people. In one squat was a wonderful black man called Ollie, who had two wooden legs. I used to sit with Ollie throughout the long boring days and we'd talk. He never told me how he lost his legs, but he talked a lot about his past, which had obviously been very colourful. And his squat was fantastic. It was mainly inhabited by musicians who would just come and go. Some would be there for two days, some would be there for an hour, some would never return. Being in Ollie's squat was like reading a William Burroughs book: everything was completely surreal. No one seemed to have any roots yet they were all leading gloriously colourful, adventurous lives.

I had six months of unemployment, which gave me time to become insecure about myself again, to lose all the grandiose stature my ego had gained from filming *Jubilee*. I also put on a lot of weight. The only comfort I had was in food. I had very little money, so I was tending to pinch Penny's food, Lee's food, and food from the local supermarket. The chip shop downstairs were very good to us. They realised we were quite poor, so at the end of the day, at about midnight when they were closing down, they let us have the scraps – you can imagine how marinated in fat those were. The chips we were eating must have been in the fat all day. One of the good things about filming *Jubilee* was my £300 fee, which bought me my first PA system: two stacks, a microphone stand and a microphone. It meant that for the first time while working with Joel I could hear myself sing. By this time, because Joel and I were taking the band seriously, we were starting to hire rehearsal rooms. We used to rehearse at the Winchester Project Youth Centre in Swiss Cottage. I had my wonderful PA system for all of a month before it was nicked from the Winchester Project. *C'est la vie* – there you go.

Life at Hornsey Road was becoming intolerable. It was too domestic. It wasn't the girls' fault, nothing like that. I just loathed being on the Hornsey Road. There was no inspiration. You looked out of the window. There was no light, no spiritual light. There was none of the inspiration of the later years, during the miners' strikes, when the women all came together and fought the system. Hornsey Road just represented poverty and apathy. There was no fight there, nothing to get your claws into. I couldn't get my imagination to work there. It was close to Joel, which meant we could rehearse quite a lot. By this time we'd recruited Nick Turner as our drummer. Nick was a wonderful boy – and he had a car. None of us could ever sleep so we used to spend the nights driving round London, ending up on Hampstead Heath, gallivanting around in the darkness at 4 a.m.

But I did have to get out of Hornsey. I had to find inspiration.

Through Glenn I met a man called Keith Hodges. Keith was an interesting character, who did a lot of film-extra work and performance art. He's the extra in *Star Wars* who famously falls during a fight scene. It happens so quickly you can only see it properly on *It'll Be Alright on the Night.* At the time I met him he lived in Notting Hill, but we both decided that we couldn't bear the domesticity of our surroundings so we went in search of a warehouse. Eventually Keith found one on the Queenstown Road in Battersea. It was down a slip road next to the railway arches of Queenstown Road railway station, so every few seconds trains rattled past and shook all the buildings. Under the arches there was a mortuary – a funeral parlour and a wood workshop where they made all the coffins. I instantly fell in love with the place. It was buzzing with life, ironically. It was a hive of activity, a hive of life and death. The hearse, and the vans that collected the bodies from the hospitals, constantly came and went carrying coffins in and out. There were second-hand-car salerooms, lots of dodgy geezers, and right at the end of our drive was a tip where the skips and their lorries would pass. It was absolutely perfect.

Steps led up to our warehouse, which was on the first floor. Inside there was no light, no windows, but we didn't care. What there was inside were some huge glass tanks that had stored acid; we decided we were going to dismantle these tanks and use the glass for flooring. It was thick and armour-plated. Keith and I set about clearing the place up. We had to scrape up the old tiles, sweep out the soot, and throw away all the rotten wood; we wanted to turn it into a massive empty space – and that's what we did, from December 1977 through to January 1978. We used to commute – me from Hornsey, Keith from Notting Hill – and it was cold and miserable. We'd get so cold I couldn't move; my fingers would just be frozen solid from scraping tiles off the floor. But it motivated us. We had something to aim for. And above all this was art. We were going to have parties. The place was never going to be empty; it was going to be full of people – friends, bands, performers and artists. We'd got the space we wanted.

Keith did the work of a hundred men. He put up partitions so we had privacy. We made makeshift beds out of old doors, and once we'd discovered more about the workings of the morgue across the road, we knew we could climb over the fence and nick the wood that they used for the coffins. Also, they actually gave us an old accident coffin, made of fibreglass; it had been used to pick up people who'd died in car crashes. I used to sleep in that. It was the only way I could keep warm. The enclosed space was ideal: I could just shove in a duvet and a pillow and be cosy for the night – although it was a little hard. It was also a bit spooky at first, but boy, was it a talking-point for people who visited the warehouse.

Joel came to see the warehouse and was hugely unimpressed. We'd painted the whole space black. We did manage to knock a window through; it was the only window in this vast space. We put in three bedrooms, a lounge area, a stage and a massive audience area. All this took time. For ages, we didn't have a toilet. We used to sneak into the pub next door, or find a dark spot under one of the arches and just crap there like dogs. It was pretty rough. There was also no bath; we used to have to go round to our friends' houses or wash in a bucket. In fact I became particularly fond of bucket baths – it's what I used to do as a child on the boat with my father. But the overwhelming thing was the cold. There was no heating and we couldn't afford to put any in. The rent was £60 a week which was about all we could afford if we were to eat as well. Occasionally we'd walk across Chelsea Bridge and have a pizza on the King's Road, but that was a real treat and would take a few weeks to save up for. But in the meantime we were having a ball. We'd joined the vanguard of the loft set and we were really going for it big-time.

One of the ways we managed to make a lot of money was by throwing parties. We'd put the word out that there was to be a party the coming weekend. We'd never send out invites – we never had to. The wonderful thing about London was that you could say to one person, 'There's a party on Friday night,' and like a Chinese whisper it would pass right through the community, from south London to north London to east London to west London, and become an event. So on Friday night four hundred people would just pour into the warehouse and they'd party till Monday morning. These parties really went on and on. The noise was unbelievable. But because the warehouse wasn't in a residential area, very few people ever complained. We certainly never had any trouble with the police. We'd make our money by selling drink and charging a small fee at the door – but that didn't deter people. They just came and enjoyed themselves. Boy George was always there. Steve Strange was always there. Martin Degville from Sigue Sigue Sputnik was always there. McLaren, the Sex Pistols, they'd just turn up. Most of the time I couldn't bear being there. I'd sit in my little room and the noise would be intolerable – plus there'd be the sound of people trying to find somewhere to pee, or the sound of people throwing up, or the sound of people having sex – so I just used to pack a bag and disappear for the weekend. I'd make sure everyone got in on the Friday, I'd leave at midnight, perhaps go home to see Mum and Dad or stay with a friend down the road, and then I'd come back on Monday morning and sweep up all the debris and throw out the unconscious bodies. There was never any bother, never any fights, never any fires, never any evidence of drugs. It just worked, and was wonderful. We had a reputation for throwing these big parties so we threw them regularly, and this was what allowed us to keep the warehouse – which by now was called Mayhem. Mayhem is my all-time favourite word. Mayhem was becoming a place in its own right.

Thanks to Mayhem my period of unemployment was becoming more fruitful. I was meeting people who were 'doers'. They were at the vanguard of the new romantic scene, the new-wave scene. These people were inspirational, and my writing took on a completely new flavour. I was plugged in; my finger was tapped in to the electricity of their creativity. It meant I was very up to date. So up to date that I could see beyond the present, could see what was coming, could see where fashions and trends were leading. Thanks to Mayhem being such a magnet to other creative people, I myself was thrust very much into the vanguard of the new-wave movement, and after moving into Mayhem I was never again surrounded by any form of banality. Mayhem was a massive mixing-pot of ideas and energy and different types of people. It was an endless source of inspiration. As I said, the inside of Mayhem was painted black. Our favourite colours as a team of people were black and red – the colours of anarchy. I had a particular penchant for shop dummies, and we had them sticking out of the walls like dismembered bodies. Mayhem was very much a punk grotto, a shrine to everything broken, picked up out of skips, borrowed and never returned. It was a fabulous mishmash of bizarre ideas.

Inspired by my new surroundings I also managed to get a new agent. Her name was Libby Glenn; she was one of the most influential people in this embryonic stage of my life. She was an American, feisty and loyal. She contacted me. She had seen me at the National Theatre, and by all accounts was desperate to have me on her books. It is very flattering when someone chases you like that; they kind of seduce you into their lives – but Libby's was a very lucky seduction. Because I was a punk, a lot of people were wary of working with me, but Libby didn't mind that her name might perhaps be put to shame in the business by her having me on her books. She persuaded people, incredibly influential people, that they had to meet me, had to consider me for roles. The day I signed with Libby was the day that my serious acting career began.

Chapter 17

Libby was a wonderfully feisty woman. She loathed that I wanted to do music. She would phone me daily and beg me to give music up. She would phone me daily and beg me to dye my hair back to a normal colour, saying my personality was enough to get me through; I didn't need the exterior to go with it. I found that Libby, like all good agents, had an air of loneliness about her. Her life was her work, and once office hours ended, it seemed her life fell into a void. In that way she was very similar to me, and that's why I identified with her so much: neither of us knew what to do with ourselves when we were out of work, we so needed to be motivated. We lived, breathed, ate our work. And Libby's energy was relentless. She never came to see Mayhem. She would have been utterly shocked if she saw how I lived, but she phoned me every day.

One day in May, Libby rang me and said that Katharine Hepburn was in town, and that Rose Tobias Shaw was casting a film that Katharine was to star in called *The Corn Is Green*, from the play by Emlyn Williams. It was to be produced by Lorimar films, who were well known for making *Dallas* and *Knots Landing*, and they had requested a meeting with me. Libby's voice on the other end of the phone could be quite terrifying. I remember the phone ringing in the bathroom at Mayhem – that was the only place where there was a phone extension – and her very serious American accent came down the line: 'You are not to go as you look normally. You have to do everything in your power to look like a young girl of fourteen.'

'Yes Libby,' I said.

'I mean it, Toyah, this is serious,' she insisted. 'Do you know who Katharine Hepburn is?'

'No, Libby, I'm afraid I don't.'

'Well, she is one of the most important actresses of all time.' And then Libby went though a list of all of Katharine Hepburn's films, which I vaguely remembered. Libby mentioned that Katharine Hepburn was linked with Spencer Tracy and then said that the film was to be directed by George Cukor. She didn't bother to describe to me who George Cukor was and I didn't bother to ask. I was to find that out later.

Even though I could tease people relentlessly, really wind them up, deep down I took advice very seriously. I realised that when Libby said that this was an important film, that I mustn't mess it up and also that it was being cast by Rose Tobias Shaw – who at that time, 1978, was the biggest casting woman around – I knew I couldn't blow this. So I immediately got on the phone to the wig department at the National Theatre, and asked if I could borrow my lovely shoulder-length brown wig from *Tales from the Vienna Woods*. They very kindly said yes. So I trotted over to the National, picked the wig up and had it with me for the next day.

The next day I was slightly ashamed to sit at Mayhem among the shop dummies sticking out of the walls, dripping red paint for blood, with all our friends, all my punky friends, while doing myself up to look like a fourteen-year-old. They laughed, and teased me, and I said, 'Well, you know I'm an actress and this is what I've got to do.' But deep down I felt as if I was betraying myself by looking normal. I'd worked so hard not to look normal that any form of normality was like catching a disease. I hated normality so much that I actually wouldn't have minded losing this job if it meant I had to look normal. So it was with complacency that I crossed Chelsea Bridge and walked to Eaton Square, marvelling at the size of the buildings, the money, the wealth, and wondering what it would be like to live in such grandiose surroundings.

I walked up to number 79 and rang the doorbell for Flat 6 on the top floor.

A voice came down the entryphone: 'Yes?'

'Hello, it's Toyah Willcox here. I've come to see Katharine Hepburn.'

'Come up.'

When I arrived at the top of the stairs, there appeared to be a butler figure holding the door. He was just letting another girl out, who had obviously been auditioning. I walked into a hallway, where I was approached by a lovely old man who said, 'Hello, are you Toyah?'

At this point Rose Tobias Shaw came out and said, 'Yes, this is Toyah Willcox – this is George Cukor.'

I said, 'Hello, George, how are you, pleased to meet you,' having no idea who he was.

He showed me into the living room, where Katharine Hepburn was sitting on a sofa having a cup of tea. Rose Tobias Shaw left us alone and I had tea with George Cukor and Katharine Hepburn. At this point I was thinking, Cor, these are just two lovely people, they are so chatty, they are so nice, so American. I talked with Katharine for a long time – by that I mean a long time by audition standards. I was with her at least twenty minutes before we actually did anything. I told her about my band, about the National Theatre, about my love of punk music, and she was fascinated. Obviously having just arrived at Eaton Square she'd had a small taste of punk from the King's Road which was only two hundred yards away. George listened in attentively. He didn't say much at all, but he watched my relationship with Katharine with an eagle eye.

I always had a knack at auditions of saying the right thing, being the right person. I was always very good at walking into a room and sensing what people wanted, what people needed, and playing up to that. But the one thing I'd learned from the *Jubilee* experience was not to be too big-headed, so I sat with Katharine on the sofa – close enough that her hand kept touching my knee in a gesture of friendship – listening to her attentively. Even though I couldn't quite recognise her face fully, I had seen her films on afternoon TV back home. I had seen the wonderful comedies she did with Spencer Tracy. But as I sat there, looking into her eyes, I kept trying to remember more clearly, trying to find a detail that I could reflect back at her, something that I could say to her that would mean yes, I do know who you are and I really respect you. But I didn't have to. She wasn't fishing for compliments.

She spent the whole time talking to me. Telling me about

herself. Everything and everyone she'd admired as a young person. And I'd bounce back, 'Yes, I love this band because they do that,' or 'I love this fashion designer because they do that.' And Katharine would retort with, 'Oh, I remember, I always got bad criticism for wearing trousers. People loathed women in trousers, they said I had to decide whether I'm a woman or a man and also that I was so thin I was unattractive.' So instantly we got on, as our histories, our social histories, had made us equals. Meanwhile George would laugh from time to time in the background, but he never really joined the conversation; he just observed.

Eventually Katharine said, 'I think we should do some work now,' and she passed me the small French's book version of *The Corn Is Green* and we started to read scenes together. That's when I really watched her. She had this wonderful shake. She wouldn't say it was wonderful. I'm sure it was Parkinson's disease. She was battling to stop shaking. But it was very endearing, and she had the strength to control it when she was working. Her voice was shaky, but she was still incredibly charismatic. As she read the lead role of Miss Moffat and I read Bessie Wattie, we had great fun together. We read as if we were having a game of tennis at Wimbledon, with the odd bowl of strawberries and cream thrown in for a bit of relaxation. I have to say we really hit it off.

I left Eaton Square after an hour. When I walked out into the hallway, there was a queue of girls who had been made late by Katharine's and my continual chatting about things we had in common. I'd forgotten that I had my wig on. I had forgotten about my normalness. It did play on the back of my mind that I should just pull my wig off and go, 'Hey, Katharine, really I'm a punk, I've got bright red hair,' but I thought no, and I left it at that. I never expected to hear a thing about the job again. I thought it had been just a lovely meeting; something I could phone Mum and Dad up about, and say, 'Hey, guess what, I've just had tea with Katharine Hepburn.' I went back to Mayhem, tore the wig off and felt my kind of normality again with my familiar red hair.

Everyone at Mayhem was buzzing to find out what had happened that afternoon, so I sat down and told them all about the tea, and of course I embellished it a bit and dropped a few names that Katharine had dropped, like Spencer Tracy, Marilyn Monroe, Cary Grant. Dropping them as if I'd known them and worked with them myself. It was a very jolly evening. We had enough money to go out and buy some beers to bring back, and we toasted bread in our little toaster and scraped the bit of butter we had in the fridge over it, and we drank beer and ate toast. It was a delightful evening.

Then at 11 p.m. the phone rang, which even at Mayhem was uncommon. I picked up the receiver. It was Libby. 'Toyah, Toyah, are you sitting down?' she said.

'No, Libby, I was just about to go to bed actually.'

'Toyah, you've got the job.'

'What!' I said, my voice going up two octaves.

'Do you realise, Toyah, at least two thousand girls were up for that part? Lorimar are looking to discover new talent and they have chosen you.'

'Ah, Libby, that's fantastic,' I said.

She said, 'Well, Katharine and George want to see you again tomorrow. They just want to sit down with you and do some more reading together. So you know where to go.'

What Libby forgot to mention was that I should go back with my wig on, but I'd already taken my wig back to the National Theatre. So the next day, full of confidence, brimming with joy, knowing that I had employment for the summer, I went back to Eaton Square looking how I normally looked.

This time George Cukor opened the door. 'Come in, Toyah, come in. We're so pleased. Would you like to take your hat off,' he said.

'George, this isn't my hat, it's my hair; my hair is bright red.'

George went very quiet. I didn't really know George at this time. I didn't really know that that quietness meant he was angry. But he kept a bemused smile on his face as he led me into the living room, where Katharine Hepburn was sitting on the sofa, reading. 'Katharine,' he said, 'would you believe that this is this child's hair?'

Katharine's face burst into a huge smile. Her mouth dropped in a kind of wonderment. 'Oh, Toyah,' she said, 'oh, I'd have loved to have hair like that when I was your age. It looks like feathers.'

She spent the whole afternoon running her fingers through

my hair. We got on even better after that. George kept a permanent expression of doubt on his face, but we all got on really well.

My punky appearance didn't lose me the job. It raised a few eyebrows, but a wonderful thing about American people is how accepting they are of different quirks and different types. So I was accepted. I was in, and I was going to be Bessie Wattie in *The Corn Is Green* with Katharine Hepburn.

Also starring in the film were Patricia Hayes, who played my mother; Anna Massey, who played the schoolteacher; Bill Fraser and a whole heap of other wonderful names. That afternoon George Cukor did the talking. I discovered that he had directed Marilyn Monroe and worked with James Dean. I also discovered that he is probably the most important director for women of the last century. I left Eaton Square that day full of respect for both of them and full of hope for the future.

All this happened the week before I turned twenty. On my twentieth birthday I was alone at Mayhem with Eve and two friends we'd acquired, two young boys – Kevin Mooney, who went on to play in the Adam Ant band, and Mark K. We got very drunk that night and, as was usual among all my friends at that time, the whole group were bemused that I was still a virgin. It seemed wrong that on my twentieth birthday I should remain a virgin. So that evening I ended up in bed with Mark K and it was the most fantastic night of my life. My experiences of male nudity on *Jubilee* didn't come anywhere near my experiences with Mark that night. It was a beautiful night. It reinforced my belief in men. It was everything a virgin could ever have dreamed of. The most perfect night.

The following weeks were a succession of medicals and tests. When you do a feature film you have to prove to the insurers that you're neither ill nor pregnant, nor about to be ill. It's a process that can make you feel really guilty. You have lots of blood tests. You go and meet a doctor who asks you lots of questions. You have to fill in sheets of questionnaires. I was actually feeling quite guilty that I'd lost my virginity, and at one point I was terrified that that might be one of the questions that the doctor would ask. When I turned up at Harley Street I was in a cold sweat – partly full of guilt, and partly just because I'd have rather been back in bed with Mark to be honest. But everything went well, and two weeks later I was off to Wales to make *The Corn Is Green*.

A lot had to be done in those two weeks apart from having medicals. The wigs had to be made. My costumes, which consisted of really tight corsets and full skirts, needed to be fitted. In those days, for authenticity, you wore everything from knickers through to corsets and petticoats to the outer layer. Everything was for real.

On my birthday, a friend called Alan had given me a white rabbit by the name of Banacheck. Dear little Banacheck couldn't stay at Mayhem while I was going to be in Wales. So my father came down and picked Banacheck up. For the first two weeks of his life with me, Banacheck had lived in my room at Mayhem. At this time I had a love of mangoes. They were my big treat. And one night I went out to the pub leaving two mangoes on my bed with Banacheck locked in my room. When I came back I found Banacheck on the floor with his little stomach swollen like a football, my two mangoes completely consumed. And by the morning, dear little Banacheck had covered the whole of my room in diarrhoea. So it was just as well Mum and Dad were going to look after him for me.

Patricia Hayes, who was playing my mother in the film, drove me to Wales in her Mini. It was wonderful travelling with Patricia. People in every car we passed recognised her. People in every place we stopped at for petrol recognised her. She had a *huge* following, mainly from playing with Benny Hill in *The Benny Hill Show*, but of course also for starring in *Edna the Inebriate Woman*, which I consider to be the greatest piece of drama I have ever seen in my entire life. So here I was sitting in a Mini with my first heroine in life, Patricia Hayes. Everyone looking in. Everyone waving. And if she got a chance to speak back to anyone she would introduce me as 'Toyah, my daughter, the punk'. I loved Patricia. We had a wonderful time.

We were based in Betws-y-coed in north Wales. It was phenomenally beautiful. Sadly, I hardly dared leave the hotel with my red hair – they'd never seen a punk in Wales. And when I did venture out of the hotel, cars would stop, people would stop, mouths would drop open and everyone would just gawp at me. Because of this predicament, many of the cast just didn't want to go out with me. Only Patricia dared walk the High Street with me, again introducing me to strangers as her daughter with great pride.

Our place of filming was a remote farmhouse on a hilltop, where you could see no sign of modern life; in fact the only intrusion from modern life was that every half-hour or so a Harrier jump-jet would fly over, about six feet above the roof. The production manager phoned the RAF and begged them to change their route. But no, they didn't. Just more planes came and sometimes I'd swear that I could see the pilot waving at us out of the window. The whole building would shake, these planes flew so low.

Filming was very intense. George could be a tyrant on the set, and his patience with my lack of filming technique quickly wore thin. But his perseverance got a very good performance out of me. He was often irritable with me and often shouted at me. When we rehearsed a scene, sometimes he was cross with me before I'd even said anything. I don't think this was helped by the fact the Anna Massey was dismissive of me. She was very very open about her feeling that I couldn't act and that I lacked talent; she was frank about it. If I didn't overhear her saying so, she would say so to others and others would tell me. In the whole of my career I have never worked with someone who has hated me so openly. But there you go. I actually found it did nothing other than focus me. And Katharine was a wonderful support and would not take any rubbish from anyone. She was wonderful to every member of the cast. She was wonderful to every member of the public who came up to her, and to every member of the crew. She really made the whole production work.

A different kind of acting was called for in this film. In *Jubilee* I could just be like a wild dog set loose in a room tearing at flesh. With this I had to be refined, totally controlled. It was a period piece, after all, set in the late-nineteenth century. I had done period acting before at the National Theatre, but this was a great learning curve. With George Cukor's experience and Katharine's exuberance it was hard to go wrong. All right, I was way down on the scale, but they allowed me to grow, albeit in a very disciplined context.

The filming in Wales flew by. We were only there for about a month before we moved into the studios in Wembley. When this film started, Joel and I had already got a manager for the band – Howard Abrahams, an accountant, who offered to manage us. Things had moved really quickly that year. We'd been playing in pubs around north London and had won an audience, followed by press recognition in the likes of *Record Mirror*, *Melody Maker* and *New Musical Express*, so there was interest in our doing more concerts outside of London. Howard Abrahams knew that I was based in Wales making this film, but he went ahead anyway and booked a seven-date tour while I was still filming. I said to Howard, 'I think it's impossible that I can get to any of these gigs – I can't have time off.' This was the beginning of a conflict of interests that really has followed me for the past twenty years. If you want to act and sing there is going to be conflict.

On the last day of filming in Wales I was supposed to be playing at the Angel in Islington. Filming finished at 5 p.m. That was fine. Theoretically I could have caught a train and got to London – but I missed the train. The film stock was to be collected by a driver and driven to Borehamwood. So I decided that I would get a lift to Borehamwood, then take a taxi to the Angel and be on stage with the band by 11 p.m. Eight o'clock came. The driver was still having a cup of tea at the production offices in Betws-y-coed. I said, 'Look, I really am in a hurry here. I've got to get to London.' He assured me, 'Oh, it will be fine, you'll be in London by eleven o clock.' Little did I know. I didn't drive, so I had no idea how many hours away I actually was. Once we had finally set off, every time we stopped for petrol, I phoned Howard. But eventually Howard was out of touch because he was at the gig. Eleven o'clock came. I think we were just about at Birmingham, and I had this awful feeling, this awful knowledge that the band were standing on stage waiting for me, not knowing if I was going to turn up any minute. I finally got into London at 2 a.m.

The next morning, Sunday morning, I phoned Howard and apologised profusely. Apparently the band did go on at 11 p.m. The pub was completely full, no one had any idea where I was, people were both bemused and impressed that I hadn't turned up. I imagined it would have been a bit like a dream come true for Joel. At last he'd had an audience and the band to himself.

He could play 'Free Bird' for at least three hours and have a captive audience. But no, Joel had actually been worried sick about my safety. Howard said the show had gone very well without me but I had been missed and would have to pay every member of the band for not being there. Oddly enough, Howard didn't take any of the responsibility for having booked the gig in the first place while knowing that I was in Betws-y-coed. It's funny how managers think that way. He blamed me totally, and like an idiot I took the blame totally, feeling guilty for a long time afterwards. Joel was more forgiving, in fact I think Joel was just relieved that I was still alive.

I had a week off from filming before we started the studio filming of *The Corn Is Green* at Lee International in Wembley. It was good to be based in London again. I had the contact with my friends at Mayhem, the support they gave me in the evenings, as well as the work at Lee International in the daytime. There was very little help from the film company during the studio filming. Getting from A to B was my own responsibility, which meant a journey right across London. I didn't drive, and catching taxis and buses was very unreliable, especially as I had to be in make-up by 6.30 every morning. The number of mornings when the taxi didn't turn up – or if it did turn up it had run out of petrol, so we had to stop to fill up – was mind-blowingly frustrating. But most mornings I would get a taxi in, and most mornings my taxi would pass Katharine Hepburn on her bicycle cycling to Wembley. That woman was utterly amazing.

Up until this time my only studio experience had been when I was filming *Glitter*, two years earlier, and now it felt not a day too early to be back in a film studio with the big lights above my head again. With the noise and the racket of the crew building sets all around. With all the stars from other productions in the canteen. It was buzzing. It was a drug – you got high on it. Everywhere you went was a wonderful experience. Katharine was always inviting me into her room to talk to me. I had to call Katharine 'Miss Hepburn'. On one occasion on the set when it slipped my mind and I referred to her as Katharine, George Cukor went for me. He smacked me at the back of the head and said, 'Miss Hepburn to you. It's always Miss Hepburn.'

Katharine jumped to my rescue and said, 'George, don't be such a fuddy-duddy. It really doesn't matter.'

Katharine always stood up for me, in many situations. Sometimes when we rehearsed a scene and it wasn't working, George would just blame me, even when there were a few other actors in the scene. I'm not knocking George; his scolding was gentle and he was, after all, responsible for getting the best possible performance out of me. Katharine would come to my defence. She wouldn't let George use me as a scapegoat. It wasn't that George was an ogre. George was a perfectionist and I really respected him, he taught me so much. But he was from a different period. Discipline in performance – I have seen throughout my career, in other performers, the younger they get – is slowly breaking down. George's generation were full of respect. Tipping the hat. Calling people Madam. Yes sir. No sir. In my generation that had gone; and now, in the year 2000, when I work with children, you consider yourself lucky to get a grunt out of them as a form of hello. Well, it's not that bad really, but I hope you get what I'm saying.

There was one scene that we shot at the studios with Katharine, Pat Hayes and me, where Katharine and Pat were having a conversation and I was just sitting in the background eating a piece of bread and jam. It was a very long scene and the camera was on a track which tracked round the kitchen table and all three actors. At the very end of the scene, I just had to throw in this one line which was a put-down about another actor. We rehearsed the scene, then we went for a take. We got to the end of the scene, when I accidentally choked on the bread and jam and George had to shout 'cut'. And again he flew in at me and called me an imbecile, said I was incompetent, what did I think I was doing, when Katharine chipped in and said, 'Look, George, she only choked on her bread and jam. Just leave her alone.' I'm not painting a very good picture of George, but he did laugh an awful lot as he told me off, and he was always ready to tell me about Monroe and other stars such as Laurence Olivier whom he directed alongside Marilyn. George was fabulous. I just think modern times were frustrating him.

Katharine would often call me into her dressing room; I'd sit and talk to her, and she'd tell me about her past. What really moved me was how, in the past, she had suffered because of the press. Not the press as we know it today, but the press as powerful critics. She started off as a stage actress and the critics would say she looked like a man. She sounded like a man. Her acting was wooden. She was too thin. She was ugly. She'd tell me she would find the criticism so personal that it was offensive. It was abusive, in fact, and there was nothing she could do about it. Ironically, it didn't seem to occur to her that the greatest way to get back at her critics was through her success.

She wasn't vengeful. She never talked about her success as a form of vengeance, in fact she never talked about her success, full stop. She mainly talked about Spencer Tracy. I loved sitting in the chair next to her, with her make-up mirror lights on; she'd look into the mirror, looking extraordinarily beautiful, and she'd talk about Spencer. There'd be a light in her eyes, as if he still lived in her thoughts. The love she felt for him was definitely still alive. She'd wear his clothes sometimes. She'd say, 'You see this jumper, Toyah, this was Spencer's. I can still smell him in the clothes.' She'd talk about their work together and how difficult their lives were together. Spencer was married. He didn't want a divorce. Wouldn't divorce. He was Catholic. His wife had a mental illness. So Spencer and Katharine used to keep a hut at the bottom of the garden. I can't remember whose garden it was at the bottom of, I imagine George Cukor's – there was that kind of bond between George and Katharine; you knew that their life spilled from the studio into a personal life as well. And Katharine and Spencer Tracy would meet secretly. The whole world knew they were an item but they had to keep their love secret.

She talked to me about her family, which wasn't a happy subject for her. There were many difficulties. And she would also talk to me about my future. She was phenomenally generous as an actress as well as generous as a person. She talked to me about my weaknesses, about my need to know the camera as a third person in a scene, always to let the camera see what I was thinking. Because on many occasions when I was acting with her, I was so involved with her as a person that I'd be looking into her eyes – I love having eye contact with actors – acting to save my life, and she'd go, 'Toyah, your back's to the camera, turn your head, darling, no one can see you.' I was so involved with her that I had forgotten about the camera. I had forgotten about George Cukor. I was just kind of making acting love with Katharine Hepburn. But she was shrewd. If a scene was favouring her too much she would say, 'George, we're not seeing enough of this girl's beautiful eyes.' And that was it. The camera would then favour me, and then she'd insist that I get a close-up and a mid-shot, which I didn't always get.

There was a passion between me and Katharine and I think it existed because neither of us ever fitted into any kind of system. Katharine never really fitted into the Hollywood system. She was far too independent. She was a true feminist – is a true feminist. And there is something about her that meant she didn't need adulation. She didn't need sycophants around her. In fact she had no entourage around her at all. I've met lesser stars who have thirty people around them. Katharine is the biggest star I have ever worked with, and the only person she had around her was George Cukor. There might have been some staff tucked away, but you never saw her with them. She was truly independent. She undoubtedly saw in me the person she had been in her youth. And the parallels were so close, even though our youths were forty years apart. My day-to-day existence uncannily reflected hers at the same age forty years earlier.

There were two events during the filming that really showed what a very special human being Katharine Hepburn was. One was in Betws-y-coed, when my parents came to check that I was all right and brought Banacheck the bunny rabbit with them. We went for a picnic with Patricia Hayes in a playing field by a river; the rabbit was running around playing in the daisies and we were in deckchairs having tea. Katharine was filming in the nearby square in Betws-y-coed, so I took Mum and Dad round to watch the filming. When Katharine saw me with them she said, 'Toyah, are these your parents? I want to meet them.' And she grabbed my father and my mother each by the hand and ushered them into her house – she'd been allotted a house to hide in – and once inside she showed them round and made them tea; it was just fantastic. This was Katharine Hepburn showing my parents round her house.

She was glorious. What made this episode even more glorious was that Katharine's dresser – whom I kept mistakenly calling Joyce – absolutely loathed me. This dresser and Anna Massey were in league against me. When the dresser saw Katharine treat my parents like this, you could almost literally see her run away with her tail between her legs. It was a wonderful moment.

Then later, when we were at Lee International Studios, one day when I was filming this huge conflict scene with Katharine – it was my biggest scene in the film, one that Katharine was particularly supportive about, making sure that I got the best angles, and that George gave me mid-shots and close-ups, so that I was featured equally with her during the scene – I looked over across the studio, and there was my father who'd sneaked in. That's something I love about my father. He could turn up anywhere. If I was in Buckingham Palace having tea, my father could get in. Anyway, I looked over and there he was. He had no intention of letting me know he was there. And again Katharine saw him and she said, 'Oh, Mr Willcox, how are you? Come and have a look at my dressing room.' And she showed him round and Dad had the most wonderful day. He used to smoke a pipe back then; I can remember him in the studio sucking on his pipe. You're not allowed to smoke in studios so the pipe wasn't lit, but he was just there chewing on this pipe with a big smile on his face. He was so proud and in a way I was proud of him. He had come all the way from Birmingham, had got into Lee International Studios and was watching Katharine Hepburn work. How many people manage to do that? He was also watching his daughter work, but I still think it was an achievement that he got in there.

Katharine wanted to give everyone goodbye presents at the end of filming. Not just any old presents, something utterly unique. She gave a lot of people sweaters, saying they had been Spencer Tracy's, and I believed her. I think she was a very genuine woman. To me she gave the blouse she wore as Miss Moffat – a tiny, beautiful lace blouse with metal bones in the neck which held the head high. I still have it today. She knew I'd treasure it, and I will treasure it for ever. To have something that she wore and was creative in is so much more special than any other type of gift. I suppose that is the essence of Katharine. That is what I want to keep for ever.

Chapter 18

Having experienced such a long period of unemployment after *Jubilee* I did not want to tread that path again after *The Corn Is Green*. I'd learned to become pushy in the right way by now. Being seriously ambitious, I'd kept my ears to the ground and had heard about the Who's upcoming film *Quadrophenia*. I phoned Libby from Lee International Studios and said, 'Libby, there's this film being made. Could you find out if there's anything in it for me? It's being directed by Franc Roddam.' So Libby arranged a meeting between me and Franc which happened in a pub on the King's Road. Franc brought along Johnny Rotten, to see if our chemistry would work.

Luckily, Franc was very interested. I was to screen-test for the lead female (eventually played by Lesley Ash) alongside Johnny Rotten as lead male. Franc was concerned that Johnny had never acted before, and asked that I should coach Johnny through the screen test. I had met Johnny in the pub with Franc, but never before that; I'd idolised him for years and the idea of meeting him was scary. I was wondering how awful he would be. In fact he was far from awful; instead here was this quiet, self-effacing, very attractive man. Nothing like the punk I'd seen on the now notorious Bill Grundy interview. Nothing like his stage persona at all. He was very modest and very shy. Franc was the mediator between us; it was arranged that I should go round to Johnny Rotten's house and give him acting lessons. Me give Johnny Rotten acting lessons! Terrifying thought.

Johnny Rotten lived off the bottom of the King's Road at World's End in a three-storey terraced house. When I arrived at 12 noon it looked as though a bomb had hit the inside of the house and bodies were casually strewn where they had landed after the blast the night before. There were people lying everywhere. I suppose midday was still very early. As I waited for Johnny to come downstairs, I sat trying to be invisible, soaking up the atmosphere. It was kind of nice just to be there, thinking about the Sex Pistols and everything they had done. And here I was in their domestic surroundings. I found it quite strange to think of Johnny Rotten living in a three-storey terraced house. Ari Up from the Slits was knocking around with a very obvious hangover.

Eventually Johnny came downstairs. He was just delightful. We went through the scenes we had to do; we had two scenes together. I was to play his girlfriend and he was to play the lead (the part that Phil Daniels eventually got). And it was fine. You can only do so much. We just went through it again and again. I told Johnny what to expect, what the filming process was like, and tried to give him some of the advice Katharine Hepburn had given me – to be aware of the camera, the camera's eye, and not to lose touch with that.

I stayed about two hours and then left. I didn't see Johnny again until we went to Shepperton where the Who had their studios. This was altogether a very unnerving experience for me. I hadn't had to screen-test for *The Corn Is Green*. I certainly hadn't had to screen test for *Jubilee*. And here I was in these very testing surroundings with the massive camera, the full film crew, knowing that I hadn't got the job yet, that my neck was really on the line. Johnny was just as nervous as me. We went to make-up. I'd already had to bleach my hair to get rid of the red so that it was a grey-blue sixties blonde. Johnny just had his hair greased down a bit and we were both made to look like Mods. Then we went out into the Shepperton grounds where a camera track had been laid, and did our scenes. We just had to walk and talk together. Johnny was very good. I'd thought he would be a nervous wreck. He probably was nervous; I think he really wanted to do the part, he really cared and he was very responsible. He had learned his lines, and didn't have a hangover. He was very disciplined, and quite fantastic once the camera rolled. He was charismatic. He really had what it takes and I enjoyed every minute of acting with him. And that was it.

We said our goodbyes to Franc. I said my goodbye to Johnny.

Then I expected to hear some kind of news. I actually thought we were both very good for the parts, but for a couple of weeks I heard absolutely nothing. Instinctively I knew something was wrong. I kept begging Libby to phone Franc Roddam to see if there was any news. So she would phone him, then phone me back and say, 'No, there's no news.' Yet I knew that they had cast some of the other roles. And when you know that some principal roles are cast, you know that the film is on a roll, so to have no news is actually a bit of a lie. But Libby couldn't give me any information, so I decided to go round to Franc Roddam's office – which ironically was in the Lee International buildings where I'd filmed *The Corn Is Green* – and confront him.

I caught the tube, walked along the outside of the building, saw Franc in his office and knocked on the window. He opened the window and I said, 'Come on, Franc, what's going on?'

So he called me in. We sat at his desk and he told me that Johnny Rotten was really very good but the insurers wouldn't insure the film if he had anything to do with it. So they had to drop Johnny.

I pleaded with Franc: 'Come on, if Johnny Rotten does it you know it's going to be a major hit and he's going to behave. He was disciplined when I went to give him his acting lessons, he was disciplined throughout the film test, he really isn't going to mess around.'

Franc said categorically no. Absolutely no way was it going to be Johnny.

In fact it had already been cast with someone else. I asked Franc who, and he told me Phil Daniels. I said, 'Franc, I know Phil Daniels, I did my first ever acting with him.'

Franc then went kind of quiet and embarrassed. 'I'm really sorry, Toyah,' he said. 'The lead female has been cast as well. It's gone to a girl called Lesley Ash.'

I sat there and ummed and ahed and I thought, I'm not going to be negative about this. 'Franc,' I said, 'is there anything else I could play?'

'There's a small role,' he answered, 'but you're not going to want a small role, are you?'

'Franc, I'll make the tea. I want anything. Please will you see me for this small role?'

He said, 'Well, its the part of Monkey, I'm not sure you're right for it. In fact I haven't been able to find anyone to play her yet but I don't think you're Monkey.'

'Please Franc,' I insisted, 'will you see me for Monkey?'

Franc said, 'OK, hang on here a second,' and he went out the room and returned with Phil Daniels.

'Hi Phil,' I said, 'how are you? Haven't seen you for a long time.'

Franc said to me, 'OK, if you snog Phil here and now you can play Monkey.'

I said, 'That's really not a problem, Franc.'

So Franc threw us both a script, and we read the scene where Monkey is selling Phil's character drugs at a party. We read, we snogged. Franc didn't commit. I reluctantly went home.

A few days later I phoned Franc and, all credit to him, he picked the phone up to me. I said, 'Franc, have you cast Monkey?'

'No, Toyah, I'm really not sure. I don't think you're right.'

'Franc, you know where I am.'

A few days later the phone rang. It was Franc. I got Monkey.

That was the first time I realised that you can actually fight for a part, because people aren't sure. Franc, I think, would in desperation have cast anyone; if it hadn't been me fighting, he'd have cast the next person along who fought hard enough to get the part. I'd got the part of Monkey. I was in *Quadrophenia*. It hadn't even started shooting yet and I knew it was going to be one of the most important films of the decade. Who was a happy girl?

The week after I got the part in *Quadrophenia* came some shocking news. Keith Moon, the Who's drummer, was dead. He'd drowned in his swimming pool. This frightened the hell out of everyone. We thought the film wouldn't go ahead. But Pete Townshend decided that everything must go on as normal. The Who threw a pre-shoot party for the entire cast – and it was a very impressive cast: Sting, Lesley Ash, Phil Daniels, Phil Davies, Mark Wingate, John Aldman, Gary Shail and many more who were to go on to become big names. It was a great party, a generous party. Roy Baird the producer was there. Verity Lambert was there. Everyone had a fantastic time. It was more of a wake for Keith Moon than a pre-shoot party for

Quadrophenia. You can imagine the main topic of conversation was Moon's behaviour, Moon's drumming, how greatly missed he was, and what a tragedy that none of us ever got to meet him. Roger Daltrey, who turned out to be a real darling, admitted that he'd fought for me to play the lead. Not because he had anything against Lesley Ash, in fact like everyone else he thought Lesley Ash was drop-dead gorgeous, but he felt that I suited the period more. I was short, chubby and had quite a bombastic attitude on camera. He said I was exactly like his first girlfriend. I really looked the part, but hey, that doesn't necessarily sell a film, does it?

All the cast very quickly became a family. We were sent out to have dancing lessons, to learn the dances of the time. We'd turn up at a studio in Soho, look at ourselves in the mirror and learn to do the Mashed Potato, and other dances with similarly quirky names. Then we were sent off to an army base west of London to learn how to ride scooters – an adventure for all. Dear Lesley kept falling off hers but that was probably because she kept riding it at maximum speed towards walls. Sting looked great on his immediately, and Phil Daniels looked as if he had been born on a scooter. Franc Roddam had done his job really well; he'd cast *Quadrophenia* brilliantly.

We were a mass of egos in a big melting-pot. There was a wonderful tension in the air because we all wanted to be the centre of attention. Sting was remarkably modest for someone so beautiful and talented – his talent was evident even at this point, yet he was still an unknown. We all enjoyed taking the mickey out of him because we were dead jealous of how good-looking he was – when he got on a scooter he just looked like a god. Lesley didn't have an ego, but she certainly was the centre of attention – again astonishingly beautiful, and very popular and just lovely to be with. She was a giggle, and had such a naughty sense of humour as well. Phil, as usual, was completely down to earth and was just Phil – immensely talented. And the rest of us were scurrying around like friendly hyenas, laughing all the time and ready to jump on our prey. We were full of ideas. We all had bands. We wrote music. All wanted to act and sing. Was Brighton town going to be big enough to house our egos? Well, we were about to find out.

* * *

Every job, every life experience is a learning curve, or should be a learning curve. But *Quadrophenia* was more like a learning right angle. There was nothing subtle, nothing slow about it. It was like stepping on a fast train with no glass in the windows, no doors in the doorways and no seats to sit on. We just stood there, with all the other passengers, like sardines in a can, hoping none of us would fall off. My little gang, the family at Mayhem, were all buzzing and happy that I was doing *Quadrophenia*; it was the film to be doing. Soon I discovered that whenever I was about to embark on a job that everyone was talking about, Mayhem became busier.

A band called the Pleasers had been rehearsing at Mayhem and they had a roadie called Gem, who I was particularly fond of. Gem was a walking encyclopaedia. Not only that, he was witty, kind and great company. Gem was a shortish, stocky man who had a wonderful face and kind eyes; when you looked into them, you kind of got lost in his world. I was deeply enamoured with Gem but I didn't know how to get closer to him. My only real experience with a man had been on my twentieth birthday with Mark K, and Mark came as a gift. I think Mark stayed the night with me more out of sympathy than anything. So I had no technique for chatting anyone up.

Gem and I were both equally playful. We used to love playing tricks on each other, practical jokes, locking each other in rooms at Mayhem. On the evening before I left for Brighton, Gem and I were having one of these particular rough-and-tumble fights where we would be laughing our heads off, pushing each other around, when accidentally I pushed Gem against a wall that had a nail sticking out of it. The nail got embedded in Gem's head. It was the most bizarre seduction I've ever engineered in my life. The nail, as well as being extremely dangerous to Gem's life, was also my best friend. It meant I had to hold Gem in my arms while I tried to stem the flow of blood from his head. Gem was remarkably forgiving, and that night we ended up lovers. It was a relationship that lasted two years and meant the world to me. Gem had so much to teach, so much to say. He had so many opinions and in a way he shaped my thinking. He shaped the course of my life and I'm incredibly grateful that I spent those two years with him.

Gem drove me to Brighton the next day and stayed the first

night in the hotel with me. He was probably more aware than I was that up until this point I'd always been the youngest person on projects. At the National Theatre I was the youngest person in the theatre; on *Jubilee* I was the youngest person in the film; and on *The Corn Is Green* I was the youngest person in the company. This meant that I got a special kind of attention, a special kind of forgiveness for my hyperactive nature. People tolerated me. This wasn't to be so on *Quadrophenia*. The moment Gem and I walked into the hotel, it was obvious that it was full of people my own age, and he probably realised before I did that this was going to be a tough one for me. I was no longer special for my naïvety and immaturity. I was going to have to fight to be noticed like everyone else.

The *Quadrophenia* company literally took over Brighton to the point where when you were walking along the seafront you didn't know who were civilians and who were actors. Most of the main actors stayed in the same hotel; Lesley Ash and Phil Daniels stayed down the road with Franc Roddam in a much posher hotel. Our hotel would rock all night and fall silent in the daytime when we went out working. One of the hardest things was just trying to find somewhere and something to eat. There were so many of us that we had to be given tickets: extras got a green ticket, actors a pink ticket. These tickets were rare; on the first day's filming, I queued up to eat – but I had no ticket, so I didn't eat that day – and complaints got you very little sympathy from any of the ground staff. There were just so many people and too few organising. It really was quite shambolic to begin with.

One of the first scenes to be shot was the riot scene. For this, Franc Roddam and the producers had put out an announcement across the country for all Mods and Rockers to converge on Brighton to re-enact the famous riot scenes of the sixties between rival gangs of Mods and Rockers. I expect they naïvely thought that five hundred or so people would turn up. In fact on the morning of the shoot five thousand Mods and Rockers turned up. Everyone looked at each other in amazement and no one knew what to do.

Somehow out of this chaos, form took shape. There were two film units because there were just so many people. There were cameras everywhere. In fact, when we were shooting one of the sequences I didn't actually know where the camera was – but that's the glory of nitty-gritty realistic film-making. You just live the action and hope the camera catches it. The main riot sequence took part on the promenade, the seafront. We'd all be herded into one huge gang down one end and then told to run and keep running until someone shouted 'cut'. We got very fit that day – we ran the promenade about ten, twenty times, I can't remember. It was one of those days when you had to accept you were a member of the herd and just go with the flow. For the next sequence we moved into the side streets to re-enact members of the gangs breaking off, getting into fights with and being arrested by the police. There was only one problem. Once we were in the side streets we really didn't know who were civilians, who were real police and who were actors. We just went hell for leather. Franc shouted 'action', I ran down one of the side streets and a policeman got me round the waist; a police van drove right up towards me so I just kicked the police van, sending the policeman and myself rolling backwards, then I ran off. When the magical word 'cut' resounded around the street, I actually had to ask whether that had been a real policeman or an actor.

Inevitably some civilians were caught up in the crush, not knowing what the hell was going on; I've never shot a crowd sequence like it. There were so many people and everyone was totally dedicated to making it as realistic as possible. In many ways I think we were all enjoying being given the right to be anarchists and we went for it whether we were being filmed or not. We were just enjoying rioting, hitting each other, and none of us really pulled our punches.

Considering the magnitude of the sequence, everything went very smoothly. There were horrendous politics. We were all very young, very demanding and had huge egos. We all wanted better hotel rooms, more attention, better food. But that kind of energy, that kind of conflict, gives a better creative result in the end – although I did find it incredibly hard working with my own generation, who were all as fiery and ambitious as me; I started to feel invisible, if not slightly swamped, even drowned by their talent.

Sting was in our hotel. Sting was just so delightful he was close to unbelievable. We used to tease him because he was so polite, so refined, so educated. He could talk to anyone, get on with anyone, and all of us were slightly jealous of him. He'd formed the Police by this time; what none of us realised was how big the industry believed the Police were going to be.

Sting had a lot going on while we were making *Quadrophenia*. He had to go off and do *The Old Grey Whistle Test*, he'd do the odd concert here and there and there was a lot of promotion to cover as well. For *The Old Grey Whistle Test*, he needed two backing singers to sing on 'Roxanne'. He called me and a girl called Tammy to his room and we sat on the bed with Sting, his new-born baby and his first wife Frances Tomelty. Sting tried to teach us the harmonies for 'Roxanne'. I am the world's worst harmony singer. I am better now, but back then, achieving a harmony was just not a possibility for me. Sting showed such patience as I lost my temper trying to learn the very simple harmonies, with the idea that Tammy and I would go up to Glasgow with him and appear on *The Old Grey Whistle Test* as his backing singers. Sadly, this didn't happen, but Sting tried really hard. (In fact, when Sting got up there he made the mistake of spraying hairspray in his eyes, so he made his first television appearance in the Police wearing sunglasses, which ironically made him look more fabulous than ever. A lucky mistake, I'd say.) Sting seemed such a happy family man. Frances Tomelty was obviously a driving force behind him. It came as a shock to me in later years that they broke up, but I suppose when you reach Sting's level of fame it must be pretty hard to keep any relationship together.

A lot of preparation had gone into *Quadrophenia*. By the time we actually started filming we had all met original Mods and Rockers, who later came down for the filming of the riot scenes – to play adults in the scenes depicting events they had in reality witnessed as teenagers. Franc Roddam arranged for us to go round to some of the Rockers' houses, learn some of the dances and go on the bikes. One particular Rocker couple whose house we went to still looked exactly how they must have looked in the sixties. The wife had bouffanted peroxide-blonde hair, she and the husband both wore black leather and they offered us lots and lots of amphetamines, mainly 'blues', which in the late seventies were still quite common. Blues were used as diet pills; basically they just speeded you up so you talked a lot and didn't eat, so you lost weight.

One old Rocker I'd once met at a party had taken me for a ride on his bike around east London, a very built-up area. I think he reached 90 m.p.h. on one of the back streets. Zooming between the cars. I've never been so frightened in my life. So if you can imagine these original Rockers, who were still Rockers at heart, fifteen years on, going round the streets of Brighton . . . Brighton was just buzzing with noise, energy, pent-up anger and nostalgia revisited.

One of the bones of contention for everyone during the filming was that Franc Roddam, because of the sheer workload, the sheer number of people he had to deal with, was no longer accessible. This was sad for everyone because during the rehearsal period we had all been very close and Franc had been incredibly approachable and chatty, but now he was this distant figure on a camera crane. In many ways we all missed him and we missed contact with him. He did allow us to see some of the rushes – sequences of film shot the day before or on that day – which would be shown on a makeshift screen in the hotel. I remember watching some of the rushes and being hugely disappointed at how I looked. It's funny, you always think you're taller than you are, slimmer than you are, and sound better than you actually do. Suddenly to see yourself in the middle of a fight sequence where you felt like Boadicea, when actually you look like some wally in the middle of a pub brawl, brings your ego back down to size.

There was so much buzz about *Quadrophenia* being made. The Mod movement was on the up and the up. Punk was still going, but the Mod craze had replaced it in many ways, so the film attracted a lot of attention from young people across the country. Magazines were regularly visiting the set. We were being featured as the stars of the future. Conversations between members of the cast off camera were always about who was doing what next. A film called *Scum* was soon to be made, and most of the male cast of *Quadrophenia* were to be in it. This didn't sit well with the women – we all wanted to be moving on to another film after *Quadrophenia*.

I was lucky enough to be cast opposite John Mills in a new TV series called *Quatermass*. There was just one problem. *Quatermass* starting shooting while *Quadrophenia* was still in production. When all the external scenes had been shot, we left

Brighton and moved into the studio again – Lee International in Wembley – to shoot all the internal scenes. Party scenes, domestic scenes. Being back in London gave us a respite from each other, which was very valuable as we were all starting to get on each other's nerves, and a lot of sexual relationships had come and gone between members of the cast. It also theoretically meant we could resume some normal kind of nightlife after filming. My problem was that *Quatermass* was all night shoots. So I'd be working on *Quadrophenia* in the daytime, then I'd go off to do a night shoot with John Mills in the middle of Wembley Arena. I had fourteen days and nights of this in a row, and when *Quadrophenia* needed to move to night shoots, such as for the café scenes in Islington or the nightclub scenes in Barnet, *Quatermass* ironically moved to daytime shoots, so it was relentless.

It wasn't just the filming schedules that were hard. It was the fact that no one ever sent a car to pick me up, so I had the problem of getting from one shoot to the other by public transport or by taxi. By the end of this sequence of shooting I was ill. I wasn't aware what was wrong, but one morning I came in coughing so badly, my lungs so full of liquid that the make-up woman could hear it gurgling as I breathed. She insisted that I see the nurse, who took one look at me and took me off to the nearest hospital where I was diagnosed with pneumonia. Being a typical actress, I was terrified that I would be laid off, would lose my job, so I begged the nurse not to tell anyone. Instead I carried on working this ludicrous schedule but made sure I ate better, slept between scenes and took lots and lots of antibiotics. Eventually the filming of *Quadrophenia* slowed down and became more sporadic, which meant that I got days of rest.

Quatermass didn't take very long to film. It was lovely working with John Mills; he was such a gentle and delightful man. We were all playing futuristic travellers, all in search of a new god, and John Mills was *Quatermass* the scientist. Just like Katharine Hepburn, John Mills was very much part of the older generation of actors. He was kept apart from the rest of us – probably not through his own choice but by those who looked after him – and then when he was brought on to the set he would delight in talking to all of us, finding out about us, what we liked, what we thought of this, what we thought of that. It was almost as if he was lonely and needed someone to talk to, but his lackeys wouldn't allow him to make contact with the outside world.

One of the many interesting things about working with these older-generation actors was seeing their frailty. For me, being very young at the time when I worked with them, it was fascinating to see their spirit, their fight. Katharine Hepburn and John Mills had a great lust for life; they each put up a brave fight against their body, as if their body was letting them down. Their minds were still vital, vibrant, full of ideas and full of dreams and goals they wanted to achieve, yet their bodies were becoming frail. I found that a great lesson. I've always believed that life is a lifetime's experience. I think that the idea of retirement, of spending your last days doing nothing, is an absurd obsession, unless of course you're working in a job that you really despise. But who could despise acting? Who could despise singing? These are things I want to do until the day I die, so watching these people dealing with the frailty of age, and dealing with it very well, was a valuable experience.

Chapter 19

One would think that making *Quadrophenia* and *Quatermass* at the same time was more than enough to do. It was! But without realising it, I had an entourage of my own. A team of people working on my behalf, as well as their own behalves. There was Howard Abrahams, the band's manager, and there was Joel, keeping the band together and writing new material while I was away working.

Joel and I had managed in a small space of time to go from playing obscure northern nightclubs and pubs around England to heading the bill at rather healthy venues like the Nashville in West Kensington. This was the venue where the Human League played with David Bowie in the audience, where Dexy's Midnight Runners played, Adam Ant, Siouxsie Sioux. It was *the* venue in London. It was small, but not that small; everyone loved going there. We were a huge hit when we played the Nashville, and even though we didn't have a record deal the press was buzzing about us. For an unsigned band we were starting to become unignorable. Our audiences were getting as large as two thousand people wherever we appeared. We were doing sell-out concerts. We obviously could have been playing bigger venues and had huge potential for record sales.

This was the time of the launch of the indie label. The big corporate labels were becoming unfashionable. The Sex Pistols had walked out on EMI. Chrysalis, although they had Blondie, were a bit too big to be considered indie-credible, Polygram was no longer credible and Virgin wasn't to be credible until they signed Boy George about five years later. We started to be approached by indie labels. While I was finishing filming

Quadrophenia Howard Abrahams called me and said that we needed to do a showcase for a label called Safari. Joel was very wary of any of Howard Abrahams's suggestions – not because of Howard Abrahams, but because Joel quite naturally is wary and wants to explore all options. But Howard rented a rehearsal room. I took an afternoon off from *Quadrophenia*; I was shooting a scooter scene in the morning and then had to be rushed by car to the rehearsal room, where we did our set to the Safari executives, John Craig and Tony Edwards. They signed us on the spot. It was the beginning of a very lucrative and creative partnership that lasted many years and many albums.

The cast of *Quadrophenia* were happy for me that I'd eventually been signed to a label. We all had such equal ideas. They all wanted their bands signed. There was an equal amount of interest in them as there was in me. So it became a race as to who would be signed first, who would play this or that venue first, whose single would come out first. We'd all become very, very competitive.

Knowing that I was signed to a record label was a fantastic feeling. I felt plugged in, as if I was part of the buzz. I belonged; I felt I was a professional singer-songwriter. John Craig and Tony Edwards became an ever present force in our lives. They nurtured us, wanting to hear all our demos, wanting to know that we were constantly writing. It was exactly what we needed, a wonderful spur that kept us going. The days of slobbing in front of the telly, going out for a casual drink, were well and truly over. We had been plugged into the juice of creativity, and we had to prove ourselves or get left behind. This was an opportunity we could not blow. We either took the contractual money and lived off it like parasites or we turned it into our future, and both Joel and I knew what we wanted. We wanted a future.

The day we signed the Safari contract a press release went out and our lives went through a big change. It was as if I, Toyah Willcox the person, could step aside and see myself become Toyah Willcox the product. For many years I'd been my own press person. I'd been my own voice, my own advertising agency. But now there was a wheel of industry behind me; all I had to do was give the industry clues as to who my public persona was and they would take those clues and sow them like seeds. Initially this was very exciting, it was everything I'd ever wanted. It was only in later years that I learned to despise the fact that I was a product rather than a person. But at this time this was exactly where I wanted to be and I went with it all the way, utterly willing, a very happy victim.

Joel and I were very much the driving force of the band. When it came to signing contracts, I knew nothing about publishing. Joel knew more than me but he still wasn't an expert. And even though we desperately needed this contract, at a time when we were watching so many of our contemporaries – Adam Ant, the Clash, Siouxsie Sioux, X-Ray Spex, do well, Joel and I were starting to feel so left behind we would have signed anything. We'd have signed our souls away and in many ways we did. When we signed the Safari contract we not only gave them the rights to our songs, we gave them the rights for life. You'd usually only sign song rights away for about fifteen years, but we had no choice. To be honest we didn't think that far into the future. All we wanted was a vehicle to be launched upon and to mean we got seen, and that's what we got.

Like true artists, Joel and I only ever wanted to perform and write. We weren't ready for what comes hand in hand with becoming a member of the record industry – the meetings with accountants, the meetings with lawyers. Endless tedious meetings that cost a fortune and don't seem to relate to creativity whatsoever. Joel and I just wanted to be creative. No wonder we signed the rights away. We couldn't wait to get out of the lawyers' office and into the studio where we belonged.

To be ready for the studio we had to finalise the band line-up which was Pete Bush on keyboards, Windy Miller on bass, Steve Bray on drums. We tended to get through musicians like wildfire. Once we got into the studio, the pressures of studio life virtually broke the band up many times over. By the time we'd finished our first album we were ready to audition for more musicians.

I'd formed a close working relationship with a keyboard-player called Keith Hales, who at the time was in a band called Blood Donor who rehearsed at Mayhem. Keith became my guiding light. He was a technological expert, and like the members of Kraftwerk, he knew everything about keyboards there was to know. So he'd sit in on the sessions and sometimes play parts, which understandably would send Pete Bush, the keyboard-player, into a jealous frenzy. But eventually we worked things out and we all worked together. Our first recording project was produced by Steve James, the only son of the late comedian Sid James. Steve was fantastic to work with. He was exactly like his father. Full of manic energy, brilliantly funny, great ears – he could hear an off-note five miles away. He was by far the best producer I ever worked with. He was creative, nurturing and wonderful to be with in the studio. We recorded our first album in Chappell's studios on Bond Street. It was a terrifying experience. I'd only ever made demos before. Singing for me was totally instinctive – something I did in front of an audience.

Working in a studio can be very sterile. You're surrounded by four blank walls and a glass partition, with people staring at you from the other side. It's not exactly the greatest environment to make you feel confident about yourself. Wearing headphones can be the most agonising thing a singer has to do. I wish they'd invent some way of recording that would mean we could just sing naturally. You have to get the balance in the headphones between all the musicians. This is a frustrating process because once you start singing the balance changes. Your whole hearing perspective becomes different. So rather than just singing and getting lost in the song, you also have to do an awful lot of listening.

It took me years to learn to co-ordinate singing and conscious listening, because all I was used to was following my heart and that's not something you can do in the studio, it's much more technical. So making the first album, *Sheep Farming in Barnet*, and the first single, 'Victims of the Riddle', was quite a tense process. Most nights I would be in tears of frustration. I'd spend so much time trying to get the sound right in my cans, meanwhile gradually losing my voice, that by the time we came to record the song I had no voice left to sing with. I really was inexperienced, and I felt quite inadequate and ashamed in front of my fellow band members. Most nights I just wanted the earth to open up and swallow me. But when we got it right, the euphoria was fantastic and it was that euphoria that we kept searching for, that kept us going, kept us overdubbing, kept us doing harmonies. Because we knew, as the night wore on, that by the time morning came, we'd be leaving the studio with the best reward of all – that feeling of euphoria.

The songs themselves weren't so much a problem. We'd spent so much time playing and touring that we'd honed the songs into quite good shape. We knew what our audience liked, what stirred them. We knew the songs that would win us five encores. The problem was performing without the energy and the life-force of the audience, which is so motivational when you're on stage. We did eventually learn to be a studio band, but it took a whole album to do it.

Personally I had another obstacle to deal with at this time, and that was my weight. I'd managed to lose some of it – when I made *Jubilee* I'd been a good two stone heavier than I was now – but I hadn't lost enough. An awful lot of money was being invested in us and I was very much the front person – after all, the band was called Toyah. Sex appeal was incredibly important and I was all too aware of that. I'd seen it in my contemporaries, such as Siouxsie Sioux: OK, great songs, great band, but what a great-looking woman. There weren't any pudgy, stocky, slightly overweight singers around at this time. Because, I hate to say, they just didn't make it.

One way of doing something about my weight was to use amphetamines. I didn't bother to go and see a dietitian; instead I used the sources readily available around me. Luckily we were only being paid £30 a week each as band members, so I couldn't afford any other exotic drugs, otherwise I really would have been in trouble. Blues were incredibly cheap, and one blue a day meant that I wouldn't eat for twenty-four hours and I would have enough energy to keep going. It only took about two weeks for me to get down to the weight I needed to be for the following years of success as a rock singer. It was an incredibly important thing for me to do. Health-wise it was the most stupid thing I could have done, but it was the only way I could lose weight. I've never lost weight through dieting. Starvation and exercise are the only ways I can shed a pound. Unfortunately, blues are not good for your mental state. I became more erratic, my reactions more extreme; if anyone approached me about any kind of problem, I would have a ballistic outburst of temper, then calm down and realise that there wasn't a problem in the first place. That kind of behaviour was down to taking blues, not eating and not sleeping. I used to go three days at a time without food or sleep and then on the fourth day I would indulge in both. If I did that now I'd be dead. It's amazing what young people do and survive; it isn't until years later that you realise that you were playing a game of Russian roulette.

I don't think I ever became anorexic; I certainly didn't throw up (unless I'd drunk too much). Life was for living, there was not enough time, and eating just didn't fit into my lifestyle. I never really starved myself. OK, I wouldn't eat for three days, but that was because I wanted a flat stomach, it wasn't because I was afraid of eating. I was probably drinking too much – I used to drink to try and get to sleep because the blues kept me awake – but I never considered drinking a problem. I wouldn't drink in the daytime. Drinking started late at night; it was a way of trying to relax, trying to slow down, trying to get the brain to slow down. I was so fearful of not making it, so fearful of blowing this opportunity that the record company was offering us, that my mind was constantly whirring. I was looking out for new ideas, new inspirations. I didn't dare close my eyes in case I missed something.

One thing was for sure: once I lost the weight I got more attention. It's astonishing how the more attractive you are, the more you can achieve, because men actually sit up and listen when you walk into a room, or should I say sit up and look. Losing that extra two stone completely changed my life, my future. I'd walk on stage and the audience would be even more mesmerised than before because they were not only listening, they were looking and lusting. Rock and roll is about sex and you have to play that game. I certainly wasn't a woman for playing around. From the age of twenty, after I had become well known, I was very distrusting of men's incentives. There were plenty of men to fancy, I mean, every week there'd be a man at work who I could easily have fallen into bed with, but I distrusted their motives and what they might say about me afterwards. I loathed hearing stories from ex-boyfriends of famous women who would divulge every intimate detail about the person they'd slept with. I never wanted to be the subject of those conversations and on the rare occasions a man claimed to have slept with me, I just punched his face in. Believe me, that happened a lot. Can you imagine that someone actually has the audacity to say to your face, in a room full of people, that they've slept with you when they haven't? What these men never realised was that I have a ballistic temper; hitting men is second nature to me – well it was back then. I haven't hit a bloke since I've been married. I've certainly never hit my husband, or ever had any reason to. But in those days I found it so insulting that someone could claim they'd slept with me, boasting about what we did, what positions, what I did to him, what he did to me, what I said, when it was all fiction. I could never understand why a man needed to say those kinds of things. That kind of gossip was rife in the industry and I made damn sure that I protected myself from it.

Now, as a woman in my forties, I don't give a damn. If someone claims they've slept with me, then it adds to my reputation. But back then, it didn't quite sit right. Women were still sluts if they slept around; I didn't like to be called a slut any more than I liked to be called a dog, and those were two words that were very common back then. Two words that meant a man would get his face punched in by me if he used them about me in that context. I have to say it, but a public schoolgirl remains a public schoolgirl deep down whether she's in rock and roll or in politics.

I have never been a person to have that deep, deep kind of intellectual thought that would enable me to create something completely on my own. All my ideas have been prompted and inspired by what I've seen, what I've learned and what I've experienced. I instinctively pick little things up and piece them together, so my ideas are kind of exotic jigsaws. I've never been a deep academic thinker, but I can sit in a room alone and be self-motivated to write. I've always used imagery, always visualised; even when writing lyrics, I visualise a story and write the words to tell it. It could be because I'm dyslexic that I use visualisation rather than depth of thought. It's not that I'm a shallow person. I feel I was never taught the art of thinking, and thinking is an art. It is something you learn to do systematically. Plotting and finding ways around problems. I feel that because I'm a woman, I didn't receive that education. That was to come later when I married Robert Fripp, a great thinker, who taught me the path to deep thinking, but that wasn't until I was twenty-seven.

* * *

When *Quadrophenia* had been edited, Franc Roddam invited all of the cast to a private screening in Piccadilly. I went along with Sting and Mark Wingate; we sat in the audience excitedly waiting for it to start. It wasn't long into the film when we realised that most of our scenes had been cut. The film had taken on a completely different flavour: it had become a story centred around Phil Daniels's character rather than about a gang of seven people. I was hugely disappointed to see that my part had been marginalised, and in many ways so had Sting's. We left half-way through. I remember standing in the foyer with Sting, Mark Wingate, Gary Shail and Gary Cooper; we just looked at each other and said, 'What's happened? How could they do this?' Most of our roles had ended up on the cutting-room floor.

There were a lot of journalists around that day and we were asked to do interviews. I didn't mind; all press is good press when you're not that well known. But every one of them wanted to talk about Phil Daniels, which really irritated me. I wanted to talk about me, my experiences, my band – after all, we'd been signed and we were about to release our first single and our six-track EP. So I found myself bad-mouthing Phil Daniels in order to try and get the subject matter back to me. This is something I hugely regret because Phil didn't deserve it. Phil was absolutely brilliant in *Quadrophenia* and he was brilliant to work with. But in my efforts to get more attention I just ended up slagging him off claiming he was a big head and a pain in the arse, which he wasn't, and saying that we never saw him because he was too starry. I wrote to him in later years when *Quadrophenia* was re-released in the mid-nineties, to apologise. He didn't reply, so I don't know if he accepted my apology. We were all so blindly competitive back then; we were fighting for our lives. I didn't have the generosity of spirit to talk about Phil. All I could think about was myself, and my future, and heaven forbid that anyone got in the way of that.

Safari records very wisely released the first single, 'Victims of the Riddle', from the first album, *Sheep Farming in Barnet*, on the tidal wave of interest in *Quadrophenia*. They had to disguise the fact that I was a punk rocker because the Mod movement had become so huge. Indeed, concert audiences around that time were more full of Mods than of punks. Those few punks who dared to turn up at one of my concerts tended to keep to the sides of the auditorium in case they got beaten up. Very soon the Mods became disillusioned because we didn't play ska. If anything we were really a heavy rock band with punk influences.

Quadrophenia went on general release and was good for all of us, even though it was a film about Phil's character. Everyone benefited from being in it. Interestingly enough, the press really tried to slate it. It got terrible reviews. It must have been heartbreaking for Franc Roddam. No one tried to see the picture for what it really was, a youth statement. All they wanted to do was to knock the Who and knock the music. But as hard as the press tried to bin this film, it became a massive success. It influenced generation after generation and it's still a classic.

At the time I couldn't bear to talk about the making of *Quadrophenia* and in more recent years I still couldn't bear to talk about it. I was angry at the end result, and I was angry at the way we were treated while making it. But it is true, time does heal those kinds of wounds; they lose their intensity and eventually you can see a different truth. I was probably as much to blame for what happened to me as anyone else.

Chapter 20

Fame was so close now I was being pulled in many directions, and by the time I was twenty-one I was becoming more and more confused. I could have become a film actress, a stage actress, or a singer, or a TV presenter. Every option was open to me. For instance, while promoting *Jubilee* I visited Pebble Mill in Birmingham to do a TV interview about my character Mad. The following week the programme's producers phoned and asked me to present the series. I said yes. So every Sunday I'd travel to Birmingham, which gave me an opportunity to see my parents and a guaranteed fee of £60 a week. The programme was called *Look Here* (produced by Roger Castles who went on to produce *The Clothes Show*). It gave Duran Duran, King and Dexy's Midnight Runners their first TV appearances.

I was becoming a cult figure across England. When the first single, 'Victims of the Riddle', came out, it stayed number 1 in the first ever indie chart for over a year. But still I was not a household name, nor fully established. My generation knew who I was, the acting fraternity knew who I was, but my future wasn't safe. This made me particularly insecure. I was still infuriatingly obsessed with stardom. Gem, my boyfriend, must have had a life of hell, living with someone so selfish. We had many happy times. We laughed a lot, but boy did he suffer if anything went wrong on the work front.

To alleviate my frustration, I was probably drinking more than at any other time in my life. One night, a bunch of us – John Craig and Tony Edwards from Safari records, me, Gem, all our mutual friends – went to see Blood Donor play in a nightclub in Deptford. Kate Bush and most of Squeeze were in the audience. By the time the band came on, I'd drunk fifteen Babychams. Why Babychams I do not know. It was probably the only thing I could afford. Why so many – well, Gem's ex-girlfriend was in the audience, and this really riled me. I was furiously jealous. They hadn't seen each other for a while so there was a lot to catch up on. Funny, isn't it? You can be the centre of attention from so many people, such huge audiences, yet have so little confidence in yourself that when an ex-girl appears on the scene, you feel you are about to lose your lover. The anger in me was building up like a bomb about to blow. Somehow I had to get rid of it.

The band were on stage, three numbers into their set. Above the stage was a balcony, where some of the audience were standing, and there was a girl up there lighting matches, dropping them onto Ricky the bass-player's head. This really pushed my button. I stormed up to the balcony, grabbed her by the hair and flung her down the stairs, at which point her boyfriend punched me in the back of the head. Turning, I kicked him right in the bollocks and carried on kicking. I was so drunk I was just lashing out in a blind rage. Not just at this guy – who happened to be six foot two, and must have weighed at least sixteen stone – but at everyone who tried to stop the fight. I vaguely remember John Craig trying to stop us.

Kate Bush's bodyguards picked her up and carried her out of the club to get her away from the area. Gem tried to stop the fight. Keith Hales, Blood Donor's keyboard-player, tried to stop the fight. But it just escalated and continued right out into the street. Eventually we exhausted ourselves. By the time the police arrived I was standing in the middle of Deptford High Street in stockings, suspenders, bra and knickers. My Willie Brown dress had been completely torn to pieces. As the police car pulled up, I stood there in a blind rage. It must have looked like a scene out of *Carrie*. I simply couldn't shake the anger off, even after all the mayhem I had caused. Everyone just stood staring at me in disbelief that someone so short, so tiny, could cause so much trouble and be so vindictive.

In the morning I woke up in my bed at Mayhem and turned to wake Gem. He had two unbelievably enormous black eyes, and nail marks all down his face. 'Gem,' I said, 'What happened? Who did that to you?' He looked at me. 'You did'. Apparently

Gem had been the first to try and pull me off the men at the nightclub, so I had kicked the living daylights out of him. Then John Craig had tried to pull me off Gem. I thought, Oh no, ran downstairs, grabbed the phone and phoned Safari. John Craig was nursing two broken ribs. I'd kicked him in the chest. He was very forgiving about it. He said it added to the legend and no doubt there would be a press release: 'Artist beats up record company executive.' He managed to laugh. I felt totally ashamed, having no memory of doing that at all. I could remember the jealousy. I could remember picking the fight. I couldn't remember the end result – for example, hitting Tony Edwards, which I felt greatly ashamed of. Tony was a good deal older than any of us. I don't think he had ever been in a fight; he'd never even seen a bar-room brawl. That night kind of changed his life. It gave me a notoriety, but I felt ashamed for a long time afterwards. I never drank Babycham again, I can tell you that.

Later that morning when we went to the police station to give our statements, the police kept looking Gem up and down, astonishment on their faces. Gem's arm was around me supportively. They knew I'd given Gem his two black eyes. They must have been wondering if he was an idiot or a remarkable man, to stand next to a woman who'd delivered him such rough justice.

Giving my statement took for ever. You have to give every single detail. I'm surprised they didn't want to know what I was thinking at the time. They wanted all the details about my clothes. How I ended up in my underwear in the middle of Deptford High Street, every punch I threw – even though I could hardly remember a thing about the night before. The police did concede that I probably wouldn't be charged, because the man I hit in turn hit Keith Hales and broke his nose. Keith was pressing charges.

I've never really thrown a punch since then – only on one occasion, when a stalker relentlessly followed me home from the West End when I was starring at the Strand Theatre. I prefer to keep my fists to myself now. There was something so utterly vulgar about that night, even though it did add to the legend of who I was. People took me a little more seriously after that, but I didn't want a reputation for hitting people in the face, the groin or the ribs.

* * *

It was 1978. Punk was slowly evolving into something completely different. Some people were calling it 'new wave'. There was a hint of new romantic in the style punk was taking on. The embryonic form of the gothic movement was also evolving. No one knew exactly what was happening, but everyone was still full of energy and ideas. There was a youthful enthusiasm running England, changing fashions, changing perceptions. The gay community, who'd always been ostracised and frowned upon as some kind of pariah, were now coming into their own. Gays were being accepted as human beings, quite rightly, but also as some of the most creative people around. All those silly jokes about handbags, being effeminate, funny walks, mincing, being poofters, were going out of the window. Being gay was gaining huge credibility. Within my community, within my surroundings, gay people were proud to be gay and they were coming out in droves. This made life far more exciting. I've always found the mix of heterosexuals and gays an incredibly exciting team. The diversity makes life so much spicier. It changes your outlook and your perceptions. Nowadays, gays have never been more equal, but back then there were real barriers, barriers that we didn't want. I genuinely think punk helped break those barriers down.

In 1978 there was still vinyl, there were cassettes – there were no CDs. I'd released one of the first EPs. EPs were short-playing albums. They played at $33\frac{1}{3}$ r.p.m. but they only had six tracks. They cost little more than a single to buy and were considered huge value for money. The credibility attached to releasing one of these was huge. In London I was a cult figure; it was an exciting time.

There was a rumour of a film to be made, a rock film called *Breaking Glass*. Eventually I was asked to go and audition for it. My appointment was just after Kate Bush's. I actually thought the part was mine. That's how arrogant I'd become. I thought they couldn't have anyone else. Kate was too big a star to do it. I was on the cusp of being discovered. Who else could have done it?

As I sat waiting to go into the audition, in the reception room with me was a girl called Hazel. She was chain-smoking. She was a strange-looking girl, not conventionally beautiful but very charismatic, and very chatty. She talked non-stop. I talked about *Quadrophenia* and she talked about having got back from a tour – I think of the Middle East, where she'd been a dancer. She was full of life and confidence. Very different from me. Even though I had an ego the size of the Eiffel Tower, I was very guarded and insecure, really quite paranoid about myself. But when I went into the audition I became that other persona. Huge, brash, chatty – very like how Hazel was naturally. I left the audition expecting a phone call within a matter of hours. The phone call never came. I rang Libby and asked, 'What happened?' They'd chosen Hazel O'Connor for the lead. I cannot tell you how furious I was. I so badly needed that film. It would have been the last piece of the jigsaw in making me famous.

Thus began a feud between Hazel and me that lasted many years. The irony was that Hazel and I actually got on very well in the flesh, but the press played us against each other. Another irony was Hazel rehearsed the music for *Breaking Glass* at Mayhem. I used to sit in my room fuming, the green-eyed monster living in my eyes. In fact I enjoyed everything she did, her songs and her writing were fantastic, and later when I saw the film I realised only she could have played the part. But ambition is a strange creature. It makes you behave in unpredictable ways, and when the press used to ask why I wasn't starring in *Breaking Glass*, I'd say anything to justify why I wasn't, and Hazel usually became the victim. Happily, after a few years Hazel and I started to go out socially and the feud ended. She was great company. We actually became quite close.

I'd come a long way from the days of Derek Jarman making me soup in his warehouse because we were both too poor to eat properly. Derek had come a long way too. Over the past year and a half we had both built on what we had achieved with *Jubilee*: it had helped give me notoriety and put Derek on the map as a film-maker. I hadn't heard from him in a while, so when the phone call came I was pleased to hear his voice. Derek always had a giggle in his voice; he very rarely sounded serious except when he lost his temper. He said he had a new project and asked me to meet him at a restaurant in Greek Street.

So that evening I went along and we sat gossiping about *Jubilee*, and reflecting on all the troubles and the pain we had gone through getting that film on celluloid. He told me about the première, which I had missed because I was in Betws-y-coed filming *The Corn Is Green*. Apparently, bang in the middle of the film, a woman stood up in the audience and started screaming my name, saying, 'Toyah, Toyah, where are you, come speak to me.' Everyone thought that I'd set it up because I couldn't be there – that I'd actually paid someone to start screaming my name so that everyone would leave the theatre thinking about me and no one else. Not even I could have conceived that one.

This woman was to be my first stalker. She'd contact me frequently, mainly by letter or by phone; if I was working on a project she'd write to my fellow cast and crew members telling them that I was evil. Later, in 1981 when I had my first hit single, she contacted Scotland Yard and told them I'd murdered three of her friends by psychic means; I'd made them commit suicide. Scotland Yard had to investigate and I'll never forget the policeman sitting in my office saying, 'Well, did you do it?' Strange times were about to begin.

Anyway, sitting with me in the restaurant, Derek started telling me about *The Tempest*. I'd never even read any Shakespeare. I probably did one Shakespeare play at school. Shakespeare was not something I relished. It was not something I wanted to do, it was not something I was remotely interested in. But, by the end of that evening, when Derek had explained all the mysticism surrounding the film he wanted to make, I was completely enthralled. Derek, like a good teacher, brought out the hidden depths of *The Tempest*. He talked about John Dee, alchemy, magic. And that was the beginning of a deep love of Shakespeare for me. I had never realised before how profoundly mystical Shakespeare was. How Shakespeare tried to educate the common man by 'leaking' within his plays information that until then only secret societies had known.

I was quite honest with Derek about my doubts as to whether I could perform Shakespeare – having never understood a line when I'd read it. It was like sublime poetry. Derek promised that if I was to play Miranda he would guide me through every line, every word, give me the full meaning. He would not let me make a fool of myself. I went away from that meeting not exactly full of enthusiasm but more full of doubt. Because if I was going to make a fool of myself it would definitely be playing Shakespeare on celluloid. In the morning I phoned Libby and discussed it with her; she felt I should do it. I spent about three days deliberating over it, with Derek phoning regularly to give me words of encouragement. My ambitions had taken a different path since I'd last worked with Derek. I'd made *Quadrophenia*; I'd desperately wanted *Breaking Glass*. I felt *The Tempest* was almost stepping back. I wanted to be Queen of Rock and Roll, a diva, so those were the kinds of films I was looking for. Eventually I made up my mind. I phoned Derek and told him, 'Yes, I'll play Miranda in *The Tempest*.' It was the wisest decision I've made in my whole career.

I was financially very comfortable by this time. *Quadrophenia* had earned me £10,000, which was a good wodge of money back then. In all I had about £17,000 in the bank at Barclays on the corner of Queenstown Road. I wasn't very wise with money. If I'd had my head screwed on, I'd have bought a house, but the houses I wanted were in Chelsea and they were at least a hundred grand. It didn't occur to me that I could have bought a house more cheaply in the Battersea area. I had to have the best or nothing; there was no in-between. I was a person of extremes.

Unfortunately cash cards had recently been invented and I was drawing out about £100 a day – and spending it. Gem and I, whose relationship was really working, would go off to the King's Road and just shop until we dropped. One hundred pounds could last you all day. It was like having £1,000 by today's standards. On the day I was leaving London to film *The Tempest* in Coventry, we loaded the car and I went to the cash machine to get £100 to get us through the journey. My account was completely empty. This wasn't the first time this had happened. This was yet another habit. I would just spend till there was nothing, then I would save – just till I felt secure, till I had a few grand in my account – and then I'd start spending helplessly till there was nothing again.

Jubilee earned me £300. *The Tempest* earned me £3,000. God bless Derek. The filming was to take place in Stoneleigh Abbey, a burnt-out stately home on the outskirts of Coventry. The building was exactly how fire had left it eighty years earlier. It was massive. There were burnt curtains, no carpets, no heating, just many many rooms of great magnitude and great detail. When I arrived, Derek and his team had begun set-dressing, adding materials, adding strange chalk markings to the walls and floors that Prospero would have made while casting his spells. Candles burned everywhere. Thousands of candles. They turned it into a beautiful rococo-baroque palace. The only warm place in the abbey was the kitchen downstairs where the caterers cooked for everyone on the team.

My father was to be played by Heathcote Williams. Christopher Biggins was in the cast, as was Peter Bull. Yolande Soleband was the costume designer; she and I got on like a house on fire. At our first costume meeting I went to her beautiful house in Hamilton Terrace in St John's Wood. She placed a crinoline on me, then took the scissors to it and slashed all the material off so I stood there in this skeletal dress. We decided that Miranda was going to be a tribal child. A thing who appreciated beauty but had been brought up without court etiquette. With no social graces whatsoever – only the natural grace that she had been born with. She was going to be a wild child. A child of potential beauty and honourableness. My hair was still bleached blonde from filming *Quadrophenia*. For Miranda it was to be braided and plaited, and interwoven with shells that she would have picked up off the beach. I was particularly excited by this look. The whole rock music scene was moving towards a tribal look, a look that I helped to instigate, and this was very much in keeping with that, so I felt I was still in touch with the rock side of my nature.

Our accommodation was the Post House Forte on the out-skirts of Coventry. Unfortunately, Gem decided that I needed driving lessons. I'd bought a little Ford Escort, which Gem used to drive me around in because driving evaded me. It was winter, early February, when we started filming, and snow was every-where; on many occasions we actually got snowed in at Stoneleigh Abbey. Gem would sit me in the driving seat, point at the pedals, then get in the passenger seat and tell me what to do. I was a dangerous driver from the very beginning. I couldn't co-ordinate my left and my right side. Whether that's part of being dyslexic, I don't know. But I found, back then, that my left and my right hand could only do the same thing. I couldn't split them. So Gem, perhaps unwisely, put his life in my hands and taught me to drive around the dual carriageways surrounding the hotel. On one occasion, pulling into the hotel drive, I couldn't find the brake, I was going a little too fast, about 45 m.p.h. and I drove straight into the reception of the hotel. It's surprising how forgiving people are when they know you work in the film industry. Everyone just laughed about it. I almost lost my entire fee for the film paying for the repairs, but there you go.

Filming *The Tempest* was an absolute joy. Derek had evolved from an experimental film-maker into a serious director; everyone looked upon him as a god. He was always the driving force. He was always an inspiration to be with, never lacking in energy and never lacking in ideas, always totally focused. And as he promised, before I shot any scene, he'd sit with me and go through the dialogue word by word. He'd give me Shakespeare's intended meaning but he'd also give me the freedom – and the confidence – to reinterpret it.

My performance energy had to be much more contained to play Miranda; even though she is a wild child, she is nothing like Mad in *Jubilee*. This is a woman born of royalty, but who has never tasted royalty. She has no concept of male and female, no concept of sex, but at the same time she is hugely voluptuous, sensual and desperate to experience some form of touch. But there is no one around to touch. Then a prince is shipwrecked on the shore. And very quickly and very beautifully, Miranda goes from being a bug to becoming a butterfly. It was virtually impossible not to play Miranda as a magical creature. The surroundings of Stoneleigh Abbey exuded a strange energy; you felt surrounded by spirits of the past. And Derek had turned it into an even more magical place, full of colour, beauty and diversity.

Heathcote Williams was an extraordinary creature. I'd never met anyone quite like him. He kept two rats, which were always in his hair. If you tried to touch them they would just bite you, and Heathcote would laugh and say, 'I told you they'd bite.' Heathcote was kind, nurturing, supportive and patient and at the same time incredibly dangerous. This is the man who wrote the great lyric for Marianne Faithfull's song 'Why D'Ya Do It' which, when I first heard it, made me think, At last, someone recognises the extraordinary jealousy I feel whenever Gem's ex-girlfriends are near. The extraordinary jealousy I feel towards anyone who's happy or does something really well. I was at that time an incredibly insecure and jealous person. Heathcote's words captured that emotion. This was the man about to write *Whale Nation*, and who published a magazine called *Beast*. Heathcote didn't broadcast about himself. Here was I, this huge ego, desperately trying to become someone, trying to become something of depth and purpose, and here was Heathcote who had absolutely no need to shout. He just was. He was remarkable. Intuitive, intelligent, always surprising and never predictable. I loved doing my scenes with Heathcote. He was as gentle as a lover and as wise as a father.

Derek as usual wanted his quota of nudity. Ferdinand the prince mysteriously appears within the palace walls, naked, for Miranda to discover him and to be aroused by his nakedness. Derek asked if I'd do a nude scene. It wasn't so much nude, it was just a topless bathing scene. A natural scene, let's say. Derek, knowing my extreme self-consciousness, wisely took me aside to ask me this and I said, 'Yeah, I really don't mind, but please could there be as few people in the room as possible?' You always ask that, but there's never just a few people in the room. There are always at least twenty. Whenever you do a nude scene, miraculously everyone needs to change a light bulb and as you know, when you are filming there are many light bulbs. Gem, realising how nervous I was about doing this very short bathing sequence, sneaked a bottle of vodka on to the set; I drank half of it and then just got on and did the job. The thing about doing nude scenes is that you feel incredibly wobbly and floppy whenever you do them. It's funny, when you wear clothes, you feel so erect and strong, fit and firm. As soon as those clothes come off you kind of fold up and everything droops and faces the floor. It's purely psychological. Either you're born with the guts to be nude or you're not, and I wasn't.

There were many, many magical moments on *The Tempest* but one in particular still has a resonance with me today. I was filming a non-dialogue scene, where Prospero has banished Ferdinand and Miranda is no longer allowed to see him. She is sitting in her room crying from a broken heart. As I was sitting there, filming this sequence, a butterfly flew in and landed on my hand. A huge, glorious red admiral. Where it had come from nobody knew. The snow was three feet thick outside. It was mid-February, freezing. The butterfly just sat there for the whole of the scene and when Derek shouted 'cut', the butterfly flew away. Since then, the red admiral to me has always represented Derek. Since Derek died, many years later, from Aids-related illnesses, whenever a red admiral has appeared, it doesn't just fly past; it comes from the middle of nowhere, from improbable surroundings, lands either on my shoulder or on my hand or next to me, stays long enough to bring a tear to my eye and then leaves. For me, the red admiral is a bringer of good fortune and a reminder of love.

There were a lot of practical jokes going on around the set and especially back at the hotel. Dear Peter Bull – I once ordered him nineteen breakfasts for the morning. According to the staff, he was upset because he felt that he had to pay for them all. He didn't realise that the night before I had gathered up all the breakfast cards from the other hotel rooms and put them all on his door. When he woke up the next morning, some earnest member of staff had patiently piled up nineteen breakfasts outside his door. They must have thought an orgy was going on in there.

Talking of orgies, none happened on *The Tempest* the way they did on *Jubilee*. But when we came to shoot the last scene, the big wedding sequence with Elizabeth Welch, all Derek's friends turned up from London. They were all to be dressed as sailors. One of the odd things about filming *The Tempest* was that I was one of the only women present. Occasionally Yolande Soleband was around, but mainly I was the only woman. That was quite strange, because everyone else was gay – but not gay in that feminine sense; these were all masculine gays, gays who loved being men. So sometimes I found it quite an isolating experience. But when we shot the big wedding sequence at the end, the air was alive with bickering and bitching, it was a fantastic day. There was so much laughter. There were so many insights, so many little snippets of Oscar Wildeness in the air. I just sat there and gawped in sheer pleasure at everyone. Dancing round, all of us high on the ecstasy of this unique magic that Derek was able to create.

It was wonderful being locked away in Stoneleigh Abbey,

especially on the rare occasions when we were snowed in. There were no telephones, no one could find me and I could forget the pressures I'd forced on myself for the sake of becoming a star. I was really really happy. On Sundays, Gem and I would catch the train to Birmingham, to Pebble Mill, where I'd do the live show of *Look Here. Look Here* had autocue so I never had to learn anything. I'd get to see all the bands play live and we'd catch a train back to Coventry. It was a happy time. A really happy time.

I never allowed myself to stop and reflect and to feel proud. I deliberately kept myself in a state of unrest. I feared that if I ever felt content, nothing would happen. I'd just fall asleep, accept my lot and not move on. So I was my own worst enemy. I was bitter and cruel to myself so as to keep myself ambitious, in order that I should reach the top. I think in a way that is why I was also bitter and cruel towards others, especially during this period. There was a desperation that time was short. That I had to achieve something while I still had youth on my side. To do that I could never allow myself to fall asleep. So I was always full of angst, incredibly serious. OK, I was a practical joker, I loved to let energy out by laughing, but I wasn't a person you could tease or make fun of; I took myself very seriously. But during the filming of *The Tempest* I could forget myself; that experience gave me a respite from that driving force inside. It allowed me to be happy for a while.

Chapter 21

One of my main ambitions was coming to fruition, that of running two careers side by side – acting and music. I wasn't top of the league in either of these careers but I was very much on the way up, and people were taking me very seriously for that. This gave me a kind of responsibility, which made me more and more nervous and quite tense. So many people were turning up to see the band and were full of so many expectations about me that I started to lose sight of myself. Having been an instinctive person who could walk on stage, get to know an audience, warm to that audience and make that evening a unique event, I now had to think ahead, because that audience was expecting to see someone who had a reputation not only for being outrageous but for being full of energy and for making brash statements. I had to go on stage fully prepared. I had to start to conceive the Toyah Willcox that everyone was antici-pating, which was very different from the Toyah Willcox that people got on the spur of the moment. All this expectation weighed on me greatly. In fact, even today, if I get a good review it makes me really nervous about performing the show the following day because the expectation is so much greater. By this time I should have been enjoying the fruits of my success. Instead I felt they were a burden on my shoulders.

What was even more extraordinary, there was no social life. Everything was work. There were no rock-and-roll parties. There was no sex, no drugs. There was only rock and roll. The drugs I took were purely to lose weight and the drink was to try and go to sleep. The parties we threw at Mayhem had by now reached epic proportions. Steve Strange was using Mayhem every weekend for three-day events. Boy George was perm-anently at the warehouse, as was Kirk Brandon. The only way I could get any peace and quiet at the weekends was to leave Mayhem and disappear elsewhere. So I wasn't a party animal either.

I was just this workhorse, trundling on, ready to work until I dropped dead of exhaustion. If I wasn't writing lyrics I was designing clothes, designing jewellery, thinking about my next look. By now my look was really refining: it was a cross between a sphinx and a tribal child. I had created this look, and people were beginning to follow fashion, follow my taste. I'd sit in my room at Mayhem hammering out copper pieces to make shoulder-pieces little copper space-age lapels, little copper elbow-guards, little pieces of armour. I knew how I wanted to look and I didn't want anyone else to know until I appeared on stage. I'd created this space-age tribal child. My room at Mayhem – which I now had built up into three floors, the ceiling of Mayhem was so high – was a shrine to creativity. I made jewellery and clothes there, painted. Every minute of the day I was thinking and thinking, trying to progress, trying to be ahead of the tide of fashion. I'd sit on the top floor among my hundreds of books, which I adored, felt inspired by – books on Masai warriors, books on kabuki theatre, books of Geiger's illustrations of aliens. I'd just surround myself with books as if the creativity of the artists who made them would somehow reflect back on to me and push me further, help me evolve further as a creative artist myself.

There were no windows at Mayhem, so the heat in the summer was intolerable. The cold in the winter was equally intolerable. Below the warehouse was a garage where cars were repaired, so the fumes inside Mayhem were also intolerable. Our lungs must have been full of poison. All the time I sat in my room, writing lyrics or designing something, there would be a band rehearsing in the main hall, as loud as if they were playing in the middle of Wembley. Iggy Pop rehearsed there for his Passenger tour. Bowie sneaked in to have a listen. John Cale too. All my heroes came to work at Mayhem. I used to sneak out and watch them.

Iggy was a great friend. We'd go round to his house for supper, or go out to restaurants. We'd sit and gossip with him, talking about the days in America when he was just hated. He was so outrageous. He used to stand on the stage and slash himself or throw himself at the audience. Iggy was the original punk. When punk first started to evolve in England, Iggy Pop had been God, and he still was. Such a small man in stature, perfectly formed, all solid muscle, beautiful face. Eve tried to pull him. A young girl called Mitzu who was living in a squat with Boy George on Warren Street was the lucky girl who got to have a big fling with Iggy. Sadly Mitzu, who was half-Chinese and extraordinarily beautiful, died the following year from a methadone overdose, but she didn't die too soon for Iggy to pen 'China Girl'.

It was bizarre having your favourite artist rehearse your favourite album in your home. I used to phone Glenn and Joel and say, 'Get over here quickly, you will not believe who's in the warehouse.' John Cale was awesome. He used to come into my room and just sit and talk. It was as if he needed to get away from the noise every once in a while, have a touch of comparative normality. He'd just sit there going through my books, talking about something I was drawing, talking about Andy Warhol, the Velvet Underground, but never really giving anything away.

Very occasionally, if I was very gentle with my approach, I could get him to talk in detail about Nico, who was a heroine of mine from the Velvet Underground. Nico was an unusual woman, very unpredictable. I'd seen her play the Music Machine, a huge club in Camden which I later played. But Nico was unfathomable. She was a woman full of pain. A kind of poetess who didn't have great musical skills but had an extraordinary spirit, that quality that some people have when you know they have an old soul. It wasn't that I wanted to be like Nico. I was just fascinated. She had a sign above her head that said 'self-destruct' and I'm fascinated by people who want to self-destruct. I think it takes immense guts. Life is such a gift. OK, I don't think many of us are ever happy in life, I think happiness is elusive, but most of us learn to bear life. Nico was one of those people who you sensed couldn't quite bear life, and that made her mesmerising.

My band was going from strength to strength. We were playing up and down the country to record-breaking audiences.

It wasn't that we were playing in giant stadiums or anything, but we'd moved into bigger clubs, with two-thousand – sometimes five-thousand – capacity. In those days there were three stages of success. There was the small club at three hundred, the larger clubs at five thousand, then the big theatres – and of course there was Wembley. Today there doesn't seem to be that in-between stage. You either fill the small club or play the huge stadiums.

Back then we were in the middle ground. We were neither a failure nor a huge success. We were making money – just, but a lot of money was being invested in us by Safari. The publicity wheel was in motion. We had Judy Totton do our publicity. Her motto was that no newspaper was too small; she said I must talk to every publication that would agree to interview me. Judy would even have me talking to local parish papers.

The band by now were playing constantly, in fact we were permanently on tour. We'd set off on our little tour bus, all crammed in like sardines with our equipment, and head north, arriving to find a huge army of followers waiting at the venue. In those days we weren't so big that we didn't or couldn't talk to our fans. We'd actually invite them in and they'd watch the sound-check. They'd come backstage, eat our food, drink our drink. We got to know many of them by name – and they were a great way of finding out what other bands were up to. They were like spies, a network. They didn't ever seem to have jobs to go to. They were just permanently on the road following us around the country in their own little bus.

Recording was a constant pressure. Once we'd written a song we had to demo it, then to get it into the recording studio as quickly as possible. I found that there was a kind of morphic resonance at this time. If I wrote a lyric I could guarantee that Kate Bush or Hazel O'Connor or even Kim Wilde would come up with a similar subject within days. Who wrote what first? Who came up with the concept first no longer mattered. You could guarantee if I had an idea someone else had it too. So the whole process was about who could get the idea out first and therefore claim originality. It was as if we were all psychic, as if we were plugged into a universal energy which would communicate something about a particular subject and we would all pick up on it at the same time.

But usually you'd make an album, make a single and promote it, then be straight back in the studio to do the follow-up album, to keep the incentive permanently going with your audience. The follow-up album to *Sheep Farming in Barnet* was to be *The Blue Meaning*. Safari decided to send us away to a residential studio in a little town called Battle, near Hastings. It was really refreshing to get away from the pressures and the speed of London. The recording studio – and our home for the next month – was in the courtyard of an ornate farmhouse. The only unfortunate thing about residential studios is they feed you too much, so you get fat, and they always have dogs, so when you go for a pee in the middle of the night you end up tiptoeing around the dogs' diarrhoea. This happened every night at Battle.

The Blue Meaning was to be produced by both Steve James and Keith Hales. A great partnership. We arrived at Battle with only half the material written, which presented an added pressure. I've always found creativity to be rather random. It's not something you can do to order. You have to be in the right frame of mind, and that frame of mind is not something you can always control. Sometimes creativity is so spontaneous you just pick up a pen and in two minutes you have written a song. Other songs can take months to write.

My nerves at singing were far better this time; in fact I really enjoyed singing on *The Blue Meaning*. I actually did some harmonies, which for me was very brave, and I'd learned the technique of listening to the band and singing at the same time rather than just doing everything instinctively. When I sang, I liked to be alone, because when I sang something for the first time I'd always feel vulnerable. I wanted to be able to feel my way around the song and make mistakes that no one else would get to hear, so I always cleared the studio except for Steve and Keith who were my best advisers.

In the morning I'd get up as early as I possibly could, sit at my desk and just write lyrics. Sometimes this process brought me to tears of frustration because nothing would come. Or there would be disturbances. Or a dog would come in and throw up on the carpet. But you just had to learn to be patient, learn to trust the process. Learn to trust that when the time was right inspiration would come.

In the meantime, the band would be in the studio laying

down backing tracks. By this time in the band we had Charlie Francis on bass, Steve Bray on drums, Pete Bush on keyboards, Joel on guitar and me doing vocals. It was a fantastic line-up; it really worked. But there were conflicts – to do with me getting all the attention, to do with me needing more time to write lyrics. I wasn't very accessible to the band, because to be creative I always needed to be alone, and that caused a division – not a terrible division, but an 'atmosphere'. Inevitably after a few weeks living in such close confinement we all started to get quite bonkers. Studios cost money, so it wasn't as if we could go down to the sea and play for a day. We just had to keep working, whether it felt right or not.

In the evenings there would be some spectacular fights. We'd all drink too much. One night Steve Bray fell out of a top-floor window. I think he actually jumped. He was so cross with me he just opened the window and jumped. I can't even remember what the argument was about – usually arguments are about nothing, you're just fed up of each other's company. It's a band mentality. We didn't have an audience to perform in front of, a concert to let steam off through. So we'd just pick at each other like hens in too small a cage.

The main song on *The Blue Meaning* was 'IEYA'. This song already had a remarkable history. I've always believed that music is a universal language and if I was asked to define God, I'd say God is music. Music transcends everything. It's the most wonderful form of communication and proof of the existence of God. And really good music makes you transcend your natural state; it helps you evolve. The glory of punk was that it brought music down to a level where young people could find their identity, find their feet and become confident.

'IEYA' started off as a jam, a jam on stage. Some months before, we'd been playing Bath, where we had a hall full of two thousand rioting kids. The show itself had gone phenomenally well, and as usual in those days we hit the fourth encore and we'd run out of music. What we used to do was repeat a song called 'Danced', about the second coming of Christ, which would slowly build layer upon layer of sound, encouraging the audience to dance and dance and dance almost into a hypnotic state.

Well, at Bath we had a lot of trouble with the National Front.

A lot of my band were Jewish, and we all found it particularly offensive that the NF would recruit at concerts – they'd go around the audience intimidating the youngest, the smallest, the scrawniest boys into joining the NF. By the end of this concert in Bath, the NF were chanting '*Sieg heil*' at the back. Charlie Francis, our bass-player, found this intolerable, and Joel kept taking his guitar off to go and beat them up, which we all had to stop him from doing. Instead we just shouted back 'Nazi scum' and got the audience to chant 'Nazi scum'.

For the fourth encore, all we could think of doing was something that had started as a jam in the sound-check that day, which was 'IEYA'. It was a sequence of chords that grew, so every verse had more chords added to it, and it had a fantastically simple chorus, a chant, 'IEYA'. 'IEYA, I am solar, IEYA I'm the beast.' I have a habit of writing about extreme opposites: I often write about Christ and Christianity in hidden forms, and then the next day I'll write about the Devil and mankind. 'IEYA' is about mankind believing in ourselves so much that we believe we are immortal and can become our own gods, therefore challenging God as the Devil, in the form of the Devil; man being the beast. So we walked on stage and started 'IEYA', and within the first sixteen bars the audience was behaving in a way I'd never seen before. And because 'IEYA' had no real form, we'd only ever jammed it, what should have been a four-minute song went on for twenty minutes, and the audience didn't stop dancing once, and I just kept making up words as I went along. At the end of the concert the NF were so incensed that the police were called and had to get us out via the Gents window at the back and into a police van, because the NF were outside, kicking in cars, waiting for us at the stage door to kick our heads in. A full-blown riot was in progress.

When we started to record 'IEYA' in the studio in Battle, we had to put it into a digestible form and decide how long it was going to be. It turned out to be seven minutes long, which is longer than any average song. But the atmosphere in the studio became terrifying. Just like when *The Exorcist* was made, things started going wrong. Technical equipment wouldn't work, arguments would start out of nowhere, distrust would enter the studio, and I had a severe problem with writing seven minutes' worth of lyrics in what was a repetitive song. It took days for me to record the vocals. It was a multi-layered song, and the chorus had many voices – all mine. But doing the verses was murder. I hadn't quite learned by this time that the simpler I kept the subject matter and the simpler I kept the phrasing and the words, the more effective the song would be. I always wanted to make things over-complex to try and prove myself.

Eventually, after many frustrating late nights in the studio, the song was put down and we sent it back to London for Safari to hear. Safari loved it so much they played it over and over again in their office and decided it should be a single. On about the twentieth play in one day, a man appeared at the door of Safari records with a knife, grabbed Tony Edwards by the throat and said he would kill him if he ever heard that song again. Thus began the legend of 'IEYA' – the song that could turn any concert into a riot. It was just an incredibly powerful song. The question is, did we write it or did it come to us from somewhere else?

Chapter 22

The Blue Meaning was turned around very very quickly and within a month of recording we were back on the road. We toured Germany, Holland, Belgium and the UK. It's always nerve-racking performing new material. You feel quite vulnerable on stage in case you make a mistake – in case you get a lyric wrong. Your fans always know the lyrics better than you do. But this tour was a massive success. We were followed by artists who wanted to paint us. Photographers who wanted to photograph us. Writers who wanted to write about us. We were like pied pipers with an endless stream of people following us, wanting to know more, wanting to take a little bit of us away with them. It was very exciting and by now my confidence was very strong. I was starting to believe that I could be a singer.

So popular was the band that on this tour we had to take security with us. They were known as the Finchley boys. The Finchley boys were a legend in their own lunchtime. They protected Hazel O'Connor (and I do believe Hazel was dating one of them), they protected me, the Stranglers, the Boomtown Rats, you name it, if they played in London, the Finchley boys were their security. I was starting to get mobbed which was an experience I dearly loved – although Gem wasn't too happy about seeing his other half suddenly pulled away by her hair and into the audience. One member of the Finchley boys, Tom, became particularly close, purely because he was the one who always had to dive into the audience and dig me out. It's quite an extraordinary feeling: one minute you're singing on stage, totally in control, in command of the whole performance, then the next you feel a hand wrap around your ankle and slowly you're pulled into the quicksand of human beings, held under while hands just grope at you and tear bits of you off.

I was a real space cadet on stage. I used to wear a fencing suit made by the designer Willie Brown, who also designed for David Bowie. I'd made myself little copper space lapels and a huge copper disc to wear on my front, out of respect for Ziggy Stardust. Every night the audience would tear these off. I'd made these discs quite amateurishly and they were very sharp, so every night the audience would be covered in blood – their own and ours – because these pieces of copper were being hurled around and shoved from one hand to another as some form of currency. Meanwhile, the audience would be pogoing like mad. Pogoing is the best thing that ever happened for an audience. You could see the steam rising from their heads. Gobbing was also still very much a part of audience response. There was nothing worse than holding a really long note in the middle of 'IEYA' and seeing in the distance a massive piece of green phlegm flying through the air and knowing it was going to hit you bang in the mouth. Often I'd be performing on stage while retching. Apparently Siouxsie Sioux contracted hepatitis B because of gobbing. Luckily I never contracted anything but it was the most revolting experience. Some nights I was so covered in gob when I came off stage that the only thing anyone could do was put me straight in the shower fully clothed. It wasn't just me, it was the whole band – we were so slimy you couldn't get the clothes off. On one rare occasion my costume had to be cut off; it had been too gobbed. I was like a huge lump of goo. There was also the small problem of trying to find dry-cleaners who would accept your costume. You can imagine walking into a dry-cleaner's in Hull and saying, 'Hello, could you dry-clean this? It's a stage costume but could you be really careful with it – it's hand-painted so it's quite rare. And by the way it's got about ten tons of gob on it.' You'd have to go round umpteen dry-cleaners before you found one who would even take the outfit out of the bag.

During this tour I was approached by a documentary-maker called Graham Moore. He was making four documentaries about four remarkable people. One was about a disabled boy, I can't remember what the other two were about, and one was to be about me. So for most of this tour I had a documentary team following me around. At first it was rather wonderful but eventually the permanent questioning and observation started to get on my wick. Especially as my private life was getting difficult: I was starting to fall in love with T., my security man. This was a phenomenally painful time. Gem was a fantastic man. I'd been with him for two years. I hadn't fallen out of love with him but I'd kind of fallen in lust with T. and this was hard to deal with. I'd never really experienced lust before and I wasn't ready for how powerful it can be. A lot of the documentary featured my relationship with Gem, but bang in the middle of the filming it seemed that Gem was about to be ousted for another man.

The touring schedule was hectic. We ended in Berlin, which proved a little too decadent for me. After our last gig we all went off to a club. It was full of very beautiful women, which made the band extremely happy. All the women looked like young Monroes, all dressed in leopardskin, with beautiful red lips, white-blonde hair. And then one came over to me and kissed me full on the mouth; we soon realised that we'd been taken to an exclusive lesbian club. I'd never seen lesbians like these. These women were to die for. The band could have slit their wrists they were so upset.

We went off to another club, this time with Robert Plant and John Paul Jones from Led Zeppelin. I spent the evening trying to chat up T. Gem was drinking at the bar. Robert Plant was trying to chat me up. That was the only time I've ever experienced being chatted up. Can you believe it? I think people were scared of me. I was always so hyper, and usually very drunk; also I was too aggressive to be taken advantage of. So I remember this night as one of the most wonderful of my life, when I had the attention of so many people. Eventually we went back to the hotel, and T. and I slipped off into the night and became lovers.

The next day in a hungover silence, we all drove across Germany and through Belgium, and caught the ferry back to England I returned to Mayhem with Gem, feeling very very confused. Exhausted from the tour. Not knowing if I was to stay with Gem or go with T. The following day was just hell. I utterly lacked emotional maturity. I couldn't treat what was happening with T. as an affair and let it run its course and then go back to some kind of normality with Gem. I'd always been an all-or-nothing person, and within the week I'd moved out of Mayhem and into T.'s house with his mother, father and sister in Finchley.

Suddenly the whole of my life had completely changed, and I tried to hide this from the documentary-makers. In the space of a week, I'd gone from playing in Berlin to three thousand people to sharing a single bed with T. in a house on an estate in Finchley. Nothing wrong with that, but I was back to the domesticity I loathed. I think part of me was yearning desperately for some kind of normality. Life at Mayhem had been hard. A constant rush, a constant buzz. There was no rest. There was no silence, no daylight. In a way I found sanctuary with T.'s mother, a wonderful woman who ran the community, who cooked at breakfast, lunch and dinner. She was someone who you could sit down and talk to and sort your head out with. She was very good for T. I soon discovered that T. was more than just a bodyguard, he was wild.

It broke my heart to face Gem. I felt terrible guilt. He's by far one of the best men I've ever known. In retrospect I wish I'd had the maturity to stay with him; it was a vast mistake to leave him. The band, too, must have thought I'd lost the plot. Gem was so instrumental in the running of the band. He made sure we got from A to B. He made sure the band were happy. He made sure equipment was right. Gem was damn near perfect. And he was such a mentor to me. But at the time I didn't realise all of this; I was just exhausted, frightened of the future, frightened of the present, and T. appeared to be the guardian I needed.

The tour had been going well. It had thrown many surprises up. In London we played the Lyceum, supporting the Psychedelic Furs, heroes of ours. Ater the show, an announcement came over the tannoy that no one was to leave the theatre. A boy of fifteen had overdosed on heroin in the audience and died. The entire audience and all the bands were locked in the theatre until the police had interviewed every one of us. I hasten to say they didn't find any hard drugs on us or on any of the bands. It appeared the boy had already taken the fatal overdose before he entered the building and sadly died among the dancing audience; no one had noticed him until we came off stage and the audience dissipated towards the bar.

This left me feeling hollow. That a child could die in the

audience like that. And as usual I felt guilty, as if in some way I was responsible. If only someone could have noticed him. But the trouble with these concerts was there were so many people in a such small space, all dancing away, the people at the front couldn't avoid getting kind of crushed. Some would pass out from the heat, and that was where T. and the Finchley boys came in. They used to drag them out of the audience and revive them in the wings and then throw them back into the audience. Most people really enjoyed this experience; it was something to write home about. So the fact that the boy lost consciousness and lost his life in the audience didn't come as a surprise, but it did leave me wishing that something could have been done to save him.

This was the first tour when the audience included not only strangers and dedicated fans, but people from my past who I admired and had learned to respect, such as Phil Daniels and Danny Boyle – both of whom I had worked with at the ICA a year earlier on a Stephen Poliakoff play called *American Days*. It was nice knowing that in some way they were endorsing my work. Poliakoff's *American Days* made a big impact in London. It starred me, Phil Daniels, Mel Smith, Antony Sher and Danny Boyle. Danny was such a sweet man. He was quiet, modest, not a great actor but a loyal actor. Always there, always reliable. He didn't seem to have much ego, he was just a thoroughly pleasant man, and to think that he went on to produce *Trainspotting* takes my breath away: somewhere inside Danny Boyle must have been a will of iron. It goes to show that you shouldn't judge anyone you work with at face value. Something I was terrible for.

A week after the tour finished, the band members wanted a meeting in Howard Abrahams's office, in Cornhill in the City. Pete Bush, Charlie Francis, Steve Gray, Joel and I went into Howard's office and sat down. Pete started the meeting. 'We're leaving the band. That's Charlie, Steve and myself, we're leaving the band. We don't want to be in it any more. To be honest, we don't believe in you,' Pete said, referring to me. This was a monster of a shock. There was so much potential. There was so much happening. Why leave the band now? And even though the band was named after me, every band member was equally important for the end result. The sound was unique and that was because of all the members of the band. Joel was gobsmacked. I was gobsmacked.

Joel, T. and I drove to Wales and spent a week in a rented cottage. It was torture. It was a mirror image of the week I'd spent with Glenn after finishing *Jubilee* after Adam had broken up the Maneaters. I was back in the same intolerable pain, not knowing what to do. The idea was that Joel and I would write, but we couldn't write. All we could talk about was what had gone wrong. We kept dissecting the past months, trying to find out that ingredient, that moment, that something we missed that had made the band want to break up. After a few days T. left to go to work, leaving Joel and me alone. We were both used to company, used to people we could tease and play practical jokes on. We weren't great with each other, didn't really spark off each other alone. It became quite a depressing week – and to top it all, Hazel O'Connor's 'Eighth Day' was playing on the radio all the time. Spiking me, prodding me, making me feel like a failure. Everything I feared was happening. I had no band. I had no platform on which to be creative. I felt wretched.

T. came to get us and on the drive home I heard for the first time David Bowie's 'Ashes to Ashes'. Yet again Bowie gave me a song that inspired me, that pulled me from this wretched existence into the future. I wasn't going to let this get me down. At least I still had Joel, and Joel was willing to stand by me and make a go of it. Back in London we contacted Safari. John Craig decided we had to do some more demoing. This time he'd pick the songs. Keith Hales had written a song called 'It's a Mystery', which consisted of an intro and a musical 'outro'. That was it. It had to be turned into a song. We recorded it as it stood, in that arrangement. I left it at that. I absolutely loathed the song. I didn't want the song to represent me and I didn't want to represent the song. I didn't relate to it at all. I let that be known and left it with Safari.

Meanwhile I had to finish off the Toyah documentary. I was to star at the Royal Court in a play by Nigel Williams called *Sugar and Spice*. The cast included me, Caroline Quentin, Gwyneth Strong, Daniel Peacock and Carole Hayman. The documentary camera team followed me round rehearsals. By

214

now the director knew that I'd left Gem, but he wasn't too perturbed by that; more disturbing to him was that the band had split up. This was after they'd filmed the band's last concert, and an album called *Toyah! Toyah! Toyah!* was to be taken from the soundtrack. I felt we had the perfect band line-up but there was no going back. It was over.

On *Sugar and Spice* I shared a dressing room with Caroline Quentin and Gwyneth Strong. It was a dressing room full of laughter. Caroline was the greatest fun to be with – bubbly, chatty, outrageous, always witty, always happy. The play opened to catastrophic reviews. It was the first time I'd ever been in a production which was totally slated. But it was mainly my fans who filled the auditorium; they didn't seem to read reviews and they loved the play. It's a play about two gangs, 'Sugar' and 'Spice' referring to male and female. My gang obviously was the girls' gang, Daniel Peacock's gang was the boys' gang. It's about events in a flat one evening when the gangs meet and fall out and the girls become the aggressors. During the play I used to have to smash a bottle on a table – sugar glass of course – and use this as a weapon to force Daniel Peacock to strip completely naked. Then, with his back to the audience and my face to the audience, I had to deliver three pages of monologue, which always had Caroline Quentin rolling on the floor with laughter because I had to address the whole speech to Daniel Peacock's genitals. I don't know whether Daniel was nervous or whether he was athletic, but he had this ability to make each of his testicles jump up and down as if they were twitching, as if they were trying to imitate my voice or talk back at me. This happened every night, and every night I was in stitches, tears running down my face.

Outside the stage door it wasn't adulation that I met with this time. The fans had found out that the band had broken up. Many were in tears. Surprisingly, many men were in tears and full of accusations, saying that the band had saved their lives, that the music was all that they lived for and what had they got to live for now. I felt a big responsibility towards the fans; I didn't know what to do. OK, we were demoing new material, but there was still no band.

Sugar and Spice finished before Christmas 1980. I took T. home to Birmingham to meet my parents. My mother hinted that I was a slut for leaving Gem, but things were OK. T. did some decorating for them, they all got on and they seemed to accept him.

In the meantime, Safari were busy. They'd hired the services of a good solid rock producer called Nick Tauber, who put together a new band for me. This consisted of Phil Spalding on bass, Nigel Glockler on drums, Adrian Lee on keyboards and of course Joel and me. And by the new year we'd already recorded four new tracks, which were to become an EP called *Four from Toyah*. On it were 'It's a Mystery', rearranged and with additional lyrics from me, 'War Boys', one of my improvisational tracks, 'Revelations' and 'Angels and Demons'. Within a month the new band were on the road doing our first major tour. It was a nerve-racking time because I didn't know how the loyal fans were going to accept the new line-up. But it turned out to be a magnificent tour. It was a better band than the original. I felt so lucky, so relieved. We were playing universities – which are always the best places to play, because you have an utterly wild audience; the audience are familiar with each other, so they have no inhibitions.

I'll never forget Sheffield. We were on stage for two hours. We played everything we could possibly play. We got five encores. We came off after the fifth encore suffering from heat exhaustion and dehydration and still the audience were crying out for more. Phil Spalding had stripped to his underpants and was standing in the shower when the promoter told us that we had to go on and do at least one more number or there was going to be a riot. So Spalding in his underpants grabbed a bucket and we did 'IEYA' for about the third time that night with our bass-player throwing up from the heat into the bucket while playing in just his underpants.

The whole tour was like that. We put 'It's a Mystery' in half-way through the set and I introduced it as our new single and waited for the boos. I was pretty honest about it. I apologised for it. I said, 'Look, the record company wants this to be our new single. I absolutely detest it but I promise you we'll follow it up with something brilliant.' We played 'It's a Mystery' and the whole place went mad. By the third date into the tour the fans knew the words so they just sang along, but I never guessed that 'It's a Mystery' would ever be a success.

Immediately after the tour I moved to Norwich for a month to star alongside Ralph Bates in an episode of the TV series *Tales of the Unexpected.* I was so busy as a musician that this was the first acting I had done that year. It was set in the sixties and I was playing a model who had lost her looks and was losing her career. I had to pose with Ralph Bates putting his arms around me for some photos that were to appear in our home over the fireplace. When T. saw the photos he went ballistic. This was the first time that I realised I was living with an incredibly jealous man. No matter how I tried to explain to him that I was an actress, that we do put our arms around each other, actors sometimes even have to kiss, I just couldn't get it across to him, and no way would he accept that any other man could show me any form of affection. The shooting of *Tales of the Unexpected* turned into an utter nightmare, with T. spying on every move Ralph and I made, watching every scene, giving Ralph threatening looks. My popularity was such that I actually couldn't be alone any more, as I was starting to be bothered by fans, who would follow me and grab me. At those times I was grateful that T. was there, but as an actress I could see that this was going to be a very restrictive relationship.

Chapter 23

Back in London, T. and I got our first flat together. The flat had one bedroom, a lounge, a bathroom, a kitchen and a study for me. The study was essential. I was the breadwinner – which was another part of the problem in this relationship. I was a very disciplined breadwinner as well. I'd get up every morning at 7, and sit in my workroom till 2, and I would not leave that workroom other than to make a cup of coffee or get a drink of water. In that time I would make myself write.

During the filming of *Tales of the Unexpected*, the record company had been couriering up cassette tapes to me of the backing tracks that the band were putting together. They were excellent, inspirational. In between scenes I would go and sit in my car with my Walkman and just listen to the tapes and plan some of the stories I wanted to tell as a lyricist to those tracks. Now I had to put them into words. The band had come up with twenty-four numbers. That was quite daunting. Writing twenty-four lyrics to some people would be an impossible task. Some mornings nothing would come, but luckily most mornings lyrics came very quickly – partly because I had been writing constantly since the age of twelve. Whenever ideas sprang to mind, I always jotted them down. I never thought, Oh, I'll write that down in a minute, because when that minute comes you can guarantee that you will have forgotten the idea. So, tapping into a source of years of writing that summed up my frustrations as a child and as a teenager, I sat in my study and pieced together the lyrics for an album called *Anthem*.

The first lyric to come was to a song called 'Pop Star'. A song about isolation – isolation caused by fame, because by this time that's what I was experiencing. I had T. for company, and fans were something to be held at bay, whereas a year earlier, fans had been friends, they were people who could share your dressing room. Now fans were obsessive. They no longer really knew who I was. They just identified with the product I was becoming. And this isolation was setting in quickly. The sheer volume of work when you start to hit a certain stage of fame is terrifying. You're constantly on the go, constantly having to think. I used to ask my office not to phone me before 12 noon so I could be alone to write lyrics. You can't write a lyric when you've got an accountant phoning you up. And you certainly can't write a lyric when you've got your manager phoning you up demanding you do interviews. Also by this time we had a new manager.

A man called Alan Seifert had come to see me when I was doing *Sugar and Spice* at the Royal Court. At the time he managed Marianne Faithfull and Elaine Paige. He was a flirtatious creature, a flattering creature, and he pursued me. He got Marianne Faithfull to write me letters saying how wonderful he was as a manager. Then he wined and dined me and I truly believed that he was the only person who could manage me. It was a good decision. He was very, very creative. He really knew about the business, and he knew everyone in the business, and one lesson I was learning fast – no matter how famous you are, if you don't know people in the business you won't be able to pull favours in times of need.

So every day I would write till 2 p.m., then I'd phone the studio and they'd send the car. The car would take me to the Marquee Studios in the West End where I would record the song I had penned that morning. Of course, when I say song, I mean lyrics. I did no more than write the lyrics and create the melody lines. There was no room to rearrange songs. The backing tracks had already been recorded – a financial necessity while I had been away making *Tales of the Unexpected*. But miraculously none of the songs needed rearranging anyway. They were perfect. The band wouldn't come in until 6 p.m, which gave me about four hours every day to put a main vocal down. I'm a second-take wonder. I like to do the first take to get the sound right and then the second take for feeling. And then clean it up. Technology is such that you can drop in on a vocal and just clean up a sentence or a word or a note. I think we worked relatively quickly. We managed to do a song a day – including my harmonies and backing vocals. It was a gloriously satisfying experience.

In those days I'd starve myself while working. I felt that eating stopped the spirit being hungry, and that hunger of spirit was what generated charisma, what attracted people to you. They could sense that animal hunger in your performance. So come 6 p.m. I'd be ravenous. I'd phone Pizza Express and have my favourite pizza (Margherita) sent round. The band would arrive. They'd start doing their overdubs and generally we'd just run amok in the studio. There was much laughter. We were very happy. We kind of knew we had a hit on our hands.

One morning, on a very rare day off, I was lying in the bath at our flat in Hendon and the phone rang. T. answered it; it was John Craig, asking to speak to me. I got out of the bath and went to the phone. He said, 'Toyah, you're doing *Top of the Pops* tomorrow.' I said, 'What?!' He said 'It's a Mystery' had gone into the charts in the top forty which instantly qualified us for *Top of the Pops*. I got back into the bath. I was trembling with excitement. I didn't quite know what to do. I didn't know what I was going to wear. Suddenly everything became a problem. I was terrified.

I'd been working for quite a few years with a dress designer called Melissa Caplan. Melissa was extraordinary. When I first met her she was a fashion student; we'd have meetings and I'd take her my favourite books, and she created exclusive costumes for me that were kind of geometrical with hand-painted Egyptian symbols on. I loved her work. I believe she influenced the whole of the eighties look, the whole of the new romantic look. At this time she worked exclusively for me, but she went on to work for Spandau Ballet, Bananarama and Sade. Melissa was making costumes for the whole of the band, but they wouldn't be ready for *Top of the Pops*. This had taken us completely by surprise. But I did have a wonderful Willie Brown dress. I'd always worn Willie Brown since Willie Brown designed David Bowie's clothes for the Heroes tour. I would wear that tomorrow. I was so excited that that night I couldn't sleep. As I lay in bed the past, present and future, all the dreams I'd ever had, were homing in on me. I was actually about to live

Promotional shoot for 'It's a Mystery', 1981. The typical Toyah look.

Hammersmith Odeon, 1982.

Shooting the video to
'Brave New World' in 1982 at the
back of Battersea Power Station,
2 p.m. Earlier that day, at
4.30 a.m., I was in the sea at
Hastings. Glamorous life!

The Ebony Tower with Greta Scacchi
and Laurence Olivier, 1983.

With Greta Scacchi and director Rob Knights, taking a
break during shooting for *The Ebony Tower*.

The Royal *It's a Knockout*, 1987: (from left to right) Nicholas Lyndhurst, Barry McGuigan, Steve Cram, me, Eddie Grant, Christopher Reeve, Tessa Sanderson and Prince Edward. What a team!

The Royal *It's a Knockout*: John Cleese and his jester.

Pissed as a newt in my dressing room at the Birmingham Rep, with my friend Gita Jaraij, after a performance of *A Midsummer Night's Dream*, 1987.

Spot the short person. Princess Diana, Stephen Fry and me at the National Theatre, 1987.

My sister Nicola and friend on my thirtieth birthday at Reddish House, 1988.

The Taming of the Shrew for the Cambridge Theatre
Company's UK tour, 1988, with John Labanowski as Petruchio to my Kate.

On tour with Robert in our band, Sunday All Over the World, Amsterdam 1989.

Peter Pan, British tour 1993–4, also starring Brian Blessed.

Filming *Rolinda Sharples* for HTV Bristol, 1996.

At home with my rabbit. Reddish House, 1997.

The two loves of my life: Robert and Beaton. Beaton always lies at Robert's feet while he practises his guitar. Reddish House, 1998.

Richmond Theatre, Christmas 1998. Me as Jack in *Jack and the Beanstalk* with my much-loved friend Robert Duncan playing Mother.

My brother, Kim. Bristol, 1999.

one of my major dreams. I felt as if I was the focus of the whole world.

Only four months ago my world had come to an abrupt standstill with the original band splitting. The fans turning on me, blaming me. At times I had been in utter despair. One day, standing on the platform at Finchley Central Station waiting to catch the tube in to the Royal Court, I stared down at the railway track and contemplated how quick it would be to end my life in front of the next train. There was a little old man who kept buzzing around me, a little Jewish man in his hat. He irritated me at first. I knew he was looking at me and I was just waiting for him to make some kind of pass. He obviously thought punks were easy pickings. Eventually he plucked up the courage to speak. All he wanted was to know the time. I told him and he walked away; then he came back and he said, 'Smile, wait until tomorrow, all will get better.' Such a cryptic thing to say. I just laughed and said, 'Yeah, I'm sure it will,' and then the train came. That was the day before I recorded the demo of 'It's a Mystery'. And as I lay in bed the night before *Top of the Pops*, it occurred to me that that man might have been a guardian angel.

Top of the Pops was recorded at Wood Lane. We all had to arrive by 10 a.m., then sat around in our dressing rooms and just waited. The bands seemed to be kept apart from each other because of rivalry and potential high jinks. Ironically I was sharing the bill this day with Adam Ant. This made me particularly vulnerable. I hadn't seen Adam in years and by this time he'd become a major star, the biggest name in England.

Throughout the day you rehearse your number many times over so that by the time you perform in the evening you know exactly which camera is on you and when. The only time I saw Adam that day was on a neighbouring stage. As a relative newcomer in the charts I was to be one of the first people on the show. Adam, being number 1, was to perform last. We made very brief eye contact. No sign of recognition passed between us, and that was the last time I saw Adam in the flesh.

The day itself was wonderful. The air was buzzing with electricity. *Top of the Pops* was everything I had thought it would be; I really felt as though I'd arrived. But being there still wasn't proof to me that 'It's a Mystery' was the right song for us. Next to all the other artists' material it sounded slow, stilted and old-fashioned. I felt incredibly vulnerable performing a slow number. Instinctively my body wanted to burst into energetic dance but there was no hope of or reason for doing that with a ballad like 'It's a Mystery'.

When the time came for me to perform I was a total nervous wreck. I wore my little Willie Brown dress. It was a very conservative dress; it completely covered me – although it had see-through shoulders which ironically were very sexy. The dress was almost like a dominatrix dress, which was probably why it worked so well. My hair was quite short, cut in a little bob, bright red and yellow. We performed, celebrated, went out for a curry in Shepherd's Bush afterwards and then went home. I had an overwhelming fear that this was it. That there would be nothing following. That that was the zenith of my music career. The song would go nowhere. I'd never see *Top of the Pops* again. Goodbye music. I was so frightened of being a one-hit wonder.

The show went out on a Thursday; by the end of Saturday you would get a chart prediction from the sales in the shops around the country. The prediction was very good. We knew that the song would go up. In those days the new chart came out on a Tuesday; you didn't know your new position until about Tuesday lunchtime. What I didn't expect was a phone call from John Craig telling us that the single had gone all the way up to number 4. It was a massive success. John Craig admitted that being an independent record company they were having trouble getting products into the shops. The factories were working overnight pressing the EP *Four from Toyah* which featured 'It's a Mystery'. The demand was huge. We were selling something like 75,000 units a week.

To put that in perspective, today you can get to number 1 selling as few as 2,000 units a week. Record sales then were much, much bigger. Suddenly my life became a strategy. I'd gone up to number 4. I wouldn't be able to go on *Top of the Pops* that week; you could only appear every other week. So it meant keeping the sales alive for another two weeks so that I'd get that second appearance on *Top of the Pops*. I needn't have worried. The single sold and sold and sold and gave me three more appearances on *Top of the Pops*.

* * *

I'd learned my lesson through *Jubilee* not to put all my eggs in one basket. So life became a constant worry of holding that bubble up in the air and not letting it burst. There was no security, no guarantees, and I certainly didn't want to be the reason anything should fail. As soon as the single hit number 4, my life became a constant whirl of interviews. I'd do about fourteen a day, and at least one photo session a day. Suddenly song-writing took a back seat, and that was a huge mistake. *Anthem* was due to be out by May. That's when we were doing our next major tour – a massive tour. We'd gone from the university circuit into the big theatres. We'd be touring a lighting rig, a stage set, caterers, wardrobe department, the lot. We'd made it. We were there.

I had to do something about my weight in a respectable way this time. I've always had to keep my weight down. I've always liked my food, and even though I'm active and never tired, always full of energy, I have a tendency to be of a robust build. So Alan Seifert arranged for me to see a dietitian. This was the legal way of taking speed. The dietitian gave me diuretics and appetite-suppressants and instantly put me on what was called the Scarsdale diet. This meant boiled cabbage and grilled skinned chicken once a day. That's virtually all I ate. I might have a boiled egg in the morning, then I'd have cabbage and chicken in the evening, and that kept me skinny. I was never thin. I don't think I'm capable of being thin. My body is too strong.

Every Thursday I'd go and see the dietitian and he'd weigh me. Every Wednesday I'd start taking diuretics. These make you shed all your excess water. I'd literally pee my weight away, so that when he weighed me every week it appeared that I'd lost something when really I hadn't, it was all false. I was starting to feel not only physically but mentally exhausted. There was no rest at night. I used to lie in bed thinking about what must be done and by the morning at the side of the bed there'd be an endless list of things to do. Then I'd phone round everyone and say, we've got to do this, we've got to do that, you've got to get me this, get me that, we need this. I had a very good team of people around me. Alan Seifert had a wonderful PA called Kate. Kate had had good training, she'd worked for the Police (as in the band), and now she was working for me and she was literally on a twenty-hour day.

There were exciting things about this time. I could no longer travel on public transport. Even when I travelled in a car, other cars would stop and people would get out and run to get my autograph through the window. Being in traffic jams was interesting because no one watched the traffic lights or the other cars, they'd just stare at me. Driving down Baker Street or down Blackfriars or down Oxford Street, I'd see my face in every window. There were posters up everywhere. I was being sold everywhere. This was extraordinary. I didn't know about any of these deals. I didn't know the photo session I'd done the week before would suddenly be available as a poster in every shop window the following week. Someone, somewhere, was making a lot of money out of me because I certainly never received any for things like that.

One of the most rewarding things was the immense pride my parents were feeling and expressing, harking back to the serious doubts they'd had for me as a teenager, when they'd sat me down and told me that acting was a career with a low success rate. Suddenly now they were seeing their daughter's face in every shop window. Their phone was constantly ringing and they were actually enjoying the fact that journalists were on their doorstep. My father phoned me one day to say he found some children going through their rubbish bins trying to find anything to do with me – old letters, food packets, anything I might have touched. So my father invited them in and gave them tea. He was absolutely loving this new attention. For the first time my parents were able to be proud of me, and that was an extraordinarily settling feeling.

Amid all this attention, *Anthem* had to be finished. The album cover had to be conceived, designed and shot, and extra tracks recorded for B-sides on singles. Ironically, one of the last songs to be finished for *Anthem* was 'I Want to Be Free'. The band had come up with this incredibly poppy backing track and I was finding it impossible to write to. Again I was over-complicating the issue. Everything I tried to write to it was too serious for the actual music. What I love about writing lyrics to a track I've never heard before is that as soon as I hear it it portrays an emotion, and that emotion tells me what to write about. But everything I was trying to fit on top of the backing track for 'I

Want to Be Free' was just too earnest. So I turned to my book of school lyrics, lyrics I wrote around the age of twelve. I wrote them as poems, there was no lyrical form, they were just simple couplets. And there I found the seed I needed for 'I Want to Be Free': 'I don't want to go to school, don't want to be nobody's fool, I want to be free, I want to be me.'

That simple little section of words triggered the whole of the song. When I'd finished writing the lyric I phoned Nick Tauber and said, 'Nick, I've got an idea for that backing track, but you have to promise me you won't laugh when you hear it.' This intrigued Nick, and by the time I arrived at the studio and sat in front of the microphone, he couldn't wait to hear what was going to come out of me. Everyone was half-expecting to be totally embarrassed. I *was* totally embarrassed. The anticipation was embarrassing me. I'd never written anything as commercial as 'I Want to Be Free'. My songs had always been weird and strange and this was just blatantly in your face and written for a youth market. We ran it once and I sang with my back to the mixing desk because I didn't want to see anyone laugh. At the end of the song I turned round and looked at them, and got a huge thumbs-up – they loved it.

I put the main vocal down and then we got the whole band in for the backing vocals. Joel was bemused. He agreed that it was like nothing we'd done before and was very commercial, but I think we all felt we needed it on the album. In those days we wanted to give value for money. We refused to let Safari release single after single off the album. We'd only allow them to release two, and it was pretty obvious that those were going to be 'It's a Mystery', which was already out, and 'I Want to Be Free'. There were plenty of other potential singles on the album but we weren't going to let them rip the fans off. In retrospect I think we should have released more. The album itself sold incredibly well – it went to number 2 in the charts – but we could have kept it cooking for longer. Instead, we let it go and by July were releasing new material.

I had my first invitation to meet Royalty. I was invited to tea with the Queen Mum at St James's Palace. I half-expected to arrive at her private chambers and sit at the table with her eating finger sandwiches but it wasn't quite like that. I'd say I was one of at least five hundred people there. When the Queen

Mother arrived she was absolutely tiny, tottering on three-inch platform heels. You could see her coming from the end of the huge hall in St James's Palace. Her entourage eyed me warily as they set up a group of people at a time so that the Queen Mum could come past and give them all the Royal handshake. When they got to me, one took me aside and said, 'You will behave yourself, won't you?' I think they half-expected me to spit at her or something. As I was lined up, all the entourage kept their beady eyes on me and no one else as if I might nut her as she passed. The Queen Mother took one look at me and went, 'Oh, how extraordinary, what a wonderful colour!' referring to my hair. And that was my first meeting with Royalty.

The event was to celebrate youth clubs across Great Britain but it was terribly formal. Coachloads of children and adults had travelled from all over the country for that one moment, standing in this great hall with canapés being handed around. It wasn't a bad event for my first turn as a token celebrity. I think the real reason I was invited was to take the strain off the Queen Mum, because the kids would all be looking at me. And they were.

Chapter 24

For the past five years music had meant everything to me. Now suddenly my image was becoming more important than the music. I suspect there was more money to be made from my image than from the music; the music was becoming a good excuse to take photographs and create merchandise. But I had always intended to be a visual artist as well, and this was the greatest opportunity. Safari records gave me enough leeway and enough finance to put together a good creative team. Robert Labetta created my hairstyles and Pru Walters created my make-up. We were a good team. We used to meet up together, paper in front of us, pens and pencils in hand, and we'd just draw and draw until we found a look that we all agreed would excite a young generation; then the next week we'd go into the studio and translate that look into reality, using me as a canvas. This also created great press opportunities. The press liked nothing more than to announce weekly that Toyah had a new image.

To set up one of the images would take a whole day – four to six hours for make-up, and the same again for hair – and then it would be shot in a matter of half an hour. It was a long and frustrating day and it took a lot of patience. I couldn't eat during the day. If you're photographed after eating, your eyes look completely different; they sparkle far more if you haven't eaten. No wonder models are thin.

Another luxury of achieving some form of success was shooting rock videos, which I absolutely adored. My main directors were Godley and Creme, the partnership that emerged from 10cc the group. We would sit down and devise madcap ideas and see if the budget could stretch that far. For 'I Want to

Be Free' I wanted to sing sitting on top of a Sherman tank driving down Oxford Street early one morning. We could neither afford to hire Oxford Street and close it off nor persuade the GLC to let me drive a tank down it pretending to blow up all the shops. So instead we opted for a simple studio shoot.

It's cheaper if you can shoot a video in a day, so I'd be in the studio by 6 a.m. This would be having played Southampton the night before. Make-up would take until 10; then we'd start shooting and keep shooting until we finished. Sometimes that was twenty-four hours later. Then we'd go on to the next concert. Life was made easier by an awful lot of 'yes' people. People seemed to believe that what I said was right and must be done, which was very flattering, but I wasn't infallible. I did make mistakes and occasionally it would have been good if someone had said, 'No, stop there, we're going to do this,' but no one dared do that. I was very much running the show with very little critical input at all. So if I started to wane, if my energy started to wane, then the whole machine started to wane.

'I Want to Be Free' came out mid-tour, mid-May. It was to become a political song across the world. Stories reached me of how it was adopted by anti-apartheid demonstrators in South Africa and even by prisoners in the Maze prison in Northern Ireland. But that was later. When it was released, in 1981, I remember sitting with Alan Seifert in the passenger seat of the car, myself in the back and hearing it come on the radio for the first time. The sheer joy in knowing I wasn't a one-hit wonder gave me a huge boost of confidence, and believe me, I needed confidence because sometimes I felt I was no more than a publicity machine.

Everywhere we went we were mobbed. Fans would be fighting to get into the studio where we were shooting the video. When we arrived on the tour bus at a venue, the bus would be mobbed by fans. When we left the venue, we'd be mobbed by fans and most nights we were mobbed on stage by fans. The band and I came to expect riots at our concerts. We came to expect to leave the building with a police escort. We'd be on stage for two hours and most nights there'd be a further three hours of signing autographs at the stage door.

On one occasion in Liverpool I was in the car with Alan Seifert and the driver on my way to do a radio interview. I was late. We couldn't find the radio station, so we pulled up in a street and all I could see were crowds and crowds of people. I said to Alan, 'There must be a fire or a bomb or something. These people have been evacuated. Hang on, I'll get out and ask.' So I got out and asked someone if they knew where the radio station was. This person turned to the crowd and said, 'She's here.' And five thousand people converged on the car. It took an hour to get me into the building and then I just stood on a balcony and waved to people, a sea, a mass of people, blocking the streets of Liverpool; no traffic could move. I can tell you, that experience is better than any drug. It never wears on you. It always surprises you. And the amazing thing is none of these people really knew me. They knew an image.

It was around this time, late May, that I started to suffer something I'd never experienced before on such a level and that was guilt. I remember waiting in my dressing room to go on stage at the Ipswich Gaumont. The support band were on stage – we always took a support act with us – and all I could hear was the crowd chanting my name. It went on and on and on. You couldn't find any silence. And that weighed on me. Again, it was that old thing of the audience's expectation making me feel inadequate. But then I'd walk on stage and the roar was so loud it knocked me back. I'd start performing, then I'd see the front rows being crushed and the security lifting out the unconscious children and teenagers. And that made me suffer immense guilt.

The same happened with being mobbed. Arriving at a radio station, seeing thousands of people who had been waiting there all day. I just felt incredibly guilty. I felt a kind of responsibility and there was no way of either extinguishing that responsibility or taking it. Usually I'd arrived on time, I hadn't kept them waiting. But I felt as if I was the reason that these people were in some way being hurt. It took a long time to get over that feeling. In fact I never really have.

Later that year I played Drury Lane. It was Christmas Eve, a live TV performance to twelve million viewers. After that show I just sat in the auditorium with a bottle of whisky in my hand and cried and cried and cried. Kate came to find me and she asked, 'What is the matter?' and I said, 'Well I just can't handle this. I can't handle this sea of faces full of expectations. I can't help them as individuals.' I don't think Kate quite understood what the problem was. It was just like the feeling I used to have when I was younger after my recurring dream about my mother in a car on the top of a cliff, waiting for me, full of expectation, ready to drive the car over the edge if she didn't realise I was there. This was exactly the same experience. I couldn't nurture this crowd. I couldn't be a mother to this crowd. And this crowd all wanted something from me and instinctively I knew it wasn't music alone. So increasingly I was left with an empty feeling after performances. It wasn't fashionable to see shrinks in those days, so I kept my feelings mainly to myself.

I was beginning to have stalker problems after the release of 'I Want to Be Free'. A couple, male and female, had found out not only where I lived, but also my phone number. They would sit outside my house in their car every single day. T. used to try to dissuade them but that didn't get rid of them. They'd leave gifts on the doorstep and they'd phone every five minutes. And it wasn't as if they wanted something. They just wanted contact. You couldn't have a conversation with them. It would be 'What are you doing now? What are you up to? Where are you?' This really sent me over the top. I started to feel vulnerable if I was left alone, and it wasn't just this couple who were making my life hell. Children had found out where I lived too, so there were constant faces at the windows. I lived in a ground-floor flat, which meant that they could put their hands through the windows. If I bolted the windows shut they'd just break them open. Lyric-writing became impossible.

Another extraordinary thing about singing is that you continually have to save your voice. Except for people like Madonna who can afford to do one or two shows in a row and then have four days off, most singers are singing every night. And after each concert the voice completely shuts down, which means you have to remain constantly silent until the show the next day. Even then you don't know if you're going to have a voice. It's like a muscle that stiffens up and you have to get it flexible and moving to get it to work again. So contrary to popular belief, there was no partying after the shows. I would come off stage and go into a world of silence. The only person I'd whisper to was T.; he was very good at not making me talk. On the rare occasions I did try to have a drink with the band after the show, you could guarantee a confrontation would erupt in the hotel bar. T. was possessive and unbelievably jealous, and if any man tried to talk to me or make a move on me, T. would get into some kind of conflict. So life was easier if I just stepped straight off the bus after the show and went to my hotel room and soaked in the bath for two hours – in silence.

If I was to change anything in retrospect, I would change that. I would have partied more. I would have made sure I was a single woman. I would have had more lovers, been more experimental; I would have gone out and seen how trends were changing and how the world was changing around me. Instead, I was living in a bubble, and I was believing that the world was revolving around me, and it wasn't.

The rest of the year was constant touring – Germany, Holland, Switzerland, Norway, Italy, flying to all of them, a different city every day. In Italy, I was to play Milan Castle. It was a TV show and I was to be there on my own, to perform to a backing track.

Italy has a reputation for being somewhere where if more than four people gather on a street, the riot police come out and start shooting tear gas at everyone. This day was no exception. As I waited backstage to go on and perform 'I Want to Be Free' – it wasn't a sophisticated backstage area; we all had tents as dressing rooms – the audience climbed the castle walls and started throwing buns and cakes at all the artists. It was quite humiliating really. Funny in retrospect. Hundreds of people were trying to get into the castle grounds over two small, ancient drawbridges. The heat was intense. The Italians were impatient and started pushing each other – and then the riot police arrived and started shooting tear gas at them. Why, who knows. It was idiotic.

Before long the audience were starting to riot inside the grounds, and it was decided that the only way to calm them down was to get on with the show. I was to go on next. This was the first time I'd ever performed to a backing track on my own. It had been bad enough travelling to Italy without my fellow musicians – now suddenly I missed their company more than ever. Alan Seifert just looked at me and said, 'You've got to go on.' The audience were using anything they could find as missiles. The air was full of rocks, cans, glass, tear gas. My heart was in my throat. It was exciting and at the same time terrifying. The authorities were looking to me to calm everything down. I was a novelty in Italy. The press loved me – even though whenever I arrived in the country and faced the press conferences they always held, when they asked me about Italian politics I could never answer one question.

I always tried to be witty, learning that one from the Beatles. If in doubt, tell a joke, try and win your audience that way. The Italians were fascinated by me. To start with, my name Toyah was close to their swear-word *troia*, which means 'bitch pig'. So I used to come on stage to a deafening chorus of '*Troia, Troia, Troia*', and everyone laughing. They didn't seem to think it would insult me; it was just all one big joke. I realised the only way I was going to get their attention was to shout for it. 'Hi, there, Milan,' I shouted. You know, the usual cliché. Hello, Milan, we love you. Always open a show by naming the city that you're actually in. That's if you can remember the city you're actually in. The number of times I've walked on stage in Birmingham and gone 'Hamburg, I love you' I've lost count of.

It worked, I got their attention. The majority stopped fighting. I think the minority were just anarchists who kept on fighting throughout the entire show. I performed as if it was to save my life. Taking over the whole stage. Another lesson I'd learned was always to fill a stage. Never stand that still. Not in venues as big as this. Eventually the crowd calmed down, and by the end of my one song I had them all in unison, dancing, chanting, singing. Everything seemed to have reverted to normal. I looked at the side of the stage and Alan Seifert gave me a huge thumbs-up. So did the head of the Italian record company. It seemed to have worked. It was a success.

As I walked off stage back to my dressing-room tent, it became evident that something very serious had happened outside. One of the drawbridges had collapsed with about thirty people on it. Three apparently had been crushed to death. This was devastating. The head of my record company, Arista, wanted to get me out of there as quickly as possible. The audience in the castle grounds were dancing away, completely unaware of the catastrophe that had happened outside. Outside, the entire castle was surrounded by riot police. It seemed as though we were going to have to revert to bribery to get out.

Fortunately my record company representatives managed to talk us out of the grounds. It was quite late by now and Alan Seifert decided he wanted to get me out of the country as soon as possible. So a waiting car took me straight to Milan airport. I had a lot of trouble in airports in those days. Not many people with bright pink hair travelled. I was instantly presumed to be either a drug dealer or a prostitute. The police didn't let me down at Milan airport. As Graham, the record company boss, and Alan went to buy me a ticket, I was left standing alone. A policeman walked straight up to me and started questioning me in Italian. I kept smiling and saying, 'I'm really sorry, I don't understand you,' but he just kept questioning, and after a while he got really nasty. He pulled his gun out, held it to my head, and called me a British whore. This might have been triggered by my telling him my name, which could possibly have made him think I was taking the mickey, pointing to myself and saying I was a bitch pig. That might have just sent him over the edge. He grabbed me by the arm and started to try and drag me towards the police headquarters in the airport. I really panicked now, shouting for Alan and Graham.

Graham ran over and started talking to the policeman. It was evident that they were going to arrest me – what for, no one knew. But Graham pleaded with him, saying that it would be somehow or other diplomatically embarrassing. I could tell Graham was lying through his teeth. Anything to get me out of the grips of this policeman, who was now joined by six others, who were also determined to drag me off. Graham eventually succeeded. I think cash changed hands, but I didn't see that. But he must have done something remarkable. The police let me go.

By this time Graham was getting very worried. It had already been announced on the radio that three people had died at Milan Castle and he was scared that I might not get out of the country at all. It was quite possible that the police would blame the artists for inciting a riot, even though at the time of the deaths there were no acts on stage. Graham didn't want to risk it. He didn't want that kind of notoriety attached to my name. So he arranged for a car to drive me out of Italy that night.

It was a lonely and bittersweet journey, travelling through the winding roads of the Italian mountains. Roxy Music's *Siren* was playing on the car cassette. I kept looking at Alan. Alan was very quiet. This was the show that we needed to break me big-time, and it looked as if it was the show that was going to finish me off in Italy. I just looked out of the window, watching the night stars and the passing traffic. Secretly wishing for some sort of normality to come back to my life, again feeling guilty and responsible for what had happened at Milan Castle.

Back in England the next day, the story had already broken. And of course it was being sensationalised. I just felt numb. I did what I always do in situations like this and just buried my head in work, went to my room and started writing. I was starting to find it quite difficult to write positive lyrics with all this going on around me. I felt as if my fame was a bright light attracting negativity, as if because of my achievements, others had to suffer.

As a lyricist, I always tried to write words that motivated people, being fully aware that my audience were at a transitional stage in their lives, going through exams, starting careers. But I was starting to find that my words were becoming quite morose, reflecting my inner guilt. If my words had been angry, they would have worked, but they weren't. They were malancholic. I kept wishing for someone to come and help me put my life in perspective, explain what was going on and where I should be going. I wished that the silver man who had appeared in my dreams when I was young and given me advice would appear again and just guide me. Show me which direction to go in. There were so many possibilities. So many options. It was as if I was faced by myriad choices and only one was right, but I just could not find the right one.

I'd become a regular on *Top of the Pops*. It seems I was there at least twice a month and they were all like family to me. But one incident happened that I think caused me great problems for the future. I was walking from my dressing room at Wood Lane into the *Top of the Pops* studio when a fan who had got into the backstage area ran up and grabbed me. He got me in a complete bear hug and just kissed me smack on the mouth. T. grabbed him by the hair and pulled him off. This was in front of the producer and director at the time, Michael Hurll. I can remember T. being protective, but such extreme jealousy really was a problem. Michael Hurll took T. aside and said, 'Don't you ever do that to a member of the public again.' The next day, Alan Seifert got a phone call saying that we were to be banned from *Top of the Pops* if behaviour like that was ever seen again. After this incident, politically it was harder for me to appear on the show. A high chart entry was no longer a guarantee. The worm was beginning to turn.

This was 1981. The year that Princess Diana got married. Thatcher was Prime Minister. Everything was rosy. Materialism ruled, and everybody wanted as much as they could get. In a way I was becoming a symbol of that. Money was pouring in – even though at this time it wasn't actually in my pocket, it was there. I was becoming a symbol of success and excess.

'Thunder in the Mountains', my third single of the year had fantastic record sales in its first week and everyone believed that it would go straight to number 1. It went straight in at number 4 and stayed there. That wasn't a problem – I was pleased it entered the charts at all. Even though by now I was fully established and everyone believed that my career was set in concrete, that I was going to be around for ever, I never quite felt secure. That probably showed when I met other stars. I was always starstruck.

I travelled to San Moritz where I was to appear on the same bill as Grace Jones. I was in the car, trying to get to the huge circus tent in the town, traffic and audience jamming every road. I could see the tent but no cars were moving. I was due on stage in twenty minutes and my car was at least five hundred yards away, surrounded by fans; there was no way I could get out and walk. The car in front of me contained Grace Jones. She lost her patience, got out of the car, went to the nearest police car – which was also stuck in the jam – got in the back and told them to escort her to the venue. I was running behind with fans following me, trying to hitch a lift with Grace and the police, but they wouldn't let me get in. Later, backstage in the dressing room which I shared with Grace Jones – who was absolutely fantastic, very much the diva of Europe – she turned to me, looking at me in my Melissa Caplan mock-samurai outfit, with my bright pink hair, and said, 'You're a very brave girl to go out there like that.' I took it as a compliment, but I suspect it was meant otherwise.

The year was passing very quickly and the Christmas tour was upon us. That Christmas I signed ten thousand Christmas cards. The year before I think I sent thirty-two. Our fourth single of the year, 'Good Morning Universe', was due out at the end of November. Again it was to be a four-track EP – *Four More from Toyah* – as a gift to the fans. Sold for the price of a single. Huge discontentment set in among the band when we were sent off on a European tour; the single was due out in England first, yet we weren't there to promote it. Also there was no video to back it up. Safari records felt that the single didn't need any promotion, it would sell on my fame and its own merit. Well, it did, initially, it went straight into the charts at number 14, but then it didn't move. Meanwhile, we were touring Sweden, Norway, Denmark and Germany, all the time knowing that we should have been back in Britain pushing the single, because the higher we got it in the UK, the higher it would go in Europe.

We returned to England Christmas week to do five dates, by which time 'Good Morning Universe' was moving down the charts. As far as the radio was concerned, it looked as if the bubble had burst. As far as the concerts were concerned, it hadn't. They were huge, as exciting as ever. The audiences were as brilliant as ever. The year was to be rounded off with a great accolade: to appear live on Christmas Eve on *The Old Grey Whistle Test*. This wasn't just doing three songs. This was to be the whole concert. A whole hour of televised concert. It was the best thing that could have happened to us.

My voice was knackered after the tour. It's unnatural to sing for that many months, for that many hours a day. Guitar-players can change their strings, but singers can't change their vocal cords. So by the time Christmas Eve came, not only was I nervous and tense, which always shows in my voice, but I'd actually lost my top range. But there's a small miracle that happens when you go on stage. It's called 'doctor theatre'. No matter how lethargic or nervous or nauseous or sore in the throat you feel, once you step on that stage none of that exists, and somehow out of somewhere you manage to find your voice.

This was the culmination of many years of the band's hard work. There was no way we were not going to enjoy it or to let the small problem of my voice being knackered get in the way. This night we were going hell for leather. To say thank you to our fans and to say look, world, we're a band who can actually play. And we could play. We were always better live than in the studio. There was no room for modesty with this band. We were extraordinary live. The energy was rare and unmatchable. As I stood on the stage half-way through the set, and the intro to 'It's a Mystery' began, I had to control the tears running down my face. This was the song that had started it all, the song I'd so loathed – but tonight I really loved it. I was aware that my parents were watching, my schoolfriends were watching, my teachers were watching. All those who believed in me and all those who never did. It was an incredibly satisfying feeling. If ever I wanted to hold a sign up to a camera saying 'Hello Mum', this was the night. (I didn't.)

When the evening was over, the band looked at each other and we ran around the room screaming and hugging, crying and laughing. It was a fantastic end to 1981. A big party was held upstairs. Not only was this show over but the tour was over and we had Christmas off. As the party rolled on, I sat in the empty auditorium, bottle of whisky in my hands, and just cried and cried and cried. Partly through relief and happiness, partly through confusion. What do we do after this? We have twelve million viewers that night. Where did we go from there?

T. drove me to Birmingham. Dad was waiting for us. It was about 3 a.m. when we arrived. Dad made us a cup of tea and said how wonderful the show was. He was so immensely proud. I went to bed that night in full hair and make-up – and woke up in the morning, Christmas morning, looking like a gargoyle. I had no voice for Christmas Day, it completely packed in, but I had a great Christmas. It snowed. My brother and my sister, their spouses, T. and I all went tobogganing. I had a bottle of whisky in my hand as I sat on my toboggan going down the Lickey Hills. I had sunglasses on. My hair was wrapped up in a scarf. As I passed people they were going, 'That's Toyah Willcox.' I was pissed as a newt and euphoric.

My first paycheque, my first evidence of earning money, came that Christmas. Safari records gave Joel and me a cheque each for £6,000, as an advance on publishing. I'd never held so much money in my hands. They also gave us a VHS video recorder. Again, I'd never owned anything so expensive. Back then video recorders were very pricey, big and chunky. I gave both to my father. The £6,000 would help him wipe off some of his debts, which he had had since I was a teenager. And the video recorder could bring him and Mum a lot of pleasure.

I knew there was more money to come. We'd had four top-twenty singles. I knew there was more than £6,000 in the kitty. In the New Year, Safari records gave Joel and me a cheque each for £49,000. This enabled me to buy my first house – a three-storey terraced Victorian house in Whetstone, near Barnet. T., my brother and I set about doing it up in every spare moment. It was my first real home.

There was a kind of lull after Christmas. 1981 had been such a whirl. The beginning of 1982 was relatively quiet. The record company were leaving Joel and me alone to be creative and to gather our thoughts. A new album was due.

A very important habit in my life was prayer and visualisation. I've never been one for going to church, even though I adore music – all kinds of music, and especially church music. I've always viewed hymns and recitals as a language of God. But in my study I always keep a wax effigy I carved when I was eleven years old. It's an effigy of the silver man who appeared in my dreams. I love icons; I feel they bring you closer to God. This wax effigy I guarded with my life. If anyone ever touched it I would literally go for their jugular. This was the link between me and God. I'd hold it every morning and pray towards the eastern sun – for creativity, for happiness, for health, for the protection of my family. I've always been pantheistic. I've always believed everything is God. This wax effigy pulled focus and allowed me to visualise God as a nucleus, a body one could talk to directly.

There wasn't much Christian influence in my prayer, other than that of the ten commandments, never wishing others harm. I always begged forgiveness of my jealousy of others. But I found it incredibly important to visualise where I would like to be, where I would like to be standing in the future, how I'd like to be feeling, how I would like to portray myself to the outside world and be perceived by others. I'd visualise a huge audience in a huge stadium. All happy and smiling and in some way being healed by the experience I was offering them. Healing has always held great importance to me. I believe we all need to be healed one way or another. And we are all as individuals capable of healing others, whether it's through a small act of kindness, an unprompted gift, an observation shared without negativity, or an honest piece of conversation. We are all capable of healing.

One of the strongest images I was ever given as a child in my Scripture lessons was that of hell. Hell was full of food yet overrun with hungry people. They all held forks, but each person's fork was three feet long, so although they could reach to pierce their food, they couldn't reach the forks back into their own mouths. It didn't occur to them that they could feed each other. That's how I've always felt about my place in the community. Even though I can be extraordinarily selfish, stubborn, materialistic, I've always understood the karma of that story. There is no need to take, because if everyone gives, then we all receive.

Chapter 25

Ever since 1979 I'd been winning a lot of polls. Magazines had polls for best singer, worst singer, best dressed, most sexy. I was managing to win all the positive ones. In February 1982 came the Rock and Pop Awards – the biggest awards in the UK – and I was nominated for Best Female Singer alongside Kate Bush, Hazel O'Connor, Kim Wilde and Randy Crawford. The idea was that members of the public wrote in and voted for their favourite singer. I was desperate to win this, as you can imagine. The results were a closely guarded secret. No insider information could offer any clues as to who was going to win, or even as to who were the favourites.

I was to perform 'I Want to Be Free' at the ceremony, which was held at the Lyceum Theatre in London. Pru Walters, Robert Labetta and I were there all day, braiding my hair, Pru painting tattoos on to my face. I had an inkling I had won, just by the way the rehearsals were going. In rehearsals I'd rehearse my number and then there would be a gap, as if to allow an event to happen on the night, then on with the show. When the evening started, the Lyceum was full of the biggest names around. Hazel was there and we got to sit together and chat, make friends again and realise that we actually were very fond of each other. The Human League were there, wonderfully pissed, very giggly; Altered Images with Clare Grogan; Duran Duran, who were just making it big; and hundreds and hundreds of photographers – it was just a sea of lenses. The band and I performed 'I Want to Be Free'. I can't tell you how many times I'd performed that song in the past year. You perform a song so many times when it's a single that you become numb to it.

As we left the stage, cameras were following us off. It was at this point that I knew something was up. Dave Lee Travis, who was presenting, called Leo Sayer up to announce the Best Female Singer. I was standing backstage with cameras all around me. They announced me. The cameras homed in. I was so bloody excited. I headed to the front of the stage, to the podium where the awards were given out, and Leo Sayer passed me my award. Best Female Singer – Rock and Pop Awards for 1981. I'd won many polls – but actually to have an award in my hand . . . it was fantastically heavy.

I wanted to run straight off stage and phone Mum and Dad and say, 'Did you see it? Did you see it?' Instead, the photographers grabbed me by the arm and started pulling me around as if I was a piece of meat. It was a dehumanising experience. I didn't know them. They didn't know me. They needed a picture of me or they weren't going to be having any supper tomorrow night. They were all shouting, 'Look at me, look at me, smile, not a funeral.' None of them was particularly happy. None of them was sharing the joy I was feeling. All they wanted was their picture. 'Come on, do something, don't just stand there.' It was a verbal equivalent of being stoned in the biblical sense. A hail of commands was falling down on me when all I wanted to do was go and celebrate. Alan Seifert was nowhere to be seen and the band had been sidelined, so there was no one to save me. I was just stuck with these hyenas. But the *Daily Mirror* – as always in those days – did me proud: the next day I was on the front page as their winner.

Once I'd eventually got away from the press I spent the rest of the evening pissed out of my head with Hazel O'Connor and Simon Le Bon. I was so smashed I was carried unconscious from the building at about 3 a.m. A chauffeur delivered us home, carried me inside and put me to bed where I stayed all the next day, nursing a mother of hangovers, vomiting in every receptacle available, with poor T. sitting at my bedside wondering if I was going to survive.

You couldn't get better publicity than winning an award like that, and this was the time for making deals. Alan Seifert arranged for me to meet a merchandising company from Scotland who produced make-up. They were going to produce a line of Toyah make-up. I said to Alan that I wanted a creative input – after all, I'd been using make-up since I was twelve. Some company representatives came down to Alan's office in London and we had our first meeting. I wanted the line to be called Soul-Catchers. I wanted the make-up to reflect the soul. I always felt the need to look different on the outside because I felt different on the inside; I felt clothes and make-up should reflect your individuality, not reflect the norm. The company came out with extravagant predictions, such as that I'd earn £16,000 a week from the sales of this make-up. I didn't really care about the money. What I cared about was – since I'd already become a product name – that the product should be good. I wanted it to be exciting and to be unisex. Boys were starting to wear make-up, thanks to the new romantic movement, and I didn't want them to feel excluded from this range.

I flew to Scotland to see the factory, to meet the workers and to talk about colour with the colour-mixers. All in all it was a very satisfactory project. The end result looked fantastic. It was relatively inexpensive and my fans loved it. But this was a partnership that did not remain sweet for long. A journalist from the *Scotsman* went to the factory to interview some of the employees. Unbeknownst to me, they were on a minimum wage – £30 a week. The headline in the *Scotsman* read 'Toyah rips off the school-leavers'. This was my first taste of negative publicity. I hadn't earned any money from the make-up deal as yet. The £16,000 a week never materialised. Publicity like this did not help sales. Also, the company signed Adam Ant immediately after signing me and started selling an Adam Ant range of make-up – which I regarded as incompatible with promoting my product.

I had a meeting with Alan Seifert and told him that I wanted out. I didn't want to be involved with a company that underpaid its staff. I had a reputation for supporting young people, for inspiring them, and motivating them to make the most of their lives, and this was exactly what I didn't need. There's a saying in the business, 'Where there's a hit there's a writ' – and soon a writ was served on me. I'd done a photo session for *Jackie* magazine wearing no obvious make-up. They'd wanted a natural shot, as obviously that would be an exclusive, since I'd spent the last three or four years covered from head to toe in highly decorative make-up. My make-up company used this as an excuse to sack me, saying that the sales had dropped because suddenly I'd appeared *à la nature*. It was all very ugly, and time-consuming and exceedingly boring. Like most performers, I only wanted to be involved in the creative processes of life, not the breakdowns of life. This bad episode seemed to have a chain reaction.

In the past year, I'd been fighting off invitations to be interviewed from every magazine in the country. You couldn't pick a magazine up without seeing me in it – monthlies, weeklies, everything from *Cosmopolitan* to *Just Seventeen* to *She*. Judy Totton, my publicist, would beg me daily to do at least ten interviews. Suddenly, almost overnight, after the bad publicity of the make-up venture, no one wanted to talk to me. Ironically, this spurred me on. It was the challenge I needed. I was fed up of people expecting me to be outrageous, to look outrageous, to wear outrageous clothes. It had all become so predictable. Now it seemed they wanted me to be like that so they could ridicule me. What they didn't realise was that having been the victim of bullies at school, I'd learned how to deflect ridicule. So inadvertently, they fed my fighting spirit and I set about fighting back.

This is when I really started enjoying life. It was a strange kind of enjoyment. I was mentally tortured by the criticism I was receiving but at the same time fuelled by a fight for survival. I've always existed on conflict. I've always had to create conflict if it wasn't there. This was the first unpredictable conflict I'd come up against. And even though I was immensely unhappy, lying awake at night my thoughts twisted with confusion and self-accusation, I'd actually never been on better form. They wanted a fight. They were going to get a fight. A fight that they weren't expecting.

Joel and I consciously decided that *Anthem*, as wonderful an album as it was, was a little too 'poppy'. The singles were a little bit too youth-orientated. Our next album had to be darker. All through our early touring days, through East and West Berlin, driving down Germany's autobahns, we'd played one cassette tape many more times than any other and that was Peter Gabriel's second album. It kept our spirits up. It was a magnificent piece of work, produced by a man called Steve Lillywhite. So Joel and I decided we'd like Steve Lillywhite to produce our next album. It was refreshing having a meeting with Lillywhite because in the first few months of 1982, Joel and I had had nothing but accountant meetings that went on all day, every day. We were fed up with the bureaucracy of having earned a lot of money. Surprisingly, Lillywhite was up for working with me. My name was dirt by now, but people were bemused and still interested in me.

Before we started recording this album, one of the great disappointments of my life happened. Around the same time that the press turned on me, I turned up one day at Alan Seifert's office, opening *Record Mirror*, and there was a picture of me singing at Brighton. I was high up on the stage and the camera lens was by my feet, and the picture made me look as though I had not only two double-chins but a pot-belly. Underneath it said, 'Shock, horror, Toyah grows fat and old.' At the age of twenty-three. But that wasn't the problem. I sat at Alan Seifert's glass-topped desk and he said, 'I have some bad news. Nigel Glockler has just phoned. He's left the band.'

This absolutely broke my heart. Glockler was such a friend. When there were tensions among the band, he soothed the tensions. He had great humour. When my relationship with T. really started to deteriorate, Glockler was brave enough to stand between us and calm the situation down. When I had stage fright, Glockler was there to talk me out of it. I was absolutely mortified. I'd lost my best friend. And then, following Glockler leaving (to join Saxon), Adrian Lee, our keyboard-player, decided he wanted to go solo. Adrian Lee was the most brilliant arranger. He was fabulous at pointing out vocal mistakes I made. Joel and I were a wonderful partnership, but we needed their input. Their input perfected our ideas. Suddenly, Joel and I were no longer a band.

For the new album, called *The Changeling*, we took on board Simon Darlow, yet another wonderful keyboard-player, who wrote Grace Jones's hit 'Slave to the Rhythm' with Trevor Horn, and we hired on drums Simon Phillips. In the music world, Simon was legendary. He was a very strong move. Having Simon Phillips on board made the industry sit up and listen. Joel set about making demos in his little home studio. He only lived down the road from my new house so he'd just drop the tapes in. I was under great pressure because the public perception of me was changing. It was no longer a question of writing crowd-pleasing lyrics; I had to go much deeper, but I was finding I had a tendency to be melancholy rather than strong. When you write something you instinctively know if it works or if it doesn't. And I knew that the majority of what I was writing at the time didn't work.

At the same time, I was trying to create something new. A new persona, a new sound and a new approach. This was not the easiest or wisest thing to do. Many bands find a formula, a sound, and stick with it for the whole of their careers. Also the public have a tendency, when they find something they like, not to want it to change. I think generally, as a society, no one likes change much. It's an odd contradiction in terms: people like to discover someone new and for that someone to stay fixed in time. Very few artists manage to evolve. It's possible to stay the same and be successful, but that's not what I call living. For me, living is about change. Shedding your skin, starting again. And this was what I was trying to do with *The Changeling*.

Because I wasn't very grounded or very settled during this period, I found I had writer's block. My efforts to write were briefly interrupted when I went off to the BBC to star in the TV series *Dear Heart*, a teenage comedy show featuring a series of characters in a series of sketches. It was universally panned. The BBC at the time played safe with humour. *The Young Ones* was to start later that year, and change the face of British humour. *Dear Heart* was good, clean, healthy, Blue Peterish, Crackerjackish-type fun and my audience hated it. So I had that failure to deal with as well.

Another problem, once we were in the studio, was that Steve Lillywhite wasn't particularly interested in me as a performer. I was used to being the centre of attention, but Steve and Joel got on so well that I'd often arrive at the studio to find they'd gone out for a meal and then they wouldn't return for three hours, so of course on their return I'd be livid. I felt ignored and sidelined, and it was even harder to be creative when this was happening, but what it did add was an incredible sense of anger to my work.

I shocked everyone during the making of *The Changeling* by sacking Alan Seifert. Alan had become too possessive. He was determined I should leave T. In retrospect he was right, but sending a chauffeur round to my house with a suitcase and a heavy was not the right way to do it. I suspect Seifert would have liked to be romantically involved, but I was preoccupied. I had too many problems, at home and at work. Seifert didn't do too badly from the break-up. Joel and I paid him £75,000 for the privilege of losing him. Then, while still recording *The Changeling*, we had to set about finding new management.

We had meeting after meeting with people we really knew nothing about. Joel and I were always insular in our work, so we didn't know the industry inside out. We didn't know who was hot and who wasn't. We eventually found a company who had some great artists on their books – Brian Ferry, Roxy Music, Eno, Robert Fripp, King Crimson, Pat Metheny – and to whom Joel and I were more than happy to be signed.

Eventually, *The Changeling* was finished. It wasn't the album I wanted it to be. The record that inspired us to employ Steve Lillywhite in the first place, Peter Gabriel's second album, was obviously created by Peter Gabriel. There was plenty of animosity between me and Lillywhite. I don't see how it could have been any other way. Lillywhite later said that he regretted making the album. But in retrospect the album isn't that bad. It won us a new audience. Music was changing rapidly by this time. The new romantics were in. The gothic movement was starting, as was dance, in the rave sense of the word. *The Changeling* fell under the banner of gothic purely by accident. It was a dark and sinister album about alienation, about standing outside society, about wanting to shed your skin and emerge the reptile you felt you were. It was a very spooky album with very little joy and a lot of angst. It helped us shed a super-young audience and gain a more solid audience of twenty- to forty-year-olds. The tour following the release of *The Changeling* was the largest we'd ever done.

Having Simon Phillips on board, on drums, turned it into a real spectacular. Simon didn't just play drums, he exuded rhythm with a kind of sexuality that was mesmerising. What I loved about working with him was that if I shifted a phrase in my singing, he would shift the drum around it. We could actually have a dialogue on stage in the middle of a song. It was like having musical sex. It was so exciting to have this drummer who could play the most intricate of rhythms, but at the same time was listening to every member of the band; who was so heightened in his awareness that he could pick up when I was about to drop an improvisational sequence in and play with what I was doing.

The culmination of this tour was four nights at Hammersmith Odeon. These concerts were to be recorded in preparation for a live double album called *Warrior Rock* – which was later critically acclaimed as one of the best live albums ever made. In later years I learned, disappointingly, from our promoter at the time that he regretted not putting us in Wembley. Four sell-out nights at Hammersmith Odeon meant we played to sixteen thousand people in all. Our promoter admitted that we could have sold that many tickets four times over. He just didn't have the guts to go with it in case it failed. If he had gone with it, our future would have been very different. We'd have moved up to the next league. But it wasn't to be.

The Hammersmith Odeon concerts were phenomenally successful. The reviews were begrudgingly good. For example, they would say, 'Toyah performed with verve and energy. She sang with an incredible vocal range – if you like that kind of thing. The band were competent. Simon Phillips was phenomenal – if you like that kind of thing.' This severely affected our chances of playing in America. If the *NME* or *Melody Maker* slated you, the promoters in America took more notice of that than of your record sales or the fact that you were selling out Hammersmith Odeon four nights in a row. We were due to play New York when one scathingly bad review came out in the *NME*. The same day that review was published, the promoter in New York pulled our gig.

T. tried to alleviate my frustration by getting me out of the house – although this wasn't without its own frustrations. Everywhere I went there was an entourage of uninvited people. Shopping became an adventure: I'd get followed into and around the shops, which often made shopkeepers get nervous – once or twice I was even asked to leave department stores because the staff were worried that I was drawing so much attention that shoplifting would increase. The only place T. and I seemed to be able to find any peace was the great outdoors. We used to head for woodland areas and just walk and walk, dreading going home because of the telephone. And once fans found out where we frequented they'd be waiting for us on the pathways. So T. and I took to running. The fans tried to follow, but fortunately both T. and I were extremely fit and after half an hour's fast running we'd manage to throw everyone off our scent.

The rest of 1982 was really quite weird. If I was to give that year a name, I'd call it the year of my crucifixion. My sense of reality was adrift from the rest of the world. The band were playing to a certain level of critical acclaim. We knew we were playing better than ever and were one of the best live bands around, and we became very proud. We stayed proud and laughed at our critics. On the other hand, the big outside world was starting to see me as a passing fashion. The red hair that had been so fashionable in 1981 was being usurped by other colours – dull, monochrome colours like silver and black. That was thanks to the beginning of the gothic movement. My weird clothes were beginning to be seen as outdated, as designers such as Jane Kahn came into fashion and took over the look on the dance floor of *Top of the Pops*, with her huge gemstones and her short little skirts and bustiers. Also, my once outrageous look was now common on the street. Shop dummies in Harvey Nichols all looked like me. The wigs on the shop dummies in Selfridges all had geometric cuts. I had become the norm, but I hadn't quite realised it.

As I sat in my workroom one summer, Joel had presented me with a fabulous backing track to which I wrote a lyric called 'Be Proud, Be Loud, Be Heard'. A lyric about believing in who you are and what you are. An acceptance of who you are. Not putting up with others' criticisms of you. This song became a huge gay anthem. It was also the song I sang for what was to be my last appearance on *Top of the Pops* in July 1982. I designed a kimono-style coat with a huge Picasso-style splash on the back, my hair was tied up in little pigtails and I wore Masai beads. There were appearances on *Top of the Pops* in later years, but never in person; once the video age had arrived, they always used my videos.

Nineteen eighty-two was also the year when my desire to be both an actress and a singer was seriously frustrated. I'd been asked to appear in *The Beggar's Opera* on BBC2 with Roger Daltrey, but sadly the dates the BBC needed me conflicted with the dates of our short series of concerts around the country. It was a year when nothing seemed to flow. The energy was blocked. It was the year of the Falklands War. There was something wrong and destructive about this year. The whole year I'd felt like a victim, so my main energy was focused on not being one. Not allowing myself to be picked on, not allowing myself to be a scapegoat to the bullies. Perhaps my greatest weakness was that I could not be dispassionate about things I felt were greatly wrong. The Falklands War affected my writing during *The Changeling*. How could I write anything happy when on the other side of the world men were dying? My mental landscape had always been brittle, but never more brittle than now.

But if 1982 was my crucifixion, 1983 was to be my resurrection.

In January 1983 I received a phone call from Libby Glenn, asking me to go with her to the Mermaid Theatre to see a play called '*Trafford Tanzi*', a feminist play by the playwright Claire Luckham. This was the story of a northern girl trapped in a marriage to a bullying man. The whole play was set in a wrestling ring, and all the dramatic dialogue took place in the middle of a wrestling match. Julia North was the leading lady when I saw the play that night.

This was theatre at its most innovative. Here were a man and a woman, battling it out as equals in a wrestling ring. It was so exciting. And I had been asked to take over the lead. In the past two years, doing nothing but music, my heart had been aching to be acting again. I said yes immediately and thought about the consequences later. I didn't exactly relish the thought of running around the wrestling ring in a tight leotard. But I did get very excited by the thought of learning how to wrestle and having a major wrestling match at the end of the play in which my character would win every night. A perfect concept.

The Mermaid Theatre was in big financial trouble and my saying yes to the play gave the Mermaid the chance of staying open for a long time. Danny Hillier was to be my director and my co-stars were to be Neil McCall, Arbel Jones, Peter Ellis and Will Warrior. We had ten days to rehearse this show. Ten days didn't seem enough. In those ten days I had to get fit, learn the

249

whole script, and learn all the fighting techniques and the fighting routines. We had a trainer, Howard, an Olympic judo champion, who would start us off at 9 a.m. with a brisk painful run from the Mermaid down to Westminster, across the bridge, around, back over Blackfriars Bridge and into the theatre, where we would start rehearsing the play in the wrestling ring. When Danny wasn't rehearsing the dialogue, Howard was rehearsing the fight sequences.

There was so much to take in. My head was exploding, but every minute was fantastic fun. In the original play, the costumes were quite dowdy; they would have reflected exactly how female wrestlers looked up north. Just tights and a very baggy leotard. My costume was to be more glamorous. This was not what Claire Luckham intended; her play was about the nitty-gritty truth of sexism and poverty up north and what these things do to people. But all the same, the Mermaid were dealing with a pop star here and the guarantee of a sell-out run.

The Mermaid obviously realised that sex would sell. So my *Trafford Tanzi* costume was as sexy as a wrestling costume could be. I looked like a female version of Spiderman – without the balaclava and the suction pads. The European female wrestling champion Mitzi Müller was our guide and mentor; she took us to many a wrestling match where we'd sit at the front and scream on her behalf as she fought and spat and pulled hair throughout. Mitzi was divinely sexy off stage, very glamorous – and a right bloody animal on stage. The world of female wrestlers was hard and bitter. Not a world that I'd like to inhabit.

Amazingly, at the time of *Trafford Tanzi*, female wrestlers were not allowed to compete in central London. That's how sexist that business was. Mitzi saw my playing Trafford Tanzi as a major political boost to her campaign to liberate female wrestlers so they could fight anywhere in the country. The night the show opened, I was terrified. Safety was paramount. All the moves were for real, and we were throwing each other around the ring as if we were rag dolls. My main worry was just trying to remember the moves. There were so many of them; they were like a sequence of dance steps and I'd never been a great dancer.

But I had nothing to fear: the first night was fantastic. The audience was full of my favourite people. There was Rik Mayall, there were all the Radio 1 DJs, screaming and leading me on and giving me the greatest support. The play took the audience as much by surprise as it had the night I saw it. The reviews the next day were sensational. After a bitter year of battling with the press in 1982, *Trafford Tanzi* made 1983 the most critically acclaimed year of my life. As far as the press were concerned, I was back on form.

Trafford Tanzi gave me the most wonderful aches and pains. It was one of those shows where it was impossible to feel anything other than a great sense of achievement every night. And we knew it was a success when half the audience consisted of Japanese people. You can always judge a successful show by the number of tourists in the audience. So strenuous was *Trafford Tanzi*, that I was only allowed to do six shows a week. I wasn't allowed to do matinées; it would have been physically impossible. After each show I just had to go home and sit in the bath for three hours.

There was a phenomenon going on outside the theatre as well. Every single night, when I arrived at the theatre there would be anything up to three hundred fans waiting outside the stage door. These fans became like a family. They all got to know each other. Some even got engaged that summer standing outside the stage door. One idiot got on the roof of the building opposite and threatened to shoot me. He'd discharged himself from the army, said he had a rifle, got himself arrested. This was after he'd stalked me at my house in Whetstone for a couple of weeks. I was relieved to see the back of him. But the fans were leaving their impression everywhere. The stage door had to be repainted weekly because of the graffiti. The Blackwall Tunnel had nothing on it bar my name – at one point the authorities warned me that if this continued I would have to pay for it to be repainted.

But all in all, the fans were a joy. Before the show, and in the interval, I'd go out and talk with them. And after the show I'd spend at least an hour with them. They were different to the fans I'd ever known before. They weren't all mad for signatures, autographs and photos. They actually just wanted to chat. It had become like a social event. It was extraordinary. And as the summer became warmer, they started to camp outside, setting up little tents, competing for the best flower-bed to sleep on.

Every evening I went out and listened to them shaping their dreams. It was fascinating. These were really young people, people about to sit exams. They were too young to have been punks and weren't interested in the new romantic movement. They seemed to be exclusively interested in me.

Two months into the running of *Trafford Tanzi*, I had to start my new album. Joel and Simon Darlow, our keyboard-player, moved all their equipment into the gym at my house in Whetstone. Simon Darlow moved into my spare bedroom. Joel's home was only down the road, so he could go home each night. Our day would start at 10 a.m. We'd start demoing. Sometimes I'd just stay upstairs in my workplace writing lyrics, but most of the time all three of us sat in the gym composing. It was an extremely happy time. *Trafford Tanzi* was alleviating all my frustrations and negativity; I was in a really positive frame of mind. And because of that, *Love Is the Law* was one of the strongest and most upbeat albums we ever made. A lot of the lyrics were based on my relationships with the fans at the Mermaid.

'Martian Cowboy' was about an exquisite creature outside the stage door who appeared to have no past, no present, no future. He was just charismatic and homeless, and I was absolutely fascinated by him. For the title track, 'Love Is the Law', we called the fans waiting outside into the studio and got them to sing the chorus. It was very much an album for the fans who were so loyal and supportive through the difficult times.

By 4 p.m. I'd be tired of writing and I'd actually go to bed for a sleep. *Trafford Tanzi* was playing havoc with my body. It was so physical that my periods stopped and I lost a lot of weight – about a stone and a half. I found it hard to eat after the show. I wasn't really ready to do anything until 4 a.m., my body was so traumatised. Once we'd moved the making of the album back into the Marquee Studios, I'd go there every night after seeing the fans and work until 6 a.m. The fans would follow me there in convoy and sleep outside. The odd few stayed outside the Mermaid, but the majority were outside the Marquee.

This was the year I met Robert Fripp, my future husband, for the first time. My managers had invited me to a music-therapy luncheon at the Inter-Continental Hotel on Park Lane. Princess Michael of Kent was the Royal guest, and the press were everywhere. Princess Michael was obviously a fan, because she came running up to me in the VIP reception room and said, 'Toyah, I simply have to have my photo taken with you.' Then she turned round and grabbed this funny-looking man with little round glasses and said, 'Robert Fripp, I absolutely adore King Crimson, come, we must all have a photo together.' I didn't realise that my management also managed Robert Fripp at this time. I didn't know who Robert Fripp was. I'd never even heard of King Crimson.

The following week, a photographer sent me a copy of that picture, but he'd cut Robert off it. It showed just me and Princess Michael and this dismembered hand, holding a glass of champagne, which was Robert's. Ironically, that picture was in my kitchen until I married Robert four years later. But at this luncheon, I didn't even talk to Robert. I just looked at him briefly, and thought nothing of it. There was no instant attraction. There was nothing. It was just one of those brief coincidences that didn't have any meaning until I met him again two years later.

My twenty-fifth birthday fell during the run of *Trafford Tanzi*. On that night Tom Baker was in the audience, and so was Roger Daltrey, who came backstage to speak to me. He wanted to do a film with me, but we didn't think it could happen until the following year. By the end of the evening I was on cloud nine. Simon Darlow and the band took me for my first Japanese meal on Baker Street. It was the most blissful birthday I've ever had. I was so happy.

But I was desperate to change my image. I was becoming a cliché, a parody of myself. The pink hair was so expected it was irritating me. So one morning I went to my hairdresser Keith Wainright at Smile and said, 'Keith, take it off.' He refused. Instead, he gave me a Mohican, a wonderfully aggressive haircut. It was exactly what I was looking for. When I stepped on stage that night, Will Warrior, who played the referee, burst out laughing, came up to me and whispered in my ear, 'Oh my God, what have you done? 'You were so beautiful before.' I had been going through a beautiful period – my body was well toned, my hair had been like a lion's mane – but I hadn't felt right. I hadn't felt I was making a statement any more. The Mohican definitely made a statement. It was the ideal image for promoting *Love Is the Law* and the first single off it, 'Rebel Run'. It allowed me to create a tough eco-warrior persona, which was a step away from people's expectations.

Chapter 26

At the end of May, I was called to Granada TV to meet a director called Rob Knights, who was going to direct *The Ebony Tower*, a TV film adapted by John Mortimer from John Fowles's book. The story is about a famous artist, his two muses and a visiting journalist. One of the muses was to be played by Greta Scacchi, the artist by Sir Laurence Olivier, the journalist by Roger Rees. They wanted me for the second muse. I was up against Patti Love, a fabulous actress who I worked with at the National Theatre. I'm a fraction younger than Patti and I think that's what won me the role, as well as the fact that I had red hair.

The day I got the role was the same day Libby Glenn got the phone call from Granada asking if I'd be prepared to dye my pubic hair red. Libby, in a panic, wondering how she could approach me about this, phoned my managers. What I didn't know at the time was that my managers then phoned Robert Fripp to tell him about this extraordinary girl they'd just signed for management who'd just been asked to dye her pubes bright red for a film. Robert said he never forgot this. It intrigued him, made him want to meet me. Libby eventually plucked up the courage to ask me if I would do it; my instant reaction was 'no way José'. Red pubes, can you imagine what that would look like? TV advertising of Tampax hadn't even started by then. It was a taboo. I couldn't do it. It was bad enough that I was going to have to do a lot of nudity – more than I'd ever done before. I'd only ever done topless nudity in films before; this was to be full body nudity and I was pretty nervous about it. I mean, what girl in her right mind wants to do a nude scene with Greta

Scacchi. It's artistic suicide.

Trafford Tanzi finished its run successfully in June 1983. Financially, it saved the Mermaid; the theatre could stay open for another year. I was ready to leave it. I was quite exhausted and my body was showing signs of terrible fatigue. I had a week off to shoot the video to 'Rebel Run' and then immediately started rehearsals on *The Ebony Tower*. The transition to working for Granada TV was like going from driving a Ford Escort to driving a Rolls-Royce. They really looked after you. They really treated their stars like stars and this was just what I needed after a long and exhausting run of *Trafford Tanzi*. A car picked me up from my house in Whetstone and drove me to Granada's headquarters in the West End.

Making my way upstairs to a conference room, I passed Lord Olivier. He had no idea who I was and he asked me the way to the nearest Gents. I was struck by his frailty. There had been rumours about how ill he was but I didn't expect it to show so much. His body looked as if it was giving up on a very strong spirit. I suspected that like Katharine Hepburn, once the camera rolled he would be as strong as he'd ever been. Inside the conference room sat Greta Scacchi, a lovely, voluptuous, flirtatious person who seduced everyone she met – not intentionally, she just had that way about her; Roger Rees, who was very similar to Derek Jarman in many ways, in that he loved people, loved to talk about other people, was always interested in getting to know them; and the director, Rob Knights. We had lunch together and talked about the story. I told Rob Knights that I was nervous about the nudity and he promised that when it came to those scenes, he'd strip off as well. I found this amusing. Rob wasn't exactly a muscleman. He was as slim as a stick. I thought, if he's got the guts to do it, then I've got the guts to do it as well.

The next time we all met was on a Lear jet which took off from a private airfield just outside London. It was exciting, flying in a private jet; even though it only sat the four of us, we had our own air hostess, who opened up a cool box full of champagne. We were flying to the Dordogne, where the film was to be shot.

During the flight, we managed to consume six bottles of champagne. By the sixth bottle, we discovered that there was no toilet on the jet. The journey was two hours. By the time we landed, we were all cripplingly desperate for a pee. As the Lear jet pulled up on the tarmac outside the airport's main building, people were all looking out of the windows to see who it was. Usually in these circumstances, I would walk slowly into the building, posing, but as we were all about to bust our bladders, we just jumped from the plane and ran inside as fast as we could.

The Ebony Tower was shot in a magnificent château, owned by a countess who always wore a black dress with little white polka dots. She looked just like the guinea fowl that roamed the grounds. The château was old and antiquated but it had brightly hand-painted wooden beams across the ceilings. The whole place was glorious; it was seductive – perfect for John Fowles's *Ebony Tower*. In contrast, our accommodation was a motel in the nearby town. Well, at least there was a local bar. Lord Olivier stayed in an exclusive château up the road, and we were put on a rota to have dinner with him.

On the first night, Greta, Roger and I all visited Lord Olivier for dinner. He was the kind of company who liked to hold court. He enjoyed regaling us with stories of his life and I enjoyed listening to him. He was an utterly charming man, articulate, with a lust for life that obviously had never faded. He could be repetitive in his stories, but one forgave him. He was such a charmer. It didn't take long to learn what his passions were – a bemused dislike of Marilyn Monroe, an obsession with his second wife, Vivien Leigh, and a great love for Joan Plowright and his children, whom he obviously missed enormously all the time we were away in France.

It was quite easy to steer Laurence Olivier on to certain subjects. He was always willing to talk. Nothing was taboo; very little was private. And let's face it, there was so much to talk about. This was the man who had set up the National Theatre, where I first worked when I was eighteen. I loved his company. I was utterly starstruck. I wanted to absorb every moment with him. After that first dinner, it was usually me alone who would eat with Lord Olivier. The others wanted to go off and have adventures.

Lord Olivier took a particular liking to me. In the beginning I think he liked the commotion I caused walking into this super-posh château with my bright red hair and punky clothes. He enjoyed the stuffy waiters having to serve me champagne. And Lord Olivier did like his champagne. I was ordered by the producers to allow him only three bottles a night. We always managed to polish off six. By the sixth bottle I would press my hand against Lord Olivier's and say, 'Sorry, Sir, you're working tomorrow.' And he'd give me a wicked little grin and he'd go off to the toilet. He'd come back, we'd have a five-minute conversation and he'd go off to the toilet again. I thought, His bladder isn't that weak, and on his third exit I followed him out. He wasn't going to the toilet at all. In the grand hall of the château was a cupboard that housed a selection of fine brandies. Many were over fifty years old; some cost about £60 a shot. Every time Lord Olivier left the dining room, he was trying a new brandy.

Lord Olivier took being told off like a naughty public schoolboy. He knew that it was only words and that I'd let him carry on drinking as long as he wanted. But when his personal assistant, Valerie, came downstairs, she would not tolerate any misbehaving. It was very evident at these meals how ill Lord Olivier was. He had to take about thirty pills every half-hour. He had survived stomach cancer. Goodness knows what he was suffering from when I worked with him. I knew he was a haemophiliac, but his spirit was so vibrant, so full of life, and so willing to continue living. I knew his willpower was keeping him alive, and probably that alone.

Our filming days with Lord Olivier were very short; he was only allowed to work three hours a day. The mornings were spent shooting scenes he wasn't actually in, and doing our close-ups and medium shots for the scenes he was in. Lord Olivier would arrive around 1 p.m. and go through make-up, and then we'd work with him till about 5, by which time he was genuinely exhausted. He always offered to work on, but we never allowed him. We couldn't afford to push him too hard. If anything had happened to him, the film would have had to be scrapped.

Olivier had a bedroom to rest in between takes; I would often go up to this room and lie on the bed with him. It looked out over the château grounds. It was beautiful. The sun would stream in through the windows, and typically this wonderful French bedroom had billowing white linen curtains. We'd looked out of the window and we'd just gossip. I was supposed to take him through his script, help him learn his lines. We'd read the scene once or twice, then he'd get bored and start talking about his past. I don't think he told me any great secrets. I don't think he told me anything he hadn't already written about in one of his autobiographies. But I didn't care. Here I was in the Dordogne, in the beautiful French sunshine, lying on a bed with one of the most important and influential actors of all time.

I would trade stories about Katharine Hepburn and George Cukor for stories about Monroe. Unlike Katharine Hepburn, who was such a feminist, Lord Olivier was very much a gentlemanly sexist and I adored him for it. He found working with Monroe tedious. He wasn't attracted to her. He felt she had too many lackeys and he couldn't tolerate the fact that she had an acting coach on set. Her timekeeping was deplorable and he didn't think she was that great an actress. All that said, he admired her for her strength and for the attention she gave to detail.

But the one person he always talked about without any prompting at all was Vivien Leigh. He exuded such a mix of emotions whenever he talked about her. There was hate, dislike, professional jealousy and an intense love. An obsessive love. One day, as we lay on the bed, he'd grown tired of learning his lines and suddenly went off completely at a tangent. Out of the blue, he said, 'She became such an extraordinary actress.' I looked at him and said, 'Sorry, Sir?' (I always called him 'Sir', which partly irritated him and partly amused him.) 'Sorry, Sir, who are you talking about?' 'Vivien, Vivien Leigh – she went mad you know.' 'When was that?' I asked. 'We went to Hollywood, it didn't suit her. She went completely mad. She went into a mental home. I thought she'd never come out. I thought she would never return. But when she did come out of the mental home, her acting was phenomenal.'

I know very little about Vivien Leigh. The only information I've ever had about her was from Laurence Olivier. I worked out from what he was telling me that his second wife was troubled. She went mad, was put away; everyone thought her career was over. She came out of the mental institution and made a film, and she'd become an incredible actress – just like that. This really shocked Laurence Olivier – and also threatened him. What was so wonderful about Olivier was his competitiveness. He was competitive with everyone. All his life he had been the best and he still wanted to be the best. Every night he told the story at dinner about making *Marathon Man* and how Dustin Hoffman was a method actor and Laurence Olivier was a traditionalist. Dustin Hoffman wanted to do everything for real and Olivier turned to him and said, 'Can't you just act?'

But with Vivien Leigh, it was different. It was as if Olivier was still trying to work something out. How could she have become such a phenomenal actress after such a debilitating illness? He then moved on to talk about her death and he was genuinely still in grief. He told me how he'd been called to her flat in London and found her on the floor where she had fallen in her death throe. He went to pick her up and he found that she had passed urine as she died. He said this with a morbid fascination. I didn't want to reply in case part of that fascination was his fear of his own mortality. The whole reason someone like Lord Olivier is still alive after so many illnesses is that they believe they cannot die, and I didn't want to fill the room with that subject.

One evening after a day's filming, 'Sir' and I were drinking kir royales on the lawn of his château. We'd got back on to the subject of Marilyn Monroe and what makes a person sexy. I was stuffing my face with olives and putting the pips into an ashtray. After five minutes, I realised that Sir was crunching on something and I looked around the table to see if there were any nuts. The waiter hadn't brought any nuts. Olivier was telling me a story about *The Prince and the Showgirl*, and as I was putting my olive pips into the ashtray, he was scooping them up with his arthritic hands and putting them into his mouth and crunching them. In a nanosecond I had a conversation with myself. 'Do I tell him those are my pips he's eating or do I let him carry on?' I couldn't bear to think of the humiliation he would feel if he realised without my telling him. So just as his hand went to place more pips in his mouth, I said, 'Sir, those are my olive pips,' and he looked into his hand and said, 'Jolly tasty they were too,' and spat the rest out.

Greta and I had to do our first nude scene relatively early on.

It was a very simple long shot with us sunbathing naked on the lawn of the château. T. had come to visit that week – I was worried he would see me do these nude scenes because he'd made me promise I wouldn't do any. A physical impossibility considering the story is about sexually charged Bohemians. Fortunately, for this particular scene, T. wasn't around.

Being naked didn't bother me at all. In that kind of environment and that kind of heat, it felt perfectly natural. I actually quite enjoyed it and I didn't feel too self-conscious lying naked next to Greta Scacchi. When T. reappeared I didn't bother to tell him, I just thought I'd have to live with the consequences when the film came out.

T. had come over to France because I was lonely. OK, I was eating with Lord Olivier most evenings, but back at the hotel I was lonely. Greta had a constant stream of friends visiting her and the others regularly went into town to see French films, but I didn't speak French and was feeling very much a stranger in a strange land. So even though T. and I quarrelled quite regularly, it was a relief to have him around. After a few weeks, he returned to England. This was great timing because we had to shoot an epic picnic scene, in which Lord Olivier and Roger Rees were picnicking with Greta Scacchi and me – both of us completely naked. I didn't want T. around. I didn't know how he would react, so it was lucky he wasn't there.

The day we shot the scene was dull and overcast. The make-up girls painted both Greta and me a deep brown to make us look as if we'd been sunbathing for a whole summer. And as Rob Knights promised, he stood behind the camera absolutely stark-naked. It was a comical sight. The weather was cold, so his manhood had shrunk very noticeably. Also as promised, it was what we call a closed set – only those necessary were present, to minimise our embarrassment. Greta and I just kept dressing gowns on until we went for a take and then we discreetly slipped them off.

I was on my knees next to Lord Olivier, who was in a deckchair. He'd accidentally scraped his skin against a rusty bolt on the deckchair and his skin had simply opened. The nurse came on the set and gave him some pills, otherwise he would have just kept on bleeding. There wasn't much blood. The shocking thing was the ease with which his skin tore; it was like paper. By the end of the scene he had bruised terribly. As I knelt next to him, naked, shivering, feeling quite stupid, he turned to me and whispered, 'I wish I was thirty years younger.' He was such a charmer. He always said the right things. I don't think he meant it. I think he sensed my nerves. He reacted to Greta very differently. Greta was very confident and self-aware, and knew the effect her astonishing beauty had on those around her. She slipped her dressing gown off with great self-assurance and strolled over to the blanket on which she had to lie with not an inkling of modesty. She was perfectly happy naked.

I didn't notice what Sir referred to, but he turned to me and said, 'I do hate women who have hair down to their knees.' She didn't have hair down to her knees, but for some reason Greta's confidence niggled Laurence Olivier. Greta wasn't a massive star by this time – she'd made *Heat and Dust* and was going on to make bigger and better films – but she had a huge following and had gained lots of respect.

What astonished me about Greta was that at the time she seemed such a laid-back actress. She didn't bother to learn her lines till we were actually on the set, or so it appeared, much to Rob Knights's annoyance. Yet, extraordinarily, when we saw the rushes back at the hotel, she was absolutely spot on. She never gave a duff performance. Occasionally we had to do a few takes because she was learning the lines as we went along, but the takes were magical, they were fluid, effortless and totally natural. Now that bugged me, because I worked so hard, so consciously, I was so nervous and so wanted to be good. I put in a hundred per cent effort. Greta, seemingly, put in ten per cent effort and came out smelling of roses. But this is a girl fluent in four languages.

After the picnic scene, we had to shoot a sequence where Greta and I took a skinny dip in the lake. Greta had a great fear of water. Having come from Australia, she had this anxiety that all water was inhabited by sharks. None of us took this very seriously, and she was quite happy to shoot the sequence where we swim out into the middle of the lake. Again we were working on a closed set, so only the camera, sound and assistants were present. The main people to get rid of in a nude scene are the electricians. They tend not to be the most subtle of people, and you don't want beer-bellied men gawping at you when you feel vulnerable and slightly ridiculous in your birthday suit.

Greta and I tiptoed into the lake and swam out towards the centre. As we kept on swimming, the lake got colder and colder. I felt nervous because it seemed so deep. It wasn't as if I could put my toes down and rest on the bottom. The water was murky, so we couldn't tell whether fish were near or not. But Greta started to panic. She turned to me and said, 'Something's touching my feet, Toyah, something's touching my feet.' I said, 'Greta, calm down, just keep swimming.' Her breathing became erratic and I told her to try and control her breathing. She said, 'No, I can't go. I can't keep going. There's something at my feet. There's something at my feet.' Then suddenly she shouted, 'It's a shark!' I said, 'Greta, we're in a lake in the middle of France. There are no sharks here.' But in her panic she dipped under the water. This terrified me, so I dived right down and grabbed whatever I could find first – I think it was her left breast – and pulled her to the surface. I held her there and tried to calm her down, to see if I could get her swimming again. But by this time she was in tears. So I started to do the backstroke and I pulled her along with me – a technique I was taught at school – shouting all the time to the shore, 'We're in trouble, Greta's frightened, we're coming back.'

After a few yards I was exhausted. Greta was a much bigger build than me, and much taller, and I was finding it hard in the cold to battle with Greta and keep swimming. I was about ten yards from the shore when I shouted, 'I really need help, I'm tired, could someone help me?' Out of the corner of my eye I caught our divine make-up artist Suzie throwing off wellington boots, her trousers, her jacket, getting ready to dive in and help us – when suddenly out from behind the bushes came all the electricians, who'd been hiding and watching all the time. So all these men came to help us, leaving Suzie stranded on the shore in bare feet and very few clothes.

Rob Knights charged into the water and tried to cover Greta's modesty. She needed calming down; she was very, very upset. It was terrifying just to think about the possibility that she might have drowned. If she'd been out there on her own I think she would have – there was no one close by, no one in a stand-by boat in case of an emergency. I was left on my own with Suzie to cover my modesty while the rest of the team went off with

Greta to make sure she was all right. It was a bit of an anticlimax, but Sir Laurence Olivier ambled over, clasped my hand and told me I was very brave.

The next day we discovered that every scene we'd shot the day before just wasn't usable because the skies were so overcast; we were going to have to shoot it all again. This came as a blow because I had woken up that morning with a huge sense of relief that all the nude scenes had been shot. What was more, T. was due to return to France for the very week the re-shooting was rescheduled.

About half-way through filming, news arrived from England that Sir Ralph Richardson had died. Because Lord Olivier lived in a protected environment, we heard before he did, which presented the problem of who should break the news to him, and how. We were all greatly concerned about Laurence Olivier's frail health; we didn't want to do anything that might shock him, or make him feel vulnerable. His young spirit was struggling enough against his failing body. We didn't want to be the messengers who reminded him that death might be waiting for him as well.

Rob Knights and the producers decided that Roger Rees would be the best person to break the news to Lord Olivier. Roger had the sensitivity needed for this. Dear Roger, he absolutely dreaded it. He was in tears as he went off to the château. But apparently Lord Olivier took it very well. He sat there in silence for a bit, then turned to Roger and said, 'I knew I'd outlive that bugger.' This so summed up Lord Olivier. He was so competitive even with those he loved. Over the next few days he did nothing but talk affectionately about Ralph Richardson, recounting the times they'd worked together, recounting conversations, recounting their friendly competitiveness. It was as though if Ralph Richardson hadn't existed, Lord Olivier would have lost a vital spur in his life. It was this competitiveness that drove him to be creative; he needed the conflict and competition of other talent around.

We all kept a beady eye on him over the next few days, making sure he didn't get depressed. We were sensitive enough to know when he wanted to be silent, and now he wanted to be silent more than usual. So we left him alone with his thoughts; we could tell he was desperately missing a friend.

* * *

On a lighter note, I heard that 'Rebel Run', the single from *Love Is the Law*, had entered the charts at number 25, and while I was filming in the Dordogne, my video was about to play on *Top of the Pops*. I was starting to feel a little forgotten in France, so this news gave me the attention I was craving. Safari records chartered a plane and flew out a gaggle of music journalists and we all spent a day together playing in the château, me pretending to be a grand film star, and them behaving as journalists do on a great big freebie. Normally I'd be nervous if a planeload of journalists were coming out to see me, but after all the critical acclaim for *Trafford Tanzi* I still had credit on my credibility, and for this day I was put on a pedestal and treated with great respect.

A big treat was that Radio 1 wanted me to be interviewed alongside Sting. This meant I had to take a private plane from the Dordogne to Lyons where Sting was performing at the stadium. Ann Nightingale flew over to take me on this journey. It was nice to get away from the confines of the filming unit and be a pop star for a day. Ann Nightingale, T. and I boarded a tiny little prop plane and went off on an adventure. In Lyons we went straight to the stadium and stayed backstage with Sting and the Police. I hadn't seen Sting since filming *Quadrophenia*. By this time he and Frances Tomelty had separated, and he was with Trudi Styler. Trudi was very protective of him. Not that for one minute I would ever consider nicking anybody's man. And beautiful as Sting was, I always saw him as a friend, never as a lover. He was far too beautiful, far too dangerous for that. Sting was so pleased to see me, he insisted that I sit on stage with him throughout. So perched precariously behind his bass stack, I looked out over the auditorium for the whole of the concert.

And what a concert. It was perfectly honed. The band moved smoothly and effortlessly from one song to another. When Sting wanted to go from bass to guitar, a roadie discreetly walked on stage, took the bass and started playing it; when Sting wanted to go from guitar to bass, another roadie discreetly walked on stage, took the guitar and started playing it. It seemed everyone was a multi-instrumentalist. It was the smoothest, slickest, most exciting show I'd seen since Bowie played Milton Keynes in 1983. I could scarcely believe the journey Sting had made from that hotel bedroom in Brighton where the poor guy tried to teach me harmonies to this massive auditorium in Lyons. He was still the same person. He was still as approachable. But someone had sprinkled him with stardust and professionalism, and I gawped the whole night in pure admiration for what he had become.

After the show was utter mayhem. The Police had to get out of the building before the audience left the auditorium. Sting grabbed me and Trudi and we just ran. It was thrilling, running down the corridors of this sports stadium, everyone trying to grab Sting – his own staff, fans who'd managed to sneak backstage, the police (the uniformed variety) who were there to protect him. All suddenly turned on him and wanted a piece of him. He kept his grip on me. We burst out of an exit and rather than jump into limousines, the whole entourage jumped into four waiting taxis – the best way to disguise the fact that Sting was in the vehicle.

There was no one there to organise us, so Sting jumped into the front seat, pulled me in and sat me on his knee (rather an affectionate thing to do, but in hindsight, I think I was there for him to hide behind). Trudi and T. got into the back, and slowly the taxi made its way through the departing crowds, who were all banging on the window. The journey went on for ever, even though we just had to make it across town to the local radio station, where Trudi got Sting out of the car and into the nearest shower. He was absolutely soaking in sweat; he needed to get dry and warm as quickly as possible, so as to protect his voice. We sat on the steps waiting.

When Sting was washed and changed, we all went up into the recording studio and recorded our interview. It was full of friendly affectionate banter about the past, about how we'd both struggled through working men's clubs, nightclubs, pubs – you name it, we'd played it – to get where we were today. We somehow got on to the subject of families, of which I never wanted one. Sting had already started his. Out of the blue, Sting announced he wanted as many children with as many women as possible. He was always full of bravado, he knew he didn't mean it, and Trudi was just on the other side of the glass. Their relationship was relatively new so no doubt she was feeling a bit sensitive. When Sting turned to me and said that he wanted at least six children by me, I looked at the glass and waited for T. to react. Thank God he had the grace not to, realising it was a joke. Then I looked at Trudi and gave her a big smile, aware of how vulnerable she must have felt – trying to let her know that I had no intention of having any children with her partner!

After the interview, we bundled into big black limousines which drove us across the border into Switzerland. It was a long drive, two hours. Once in Switzerland, the night was so black I couldn't see where we were, but we kept ascending and ascending and ascending until eventually we reached the castle where the rest of the band and the crew were already partying. I didn't know anyone at this party, and I was quite tired. I'd been filming earlier that day and I had to fly back to the Dordogne the next morning to be filming again by midday. Sting disappeared and the only other person I recognised at the party was Andy Summers. So T. and I disappeared to our room for a good night's sleep.

All my life my dreams had been so vivid that it was hard to tell if they were real or not. That night, sleeping in a converted barn next to the castle, I had such a horrendous dream about three witches who were decapitated and burned that I had to wake T. The witches were trying to tell me something, and every time I tried to slip into a peaceful sleep, they were back there as vivid as ever, bloody, wretched and angry. After three attempts at sleep, I got T. up and we went out into the grounds. It was 6 a.m. and still dark. I was so frightened I couldn't face sleeping again. Walking around the grounds, we found our way into a maze, in the middle of which was a life-size chess set. I was pretty freaked out by now, and seeing these tall, still figures, all I could make out in the darkness, just added to my paranoia.

In the morning I told Ann Nightingale about my dream. She did a bit of research and discovered that yes, three women had been burned for witchcraft at the castle. The trial had been in the barn where we slept. The message that they had been trying to convey to me was that they were innocent. They were just maidens, picked on by the married women in the village. As our car drove us away, I felt hugely relieved to escape from the castle and be returning to the Dordogne.

On the film set, all were beginning to get restless. As beautiful as the location was, everyone wanted to get home. Everyone except me, that was. I loved the escapism. It allowed me to forget the product I'd become and just to be myself. I kept trying to entice T. to go home early on his own, knowing that we had to re-shoot the naked picnic scene. But he was all too aware of the pressure I was putting on him, which made him even more determined to stay. I was living in a state of anxiety, knowing how he would react when the time came. Well, I thought I knew – nothing could have prepared me for how he actually did react.

I started not to discuss the next day's filming with T., so he never knew where I would be. This was out of character for me. T. always knew every move I made. In England I didn't mind this at all; I needed his protection and needed him around. Before I came out to France he had insisted that in no way should I do any nudity, and in no way should I shoot the picnic scene. But I was an actress. I really didn't give a damn about nudity. OK, I felt shy doing it, but I saw no reason not to do it. It was an integral part of this play and I really disliked T. for trying to influence me.

This was the beginning of the end of our relationship. The more I tried to detach myself from him, the more obsessed with me he became. I started to feel very claustrophobic in his company and we began arguing more and more. The day of the re-shoot, I didn't tell him that the whole crew were going to decamp to a lake an hour away from the château, hoping that in no way, if T. got scent of what we were doing, would he be able to find us. I would just have to face the consequences later.

The day was a complete duplication of how we had filmed it before, except this time there was glorious sunshine. It was also our last day's filming, so even though everyone was tired, we were all happy at the thought of going home the following day. The make-up girls had painted Greta and me from top to toe in fake tan as we stood naked in the forest. By this time we weren't so shy, which made the whole event much more relaxed. Again I knelt at Lord Olivier's side, completely naked.

We were half-way through shooting this scene when suddenly there was a commotion behind me. T. had found his way to the location and obviously had been watching, getting more and more agitated. Suddenly he ran on set, grabbed me by my arm, pulled me to my feet, called me a fucking slut and wrapped me in a dressing gown. I felt intense humiliation and embarrassment as T. tried to drag me away. I knew exactly what he was going to do: take me to the car and drive me away. Rob Knights tried to stop him and there was a terrible row, at which point Laurence Olivier gently touched my hand and said, 'I'm so dreadfully sorry.' I looked at Olivier and apologised profusely. The poor man was ill and tired and here was this shit going on. Eventually some of the electricians, with whom T. had become friends, managed to calm him down, and get him off the set, by which time both he and I were in tears.

We continued filming the rest of the scene and then wrapped the entire film. It wasn't a happy wrap. The entire company knew the tirade I was about to face and they were helpless. They couldn't intervene. I said my goodbyes to Rob, Greta, Roger, and Lord Olivier, then sat wordlessly in the car with T. He insisted that that night we drive to the coast and get the ferry back to England. I sat in silence. I couldn't speak to him. Michael Jackson's *Thriller* played on the car cassette and we drove through the night. On the ferry, I tried every minute of the crossing just to get away from T., to stand on the deck and watch the sea as the coastline of France disappeared. I had to, had to get away from him.

Chapter 27

This was the end of our relationship, but it was impossible. Whenever I tried to go to work alone, he would follow me. Whenever I phoned someone from the house, he would sit and listen. Even when I decided to act normal in an effort to get him to ease the pressure, he remained suspicious. Deep down he must have known I was doing all I could to get away from him. It actually took another two years – and the intervention of the man who was to eventually become my husband – for me to be free of T. In the meantime, our relationship went from bad to worse, which in turn affected everyone and everything around us.

Throughout the rest of the year, I lived in an uncomfortable silence. The outside world perceived me as a happy, successful, rich superstar. But at home I was walking on eggshells. Every conversation had to be preconceived. I had to make an extra fuss of T. in order for him not to feel I was about to leave him. I'd lie awake in bed, staring at the ceiling, praying for something, anything, to intervene, because I did not know how to get out of this situation. I couldn't drive. I couldn't exactly just walk out of the house, and I didn't know where to run to or where to hide because I knew that if I disappeared T. would seek me out. So I decided to sit it out.

This was made extra difficult by the press's fascination with the filming of *The Ebony Tower*. They all wanted to know about the nude scenes. They all wanted to know what it was like to be naked next to Laurence Olivier. I've never been one to be shy of the press and I hated having to censor my personality and my words. The press were particularly interested in John

Mortimer, who adapted the story for film. John was present on the last day of filming. He was a wonderfully gregarious man, full of life and conversation, and he was quite open about the fact that he'd like to see the filming of the picnic scene. I made the huge mistake of mentioning this to the *Daily Mirror*, who lapped it up. Joking, I called John Mortimer a dirty old man. I'd have said it about anyone and everyone present on the set. It was a Toyah-ism. It was an affectionate expression about a man I really respected. That weekend, the middle-page headline was 'John Mortimer was a dirty old man'. John was very forgiving of me. He realised that it was a saying taken out of context, but it was the beginning of a long and bitter battle between him and the *Daily Mirror*, and I'm sure that somewhere along the line it has affected me in the professional world. That day I learned my lesson not to give the press too much, certainly not at the expense of my personal relationships.

I was under so much emotional strain that I felt I needed to escape from my image, so I went to my loyal hairdresser, Smile, and asked them to cut my hair short and dye it black. Joel was at my house when I returned and when he opened the front door to let me in, he stared at me in disbelief. He'd never seen me look normal. He was a perfect gentleman. After a minute's silence, he said, 'Oh, you look wonderful.' And all the time I could tell he was thinking, My God, she's really lost the plot. We were getting ready for a short Christmas tour. It was cold and miserable, the worst time to be singing. Our new management didn't treat us with kid gloves: they were a hard and raw company who saw our temperament as a result of spoilt behaviour, so they made sure never to spoil us. This tour was difficult because we didn't have anyone mollycoddling us. Some of the venues weren't even heated. We weren't used to this. We'd been used to the real star treatment. But we just had to get on with it, and we did.

By this time, tours were blurring into one another, but one incident held this apart from the rest. The culmination of the tour was a show at London's Shaftesbury Theatre. This was one of the venues that hadn't been heated; as I sang, I could see my breath vaporise in front of me. The audience were huddled together, still in their coats. In the audience were two boys who

271

looked like wonderful peacock Mohicans, adorned in effervescent colours, beautiful jewellery, beautiful clothes and fantastic make-up. These boys talked throughout the show. Through the quietness of the intros and the introspective parts of songs, all I could hear was their talking; it was as if they were taking the piss out of me, and it really annoyed me. No matter what I was going through on a personal level, how oppressed I was feeling as a person, I was still a control freak. But nothing I could do could get these boys to stop talking. Every time I looked at them, in the quiet moments, hinting for them to shut up, they just talked more. My attention made them more excited. So I went up to my dressing room that night feeling particularly riled.

Outside, the street was full of fans. The London shows always turned into a bit of a party for them. They were climbing the fire escapes. We had to move from room to room to get away from them, also to discourage them in case one of them fell. As I sat with Joel in a quiet dressing room, there came a knock at the window. I looked at Joel and thought, Oh my God, we're three floors up. Looking out of the window, to our astonishment we saw the two fabulously decorated boys. Joel and I jumped to open the window to save their lives and pull them into the room. They were so excited, they were jabbering gibberish. Neither Joel nor I could fully understand them.

Then, to my horror, I realised they were both deaf. One of them, Mark, would lip-read what we were saying then translate in sign language to his friend. I hadn't seen this from the stage, but in the dressing room it was evident that they were a partnership. The one couldn't exist in the outside world without the other. They explained to us that they were trainee hairdressers; that they loved my lyrics and loved the music – they felt the music through the body and received the lyrics by watching my mouth. The noise and the commotion in the audience that night had been Mark signing the words of the songs to his companion, for when Mark signed he'd verbalise as well, not realising how audible he was or how incomprehensible were the sounds that came out of his mouth. This moment taught me such a lesson. I was so ready to prejudge people, to prejudge situations. I was on the defensive all the time. Not only because of my personal life, but because of my work as well. I had started to project negatively about everything, and that attitude had to change.

Around the time I met these boys, I was receiving paintings from an eleven-year-old girl called Rachel. They were extra-ordinarily naïve paintings, very beautiful, and like all naïve art they held a very personal truth. Rachel would send me paintings of landscapes with rainbows on the horizon, but her rainbows didn't consist of the colours one would expect. Everything was jumbled. Her landscapes were purple and green and pink and blue. Rachel was blind. But she had developed in her mind's eye a sighted world, a world where she decided what colour a tree was, what colour a field was. I used to get wildly excited about her paintings, just as she got wildly excited about my lyrics and the music from the band.

I now saw that disability is a false word; after all, aren't we all disabled by the fact that we're going to die? Rachel had turned her so-called disability into something unique. Mark and his companion had turned their disability into something that made them unique. All that was disabling them was the attitude of society. We were living in a time when we couldn't accept diversity as a gift to teamwork. It wasn't yet 1984, yet we were all so happy to live George Orwell's dream of uniformness, of sameness, of safe identity. Yet here were people, the essence of individuality, who, if we could involve them in our everyday lives, would change our habitual way of thinking. Everything had to be so black and white. Everything had to be categorised, and noted on paper. We were surrounded by bureaucracy and sameness. On the night of the Shaftesbury Theatre show, I realised that this was my problem. Life wasn't all about external image. I had to start to think differently. I had a desperate need to evolve. I was stuck in a quagmire of jealousy and possessive-ness and the world was projecting on to me an image I'd outgrown and a role I was no longer prepared to live. It was going to take time, but I had to change, I could change, and it probably wasn't going to be easy, it probably was going to be painful.

Early in 1984, I spent some time in Switzerland, doing the usual rounds of TV promotion, still singing 'It's a Mystery' and 'I Want to Be Free'. On a rare occasion I went to a nightclub after a TV show; my hosts were two photographers, who proudly called themselves paparazzi.

With great pride and much laughter, they told me how they had used to earn a fortune stalking Princess Diana, how they followed her through a skiing holiday, getting as many close-up shots of her as they could, driving her to tears. I found this really ugly and shocking. I sat there listening in disgust with a false smile on my face, trying to work out how anyone could be proud of doing anything like that. They didn't see Diana as a human being. They saw her as an income. They had no sympathy for her whatsoever.

I arrived home from Switzerland to some pretty terrible news. A friend of ours, Stephen Waldorf, a video director, who was one of the Finchley boys who acted as security men, had been shot in the chest by police while driving along Kensington High Street. It was a case of mistaken identity. The police had thought he was an escaped convict, a dangerous man who dealt in arms. On hearing about this, I broke down into tears, at which point T. turned to me and told me to stop being so melodramatic. 'Why are you so upset?' he said. 'It hasn't happened to you.' We set about trying to find out what had happened to Stephen and where he was. We were particularly close to his sister Miriam and her boyfriend Lester. Lester had been in the car with Stephen when he was shot, and in his fear had run off and left him there. Stephen survived the shooting and the police were very embarrassed. They had almost killed an innocent civilian.

I didn't want Mum and Dad to know how unhappy I was. In fact, no one knew how bad it was except Joel, and Joel and I were soon to be parted for ever. Joel was making noises that he wanted to work with other artists. He didn't want to work exclusively with me. I was very possessive of Joel; it hurt me that he felt he needed to work with other people. Our management were also making noises that I would actually make more money for everyone if I was a solo artist and not a band member. So heavy hints were being dropped suggesting that Joel should go his own separate way. What no one realised was that Joel was an integral part of who I was.

A little light relief came during this period when I met a film producer called Mona Bauwens. Mona was a young Arab girl who looked all of twenty-two, but it was hard to tell her real age. On her twenty-first birthday she had reputedly inherited £20 million from her father, who was the treasurer of the PLO. Mona lived in a block of flats owned by the family on Curzon Street. She was producing and financing a film called *Murder, the Ultimate Grounds for Divorce*, in which I was to play Roger Daltrey's wife and Lesley Ash was to play his lover.

The film was shot in Hastings and it gave me six weeks of bliss. It was an utterly unremarkable film, even though Roger, Lesley and I worked our rocks off. The director was cracking up during the making of it; my solicitor was part of the production team and I have to say he was eccentric; the film was beset with problems – but we, the cast, had a great time. And out of it grew a wonderful friendship with Mona that lasted many years.

Mona was remarkably generous. She'd phone me up and say, 'Toyah, darling, come round, we'll get a takeaway in.' So I'd go round to her apartment. The takeaway would consist of a knock at the door followed by the entrance of fifteen staff from the White Elephant club across the road, all dressed as butlers, carrying half a side of beef, dozens of chickens piled up on top of each other, fruit, veg, massive desserts. They'd place all this on the table and Mona would say, 'There you go, Toyah, help yourself.' I'd laugh my head off, saying, 'Mona, it would take two of us a year to eat all of this.' She'd say, 'Don't worry, take what you want and then I'll call the staff in.' So we'd eat what we wanted and lo and behold, all the staff from the rest of the building would come and finish the takeaway off.

Mona simply dripped money. On one occasion, I went shopping with her in Knightsbridge and she forgot her credit card, so I said she could use mine. Within half an hour in one shop alone she'd bought £2,000 worth of jumpers. She wanted me to go to Monaco to a ball being held by the King. She said, 'Of course, Toyah, it's fourteen nights, a party every night. You'll need a different ballgown every night. And, if you're to be one of the in-crowd, each ballgown has to cost at least £10,000.' I said, 'Mona, not in my wildest dreams could I afford that.' She said, 'Don't worry, you can borrow mine.' I never went to that ball. Mona must have paid in the region of £140,000 for the privilege of being there.

She introduced me to Imelda Marcos, who brought her

daughters to Mona to be introduced to London society. Imelda Marcos didn't look like a dictator's wife. The only thing I remember about her is that she refused to smile because she thought smiling would give her wrinkles. So every time I cracked a joke, she would laugh from the head down: her face would remain perfectly unchanged, while the whole of her body shook with laughter.

For a year I went everywhere with Mona. I could talk to her about T. She was also kind enough to get on with T. and never stirred it between us; in fact, she was a bridge between us. We'd all go and watch Prince Charles play polo, we'd sneak into the White Elephant and watch Roger Moore gambling at the casino tables, we lived a life of excess together. This was the materialistic eighties in full swing.

My management were very much a conservative management. Of the two leading figures, one was an heir, the other the treasurer of a high-powered organisation. They were very much Thatcher's stars. This Thatcherism was rubbing off on my lifestyle, and my fans were becoming greatly disgruntled with me. I had always been a spokesperson for the underprivileged, for those who were different, for those who needed a voice to stand up for them, and now suddenly I was living like a queen. I didn't realise it but I was snubbing them. I was desperately looking for a way out of my intolerable home life. Also, I felt I'd worked hard for many years and now I wanted to party. In retrospect, I realise that I was running away from problems rather than facing them; meanwhile the problems were just getting bigger and bigger.

It was evident I'd gone as far as I possibly could with Safari; they were still a small independent record label. The only way for me now was to enter the big league and sign with a major. I started to have meetings with CBS records, which had a particularly good track record for women singers. Its president, Maurice Oberstein, had set about making his dream come true – for CBS to sign all the great female artists in the country. He'd signed Alison Moyet and Carmel, to name but two. It was A & R man Muff Winwood's job to go around the country and sign the rest. I was one of them.

CBS didn't want me as a package with Joel. They wanted me as a solo artist. This really hurt. I was desperate to make it to the next league, but was torn between commitment to Joel and commitment to my life dream. Joel was already becoming a little spiky to get on with. He was no longer a person I could see any time of day, any day. One had to book ahead because he was working with other singers. So I bit the bullet and decided to sign with CBS without him. My last conversation with Joel on the phone was bitter and sad. It was the only time we ever had a real disagreement and it was many years before we were to talk again.

I took comfort in the fact that CBS also had Paul Young and Bruce Springsteen. They were setting up a new label called Portrait; I was to be the first artist released on that label. In retrospect, it was an act of madness to have gone with that. New labels have teething problems and those teething problems would reflect on me. But they put me in the studio with a fantastic producer called Chris Neil who had a history of working with women – such as Cher, Sheena Easton, Elaine Paige – and that gave me confidence. I spent the whole of the summer of 1984 writing and demoing, meeting as many writers and co-writers as I could, piecing together the album that was to become *Minx*.

Not only was home life difficult, but life with my management was becoming increasingly difficult. They were of the opinion – unless it's the best, don't do it. They'd set me up with the acting agency ICM; it was felt that unless it was to be on a major feature film, I shouldn't work, and of course these major feature films never came. Not even off the back of the success of *The Ebony Tower*. My management also turned down my chance to perform on the Live Aid single and at Wembley. They just scoffed. They said, 'Oh, it's a charity thing. You don't need to be seen to do charity work.' It wasn't until they turned down an artist called Madonna that I realised that perhaps they had lost the plot as well.

I was feeling quite numb not having Joel around. The recording of *Minx* which took place just off Baker Street, was very luxurious. We had full orchestras, the best musicians in the world, the best songwriters, the best song arrangers. I started to have singing lessons so that my voice would be at its peak. It was a well-honed album, but it was not what my fans expected. My fans had evolved with me throughout the punk era into the early eighties; they still expected a raw quality. The last album they had heard was *Love Is the Law*, a good, raw, simple gothic album. *Minx*, by contrast, was a highly polished theatrical album. Even though I liked it, it was a massive departure from what my fan base was used to.

The promotion for *Minx* was really slick. I starved myself for weeks to shed a stone in weight, going to the gym constantly. I found the most amazing dress in Hyper Hyper on Kensington Church Street. It was a small black rubber dress that fitted like a second skin, and once on had to be polished with Mr Sheen to make it shine like liquid rubber. This was the dress I wore for the first single, 'Don't Fall In Love'. The promotional shots were done by Terence Donovan, who later also shot the video. I was starting to look like a mature woman. It was a very classy and classical look, a look that gave me great confidence. I immediately started travelling Europe, promoting 'Don't Fall in Love'. I travelled with just my personal assistant, Kate. It made the experience a happy one.

Kate had the awesome job of zipping me into the rubber dress. I had to be completely starkers under it and covered in talc. She never protested. She was a very patient and supportive person. My first shoot was for a TV show that took place on the set of *Das Boot*, the huge German TV hit at the time about a German submarine. While shooting the video for this programme, we allowed tourists to continue the regular hourly trips around the set of *Das Boot*. These took place on little trains, which travelled past piled high with hundreds of eager tourists with cameras in hand. As we did the many takes on 'Don't Fall in Love', I grew accustomed to the tourists trundling past and I just ignored them.

It was very hot under the lights and I started to sweat profusely. Rubber doesn't exactly breathe. The first problem we encountered was that of sweat running down my legs. This greatly embarrassed me. I didn't want people to think I'd suddenly become incontinent. So we kept having to stop mid-take to towel down my legs. We soon gave up on that and just accepted that the sweat couldn't be seen on camera anyway. Wearing this black rubber dress was like being inside a sauna. As I sweated more and more, the dress started to move around my body. And exactly on cue, as if with a consciousness of its own, just as a train full of tourists came past and stopped for them to take photos, my dress decided to exit my body. With the power of a rubber band retracting, it pinged from my body down to my ankles, leaving me standing there completely naked. My audience whooped and cheered as I tried to pull the dress back up but the dress had a vengeance. Having left my body, it had cooled and shrunk to the size of a pea and decided to stay firmly shrink-wrapped around my ankles.

Chapter 28

In May 1984, I shared a cab from my management office with Robert Fripp, a man I'd met only briefly before. We were going to a hotel where we were to be guests at a music-therapy lunch. I decided to tease Robert all the way. My managers were quite shocked by this, knowing that Robert was rather an earnest character; they weren't sure how he was going to take being relentlessly teased for half an hour. Robert took it very well. He's like a little professor, gentle, witty, capable of piercing sarcasm, never predictable and always surprising. We arrived at the hotel being photographed together by the paparazzi and disappeared inside. In the reception room, Robert asked me if I would appear with him and Sting on a charity album he was making for a school in Washington DC where he taught. I was very flattered by this and said yes, of course. So we tentatively arranged a date for the following month, June. I thought little of it and went about my life as usual.

I was working with Tony Banks of Genesis on a song for a science-fiction film called *Redwing*, in which I was to appear as a holographic star. Tony Banks left me to my own devices with the lyrics and vocal arrangement; it was a very satisfying piece of work. After this I was to join Robert at his house down in Dorset, to work on an album of children's stories. I was to be the narrator. The album was called *The Lady and the Tiger*.

There was much intrigue in the management office about my working with Robert Fripp, and I couldn't understand why. My managers told me to be careful. They said Robert had a reputation. They accused him of being a dirty old man, and said he'd spy on me at every opportunity. He'd ask me to dress up in strange clothes and expect me to participate in strange practices. I didn't quite know what they meant; I was remarkably naïve. I'd only ever experienced two long-term relationships, neither of which was particularly unusual sexually.

Robert arranged for a car to pick me up from my house. T., unusually, let me go on my own. The car drove me from north London down to Dorset, to a small country village called Witchampton. I'd never been to Dorset before and I found it rather spooky. I instinctively thought it was called Witchampton because witches had been burned there. We pulled into the drive of Robert's house, which was a large country affair, and the driver decided to go and knock on the front door to make sure we had the right house. He came back with an odd look on his face. He said, 'Are you sure you want me to leave you here, miss?' And I said, 'Yes, why?' He said, 'Well, the gentleman's just come to the door in a bathrobe. Do you know him?' I said, 'Well, no, I don't really know him.' Suddenly my managers' warnings came flooding back into my head. I said to the driver, 'No, I'll be OK, I'm sure it's all all right.'

Robert showed me up to the top floor of the house which was to be my home for the week. He was still in his bathrobe. As we hit the steps of the top floor, he said, 'Do you like dressing up?' and I thought, Oh my God, what have I got myself into. I said, 'Well, only when I'm on stage.' Robert opened a wardrobe and showed me his clothes and said, 'Well, there's some clothes here – if you fancy wearing them, they're there,' and then he disappeared, leaving me for half an hour to unpack. I kept looking around, in case he was spying through a spyhole; by now I was really suspicious. Not wanting to disturb any of his belongings, I just sat on the sofa and looked at my surroundings.

I was in the attic. It was an enormous attic. It wasn't a normal attic. It had been completely refurbished. It was a warm and sunny with many windows. The walls were covered in bookshelves and there were pieces of furniture and plants everywhere. In the corner was a mattress on the floor, and on the far side was a bathroom which had a window facing into the attic room (now that made me nervous). It was a completely self-contained attic, with a kitchen as well. I just sat there looking about me, feeling a great sense of peace at having escaped my house in Barnet. There were also the beginnings of nerves about starting work with Robert Fripp, who by now I knew more about and realised was a bit of a legend.

While I sat and waited for Robert to return, a woman appeared from behind one of the many bookshelves. I said, 'Hi,' but got no reply. She was dressed completely in black except for a white lace hat. Watching her walk around the room, I assumed she was Robert's wife. Then, out of the blue, she walked straight through the bathroom wall. I jumped to my feet and shouted, 'Oh shit!' This brought Robert up the stairs. I said, 'You'll never guess what I've just seen.' Robert wasn't surprised at all. His house was so haunted, workmen would not stay inside unless accompanied by another living soul.

All I had to do that week was narrate children's stories to music Robert had already prerecorded. It was not a difficult task. Robert was charming to be with. He was a healing influence and I needed a lot of healing. T. phoned regularly to make sure I wasn't up to anything. Robert was a perfect gentleman on the phone and gave no cause for concern. He wasn't that interested in talking about T., but he acknowledged he knew of a problem.

Instead we talked about our dreams and aspirations. Robert had had a very varied and colourful life. To me he appeared boastful about it – about the conquests, the sheer quantity of women he'd had relationships with. Robert was twelve years older than me so he'd had a lot more sexual practice than I had. In later years, he said he was trying to prove himself to me, to prove his masculinity. What he didn't realise was that as he described one conquest after another he was making me distrust him more and more. I couldn't quite marry the image of this little nutty professor with someone who'd had a sexual past equal to Hugh Hefner's. The only stories I could swap with him were stories of violence and alcohol excess. In this strange way, sitting up into the early hours of the morning, we got to know each other.

At the end of the week, Robert gave me a big hug and made me promise that I would come back in a month's time and actually write some new songs with him. I was very happy to agree to do this. We were good friends. He was wonderful company, and I felt safe with him. What I didn't realise was that in that month, he went over to America and told everyone that he'd met his wife and was returning to England to marry her.

When I returned to his home a month later to write, our relationship intensified. We used to sit up all night talking, but this time the stories of his sexual conquests took a back seat. We talked more about him, the real person in the present day. We wrote two beautiful songs. They were songs written by two people falling in love. The first was 'Mothership' – about the first experience of touch in the moments of first love – and the second was 'Freedom', which reflected my desperate need to be exactly that. That week together was so special. It was an unrealised courtship. At the end of the week, Robert turned to me and said, 'I've known all along you were my wife. I don't want to waste any time. Will you marry me?'

I was totally shocked by this. I was desperate to find some space and heal my mind. I'd spent five years in a pretty intense relationship. OK, it did have happy and wonderful moments, but the last few years had been intolerable; what I needed now was some space. I had no wish to hurt Robert. So I said, 'I just need a little time. I have a major problem to deal with. A major obstacle in the way.' Robert was very understanding. So understanding that he came up with my route of escape.

With the help of our management, we were to put it to T. that I was to go away for a few days to Berlin on a promotional tour. In the meantime, I started secretly to remove clothes from the wardrobe and the drawers at home and hide them at my management's office. My passport was updated. Kate went out and bought me new underwear – the one thing I couldn't make disappear without T. noticing. I started to get really nervous and feel terrible guilt. I knew that this experience was going to be painful for both T. and me, and I was dreading the moment when I would have to phone him and tell him I wasn't going to return.

There was also the problem of property. I owned the house. All my collateral was in that house. For the moment, my management arranged a bridging loan and I bought a penthouse in Wapping, overlooking the Thames. This would be where I would live when I returned. Everything was like an undercover operation. I had to check myself before I spoke in case I gave anything away. The pressure was so bad, I felt as if I was on the verge of a nervous breakdown. But what kept me going was the hope of freedom. The hope of living a life where I could be myself, and wouldn't have to check myself every minute of the day in case I said something that would upset someone who by now was as unhappy as I was.

The big day came. A car was to collect me to take me to Heathrow. There I was to pick up my tickets for Washington. I hadn't been to America before; that was awesome in itself. I hadn't flown alone before; that was making me nervous. I gave T. one last hug and kissed him on the cheek and told him I'd be back from Berlin in two days. I stepped into the car, which had already picked up my luggage from my management office, and I cried all the way to Heathrow.

Kate had given me a cassette to listen to on the flight over. It was Kate Bush's *Hounds of Love*, the greatest album of the eighties. Not only did I cry all the way to Heathrow, I cried all the way from Heathrow to Washington. I'd spent five years of my life with T. It was one hell of a five years. I'd gone from obscurity to fame, from rags to riches. We'd had some phenomenal times together. The beginning had been good. He'd had to live in my shadow for the whole of those five years, and that had tormented him. I felt terrible grief at what I was about to do to him. I kept praying and praying that he would get over it and rebuild his life. Because no matter what we had been through, I really didn't want to hurt him. But the only way for us to start our lives afresh was to be separate, and we just had to face the pain of that hurdle.

Sitting next to me on the plane was an official from the White House, who couldn't help but be aware that I was crying non-stop. He never pried into the reason for my tears. Instead, he talked to me about what it would be like in America. I told him I was meeting someone very special to me, and I was. I stepped off the plane and there was Robert Fripp, waiting for me on the other side of customs to help me begin my new life.

I'd left England without telling anyone what was happening. It was of the utmost importance that none of my friends knew that I was leaving T. It wasn't that they weren't trustworthy, but at the slightest slip of information T. would definitely have come after me and just brought me back. And I never told my parents about any of my problems. I wanted them to think that my life was happy and hunky-dory. They had enough problems of their own, and, like most parents, if they'd known what I was going through they'd have worried themselves to death.

Leaving someone you've known for five years for a man you've only known for a number of weeks, flying off to a country you've never been to before, could understandably be thought to be an act of madness. But Robert was like no one I'd ever met before. He had an incredible wisdom and the gentlest nature. He didn't frighten me, and that, above all, was the most important thing. I could talk to him about anything, and he had a great ability to sort my head out. I'd reached the point where I could no longer think. So many things were troubling me from my career right through to my personal life. The whole spectrum was troubled and blurred and I just couldn't see into the future. This escape was the only solution.

When I walked out of customs at Washington, I was so relieved to see Robert. I wouldn't have known what to do if he hadn't been there. But he was, as reliable as ever. Back then, Americans still drove huge cars, and America looked exactly how I'd imagined it from the Jack Kerouac novels. Everything was excessive. Everything was super-large, including the people. Everyone had that bit more energy than the British had. There were so many things to see, I couldn't take it all in. It was incredibly exciting.

I had three months in America while my management tried to sort out the mess back home. At this time, Robert was living and working in a school outside Washington called Claymont. Robert was not a religious man, but he was a man of discipline and he followed an Eastern philosophy based on the teachings of Gurdjieff. In the early seventies, Robert had crashed just like me. After a long period of success, he had become disillusioned and entered a community run by a man called J. G. Bennett, who'd worked with Gurdjieff and Ouspensky. Robert still spends a lot of time promoting Bennett's work. In retrospect, it seems a simple philosophy – the human race has evolved so much in the last thirty years that we've almost all become Gurdjieff people. It's a system of breaking out of your cast and working consciously to become a more aware race. Bennett wasn't a cult. Bennett was a way of working in the world, so I didn't feel threatened by it at all. My head needed serious sorting out. I was of no use to anyone in the state I was in when I arrived in Washington.

Robert drove me through the American countryside to Claymont, a huge, rambling mansion, exactly like the ones in the film *Gone with the Wind*, except it had fallen into disrepair. There was very little money. The Bennett organisation wasn't about making money. It was actually about stripping yourself of material wealth or, should I say, leaving it back home, coming to this place and living on the basics. No one asked you to give your money to a leader. It was nothing like that. It was about rediscovering yourself. For the first few days I shared a room with Robert that contained just a bed and a wardrobe. It didn't even have the style of Shaker minimalism. It was more MFI, make do with what you have. I didn't care. I'd escaped. My dream of the past few years had come true; I was free. The only black spot on the horizon was knowing that I still had the responsibility of phoning T. and telling him I wasn't coming back. It was a responsibility I would rather have avoided, but only I could be the bearer of that news.

The embryonic stages of my relationship with Robert had been perfect. I knew so little about him and he knew so little about me. We didn't have to deal with the baggage of the past. All we had to do was to get to know each other and flourish in each other's company. On the night he first made love to me, we stayed up till 6 a.m. talking, each terrified that if we made a move, we might be rejected by the other. As we had on so many evenings before, we sat on the sofa and talked and talked; time just melted away.

The moment came when Robert got down on his knees and kissed my feet, an act that for me was almost unbearably intimate, because, believe me, I hide my feet at every opportunity because of the scarring from childhood operations. He expressed his love to me in the most potent way possible: he looked up and said, 'I love your feet.' This so took me by surprise, I blurted out, 'You can't possibly love my feet, no one loves my feet.' But that night he proved he did. He erased my fear, a deep subconscious fear I'd always had that I was unworthy of love because of the condition I was born with. Because my legs weren't perfect and my feet weren't perfect. But Robert said that was ninety per cent of the reason he loved me. He loved the way I limped. When he said that, I laughed and laughed and laughed. How could any man, any woman, love a limp? It's something I'd always been ridiculed for. It's that thing people always pointed out before thinking about *why* I might limp. People always criticised the shoes I wear without thinking why I wear those shoes. And here was a gentle loving man saying he loved me for the one thing that had made me hide my affections all my life.

Robert's father had polio, so Robert was used to loving someone with an imperfection. He didn't see it as an imperfection, he saw it as part of the whole. Robert's ideas of beauty were not to do with youth, slimness and prettiness. They were to do with the whole, the mind, the soul, the zest for life and the physical.

After two days at Claymont, Robert and I drove to Chicago for a meeting he had to have with some friends. Chicago I found far more frightening than Washington. Robert is well known in America; I was shaken when some weirdo stalked him as we walked down the main street. And it was shocking to see the extremes of wealth and poverty. Within a stretch of fifty yards, you could pass an entire family living on the street. They'd be just sitting in their armchairs on the street, watching a TV run by a generator. I wondered how a civilised society could allow this to happen. Then a little further up you'd pass a woman who'd had so much cosmetic surgery she looked like an ape, a shaved ape, with her chauffeur carrying her shopping from the department store into a big black limousine.

I felt unsafe in Chicago. It was also from Chicago that I phoned T. When he picked up the phone and I said, 'Hello, it's Toyah here,' he already knew something was wrong.

'Where are you?' he said.

'T., I have something to tell you. I'm not coming back.'

It was as if he'd been waiting to hear this for some time. He burst into tears and said, 'Why, what's wrong, what's the matter?'

'T., it just isn't working and I'm not coming back. I've left the country.' Then I lied to him. I told him I was in Canada.

A long argument ensued. He went from trying to persuade me to come back to threatening me. We were both crying uncontrollably throughout. There was no way I could express to him the relief I felt being away from him. Nor was there any way I could try to be a friend to him, try to explain that we were destroying each other. After five years of living in my shadow, suffering the frustration of having to live by my timetable, off my money – and yes, that is a frustration, there is nothing worse for a man than not to have his own money – he still couldn't see that in time he'd be better off without me. Eventually I put the phone down on him. We only talked through lawyers after that.

He managed to discover my hideout in Wapping; he was found roaming the corridors trying to find me. He still didn't realise how long I was out of the country for. Once I knew that he was aware of my new home, it went back on the market. I'd owned it for all of three months. As for my house in Barnet, T. refused to move out. So a long waiting game was in progress, with me in Washington and him in Barnet. In the meantime, I had problems of my own to deal with. Deep inner problems. I needed to strip everything away to find that vulnerable little soul who still existed, and work on giving her strength.

Claymont was by no means easy. It had people there who lived there long-term. They were the most fucked-up people I have ever met. Seventy per cent of them were certifiable. Thirty per cent were saints. The whole point of the Bennett philosophy is that you live and work with other people's diversities. But I was so mentally vulnerable I found it impossible to be a good Samaritan – especially when the seventy per cent who deeply needed some kind of psychiatric help were hell-bent on pulling me and Robert apart.

Robert had spent many years at Claymont, so he had a lot of history there and a lot of former girlfriends. All willing and happy to tell me of their past; all willing and happy to share my experiences and compare them with theirs; and all keen to point out that their relationship had been short-lived, therefore mine must be too. Robert, knowing that he'd thrown a cat among the pigeons by bringing me there, didn't want anyone to know that we were to be married. He felt this would tip the apple cart completely. I felt that this simple fact would shut the whole lot of them up. But he still had one ex-mistress there, a recent mistress, who was married but still very attached to him, whom he didn't want to hurt too much. She was the bane of all our lives.

So Claymont was not good for me. I was having to do a lot of work on myself. I was studying a lot – psychology, psychoanalysis, anything to understand why I had got into such a mess in the first place. Then I was made to feel insecure about my relationship with Robert. I was made to feel like a hick from out of town. A lower caste. Someone who hadn't evolved. In retrospect, one can appreciate that the one good thing about this kind of pain is that it makes you sit up and listen, it makes you sit up and do something about yourself. This was exactly what I needed. I stripped myself of my material possessions – all I owned were the clothes in my suitcase and enough money to phone home – and for three months I sat in a cloud of whirling memories and emotions, trying slowly to pick particles from that cloud, analyse them, and find out why they were there. All the time, people back home thought I was living the life of Riley.

All my friends thought I had run off with this millionaire guitarist and was living in a big mansion in Washington. Yes, I had run off with a very wealthy, very well-respected man, but what they didn't realise was this was a man who had a different kind of wealth. It was a psychological wealth. He had no tolerance of material needs. He felt they were all gratuitous, and this was such an eye-opener for me. He had no interest in fashion, no interest in swimming pools, jacuzzis, sunbeds. These were all vanity. I had to strip away the vanity, the ego – and I was quite happy to do that. But the whole reason a human being has an ego is for survival, so you put up a fight with yourself the minute you start trying to deconstruct yourself. Your shadow, your inner self, starts kicking back hard. Eventually, you're living in a pure form of inner conflict.

I was twenty-seven when this happened. I am now forty-two. It has taken me all these years to recover from that experience. But I wouldn't be who and where I am today if I hadn't been through it. Because of my past and because of the so-called psychic experiences I had as a child, I'd learned to shut myself away. I stopped the experiences happening. They not only frightened me, they were very antisocial. So every time I felt these things emerging I submerged them. I'd suppressed so much of myself that things were starting to appear that took me by surprise, and the Claymont experience opened all that up again, making me even more vulnerable.

One of the many good things Claymont taught me was how to control these so-called psychic experiences. It taught me that the reason why I get messages out of the blue, why I see things that no one else can see, is that this is simply part of our animal brain. Some people have it, some people don't. It taught me how to use it to my own benefit, rather than have it use me like some kind of mental illness. Being psychic is a fact; I truly believe that in future generations it will be the norm. Now I can suppress the anger and the hate that come through on one level – for in our existence there are many levels of spiritual life, the very lowest being anger and hate, the very highest pure love. I can now silence them, those lower orders, those demons. Now instead I just allow the signals to come through that warn me of danger, or warn me of someone's needs, or advise me on a decision.

How many people in this world have this ability but have stifled it, when really it could help them in their lives. I'm not talking about sitting down, holding hands and contacting the dead here. I think the dead should rest in peace; we should learn to live with our memories and let that be enough. Nor am I talking about the kind of fortune-telling that predicts the winning lottery numbers. What I'm talking about is on a much simpler level. I now know how to use this inner voice constructively.

In the past, this voice used to give me far too much information. For instance, I'd be sitting in a restaurant and the voice would harp in from nowhere, saying, 'Tell the lady next to you she's got to paint the brown bedroom door blue,' then it would give me a whole vision of her bedroom and I'd turn to her and say, 'Is your bedroom door brown?' and she'd go, 'Yes.' I'd say, 'Well could you paint it blue, because it would completely change your life.' We'd swap phone numbers and the next day she'd paint her door blue. Within an hour her phone would ring with the offer of a job in another country. The job she'd wanted all her life.

That's the voice I've learned to suppress. I don't think it's right to interfere in other people's lives. But Claymont, because it dealt with the mystical side of religious knowledge, helped me redefine this side of myself. Now this mysterious little voice gives me snippets of information that are exclusive to me. The only reason I'm telling you this is that I believe we all have this voice, and for us to become a better world, a more united human race, we need to develop this voice. So rather than get messages like 'Your grandmother tells me her favourite chair is blue', I get messages like 'Slow right down now, there's an accident around the corner', or 'Phone your father now, he needs your help'. We all have this voice; I know most women out there understand what I'm saying.

At Claymont Robert ran what were called Guitar Craft classes. So I had three months of learning to play guitar, which helped focus me. Within this three months, we drove across West Virginia, playing impromptu concerts in record shops. There were eighteen of us in all; we'd sit in a huge circle around the audience, who formed an inner circle, and play bizarre pieces of music. I was an inexperienced guitarist, so I was only allowed to play bass lines, but this kind of ensemble work was a great comfort to me. I wasn't the focus of attention, but I was still performing.

I had a lot of jealousy to deal with. Robert's ex-girlfriend attached herself to us. She wouldn't let us out of her sight; I think she was waiting for the bubble to burst between Robert and me so that he'd go back to her. What Robert wouldn't do was ask her to leave us alone, so I had to accept her company and play for time. This was not an ideal relationship for me. So when Robert and I packed up to leave for England, I was hugely relieved that we left her behind.

Chapter 29

We arrived in England amid a storm of attention. Everybody wanted to know what was going on. *Minx* was out on CBS, so my profile was reasonably high; even though this album wasn't a huge success, it had a lot of media attention. Robert's and my management had arranged for a car to be left for us at Heathrow. So we drove down to Robert's house in Dorset, then set about phoning people, explaining ourselves, and letting those we trusted know where we were.

Before leaving England three months earlier, I'd lived in a world where I was the centre of attention. Where I was head honcho and called the shots. Now I was living in Robert's world, the world of an established guitar legend. Suddenly I'd become the blonde bimbo girlfriend. None of Robert's close circle of friends really knew anything about me. They were all into progressive rock; they certainly weren't into punk or pop music. So after my three months at Claymont, stripped bare of my ego and self-pride, I arrived into Robert's inner circle of friends who were quick to point out that I was not of equal intelligence to Robert. Some would even go as far as to ignore me completely and not include me in the conversation at all. Then I realised that they were all ex-girlfriends.

By entering Robert's world, I'd entered a world of women who were all waiting to marry Robert. In retrospect, I can see how sad they all were, but at the time, because I was feeling so vulnerable, I felt threatened. Robert couldn't see this at all. He just felt he had this remarkable close circle of friends who would do anything for him – from doing his washing, ironing and shopping to phoning him at midnight to ask him if he needed anything. It really didn't occur to Robert that they were all waiting for proposals of marriage. And suddenly I came along, I was much younger than them, and I was destroying their dreams. If I could go back there now, knowing what I know today, I would wipe the floor with the lot of them, but back then I had to play a very quiet, strategic, patient feline war game.

In the meantime, T. had sold the story of our five years together to the *Sun*. One morning we were out shopping with Robert's mother Edie in Wimborne, where she lived. Edie was very quiet, and out of the corner of my eye I caught her taking Robert aside and telling him something. Edie was a wonderful woman, a great friend and ally from the beginning. She was telling Robert to go and buy the *Sun*, but not to let me see it. Robert did show it to me: there, in the centre pages, serialised, was my past with T. It wasn't terrible and it wasn't catty. It was sad. And there was no gossip there. T. and I, apart from fighting with each other all the time, never did anything out of the ordinary. We were too busy; we were always working. That was probably why the *Sun* refused to pay T. a fee.

I sorted T. out in the end. We managed to sell the house in Whetstone, and settled by my giving him enough money to set up in business.

All this apart, when Robert and I were actually alone together, we were blissfully happy. We were made for each other. It's amazing that for so many years we had so much in common, yet never met. We even had mutual friends, but fate and time kept Robert and me apart. You'd think that others seeing us this happy would be happy for us; we were both taken aback by our managers' insensitivity. This manifested itself in quite bizarre ways. Robert told me that in the middle of a meeting he had with them one day, they suddenly brought up the subject of an ex-girlfriend, reminding him of their sexual relationship. Another time they brought up the subject of a sexual liaison he'd had, a one-night stand, and reminded him how much he'd enjoyed that kind of bachelor life. Robert always told me about these conversations, and I started to see my managers in a different light.

Initially Robert wanted us to get married after a three-year engagement, but it became evident that we needed to commit earlier than that. Our relationship was met with extraordinary cynicism not only from the media – which was very entertaining and quite laughable – but also from friends on both sides. Some people were going to extraordinary lengths to dig up Robert's ex-girlfriends and encourage them to be in communication with Robert. And out of the blue quite unexpectedly, men I'd known for years were suddenly declaring their love for me. I think when I phoned around my male friends and colleagues, on two occasions I was greeted with tears and on one I was begged to reconsider. I found this absolutely bizarre. No one had ever showed any romantic inclinations towards me in the past – I think I'd always been seen as some kind of ice maiden – and suddenly it was all surfacing. So because of both these pressures and those of being kept apart by our work, we decided to get married within nine months of meeting. This was incredibly important to me. In hindsight, I think if we hadn't have got married then, hadn't made that commitment to each other, we would have broken up within a year. The commitment helped me to trust Robert. We often talk about this, even today, and he says there's never been any doubt in his mind that I was his wife nor, once he'd realised this, that he was exclusively mine.

We had many discussions about whether we should tradition-ally marry or just take vows. We did feel that the wedding was not only for us but also a proclamation to the outside world and to God. Both Robert and I have beliefs, although they're not traditional beliefs, not by Western standards. I have no problem with Christianity; I think it embraces all the world believes in one way or another. Robert follows an Eastern philosophy based on the teachings of Gurdjieff which embraces God in a similar way to Christianity. Culturally we'd been brought up as Christians, so it didn't feel hypocritical to decide to have a Christian wedding. Bearing in mind that both of us have continual dialogues with God in our own heads, what better place to say our vows in the presence of God than in a church? I once said to a vicar, 'Why do I need to go to church to pray, I can pray wherever I am?' and he said, 'A church is a building that pulls focus, focus not only for you and God, but focus for the community.'

My parents didn't get to meet Robert until after Christmas when we'd returned from America. I'm sure in their mind's eye they envisaged him as some multimillionaire rock star. When I used to call home, they'd ask, 'Is he rich?' and I'd say, 'Mind your own business.' 'Is he going to support you?' and I'd answer, 'I sincerely hope not. I've supported myself up till now and that's how I'd like it to continue.' It took a long time for me to convince Mum and Dad that I wasn't marrying Robert for some kind of material wealth.

When I did eventually take Robert to meet my parents, they couldn't stop laughing. My father kept disappearing out of the room in fits of giggles. I could hear him and Mum laughing in the kitchen. When Robert went into the kitchen to ask them for my hand in marriage, my father could control himself no longer and he said, 'Why on earth do you want to marry our daughter? Do you know what you're letting yourself in for? You're such a nice man. Are you sure you don't want to reconsider?' Apparently what had tickled my parents was that they saw Robert as a lovely, educated, middle-aged man who surely had more sense than to marry their troublesome daughter. Unswayed by their reaction, Robert explained he had known I was his wife since the first moment he saw me. And he had every intention of marrying me.

After that we faced all the usual decisions. Robert is a very quiet, retiring type and doesn't like being in the public eye. He didn't want a huge showbiz marriage, he wanted only close family. I, on the other hand, would have loved a showbiz marriage, something big and glitzy that went on for days. So we had to compromise. Well, it wasn't much of a compromise – we went with Robert's idea, otherwise there probably would have been no wedding. He just wouldn't have turned up. Also, Robert absolutely loathed having his picture taken. So we agreed that my brother-in-law, Frank, could video the ceremony but there would be no photographers present. Another bone of contention was children: as neither of us wanted to have a family, we felt we didn't really want young children running around the church. Aware of how harsh this might appear, we agreed that children could be outside the church playing under adult supervision, but we would like to take our vows in silence. We decided there'd be no music for the ceremony; we just wanted a contemplative silence in the presence of God. So immediate family were invited, and friends would come to the reception.

We had to keep all this under wraps, and trust that no one was going to tell anyone; if the press turned up I knew Robert would do a runner.

We were to be married in the little church in Witchampton where Robert's father had been buried the year before. We sat with the local vicar and chose the ceremony we wanted. I didn't want the vow 'I will obey', but somehow on the day it miraculously appeared and I looked at Robert and laughed when I said it. I prepared all the food for the reception, keen to prove that I was capable of being a good wife and feeding my spouse. A family friend, Bob Lewis, made a spectacular wedding cake.

The one problem I had was what to wear. I couldn't exactly just go into a wedding shop and buy a dress; that would have given the game away – by now there was a lot of interest in Robert's and my relationship and people were waiting for some kind of announcement. So instead I went to the local ballgown shop, frequented by the county set, and picked the first dress I saw. It was a little pink off-the-shoulder, Bo-peep affair. It was really quite gross, but I so wanted to be a feminine ideal when I walked into the church. I wanted to be the most beautiful woman Robert had ever known. I'm not a dress person, so this was a big step for me. The ultimate compromise.

In the days before the wedding I was unexpectedly gripped by nerves and fear, and I think Robert was too. This was the ultimate commitment, and neither of us was entering into this ceremony thinking that if it didn't work out we could get divorced. This was for a lifetime. The anxieties going through my head were stupid and pointless – probably just natural self-doubt. Robert and I had never been happier. We loved each other's company; we were soulmates, and felt incredibly lucky to have found each other. Our mutual managers, who'd known Robert for fifteen years or more, were to be best men. According to tradition, we planned to spend the night before the ceremony apart, Robert with his male colleagues, I on my own – I had no friends in the area, and I couldn't tell any of best friends back in London about the wedding because they all worked in the media. But our plans were scuppered when our management told me that their pre-wedding gift to Robert was going to be a prostitute. It's amazing how some men can completely lack tact, spirit and goodwill. Looking back, I'm sure this was a joke, but was I supposed to allow this? I was so upset that Robert decided that we'd spend the night before the wedding together.

The morning was the most perfect morning you could have. It was Robert's fortieth birthday, and the sun was shining – the first time we'd seen sunshine all month. My family arrived and clucked around me all morning, driving me bonkers. They kept searching the house; they'd never seen my new home before. I was worried that Robert might find them looking in cupboards, under carpets, checking for dust. But on the whole, as families go, they were well-behaved.

Unbeknownst to Robert and me, the large manor in the village, right opposite the church, was having a contents sale. The owner had died earlier that year and all her possessions were being sold, at a massive auction to which people were travelling from all over the country to buy rare antiques. The police had cordoned the road off so that the press and VIPs could get to the manor. This made things difficult for us because by midday I was dressed as a bride and we didn't want anyone to see what was going on. So we notified the police, telling them it had to be top secret, I needed to get to the church without anyone seeing. It was decided that our guests would walk along the road as if they were walking to the manor sale, then discreetly take a left rather than a right turn. Twenty minutes later, my father was to drive me straight up to the church gates, which were bang opposite the entrance to the manor, where I could sneak in quickly and, with luck, unseen.

I was so proud of my father that day. He was perfect. He was calm, collected and never stopped smiling – every time I looked round, there he was, beaming away or giggling. As I walked into the church I was shaking from head to toe; I so didn't want to cry, but tears kept welling up as I walked up the aisle with my father. I was greatly relieved that there was no music. I find church music so beautiful it has me in floods of tears within four bars. When Robert saw me, *he* burst into tears, bless him. He'd never seen his intended bride look so feminine. In retrospect, I looked like a floozie out of the Billy Idol video, but at the time, I thought I looked the ultimate woman.

It wasn't a long ceremony, especially without music. When we came to say our vows, a glorious, well-timed shaft of light came through the stained-glass windows and illuminated Robert and me. It was a wonderful omen.

Afterwards, we went outside for family photos, behind the church, discreetly hidden from the manor. But when we walked round to get into the car, it was clear the press had cottoned on that something was happening. One eagle-eyed press man from the *Bournemouth Echo* had realised that the police weren't cordoning off the manor, they were actually cordoning off the church. It was already well known that we lived in the village. He'd put two and two together, told his mates, and by the time the ceremony was over they were all outside. So instead of calmly walking hand in hand with me to the car, Robert broke into a sprint and disappeared from view, trying to conceal his face from the cameras, with our managers chasing after him. I was perfectly happy. I was beaming from head to toe, and now the deed was done all my nerves had gone. So I smiled and kept on walking, wondering when I'd see my husband next.

The following day, Robert and I were asleep at the house when there came a furious knocking at the door. This was quite unusual; we very rarely had visitors. Robert went downstairs to answer it and was faced by two *Daily Mirror* reporters. He instantly shut the door and they started shouting through the letterbox, 'Let us have a picture of you and your bride or we'll just have to print something nasty about you.' This went on all morning. As a wedding present I'd bought Robert a house in a neighbouring village where he could start his guitar school. We were due to go there this day for a meeting with the architect, but it wasn't going to be easy. The journey turned into a crazy car chase down narrow country lanes at about 80 m.p.h. Our main worry was that we didn't want to lead our pursuers to the new house, but there was nothing we could do about it. When we got to the new house, we drove through the gates to the courtyard and slammed them shut. Our meeting with the architect turned into a discussion about how to distract these determined photographers, since Robert totally refused to have his picture taken. In the end the architect took Robert away in his car; I waited an hour and then drove off myself.

The next day was my twenty-eighth birthday. We were still being doorstepped by photographers, so we decided to leave the area and go down to Penzance, reckoning that this was such a long drive we would eventually throw the press off. In Penzance we went on to a little village called Sancreed, where some friends of ours had recommended a Franciscan retreat to hide in. It was the perfect place for us to reflect on our marriage. It was run by a Franciscan monk who also happened to be a wonderful artist; he blessed our marriage, and in the little chapel I read the prayers for the day, in front of a congregation we didn't know but felt greatly protected by.

Our honeymoon period lasted a week and then Robert had to return to Claymont. It was so hard to let him go, it broke my heart. It wasn't possible for me to go with him; I had too much work in England, and the fact that our careers were split by the Atlantic was one I was going to have to learn to live with. Before I met Robert I'd very rarely been alone; my boyfriends had always driven me to and fro and come and stayed with me while I worked. Now that I was married, ironically I had a new independence, and I had to learn to be confident on my own. Life on your own in the country can be spooky – there are strange noises at night – but eventually I grew to embrace this independence. It gave me the freedom I needed to continue my career, and in some ways the best thing about our marriage is that Robert and I can be independent of each other yet still connected.

Chapter 30

The management decided that I should leave CBS. *Minx*, although only a moderate success, broke new territory abroad and moved me up to the next stage as a serious solo artist. But my management company took the opportunity to get me out of the contract as soon as they could – and immediately signed me to Virgin. There was only one problem about the Virgin deal. The day I signed, in Richard Branson's office, was also the day he left. (This kind of behaviour was rife in the music industry.) Exactly the same happened when I signed to CBS: I signed because I wanted to be with Morry Oberstein, a music legend, but within a week of my signing, he left the company to go into retirement. It's incredibly important within record companies to have fans and allies. They are the people who work for you and make sure that you're at the top of the rota, who talk about you in board meetings and make sure all the sales force are behind you. If an ally leaves the company, you're pushed to a far corner of the room, as part of your former ally's history.

All the same, signing to Virgin was an exciting move. Virgin was a young and vibrant company. It meant the possibility of a new image, a new sound and in many ways a new beginning, which exactly suited my life at that time. I set about writing and demoing with the new guitar skills I'd learned from Robert in America. It was very satisfying having a greater understanding of music, and I wanted to be much more adventurous with *Desire*. But at the same time I also wanted to step back in history and work with Steve James again, who was so understanding of my creative process. Unfortunately, my management had taken on a man called Dick Prewitt, who was to represent them at an A&R level. Dick Prewitt came with a great history: he had supposedly discovered and signed one of the most successful bands of the eighties. With a claim like that he commanded instant respect. But five minutes into my first meeting with him at the management office, where he sat marking my songs one out of ten while placing a bet on a horse at Aintree, I realised that this man was not a fan. Mr Prewitt didn't want Steve James to produce *Desire*.

Needing a place in London, I rented Eno's flat, just off the King's Road in Chelsea. Robert at this time was returning every two weeks to Claymont. This troubled me, because it meant he'd be alone with his ex-girlfriend; I was still so jealous I didn't really believe that she was an ex. Mike Hedges was to produce *Desire* and we were to record it at Abbey Road in the studio made famous by the Beatles. Tucked away in their Abbey Road studios were the Beatles' old four-track mixers; I used to pass them every day on the stairway as I walked down to do my vocals, and I'd just gently brush them with my fingers, hoping something, anything, might rub off on me.

Desire had its complexities. I'd returned from Claymont with a much more inquisitive mind and was no longer prepared to write things of basic simplicity. I wanted to write things that explored mental states. For me the whole joy of making an album is being given a chance to try out new ideas, not to repeat old formulas. Commercially, this was probably a weakness: if I'd stuck to formulas, I'd have had formula sales let's say. But life's far too short to be repetitive; and I was always of the mind to keep moving and moving on. Don't backtrack.

During the recording of *Desire* I was asked to audition for Gillian Lynne, to take over the part of Sally Bowles in *Cabaret* in the West End. Gillian was also seeing my old friend Hazel O'Connor for the role. The whole idea greatly excited me. It would ground me, give me something constant to do, rather than flitting about like a butterfly, trying different ideas here and there. I'd never appeared in the West End, only at the National Theatre; this could be the vehicle that I needed to move that little bit further up the ladder. Making records and writing music were great fun, but that kind of work had its pressures; doing a West End musical would mean all I had to do was perform. The writing was already done and the selling of tickets was someone else's responsibility.

Cabaret was already on at the Strand Theatre, with Kelly Hunter playing Sally Bowles and Wayne Sleep the MC. Wayne Sleep was to stay, Kelly wanted to move on. So, on a cold December day, I spent a morning working with Gillian Lynne on the stage at the Strand. My voice was in peak condition because of making *Desire*: I was having singing lessons in the morning, then singing in the studio throughout the rest of the day. The songs in *Cabaret* are so me, so perfect. They're pop songs for the stage. What they need added to them are guts and charisma; I was still young and feisty enough to inject these songs with attitude.

Gillian Lynne was, and still is, obsessed with good legs. She would insist that her dancers starve till their legs were pencil-thin, lean but muscular. There was nothing she could do with my legs: they were muscular, but too muscular, and as for long, there wasn't a hope in hell. I hadn't grown an inch since I was fourteen, and I wasn't about to start growing. Not upwards, anyway. But Gillian must have been forgiving of my physique, because I got the part of Sally Bowles; I was to start rehearsing in January and performing in February.

This gave me enough time to finish recording *Desire*, which was getting a lot of attention. My marriage to Robert Fripp was causing such a stir in the music world that I could call on any musician I wanted to play on *Desire*. One was Ron Wood of the Rolling Stones. I'd written a very basic blues song with a writer called Nick Graham; we sent a demo to Ron and he said he'd come and play on it. Bless him, he turned up at Abbey Road with one roadie who drove him, a tiny Marshall amp and his guitar. He did the song, 'Dear Diary', in one take, then spent the rest of the night listening to everything we'd recorded for the album. He chain-smoked, we gossiped, we drank a lot of wine. He could have been anyone, he was so gregarious, it was as if I had known him all my life. He was awesome, yet at the same time he was the typical boy next door.

I set about serious vocal training. It's all very well being able to sing in the studio. In a studio you don't have to project; you mainly have to show control and subtlety. On stage a completely different voice is needed, a voice that can sustain eight shows a week, projecting out across an auditorium. I was seeing my vocal coach, Helena Schoenel, three times a week. She was also the support, the crutch, that gave me confidence.

Christmas that year was short-lived. I had to finish *Desire* at the speed of light. Suddenly my attention was divided. A common complaint people have about me is that I can happily go off at a complete tangent. From my point of view, I need extremes: each extreme keeps me interested in the other. *Desire* for me had run out of steam. *Cabaret* coming along gave me the incentive to give the album that last push, get it finished, in the can; then I could go off and do my stint in the West End.

I was under a lot of pressure from my A&R man to produce a hit single from *Desire*. I was no longer interested in hit singles. Being with Robert had changed my attitude towards music; I just wanted to make an album, a complete form, with ten cohesive tracks. So when the arguments started – the A&R man saying I hadn't written a song suitable for a single, me saying I had written songs suitable for me, the artist – pressure was put on me to start doing cover versions.

Back in 1986, cover versions weren't perceived the way they are now. They were considered an opt-out, an admission that one had failed to write a commercial song, so it was reluctantly and rather bitterly that I recorded 'Echo Beach' – the choice of my A&R man. Then later, I was pulled out of rehearsals for *Cabaret* and physically put in a studio and made to record the worst song I've ever heard in my life – 'Love's Unkind', which was a Donna Summer track. I have never heard anything more ill-suited, it was the ultimate proof that this A&R man should be put against a wall and shot. Many might wonder how one could be *made* to record a track – but when a budget is about to be pulled from under your feet because of your sheer reluctance to co-operate, the only way forward is compromise.

The recording of 'Love's Unkind' was a sad indication that my involvement in the commercial world of music was well and truly over. It was a mistake too far. It sat on *Desire*, an album that was quite experimental for me, like the figure of ridicule from an almost exclusively male world of A&R. I could not forgive my management for letting this happen, or for subjecting me to such a tosser. If it hadn't been for the financial problems my management were causing me, I would have left them for this alone, but I was under a contract to them and no matter how much I disliked their Thatcherite ways, their materialistic views, their attitude that everything was a possession and nothing had soul, I was stuck and I had to live it out.

Another problem was that it seemed only I, one of many artists on their roster, was having money problems with them. My husband, who'd been managed by them since 1970, considered them his closest friends. When I tried to explain to Robert that the difference between my income and what was actually going in my bank was vast, he just believed that money was simply passing through my hands like water. It seemed to escape my husband that if I was having to walk home to Chelsea late at night from the West End, it was because there was a cash-flow problem; not even I was so stupid that I'd spend so much money that I didn't have enough left for food and travel.

With this particular management set-up, I was living in a very masculine regime. The management were like a boys' club which I couldn't penetrate and certainly had no part of. By marrying their top artist, in their eyes I'd stepped back from being a major artist myself to being just a wife. If they wanted me for a meeting, they'd call Robert and ask him if I could come to the meeting. They no longer saw me as an independent individual. This put a terrible strain on our marriage. I am fiercely independent and I've worked all my life to be an individual in my own right; suddenly all that was gone. What made it even more painful was that Robert couldn't see that they were doing anything wrong. Robert has always been wealthy, very comfortable; when we married, he saw me also as someone wealthy, and, theoretically, I was – I just didn't seem to have anything in practice. We both said that we'd never live out of each other's pockets, we'd stay completely financially independent. We have never shared a bank account, and never will. So my cash-flow problem was mine alone and I had to deal with it myself. So I was talking directly to the management, their heads were turned to their right and they were talking directly to my husband. It was as if in their eyes I was incapable of running my own affairs.

All this was going on at a very subtle level; my intuitive mind was working overtime on how to deal with it and not let the problem go any further. So on one level I was a worried person, but, thanks to *Cabaret*, on another level I was a very happy person. I was being lavished with lots of positive attention, wined and dined by London's society who were far more interested in a West End star than they'd ever been in the pop star.

The rehearsals for *Cabaret* were hugely enjoyable. I spent a lot of time working alone, going through the dance steps over and over again unseen. Dance was never my forte, but I didn't want to let Gillian Lynne down. She'd shown such confidence in me, I was determined to be the best Sally Bowles she'd ever had – and believe me, Kelly Hunter was a hard act to follow. Gillian wisely decided to keep my dance routines to a minimum. Kelly had done a lot of dance work with Wayne Sleep in the show. All that was cut – partly because next to Wayne, I obviously wasn't a dancer. Also, Gillian felt that my stature and my physical build went against dancing ethics, so she choreographed my steps very much for who I was, letting my singing and acting be the focus.

The costumes for *Cabaret* weren't particularly flattering. I had curves, whereas the clothes of the 1930s were still very boyish. My good assets, my bust and my waist, were covered by unflattering straight lines. This was frustrating for everyone, but there was little we could do about it. After all, *Cabaret* was a period piece. You can't suddenly have a buxom wench in the middle of it. Ironically, my worst feature was to be featured the most – my legs, which had to be exposed nightly in stockings and suspenders. Gillian tried to be forgiving about my legs. I can't help the fact I didn't grow much in childhood, but I could do something about my weight. So I set about not so much starving myself, but not letting myself think about food. I allowed myself enough to function, but never enough to allow those thighs to expand. So it was a bowl of soup and a piece of bread at the end of each day, and eventually, I started to look reasonably good – although not before the critics blurted out how awful my legs were.

I've never liked having to sing in winter; I've always avoided touring the band in winter. Psychologically, the cold just makes me want to get under the duvet and not come out until May. Robert was away for most of this period in 1987. Typically, I've never needed him more. My bravado could only go so far; I needed someone to come home to at night, a shoulder to put my head on, someone to hold me and give me enough strength to go out the next day. This was such a toughening-up period. A period that in retrospect I'm grateful for, but at the time I wished would dissolve into a happy ending.

Robert's absence was the spur that was toughening me up. It's ironic that one becomes independent through becoming married. He was away with his Guitar Craft students, touring Israel and Europe. On the day he left for Israel, I'd been at a costume-fitting and my taxi driver got lost driving me from Putney to the King's Road. All the time I was shouting directions at her and she was ignoring me. I knew I had a matter of minutes before Robert left the apartment for Heathrow. When you spend so little time with someone, every second you can grab with them is of vital importance; a taxi ride can turn into an utter nightmare, when your directions fall on deaf ears and the taxi driver seems determined to take you to a different part of London from the one you actually live in. And you know that the man you love is stepping into another taxi, about to leave you for six weeks. This kind of experience can turn a normally tough person into a hysterical wimp – when you walk into a flat that still smells of your mate, still has his body heat, and you realise that you've missed him by seconds. It does somewhat put a dampener on your day.

I was yet to grow used to this. Eventually I did. Eventually I realised it was my desire for control that made me panic in these situations. Robert was still working with his ex, and I suppose I got upset because I wanted to see him one more time to remind him who he was coming home to at the end of his tour. Trust eluded me at times like this. It brought out the panicked child; I just wanted to grab hold of him and never let him go, claim him, own him. But over time, his being away did mean I got tougher. And one thing Robert has always been brilliant and reliable about is phoning – not just once a day, sometimes five times a day, maintaining a constant presence in my life.

Chapter 31

My managers had many strings to their bows, so it came as no surprise to me when one of them said he wanted to take me to meet Prince Edward. The Prince wished to put together a team of people who could bring an idea he'd had to fruition. We were to meet at the house of Emma Nicholson. My manager and I arrived first and waited. We knew when Edward was about to arrive because a bodyguard came into the room, looked around and sat in the corner. Then another bodyguard brought the Prince in.

Edward was very natural and very chatty. If it hadn't been for the security men, it would have been like any other social meeting. But instead it was rather exciting, sitting in this warm cosy lounge, me on a sofa, Prince Edward in the armchair next to me, and sprinkled around the room a bevy of bodyguards, who I'm sure were carrying guns. They discreetly observed the situation, keeping a beady eye on me in case I was about to assassinate a member of the Royal Family, and laughed politely at the Prince's humour. The Prince was extremely likeable. There was almost a naïvety about him. I only knew his public persona, so I had come to this meeting armed with preconceptions. But he was genuinely caring and had a great love of theatre and performance; he so obviously would have been much happier in a theatrical world than in the world of the Marines.

The idea the Prince wanted to put to me was that of a Royal *It's a Knockout*. I was blown away by the ordinariness of this idea. Considering all the things the Prince could achieve, I felt that *It's a Knockout* was quite bland. But he wanted to get stars from all over the world competing with his brothers and sisters as team captains. He wasn't sure whether Princess Diana would be allowed to take part – though she'd said she would love to head a team – but Princess Anne, Andrew and Fergie had all been given permission to be involved. Would I be prepared to come on board as an organiser and participant? Of course I said yes. I thought this was the wackiest thing I'd been asked to do since Derek Jarman showed me the script for *Jubilee.*

We met again at Emma Nicholsons's the following week. This meeting was tinged with sadness. Prince Edward had just told his father he was leaving the Marines. He arrived at Emma's in a state of shock; he was visibly shaking and I daresay he'd been crying. We all felt great sympathy towards him. Indeed, we spent the whole meeting talking about the Marines and about what Edward expected to be in the papers the following day – and he wasn't wrong. His decision to leave was every headline. Edward had found the Marines unbearable. He did hint at our meeting that he'd experienced bullying, but above all, he just felt so totally out of place. The arts and the theatre were where he wanted to be. I felt passionately sorry for him, and wondered how many other things he had to tolerate that went against his nature. But in subsequent meetings he was a different man. The air had been cleared and he was obviously finding his feet. I, in turn, must have made an impression on him, because within days of our second meeting, I received a call on my personal phone from the Brigadier who looks after Prince Philip. Prince Philip was hosting an event for two thousand young people at St James's the following day. Would I go and give a motivational talk to the group? Again, of course I said yes.

Turning up at St James's I was greeted by the Brigadier, who politely thanked me and led me up the stairs past a chamber orchestra, into a big room full of young high-achievers. As I walked in, there was a 'pssst' in my ear – I turned, and behind a curtain I could see Prince Philip beckoning to me. I went over. 'Thank you, my dear, so kind of you to help me out. These people don't want to see me. They want to see someone like you. And tell me, what are you up to at the moment? Doing any telly?' Prince Philip was just as interested in the world of theatre and television as Prince Edward was, though I suspect that on this day he'd rather have been out shooting, racing or hunting.

He made a welcoming speech, then was whisked away by the Brigadier, leaving the rest up to me.

All the time, I was learning more about how the Royal Family function. Prince Edward came to see *Cabaret* with Lady Sarah Armstrong-Jones. This was an unofficial visit, but even so, the theatre had to be checked: security came in and checked under all the seats and checked backstage. After the show, Prince Edward came back to my dressing room to say hello. Rather disconcertingly, no car arrived to pick him up. I can't tell you how embarrassed Edward was. In my dressing room, he called the palace to see if a car was coming but one hadn't been arranged and it appeared that at that time of night, one wasn't going to be arranged. The producer was in that night, so we thought it best that he drive the Prince back to the palace. Apparently, when they got to the palace gates, Edward had to get out of the car and persuade the security that it was really him. I was starting to get the impression that Edward wasn't considered an important Royal within the Royal Family. Either that, or the whole organisation was so vast that when something like this went wrong, it really went wrong, and word wouldn't make it to the Prince's mother that her son was stranded outside the palace gates.

I did something with Robert I could never have done with T. I decided that for the album cover of *Desire* I wanted to appear in the arms of a naked man. Naturally I asked Robert's permission first – he didn't even bat an eyelid. He almost expected it. I chose Carrie Brannigan for the photo shoot. She was well known in the corridors of *Vogue, Harpers' Bazaar* and *Tatler* for photographing beautiful women in luxurious lingerie. She was also an extreme New York feminist; I loved the fact that a feminist could work with nudity but keep it both sensual and strong. I had a very hard task of casting the male model. I called all my friends and we sat in this room as model after model came in. I think that day I decided I wanted to be an advertising executive. I have never seen so much male beauty in my life. Regrettably I didn't have the guts to ask any of them to strip off, but it was a bit like the male equivalent of a wet-T-shirt exhibition – you could imagine full well what was underneath.

At the photo shoot, there was only Carrie, her (female)

assistant, me, the male model and the male model's girlfriend. I think she was there for protection and believe me, her instincts were right, he needed protection. What was fabulous about this shoot was that the male model was more nervous than I was. Carrie took various photos of us in various positions, remembering that this album cover would probably be on the shelves of Woolworth's and W. H. Smith, so keeping it sensual and beautiful with soft lines. All the time I was thinking, This is definitely a new life, a new beginning. Just having the freedom to make a choice like this and to be trusted in that choice. In the past this just wouldn't have been possible. But one of the wonderful things about Robert is his trust: he trusts me implicitly. I think he was hoping in the beginning of our relationship that that trust would rub off on me.

Another remarkable example of Robert's trust was one evening after *Cabaret*, when, on a rare occasion we actually went out, we went to a restaurant, Orso's, with our album designer Bill Smith and his wife. We were quietly minding our own business, getting on with our own secret world of gossip, catching up on the past and expressing ideas for the future, when out of the blue, Wayne Sleep appeared, picked me right up off my chair and carried me across the crowded restaurant – by this time with everyone looking at us – shouting 'Steven, Steven, here she is, here she is.' After we'd passed about four tables, Wayne Sleep dumped me unceremoniously, bum first, into Steven Berkoff's dinner. I sat there in dazed confusion while Wayne Sleep shouted, 'There she is, Steven, fuck her.'

What could one do but laugh? Berkoff didn't mind that I was in his supper. I suppose I didn't mind either. I just prayed he wouldn't take Wayne Sleep at his word. I know my husband's tolerant, but really, getting laid at Orso's by Steven Berkoff was not on the menu. I picked myself up, brushed myself off, apologised and tiptoed, head down, back to my table, where I looked my husband in the eye and said, 'Wayne, really, what a laugh that boy is!' No more was said.

Cabaret trundled along agreeably. I was very happy being in the West End. It called for great discipline from me: my voice isn't naturally tough, so I had to keep quiet in the daytime, then go to the theatre and start warming my voice up again. From

Monday to Thursday audiences would be a bit thin on the ground, while Fridays and Saturdays would be completely sold out. This is a familiar pattern in the West End, where shows increasingly have an out-of-town audience. But the producer wasn't happy and was hinting at closing the show around May.

At the beginning of May there was an incident that I really had no inkling about. During Wayne Sleep's large dance production number, rumour had it that he had thrown something into the orchestra pit. The orchestra claimed it was orange peel. What Wayne was doing with orange peel in his hands while dancing a complex piece of choreography is anybody's guess, but the orchestra took umbrage and made an official complaint to the Musicians' Union. According to Wayne, the orchestra had thrown something at him and therefore he threw it back. I thought no more of it. I thought it was just mid-run grumbling. People do get pissed off with each other when they have to work in such confined spaces for so long.

Anyway, Wayne was due to have two weeks' holiday. He had been in the show touring and in the West End for over a year. So he was going to disappear for a bit and no doubt this dispute would all settle down. But it didn't. The Musicians' Union called a strike. MU members staged a protest outside the theatre. I'd never had to cross a picket line before. What greatly confused me was that I was a member of Equity and also a member of the MU. I phoned both offices and asked advice. None would commit to any. They told me I had to follow my own judgement.

There were eighty members of the company; all were Equity members and five also MU members. I decided to cross the picket line, because eighty people had mortgages to pay and children to feed. I really couldn't believe that all this had blown up out of the simple misplacement of a piece of orange peel. Whoever took responsibility for its displacement. Inside the theatre this fated night was chaos. No one knew exactly what was going on. Accusations were flying everywhere. The producer was trying to negotiate with the MU, while outside, MU members were picketing the audience. The debate was – did we not perform that night, or did we go on without an orchestra?

Gillian Lynne had made up her mind. We were to go on without an orchestra. So the debate went a little further. Did we charge the audience to see a musical without an orchestra, or did we give everyone their money back? It was decided that we'd let the audience in – those who dared cross the picket line – explain to them that that evening's performance would be exclusively without music and therefore they'd be witnessing history in the making: this would be the first musical in the West End ever to be performed without music. In the meantime, when I managed to catch Gillian's attention – so militant was she that she was on her soapbox for most of the evening, bless her, fired up with righteous indignation – I tried to eke out of her how we were going to keep time, let alone keep key. 'No problem,' she said. 'We're all going to be in the wings, humming and clicking our fingers.' Easier said than done.

I have never been so terrified on a first entrance in all my life. Many of the songs in *Cabaret* have long complex introductions which allow the performer to get on stage and in place, centre stage. All this had to be done in complete silence – with the occasional titter from the audience. Gillian Lynne's choreography is incredibly rhythmic and sexually charged. The presence of music helped one to portray this; suddenly I felt like a hot, debauched, decadent floozie, having a bit of a turn in silence. My heart was pounding so hard that the sound of blood in my ears was louder than the finger-clicking from the rest of the company in the wings. But by the end of my first number, we were already receiving our first standing ovation from the trickle of audience who had crossed the picket line.

There was a camaraderie between us and the audience; we were in cahoots. Some had travelled from as far as Birmingham to see the show that night, they weren't going home without an experience and by God were they getting it. When the cameras appeared for *News at Ten* to record this historic moment, everyone knew that we were doing the right thing. At the end of the show, the clapping went on for ever. The whooping, the cheering, the bravos, the shouts for an encore just went on and on. I was profoundly relieved. Partly I felt a complete idiot, partly I felt confused. I still didn't understand how this situation could have got so out of control in the first place. I returned home that night and fell into a deep sleep, hoping that the next day everything would be back to normal. We'd proved as performers that we intended the show to go on, and no doubt the notoriety of what we had done would boost the ticket sales.

The following day, a Friday, was one hell of a day. 'Echo Beach', the first single off *Desire*, was to be released in a week's time. The only way I could guarantee airplay on Radio 1 was to do them the favour of being in Liverpool on Friday morning to do a live interview on the ferry across the Mersey. To do this and be back in time for the show in the evening, I had to hire a helicopter. I am not fond of helicopters; they make me frightened and sick. So when I got to Battersea Heliport at 8 a.m. I downed two Valium. By the time we left at 8.30 I was happy as a socialite in *Hello!* magazine.

In Liverpool I boarded the ferry, did the three-minute interview that would guarantee me airplay of 'Echo Beach', promised the controller of Radio 1 a lift back in my helicopter and buggered off as quickly as I could. The fatigue from the night before was in every muscle of my body. By now the adrenalin had well left me from my history-making experience. Instead I was just tired and craving for my bed. The controller, my A&R man and I flew back to Battersea, where a car met me to take me to the theatre for the evening show. And that wouldn't be the end of my day.

I was booked to appear on the Ruby Wax show, *Don't Miss Wax*, at 11 p.m., so I was hoping to get to the theatre early and have a little snooze. As the car pulled up at the Strand, I saw that there was a massive crowd of press outside the stage door. Partly flattered, thinking they were there because of my glory the night before, I soon realised otherwise, when one of them asked me how I felt about the fact that the show had been closed. This was the first I'd heard of it, and I expected it to be the last. I thought it was all a massive hoax. The last twenty-four hours had been so victorious, I was on a high – not only from the Valium, but also from having had the guts to go ahead with the performance without an orchestra. The press seemed vindictive, almost gleeful, at this bad news. It brought me back down to earth with a bump.

My A&R man was magnificent in this situation. I saw a completely different side of him. He suddenly went from being a hyena to acting like a human being. Seeing that I was becoming a victim in this situation, as I was obviously tired and confused, he whisked me up in his arms and pushed me through the stage door as quickly as he could. We were both ushered to the stage, where Gillian Lynne was holding a plan-of-action meeting with the entire company. Gillian was really on her soapbox. She was magnificent. She stressed that in no way could we allow the show to close just because of this dispute. It would put eighty people out of work and we had to do something to let the unions know that this was not an acceptable solution. Her instinctive feeling was that we should have a sit-in. We should stay in the theatre, lock ourselves in if we had to, and not come out until the dispute was resolved and the show was back on stage.

In principle, I thought this was a fantastic idea. In practice, I was too mentally exhausted to face it. I had my A&R man on one side, quaking with fear at the thought of this artist, who was about to release her latest single, not being available for promotion because she was locked in the Strand Theatre in a protest. He whispered in my ear, 'Don't forget we've got Ruby Wax tonight.' On the other side I had Gillian. I came clean with her. I said, 'I'm really sorry, I'll happily do the lock-in, but I've got to go out and do Ruby Wax.' This did not go down very well – understandably. The meeting went on from 5 p.m. until 11 p.m. when my car came to take me to the Ruby Wax show, by which time everyone had decided that a lock-in wasn't the solution. They all had families to go home to. Some were single parents. It was impractical.

But what did emerge from this meeting was how convenient this closure was to the producer. There are always rumours flying around a production and producers are usually the least popular people. There was obviously some history here that I was not aware of. I went away, did the Ruby Wax show and gratefully returned home to bed, exhausted.

In the morning I returned to the theatre to collect my possessions, and discovered I was on virtually every front page. The photographers had captured me looking dazed and vulnerable; the captions said things like 'Toyah's show closed due to dispute'. There was no sense of notoriety about this, nor was there any sense of failure. But even worse than those might have been, there was no real feeling of closure. As I packed up my dressing room, everything just felt empty and sad. I felt unbelievably sad for the wig people upstairs who prepared our wigs every day. They were probably paid the least; they would also suffer the most from this closure. Then the same with wardrobe. Not to mention the dancers and the singers who had all thought that they were contracted for the rest of the year. In the light of what they were now facing, this was all very brutal.

Robert was abroad during all this, so I went home alone and slept most of the weekend. In my waking moments, I cried a surprising amount. Partly relief, partly sadness. But this was also the first time I'd been alone in a crisis. Being on my own had its good sides – it allowed me to think, to sort my head out and evaluate the whole situation. But Robert was wonderful at unmuddling my head. He talked so much sense and I really really missed him this weekend. As for Gillian Lynne's instincts about the producer, she was right. Within a month he left the country leaving the company in disarray. For me, it meant I didn't receive my VAT. I could survive that, but a lot of the rest of the company hadn't received wages in quite a while. The producer went to Argentina.

Robert returned home, which was always a joyous occasion. I felt such relief every time he phoned from Heathrow to say he'd landed safely; just knowing he was back in the country stopped me feeling so lonely. I was off doing the usual promotional rounds for 'Echo Beach', which went straight into the charts at number 20. Disastrously for me, *Top of the Pops* didn't invite me on the show that week, so when the following week's charts appeared, I had dropped. It was frustrating, but I was numb to all of this by now. Also I had the album to deal with.

Desire was an album I was proud of. It was a new departure, although unfortunately glaringly scarred by the presence of 'Echo Beach' and 'Love's Unkind'. I saw no point in keeping it a secret that I felt those two tracks threw the album completely off balance. *Desire*, as the first album I had released as a married woman, also had a new sexuality about it. In the past I'd always been afraid to express sexuality, I'd always seen it as something that had caused me trouble. Now I felt it was safe to be a woman and express myself as a woman; I was happy to explore this subject publicly.

Interestingly enough, it was at this time that I started to have stalker problems – not huge problems, but by expressing myself as a more sexual creature I was attracting the wrong kind of attention. I had been invited by the National Theatre to take over the female lead from Gemma Craven in their production of *Three Men on a Horse*, directed by Jonathan Lynn, which was going straight into the Vaudeville Theatre on the Strand. This was a year I was in two West End shows, earning substantial amounts of money, yet I was lucky if once a month £500 was making it into my account. So by the time I opened in *Three Men on a Horse* I was walking to and from the theatre every day. This made me vulnerable to stalkers.

One man in particular, a youngish City man, dressed in a raincoat, would follow me from the stage door. I would repeatedly ask him not to, I would take different routes, trying to throw him off, and when I got closer to home I'd just have to wait for a police car to come by, catch their attention and then he'd run off. The third time this happened I really lost my rag. After asking him again and again to stop following me, I waited round the corner, then as he came round I punched him smack on the nose. He stood there completely stunned, burst into tears and walked off.

Chapter 32

The Royal *It's a Knockout* was to take place at Alton Towers over a weekend at the height of summer. By now the press were in full swing, talking about nothing other than how the Queen could allow her children to be exploited in such a way as potentially to make fools of themselves in the public eye. This was not what Royalty was about. Prince Edward continually put on a brave face, saying it was about raising money and having fun, and after all, the Royal Family were human beings, so weren't they allowed to have fun? Rumours abounded that Princess Diana wanted to appear, but that Charles said it was not suitable. The press made a lot of this, hinting that Charles had snubbed the whole event, but no one really knew. That wasn't the point, anyway.

The point was that Prince Edward had managed to put together the biggest celebrity cast list any TV programme had ever known. From Christopher Reeve to John Travolta to Sheena Easton to Cliff Richard to Fiona Fullerton to Jane Seymour, he'd successfully put together an impressively enormous international cast and divided us all into four teams. I was on Prince Edward's team – the yellow team. I was his jester.

Robert drove me to Alton Towers and to our hotel, which was in the Peak District. We were to be sharing a hotel with Prince Edward and Princess Anne. In accordance with royal protocol, we arrived before them. By the time we found the tiny remote hotel, it was surrounded by security: even though we'd completely lost our way, all we had to do to find it was look for the police officers dotted around the fields and join the dots.

Our car and luggage were searched, then we went inside. It

smelt of paint. The whole place had been newly decorated for the arrival of the Royal siblings – in fact, when we arrived it was still being decorated, by a man with one arm, painting away furiously. Robert made the mistake of going straight to the Gents. He was immediately followed in by security who stood and waited at his door, then searched the loo after he'd finished. They must have run security checks on us by now and found out that we had no history of terrorism or violence, apart from me hitting the odd bloke on the street.

When Princess Anne and Prince Edward eventually arrived, there was much hoo-hah, many cars and a helicopter. The whole place was buzzing with security.

Later that afternoon, we were collected by coach to be taken to Alton Towers. In my coach were Princess Anne, Prince Edward, Prince Andrew, Fergie, Sheena Easton, Cliff Richard, Billy Connolly, Pamela Stephenson and John Cleese. This coach ride was a sheer eye-opening joy. We were driving down very narrow country lanes, passing through the occasional remote village, where villagers had lined the streets waiting for us. At one point Fergie shouted to Andrew, 'Look, Andrew, subjects, give them the Royal wave.' And Sheena Easton, bless her, sang 'Summer Holiday' all the way to Alton Towers, insisting the whole coach joined in, much to the embarrassment of Cliff Richard.

The security at Alton Towers was fit for an American President. We were ushered into our teams, given a pep talk, then taken through the games. Everything was going to be very wet, very muddy and very mucky. There was no room for vanity and certainly no room for pride. The press had tried their best to strip us all of our pride in taking part, but what they didn't realise was this wasn't about pride at all. This was about breaking down barriers and making things happen. It was wonderful seeing Tom Jones having to climb down a rope from a balcony to save Jane Seymour, then both of them falling into a huge pool of water. Jane was desperately trying to keep her hair dry – and in fact so was Tom! But their efforts were pointless. It was soon evident that we were all going to be a complete mess within minutes.

After rehearsals, we were all driven back to our hotels. There were two; Fergie and Andrew were with most of the celebs in a neighbouring hotel. We were all to dress formally for dinner, which was to be held later back at Alton Towers. Robert and I popped over to the other hotel. I wanted to see Fiona Fullerton. It was buzzing. Helicopters were toing and froing carrying celebs from London. One helicopter was even engaged in going back to London to pick up people's forgotten ballgowns. But this was the only extravagance I came across. Everything else was running smoothly and quite modestly.

That evening I had supper sitting next to John Cleese. There was no talk of *Monty Python* or *Fawlty Towers*; the conversation was all about marriage, the politics of marriage, the psychology of marriage and whether marriage was healthy in the first place. He was delightful company. The noise and commotion in that room were huge. John Travolta, who was very much a driving force among us, organising and questioning how things should be done, was rushing about among all the tables. He couldn't have possibly known who most of us were, but he was wonderfully gregarious, up for anything, a real hell-raiser. He'd started a food fight with Fergie that was really getting out of hand. As I quietly chatted with John Cleese about the benefits of marriage, a bread roll hit me smack on the forehead. My instincts were to look up and throw it back at the offender – and there was Fergie, staring at me, looking very apologetic, so I thought I'd better not. I didn't want to end up in the Tower.

The day of the games was blisteringly hot. Alton Towers was at a standstill. So many people were trying to get in. The press tent was chock-a-block. When we weren't playing games, we were entertaining the press, doing photos and interviews. Keeping morale up. Edward was the one who was most strained; I had a sense that he wasn't good at delegating. He very much was the creator of this idea and was taking full responsibility for every event. This was pulling him every which way. Edward decided the press had to stay in the press enclosure, they weren't allowed to ramble freely. Given the Royal Family's history with the press, this was understandable, but it really riled the press groups and they became quite unpleasant. I think this was Edward's first taste of having things turn against him, and he went into self-defence mode. He actually lost his temper with the press, which of course gave them an exclusive. Away from the public and press's eye, I tried my best to mollify him. He genuinely couldn't understand why everything had turned so nasty. Being needed in every camp, he had no time to defuse this situation, so by the time the games started, we'd lost our greatest allies. In the following weeks, the press were full of vitriol, spite and ridicule towards the whole project. It was portrayed as nothing more than an extravagant, overindulgent, egoistic folly.

But there are two sides to every coin. I felt that this was the beginning of the Royal Family's more human approach to their public image. I don't think anyone likes change when the change is actually happening; people from all walks of life fight change with a passion. Old habits die hard and all that. But once I'd stepped inside St James's Palace and witnessed how the regime was run, I personally felt it was better that those barriers come down. I distrust anyone who shows the public one face, then lives with another behind a screen of privacy. The Royal Family have such responsibilities, I think it's better that they show their country the true face of who they are. So all my admiration went to Prince Edward for this attempt to show not only the public, but his family, who he really was.

Weeks later, Edward threw a party at Buckingham Palace to say thank you to everyone who had made *It's a Knockout* possible. All the sponsors, fundraisers and celebs were invited. I arrived alone. Again, the protocol was breathtaking. As you pull into the forecourt of Buckingham Palace, your car is searched whether it's yours or it's hired. The bonnet is lifted and dectectives with mirrors go in underneath to search the engine. All the time, you stand by the car, just in case.

Inside the palace, we were all ushered up a magnificent red-carpeted landscape of stairs to an upper hall. Everything was on such grand scale. I couldn't stop gawping at the pictures, the plasterwork, the paintwork; everything was immaculate, covered tip to toe in gilt, or should I say gold leaf. I have no idea which two rooms we were in. One, apparently a dining room, was of vast proportions – you could have fitted a whole housing estate into it. The other appeared to be the throne room – down at one end of it, roped off was the throne. There were butlers everywhere who magically appeared and disappeared through panels in the walls. At first you thought these were simply mirrors, but then you realised they were on hinges and they actually opened. These weren't only for the butlers. Apparently they allowed the Queen to sneak in and out of events.

Billy Connolly was on top form, running amok, teasing everyone. Jane Seymour delicately walked around eyeing everything up, no doubt wondering if she could pinch some ideas for her stately home in Bath. I talked with Jane for a long time. I admire her so much. She is so astonishingly beautiful in the flesh, yet you know she's made of stainless steel, ambitious, driven and very very clever. She too had come to this event alone, and I really admired her for that. She bravely and confidently walked from room to room, looking very at home in the stately corridors. Most of the conversation, when Prince Edward wasn't present, was about the flower-embossed loo seats downstairs, the toilet roll and the ashtrays with BP on (Buck Pal, not British Petroleum). And who dared to pinch them. I suspect the ashtrays were discreetly placed on corners of Queen Anne furniture in the hope that they would be pinched and nothing more valuable.

In the course of the evening I spotted Fergie sitting on the throne, knighting Pamela Stephenson, but the most amazing event of the party was at midnight, after we'd all eaten. Prince Edward called us back into the throne room, where chairs had been set out in neat lines. We all sat down and waited. To our surprise, in walked the entire cast of *Cats*, who then performed selected songs from the musical. Now that's what I call pulling a favour. I left the party at 2 a.m., by which time it was really rocking; one couldn't help wondering if the Queen was being kept awake by the racket.

I was so lucky to step out of *Cabaret* straight into *Three Men on a Horse*. It was a period piece, set in the thirties, and I played a faded, jaded showgirl. It was a comedy, which was just what I needed – I have never known comedy ever be anything other than a joy to perform. My fellow actors were Geoff Hutchings, Desmond Barrit, Nicholas Le Prevost, Alison Fiske and Ken Stott.

The play is about an out-of-town New Yorker, discovered by some mobsters in a bar, because he has an attractive knack of picking the right horses for the races. I was the moll. Richard E.

Grant's wife, Joan Washington, was my vocal coach. It still astonishes me how at school I couldn't abide learning, yet in 1987, in my late twenties, I couldn't get enough of it. I enjoyed every minute of the day having to rethink my speech rhythms and adapt the way my body moved so I could portray that of a dancer who'd seen better days. There was so much room for parody here, but the subtler the better. There's no greater joy than hearing a member of an audience burst out laughing because they've caught the subtlest nuance of one of your jokes.

Geoffrey Hutchings was wicked to work with. He was one of those actors who had a knack of looking upstage, pulling a face at you, then turning round to face the audience and carrying on as if nothing had happened. I'm a terrible giggler, I giggle at the drop of a pin, and Geoffrey loved doing this to me. I had to do a mammoth scene with him which began with me slipping into bed with him, fully clothed, and launching into a speech about my life, and ended with me stripping off to my underwear and showing him my turn as a showgirl. A magnificent piece of writing that always brought the house down, it's one of those scenes that would be a gift to any actor or actress. And at least with Geoff I didn't have the problem that Ken Stott presented me with: Ken actually asked me not to get laughs on lines that preceded his, because he didn't like having to wait for the audience to settle down.

In this scene with Geoff I soon learned that once I was turned upstage to get into bed with him, he was going to take as much advantage of my humour as he possibly could. It started off with him making verbal farting noises so that I'd spend the whole of my three-page speech just trying to control my vocal rhythm. Then when I had to leave the bed to step out of my dress for the dance, he'd hold on to me so tightly I couldn't move, and again I'd be in fits of laughter. Maureen Lipman was gracious enough to come up to me at an awards ceremony and congratulate me on my comic timing. I confessed to her that she'd probably been in on a night when Geoff Hutchings was misbehaving. It wasn't only me who fell victim to Geoffrey. We often both had to exit stage together, leaving Desmond Barrit on his own – in one particular scene, drinking a glass of water in the silence of an empty stage, we'd run round the outer side of the set and start to make farting and burping noises through the cracks in the scenery. This was before Des was a huge star at the RSC. He's a lovely polite Welshman who wouldn't have dreamed of rebuking us. Instead he just drank his water. Suffered in silence and ended up choking.

Yet again my life got very busy on all fronts. While appearing in *Three Men on a Horse*, I landed the lead in a film called *Midnight Breaks* with Robbie Coltrane. I was also asked to be the guest speaker at the Woman of the Year lunch in October, with Princess Diana the guest of honour. I was disappointed not to have met Diana at the Royal *It's a Knockout*, so this was a fabulous opportunity to meet someone I'd always admired. By now she was coming out of her shell, losing that Laura Ashley appearance, becoming the Diana we all grew to love, independent and stylish. At our first meeting, one of five, she never remotely hinted at the inner pain she must have been in.

At the lunch, held at the Savoy, I was sat next to Diana. With us on the head table were Martin Luther King's widow, Kate Adie and Lady Lothian, who organises the whole event. Diana and I were left very much to chat alone. Our lunch was salmon and potatoes, but neither of us ate much – I was too nervous to eat and I imagine Diana just didn't want to eat. Instead we spent the whole time talking about her children, her concerns for them. She stressed many times that they were the most important part of her life and their future was paramount. Prince Charles never came into the conversation. We also talked about her other great love, dancing, and how she would have loved to be a dancer.

My speech that day was about blindness, about how I'd met blind people with more sight and vision than the sighted. I used my young fan Rachel, the painter, as an example. I also told the story of the two deaf boys who used to love to come to my concerts and lip-read the lyrics, feeling the music through their feet. After my speech, when I returned to my seat, Diana held my left hand and squeezed it, saying how moving she had found it. She really was extraordinarily beautiful. Usually you can sense if someone is insincere. Diana was totally sincere. I wouldn't use the word naïve about her. I think she genuinely had a heart of gold and loathed being hurt, therefore could not bear to hurt others. I met her on four other occasions after that, all official charity dos, and each time she'd give me a wicked little glint and grasp my hand and say, 'Here we go again.' She obviously had a great sense of humour.

Robert and I had one problem, and that was we weren't happy where we were living in Witchampton. I was afraid to be alone in the house; it was haunted, and my sleep would be disturbed nightly by awful dreams of the Devil. Also I wanted us to start our life anew. Witchampton held a lot of memories for Robert and they weren't memories appropriate to build a marriage on. This house had been his bachelor pad, as I was made acutely aware of by the number of strange women phoning up at all hours of the day and night. It was emotionally tiring and demeaning constantly to be reminded of his past. When we went out, women would walk up and remind him of one-night stands they'd had – admittedly many years before I came along. Even when these meetings didn't happen directly, Robert's friends would incessantly remind him that in the past he'd been nicknamed the Stud, thinking I would find this information amusing.

I didn't find any of this attractive. In fact it had the opposite effect – it made me distrust Robert. We were very honest with each other about this, and I started to have therapy to try and deal with it. When you love someone, you want them exclusively to yourself, and that includes their memories of the past. The trouble was, Robert wasn't allowed to forget his past. Everyone seemed to think it was wonderfully entertaining to talk about his conquests in front of his new wife. It made me feel like a token woman in his life. I no longer felt special; making love started to feel as if it was just something you did with the nearest woman at the end of the day. This wasn't the reality of the situation; my husband loved me incredibly and would do anything to save me from the pain I was in. But the pain was getting deeper and deeper. So we decided we were going to move and start again. Create our own memories, memories exclusive to us. Memories of being a couple.

One morning at Witchampton, looking through Robert's favourite magazine, *Country Life*, we saw a radiant picture of a garden. It was a house for sale – Reddish House near Salisbury. Robert turned to me and said, 'Look at that. Isn't that extraordinarily beautiful?' I looked at him and said, 'Robert, we're going to live there.' Robert always takes my predictions very seriously and acts upon them, so he phoned the estate agent. I had to go back to London to continue in *Three Men on a Horse*; Robert went to see Reddish House. There was such excitement in his voice when he phoned me that day. He said, 'This is the place. It is beyond paradise. It is absolute perfection.' When could I get down there and see it? The following Sunday I had to appear on TV AM, but I could drive down directly after that and be in Salisbury by 11 a.m.

I met Robert at Reddish House. The Chalke Valley was so unspoilt and beautiful all those years ago. Pulling into the drive of this tiny, immaculate, perfect piece of architecture was thrilling. There was already another family looking round, the Sassoon family, the grandchildren of the great late Siegfried Sassoon. The house came with a history. Sir Cecil Beaton had lived there for thirty years; he had created the garden and the interiors. It was Queen Anne grandeur on a small scale. At the time of our visit it was owned by Lady Chichester, an Argentinian woman in her early seventies, who took great pride in showing us around. Luckily that morning there was a huge article about me in the *Sunday Telegraph*; she carried the paper under her arm all the time.

Robert and I spotted three Canalettos on the walls of the saloon. Rumour had it that Lady Chichester had traded paintings to get her family out of Germany during the war. She left Robert and me to walk around the grounds alone, and we both fell in love totally with this pocket of perfection. The following day, Robert put in a bid. Shall we say it was just over half a million. This was to be a tense week. Sir Peter Hall and the Sassoon family were also interested in Reddish House and at one point the bidding was going up £10,000 a day. By the end of the week, we'd hit our ceiling and were heartbroken at the thought that we could bid no more, when the phone rang – our price had been accepted. We had a new home. We put the house in Witchampton on the market, and fortunately it was sold in no more than a month. At last, Robert and I could start a new life together.

When word leaked out that we had bought Reddish House, the press had a field day. Articles appeared in the *Independent* and the *Guardian* asking what was happening to Britain's heritage if such vulgar people as Toyah Willcox and Robert Fripp could buy into it. Unbelievable prejudice and bigotry were being aired about us. Before we'd even signed the contracts we were being accused of turning Reddish House into a base for vulgar parties and drug-taking. Luckily neither of us really gave a toss what people were saying. Once we were inside Reddish House we could firmly close the gates and shut the world out.

For the first time in my life I allowed myself to be domestic. I wanted to set up a perfect home for us. Reddish was not huge: it had four bedrooms, a very large saloon – where Sir Cecil Beaton used to entertain his guests – an entrance hall, a dining room and a kitchen. It was perfect for two people. The ambience was peaceful and romantic in a classical way. You could feel the elegance of times long gone, when people would arrive from London in open-top sports cars and would dine, gossip and play parlour games.

The garden, in comparison, was enormous. It was just under six acres of formal landscape and a water garden. To get lost in the garden was sheer joy. Every month was an eruption of new colours, new scents. Both Robert and I were well aware that we'd need to live there a couple of years before we really knew what Sir Cecil Beaton's ground plan was. So clever was his planting that the garden was never dormant. There was always something going on and, beautiful as the house was, I spent more time outside than in. In many ways, I'd at last found something to focus on – the garden, the seasons, all the possibilities. I found myself wandering around garden centres in a state of ecstasy, especially when I could find a plant that was old, that hadn't been genetically modified. The beauty of Beaton's garden was his roses; they were old breeds and they were rare.

And to put it politely, another rare old breed was the gardener who came with the house, Les. Les was magnificent. Robert and I used to sit inside the house and watch him work, every day of the year including Christmas Day. We so adored him. He represented everything England was at the turn of the twentieth century. We never really knew how old he was. He was as fit as a fiddle. As active as an athlete. When we left Reddish House in 1999, we finally discovered by accident that our gardener was ninety-two.

Les brought with him a wealth of knowledge – not only about gardening, but about the village and Sir Cecil Beaton. Les was there when Greta Garbo visited. He could remember chasing the press away as they hung over the garden fence asking if he'd seen Greta Garbo, if he'd seen Sir Cecil Beaton touching her intimately. Les, in his very charming way, told them to bugger off.

Les was our ally. He told everyone to bugger off. German tourists who just walked straight on to our property and started filming would get chased off by Les with a spade in his hand. Uninvited press would be chased off with those immortal words 'Bugger off and don't come back'. We so wanted to film and record Les's life story, but he was a secretive creature, a typical country person who generally kept his business to himself – but every now and then told us such remarkable stories that we'd run to the village shop and repeat them. Les's stories were legendary and excited everyone. He let them pass his lips like snippets of wisdom that everyone was waiting to hear.

Les was strong, too. One morning Robert was carrying a stone bench across the lawn when Les appeared in quick pursuit. He said, 'Don't worry son, I'll carry that.' He would have been eighty-two at the time. He picked the stone bench from Robert's crumbling arms and sprinted across the lawn with it. He'd hate me for saying this, but he had a quirky habit: on Friday evenings, he would go and buy fish and chips for himself and his wife, then they'd keep them till Saturday and heat them up. I've never known anyone else do this; it's one of the things I really loved about him. One of those little secrets that added to his legend.

When I remember Reddish, I remember Les. He's someone I never will forget. I value his memory as much as I do those of Katharine Hepburn and Laurence Olivier. Les was a magnificent star in his own right.

Along with Reddish came two cottages, which enabled us to keep staff. Because of fan and press intrusion, this was a necessity. It also meant – since Robert and I weren't always there – that I could keep a pet for the first time in ten years. Robert had always said he never wanted children, never wanted a family, and didn't want pets. But I drew the line at animals. I needed something to love, something to cuddle. I needed some kind of surrogate child, even though I never desired to have a human one. So one morning, we hotsy-trotted to Wimborne and I bought a rabbit, a young New Zealand white, and called him Cecil. On the way home, Cecil peed on my lap – I had to hide this from Robert; it was a sign of things to come.

Establishing a home life at Reddish wasn't exactly like establishing some kind of normality. Reddish was very much a show house. It attracted interesting types of people. For instance, invitations to lunch started to arrive from the ex-Prime Minister, Sir Edward Heath. Over the years we developed a close bond with Sir Edward that amused many in the community. I would go over to his house in Salisbury Cathedral Close for lunch, for tea. He would do me the great honour of letting me interview him on various TV programmes. Yet we knew very little about each other.

At one particular lunch, a Sunday lunch, Sir Edward had round his table me, Robert, his friend John Studzinski, Andrew Lloyd Webber and his wife, Trudi Styler and Sting. One always let Sir Edward lead the conversation on these occasions. But this time the conversation was led by Sting and Andrew Lloyd Webber. It appeared that both had bid for a Picasso in New York. The Picasso eventually sold for $54 million. I kept looking at Robert, praying he wouldn't try and join in the conversation. I had no intention of adding my voice to this particular snippet of multimillionaire life. I sat there and listened intently, hoping I wouldn't blurt out that I only had £500 in my bank account.

All the time we were at Reddish we were learning more and more about Sir Cecil Beaton. The house required constant attention, and we took on the building advice of a Mr Blick. Mr Blick lived in the village; his wife Dorothy was our housekeeper. He had worked with his father for Sir Cecil Beaton when he was a young man. In the stable yard at Reddish, Sir Cecil Beaton had his photographic studio, where he also painted. One week, Mr Blick senior was modernising the studio, when in the eaves of the roof he found a series of paintings, about seven in all. He sent one of his workmen into the house to tell Cecil's house-keeper about the find and ask what would Cecil like done with the paintings. Cecil, and apparently, without batting an eyelid said, 'Just burn them,' believing them to be old sketches. And it wasn't until the paintings hit the fire that it dawned on our Mr

Blick that these weren't Cecil's pictures. Twenty years before him, the parents of the artist Christopher Wood had lived there, and it was very likely that these seven paintings were undiscovered works by Christopher Wood. When Mr Blick told Robert and me of this, we quickly reckoned that at least £120,000 went up in smoke that day.

Chapter 33

Having spent the last ten years under constant pressure, mentally and physically, I was finding it quite hard to feel calm and confident at home, cut off from the outside world. *Desire* had failed miserably and I was chomping at the bit to get out there and prove myself. I was twenty-nine. I was in my prime. There was so much life to lead and I was starting to get very twitchy. Also, the realisation that my management weren't going to be doing that much for me was spurring me into action, because if I had a future, the only person who was going to make it happen was me.

In the big outdoors, outside of the gates of Reddish House, the world was changing very rapidly. Kevin Godley, my former video director, had set up Ark, an organisation that aimed to increase public awareness of the destruction that industry was wreaking on our planet. Ark wanted to introduce eco-friendly products on to the supermarket shelves. This prompted an enormous shift in the general consciousness. People weren't prepared to live with their disgruntlements any longer; their instincts were sharpening, and they were acting on their instincts. Thatcherism was burning out; yet again the majority were fed up being put upon by a privileged minority. You could feel and taste this shift of consciousness in the air. It seems to happen about every seven years. There are those who go willingly with it and those who fight against it. It's amazing to see what happens to those in both camps.

I've always believed that life is about evolving. It's never been about a simple pattern of go to school, get a job, go to work, retire, then die, realising on your deathbed that you've

330

missed a vital part of your life out and that's your spirituality.
What kind of evolution is that? Many of us have no choice;
situations are forced upon us. But no one is stopping us re-
educating ourselves. Making efforts to break free, to break with
habits and traditions and set our souls free. There's one key
question you can ask yourself if you want to sum your life up:
how will you feel about yourself on your deathbed? This is a
responsibility most people shirk. We don't seem to be able to
respect the fact that life serves a purpose. I believe in a greater
purpose. Because of this, there was no way I could sit in the
comfort of Reddish House and keep my sanity. I was only just
embarking on my life. I still had so much to do. So many things
needed addressing and changing. I was just revving up for the
race. The last decade had been fantastic. It had awarded me
many prizes – and left me with a few scars. But it was by no
means the culmination of my life. There were inner things to be
addressed and I was determined that as my body grew older,
my spirit and soul would grow outwards.

Working at my management's office was a young man, Alex
Patterson, who roadied for bands like Killing Joke, sometimes
for me. He had helped me move into my apartment in Chelsea.
One day while I was waiting to go in to a management meeting,
Alex and I put our heads together about what we'd like to hear
from music in the future. I talked about *Desire* and the problems
I'd had – with the A&R man forcing all his ideas on me when he
didn't really know me and didn't bother getting to know me,
and then me, as the artist, having to carry the critical brunt of
his decisions. Alex's problem at the time was that he was seen
as a roadie, not as a musician. He was already DJing in clubs
and experimenting with music, taking tapes around and trying
to get people to listen to them.

Our problems were opposites. Everyone had expectations of
me as a musician, and no one expected Alex to be a musician.
I talked to Alex about a project I was there to set up, a project
that was purely about the voice and emotional truth – definitely
not a commercial idea, but something I needed to do to feel
that I was a singer. *Desire*, like most albums in the past, had left
me feeling like a product. I wanted to be a singer again, to go
out on the road with a band, tour small clubs every night, be a
working musician. This was the album I hoped would take me

out of the commercial eye and put me back into the musical world I had started in. A world of experimentation, expression and ensemble work with others.

I told Alex that I wasn't a great musician, so I'd have to create layer upon layer of voice, using my voice as the main instrument, as a sounding board for lyrics. This really excited Alex. He said he was working with minimalism – no longer using the voice to sing complete lyrical structures, but lifting phrases and placing them within the music. As a person who had built a career out of singing songs and being a front person, I found this idea a little scary; I wasn't really in support of that kind of minimalism. But Alex and I met eye to eye about experimentation with sound and using sound to create emotions. There was nothing new here, Eno had done it for decades, but it was new to our generation.

Alex Patterson went on to found the Orb, while I went on to make an album called *Prostitute*. My management were now my publishers and record company; they refused to give me a large advance, so I made *Prostitute* for £10,000. If I remember rightly, the artwork for the album, which again was in-house – the management were in control of the packaging – cost more than the album did to make. By now there were such conflicts between us, I was at war with my management.

For *Prostitute* I hired a magnificent drummer-arranger called Steve Sidelnyk. I warned Steve that it was going to be cheap and experimental, but he was up for it. We locked ourselves away in a studio in Dorset for a week. My instructions to Steve were to create as many different rhythmic patterns as possible. I sat in the studio and said, 'Give me eight bars of this, then I want sixteen bars into that. Now give me another eight bars and do whatever you want for twenty-four bars.' So the only structures I kept to were the rhythmical structures of a lyricist, allowing Steve complete free expression and not telling him what I was going to write about. Steve didn't realise, but I was on a mission.

The meeting I'd had with my management a few weeks before was, for me, about creating this album, a piece of personal expression I had to get out of my system before I could do another commercial album. For them, it was a meeting about their feeling that really I should start a family, settle down and just go away. All that said, there was no offer to release me from my contract. That's why I decided this album had to be called *Prostitute*. I'd had enough of being treated, in my professional life, as a name without feeling and then, in my private life, as the wife of Mr Robert Fripp. My identity was being swallowed up by a man's world.

Surprisingly, my management thought I'd be happy to be relegated to the status of rock wife. No doubt they saw in me an important asset as a fundraiser, who would organise dinner parties and coax other rock wives into siphoning money out of their rich husbands for various charity appeals. There is nothing wrong with that, but bollocks to being a rock wife. I married Robert because I wanted to be his companion, in private I wanted to be his equal, his lover, and to go through my life with him, developing with him, and that's what Robert and I had. The outside world could bugger off and stop projecting its desires on to our private lives.

So, fired up by these enforced ideals, I sat in my room and wrote *Prostitute*. I based it on a wife's-eye view. The character I created as the wife was obsessive, bitter and violent, viewing life from the bed while her husband slept next to her. Her prison was the bed, her jailer the husband. What she saw from the bed was her lust for others and her lust for life, the irony being that the only creativity left to her, that of childbirth, was a path into a world of negative conflicts. The songs were built by layering the voice, layer upon textural layer; Steve and I shared playing keyboards and I played a little guitar. It was a strange and weird album, like nothing I had ever done before.

When I presented it to the management, their first reaction was 'Is there a single from it?' I laughed and said, 'You'll get nothing from this. But if you're brave enough and stick by it, the reaction you'll get will allow me to re-create myself as a singer-writer.' Credit to them, they did stick by it. Calling an album *Prostitute* is not the most advertising-friendly thing in the world to do. When their promotional team played the eagerly awaited new Toyah album to the sales force, most of the men, on hearing what the subject matter was, walked out of the room, refusing to have anything to do with it.

That was in England. In America, the response was unbelievable. First, it was seen as an anti-Madonna statement – which couldn't have been further from the truth. I've always felt that Madonna is the best thing that's happened to women. *Prostitute* was picked up as the feminist statement of the eighties. I was receiving letters from eminent professors at various universities across America, saying that I'd captured the anger and the changing atitude of women of my generation. *Billboard* reviewed me as an up-and-coming producer, and my fans loved it. It was not by any means a commercial success, but what it did achieve was to put me back in the waveband of creative thought.

By now I was so divorced from my public persona that I wasn't giving the outside world time to catch up with me. I had become completely driven and completely focused, realising that I had a lot of homework to catch up on as an actress and as a singer. Wherever I went, the common question was – and you cannot believe how often I was asked this every day – 'Do you still sing?' Of course, there's no way that people who heard 'It's a Mystery' and 'I Want to Be Free' on the radio would ever know that I'd created an album like *Prostitute*; they weren't meant to know. That album was made for true fans, fans who seek you out, make an effort to follow you. I'd stepped away from the commercial world, and the price I paid was to be asked, 'Do you still sing?' forty times a day. It was irritating, but my life was becoming, for the first time, plausibly satisfying.

I was beginning to become a private person again. People stopped asking me which toothpaste I used, who was my favourite designer, which nightclubs did I frequent, which gave me the chance to talk about changes that we all, as a society, had to address – and boy, did we address them with a passion. The fact that CFCs had to go out of household products, the fact that we no longer wanted animal testing. My past allowed me to address these subjects in public, and although there was one contingent who wanted me to remain the pink-haired singer of 'I Want to Be Free', the majority, like myself, wanted change. At least sixty per cent of this majority were women, and they responded to the message of change more than anyone else.

You could see a tide of shifting consciousness sweep through women in the late eighties. They were not prepared to accept the 'normality' that the corporate giants were thrusting upon them. They wanted a healthier, more active lifestyle. They wanted better quality, more responsible products on the shelves. Ludicrous as it sounds, consumer power is the best power in the world. Let's face it, we live in a world where everyone wants our money. If we refuse to give it, things have to change, and women started that revolution.

I also had a more personal issue to deal with. All my life I knew I would never have children. But the pressure on me now was intolerable. From all sides there was a bludgeoning inquisition as to when I was going to start a family. When you have no maternal instincts whatsoever, these preconceptions can be very frightening. You don't bring a child into the world just because you are a woman. You bring a child into the world because you have a calling – in an ideal situation. Also, I was married to a man who didn't want children. This isn't to do with a lack of love. Being with children, working with children, playing with children are far different from actually bringing a child into the world. I always trusted that if I had no biological calling, then I shouldn't force motherhood upon myself. It sounds hard, but I had an intense loathing of family life. It's something I never want to be a part of. If I were to bring a child into the world, there would be no way I could stop the child sensing that. And I couldn't bring a child into the world just to continue my blood line; that is a pathetic excuse for creating a life.

Because of these feelings, I didn't want to fall pregnant accidentally. I felt that I should take the responsibility of being sterilised. I didn't want Robert to get the snip. After all, our marriage may not last for ever, and he could meet someone he actually wants to have children with. So I made an appointment to see a gyno (who happened to be Fergie's gyno). When I went along for our first consultation, I was shocked to see pictures of all his patients covering the walls. Why is it that gynaecologists always have pictures of beautiful women all over their walls? I kept praying he wouldn't ask me for an autographed photo. But I suppose the good side is he remembers your face and not your backside.

He did a good job of trying to dissuade me from going ahead with the sterilisation, feeling that I was far too young and that once I hit my thirties, my biological clock would kick into action, but I did an even better job of persuading him there was no possibility whatsoever of that happening. So I was booked into the Harley Street Clinic and had the operation. Robert was away. I hadn't realised how vulnerable I would feel. I was torn between so many different viewpoints. I never wanted the responsibility of terminating a pregnancy; that's why I was doing this. I didn't want to take the pill. I'd had a coil, it did nothing but scar me, and there were a lifetime problems to do with my hips. If I had become pregnant, it was likely my hips could have dislocated.

Coming round after the sterilisation was particularly difficult – because of that I've never had another operation since. I can remember being conscious and unable to breathe; my whole body was convulsing. I could hear the anaesthetist talking overhead. Then suddenly, I was standing next to the bed, watching myself convulsing, listening to the anaesthetist telling the nurse to be patient, it was a reaction to the anaesthetic. I was trying to tell them that the problem was that my throat had constricted so badly I couldn't get air into my lungs, but they couldn't hear me. I was trying to suggest to them that perhaps if they gave me some water so that my throat wasn't so dry, it might relax. It didn't take long for me to realise that this was what's called an out-of-body experience. I can recall every word they said, yet looking down at the bed, I could see that my body was totally unconscious.

When I did come round, I asked the anaesthetist if he wanted to tell me anything. 'What do you mean?' he asked. I said, 'Surely you should warn me about having an anaesthetic in future?' He asked, 'Why?' I said, 'Because of the problems I had coming round.' I then recounted to him the conversation he'd had with the nurse. Funnily enough he wasn't flummoxed by that at all. He said it happens quite often. It's one of those things that surgeons can't quite explain. People just have out-of-body experiences. I've since learned that hearing is your last faculty to leave you when you die, and perhaps when you're unconscious your hearing is still very functional. That still doesn't explain how I came to be standing by the bed, watching this scene, but it explains how and why I could recount the conversation.

I didn't so much come round from the operation as get shocked out of my bed. I was back in my room, when a huge bang went off, which woke me with a start. I tried to sit bolt upright, but the pain in my stomach was too severe. Looking around the room for the source of the explosion, I saw that it was a huge bunch of helium balloons, one of which had exploded. Attached to them was a tag, on which was written, 'Tie a knot in it.' They were from Des Barrit, bless him, who was the only person to visit me. Well, put it this way, he was the only person who knew.

Before the operation I couldn't wait to be sterilised, but after the operation, oddly enough I felt as if I'd been robbed of my femininity. Why are women by nature so contradictory? Is this our weakness or is it our strength? For a long time afterwards I was in a state of confusion as to whether I was still a woman or not. I felt guilty that I'd interfered with God's conception of me, yet if I hadn't have been sterilised, I'd have felt guilty if I'd become pregnant. Is it possible that a woman can live without feelings of guilt, or are they part of our driving force? For weeks I was crying both tears of relief and tears of confusion. It's not that I'm only happy when it rains, I'm just one of those people who constantly search every possibility. It's an emotional search. I can feel both the pain and the joy, see both sides of the coin. Nothing is black and white.

Robert had spent the first three years of our marriage avoiding being in a band, working purely on Guitar Craft with his students. He was under pressure from our management to reform King Crimson, and he wasn't quite ready for that yet. But we both decided that having a band together would mean we'd have more time together. So we formed Sunday All Over the World. It was a way of adding focus to my music career, and also would prepare Robert for entering back into the mainstream with King Crimson. It's not easy working with your spouse, especially when he's equally as stubborn and opinionated as you are. Once we were touring we actually had separate bedrooms in order to get away from each other.

But the Sunday All Over the World tour was magnificent for me. This was not a pop band. We were writing contemporary songs in a post-progressive style. It was like a mixture between jazz and new wave. For the first time, I was singing in a style that challenged me, and vocally I was making massive leaps of improvement. We toured non-stop, all over Europe, and every-where we went we were whipping audiences into a frenzy. There were shouted requests for 'Schizoid Man', one of Robert's songs, and for me to do 'I Want to Be Free'. They fell on deaf ears. I'd open the show with 'Prostitute'; I was the support act as well as being in the main band, which in most European cities went down well. I only ever got booed off once and that was in Berlin. It took three people to boo me off. They were whistling and shouting so noisily it was just impossible to sing against them. When I came back on for the Sunday All Over the World set, the audience made a huge effort to let me know how welcome I really was, applauding and screaming after every vocal outburst.

In Barcelona, we played in an acid-house club. It was enormous, barn-like, and the stage was ten feet above the audience. When you're that far away from your public, you can't always tell if they like you or not. So after an hour-and-a-half set, and our usual modest one encore, we left for the dressing room where we all got changed and had a meal. Robert never eats in the daytime but he always insists on being fed immediately after the show. All through the meal I could hear this intense noise, like a hard rain falling on a tin roof. After we'd eaten, I said to Robert, 'There's something really odd about this noise. It's not mechanical, it's organic,' and I went back downstairs to look in the hall. For up to an hour, the audience had carried on applauding and were still applauding; somehow they knew we hadn't left the building. So we went back down on stage and repeated half the set in a series of six encores.

It wasn't just Barcelona that went bonkers. In Paris, where people had flown from all over the world to see us, the audience went stark raving mad. Yet back in Britain when we played, the audience's reaction was one of disappointment. Robert's audi-ence wanted nothing to do with me, and my audience wanted to jump up and down, have a good dance and a singalong. It didn't work in England. But that's fine. That's not a complaint. That's an observation.

Meanwhile, our management was in full swing, trying to persuade Robert to break up Sunday All Over the World and re-form King Crimson. My situation with the management was hopeless; I was going nowhere fast. So I moved my work away from where they could interfere: I went back into theatre, doing *A Midsummer Night's Dream* at the Birmingham Rep and *Whale* at the National; then I toured *The Taming of the Shrew* and made a film with French and Saunders and Timothy Spall called the *Tales of Little Pig Robinson*. By moving back into acting, I could take some control over my life and earn an income. I had taken to writing everything down, every fee, every penny earned. Because if I didn't know what I was earning, I couldn't trace what was actually arriving in my bank account.

In 1989 alone, I earned £73,000 from acting, but I never seemed to have any money. It wasn't as if my overheads were so high as to swallow up the majority of my income. I'm ballistic when it comes to money. Hugely protective. When I was working with Doon Mackichan on *A Midsummer Night's Dream*, she'd shout at me, 'You're a mercenary, you're nothing but a mercenary,' but she didn't understand why I had to be a mercenary. Back in London I stormed into the management office, into the accounts department to thrash out what I felt they should be doing. The head of the accounts department, who Robert and I disaffectionately called the Worm, looked me in the face and said, 'The reason you have no money, Miss Willcox, is because you squander it.' And I said, 'If I'm squandering my money, where're the flash cars, where're the holidays? I have done nothing but work for the past fifteen years.' He just laughed in my face.

The following day I sent a fax to the management saying they no longer represented me. I phoned every TV company I'd worked for and froze all my income. Because of their control over me, I had no other assets, no other accounts that they didn't know about. I put my apartment in Chelsea on the market, the sale of which I could use as collateral.

Robert returned to England the following week and we set about tracking down my creditors. By now I'd heard rumblings from doctors, dentists, studios, that none of them had been paid for their services for quite a time. First port of call was the bank manager at Lloyds on the King's Road. I owed the bank £5,000. Then we went across to my other bank, in Sloane Street, where the bank manager told us I owed them £80,000. I looked him in the eye and said, 'How can I owe you that much money when

I haven't seen it myself? Also I gave you no written consent to allow me to have an overdraft.' I saw concern in his eyes.

I was suddenly left with no income. I didn't want a court case; I couldn't afford the time. I was too busy rebuilding my career, and litigations had held back my creativity in the past. I decided to see an insolvency lawyer, sell up everything and just start again. But there is a miracle here. Within three weeks, I had tripled my income. I was earning more now than I'd ever earned in the whole of my career. It took a year to get back on my feet again financially. But the mere fact that my income went straight through the roof as soon as I'd left my management company showed me that all was not lost.

I hate to harp on about money. But when you haven't got it, you really know about it. Financial independence is your political strength. To have been in a situation where I couldn't defend my corner because I couldn't even feed myself has taught me to respect money. Money is transient but it allows things to happen. If you have millions you can change the world. If you have a few spare pounds you can help those you love.

In 1989, I'd been intending to buy my parents a new home. All their life they'd lived in the centre of Birmingham, and their house was becoming dilapidated and their health deteriorating. My parents needed my attention and my support. If I could get them in to a safe new environment where they could spend the rest of their years in a comfortable retirement it would be one worry dealt with. Now, having seen that I could earn money relatively quickly, I set my head about doing just that.

Robert in the meantime was full of fighting spirit. He had his own corner to defend. His fight took seven years to reach a conclusion, by which time there was little financial gain, only a settlement of pride. On a personal level, he felt let down by his friends. But a situation that often might break a marriage up actually made our marriage stronger. Robert never again hinted that I needed therapy if I suggested that some conspiracy was going on; he also learned to respect my jealousy and recognised that if I was suspicious of a woman, there was a reason. So instead of dealing with life's problems after the horse had bolted, we went for a more cautious, preventive approach.

Chapter 34

The legalities of getting out of my management contract meant that I had about six months in limbo. I wasn't idle in this time; I set about writing – songs, poetry, newspaper articles. The year before, I'd finished recording *Ophelia's Shadow*, my last album for this company, which received rave reviews in America – *Billboard* once again hailed me as not only a woman of the nineties, but a producer to look out for. That same year, when I was touring *The Taming of the Shrew*, a writing partner of mine, Simon Darlow, brought his friend John Roseman to see the show. John claimed to be a huge fan of mine – I was of his. He directed the *Bohemian Rhapsody* video for Queen, as well as most of the Eurythmics videos, and he'd made documentaries on the Rolling Stones. John was a real rock-and-roll character. He'd been there, done it, got the T-shirt and moved on. He was now an agent and manager for such people as Jill Dando, the Dimbleby family and other high-profile media journalists. I told John over dinner about my problems with my management. His eyes lit up. 'I'll sort it out for you,' he said. 'I'll get you a lawyer. We'll get you an accountant. We'll take on their companies and very soon everything will be clear.'

All my life, even though I've thrived on conflict, there have been certain types of conflicts I've hated. Legal conflict is like being wrapped in bindweed with your nose just above the water level; as the bindweed grows, it gets tighter around you and slowly pulls you under. I've never relished the process of hunting for clues, searching for proof that vindicates you. And so – not knowing, in any case, whether he was being genuinely kind or the bravado of the drink had set in – I thanked John and didn't take him up on his offer.

But now, a year later, seriously tangled in the bindweed of law and bureaucracy, I approached him. One afternoon I sat in his office on Charing Cross Road and told him the whole story. He kept his promise. Within two hours, I had the best litigation lawyer in the country, and the best accountant. By the next day, letters had gone to my management stating that action would be swift, fast and successful. John must have chosen the right names to represent me because within weeks we were getting somewhere.

In order to reach this deal, I had to accept a clause in the settlement contract, expressing that I would not discuss the reasons for my management split with my husband or anyone else. The financial situation is not why I left the company. Cash-flow problems had been evident for a good two years before the split. What I have chosen to talk about in this book is the effect the whole situation had on me, not the cause. In 1993, Cliff Dane published *The UK Record Industry Survey*, which minutely details all the said company's accounting, thus putting all that information in the public domain. If I cannot talk about my feelings and thus my actions, we do not live in a true democracy. The fact of the matter is, this whole scenario kickstarted my life in a totally new direction. In retrospect I thank all those involved for helping me make that journey, whether intended or not.

John set about the task of putting my main production company into liquidation. This was a phenomenally painful process for me. It was closing a chapter of my life – a chapter where I'd worked hard, and which, if I'd managed my own finances, would have led on to many others. John's kindness, support and belief in me were overwhelming. I can understand that a person loves a fight and loves to see justice, but his arm of protection went beyond being a Samaritan. It's quite astonishing that in times of real need, when one is about to break completely, life presents you with an angel. John was not without his own problems: his wife was terminally ill with cancer, and he had four very young children. I don't really know whether the battle John was fighting for me was helping him vent his anger over his wife's suffering. But ours was a partnership that worked, and in time, I and my best friend Danielle were to move in with

John to look after the children so that he could help Pearl in her last days.

Fighting the management had taken its toll on me. Robert said to me later that the light had gone out in my eyes; that he felt, looking into my eyes which are usually sparkly and mischievous, as if my spirit had died. I do think negativity can drain your life-force, which in turn can lead to physical illness. It wasn't that I was becoming ill – I'd never been more in tune; I was fighting a battle, so I was fit as a warrior. But Robert was right – my spirit had given up. The battle I was fighting was for my parents and my family. They needed me, they needed my support, and I kept going because of that alone.

I did an interview with Dr Anthony Clare for the Radio 4 programme *In the Psychiatrist's Chair*. Obviously he had to be quite prying, and this made me incredibly angry – because he hit the button immediately. His first question was: why haven't you had children? I don't know why I reacted, but I did and I remained on the defensive throughout the rest of the interview. He next asked about my mother, with whom I have a difficult but loving relationship; even though most of the time Mum and I find it hard to be in the same room together, I would kill anyone who hurt her. And then, out of the blue, after we'd stopped recording, Dr Clare asked, 'Do you suffer from depression?' I said, 'Not that I know of.' But I think he was right. I think what Robert saw in my eyes was depression. When I slept I could forget, I could forget who I was and everything around me, and the moment I awoke I felt normal, but then in a split second I remembered who, where and what I was, and the feeling was as if I was falling into a void. That must have been depression. I was going through the day functioning, but not feeling. I was numb.

Then right on cue came another surprise.

Robert walked into the house with a fax in his hand. He said, 'I don't know how to explain this. I have no idea how this person has found me.' The fax read: 'Dear Robert, Excuse this intrusion, but you should know your wife is seriously ill. I cannot get to England but if you can get her to either New York or Los Angeles, I can help you. Your wife is surrounded by so much negativity that it is impossible for her to cope. Signed Phyllis.' The only Phyllis Robert had known had worked in a record company in New York fifteen years earlier. It was possible this could be the same Phyllis, though how she tracked him down was uncertain. It turned out Phyllis had worked with Sting. She was known in musical circles as a counsellor and a healer. Her concern for me wasn't that I was physically ill, it was more weird than that – well, back then it was weird; now I understand it to be commonplace. Within the body there are seven energy points, called chakras, which align the emotional body, the physical body and the soul. They are the life-force. What Phyllis had sensed was that mine had completely shut down – a process that happens naturally when the body is about to die physically. I was in no state to argue. Robert bought air tickets and flew me straight to New York.

Just getting away from England did me the world of good. The moment we stepped on the plane I was starting to feel better. I just needed to turn my back on everything. The next seven days were to change my whole view on life. The way I thought, my relationship with the world and my relationship with Robert were about to have a radical makeover.

New York is always extraordinarily exciting. You can have anonymity in New York – no one really gives a damn about who you are; everyone ignores you. This alone eased the burden of my personal problems. John Roseman, bless him, was on the phone every day, checking I was OK and filling me in on the progress he was making with my ex-management.

The stick player in Sunday All Over the World had an apartment at 54 West Street; he and his wife Deborah welcomed us into their home, where we stayed for two weeks. The actress Ellen Barkin lived just above, and Robert and I spent much time in the lift hoping to bump into her. Robert and I had a day to explore. I was slightly nervous. Robert had lived in New York for two years, and many of the phone calls at the beginning of our relationship, from strange women in the middle of the night, had come from New York. By now, with my mental state so low and my self-esteem non-existent, I really didn't want to meet any more of Robert's exes. All had a knack of making me feel temporary in Robert's life. I'm not sure I could have held myself in check had we met one of them – I think my fists would have suddenly developed a kind of physical Tourette's syndrome and landed plonk in the middle of her unwelcome face. But away from England and our problems at last, we actually started to have fun.

We'd arranged to meet the mysterious Phyllis at the apartment on my second evening in New York. She was punctual. I don't know what I expected; all we knew of her at this point was rumour. She was a healer and a therapist of great reputation. We'd managed to track down a few musicians who had worked with her, and they had nothing but praise for her miraculous powers. I think I was expecting a mystic to walk in. Instead, through the door appeared a short, curvaceous, country-and-western-style woman. She could have just stepped right out of *Calamity Jane.* She had a broad whisky voice, loud and full of colour and character. She walked straight up to me and held me, and while she hugged me she just laughed and laughed. I was soon to learn that Phyllis laughs a lot. She whispered in my ear, 'Everything's going to be all right.' I'm ashamed to say I was suspicious of her in the beginning. I so needed to protect my inner privacy. My thoughts at the time were quite rancid; I thought ill of most people and I didn't want her to be able to see inside me, see all that festering.

We started the therapy immediately. The very first thing Phyllis did was to sit Robert and me down facing each other. Then she sat on a chair between us. This amazed me. I think I was expecting her just to touch my head and all would be well – I would be healed. But what she actually did was so practical, so common-sensical, that Robert and I would never have thought of it. She'd ask me a very simple question: 'What do you think of Robert's clothes?' And I would answer quite critically. She'd tell Robert not to respond but to listen to her. Then she'd turn to Robert and put my answer into Robert's vocabulary. Then she'd ask him a question: 'What do you think of your wife's temperament?' And Robert in turn would answer critically. I was told not to respond until Phyllis had translated Robert's words into my dialect.

This went on for a whole evening, and slowly it dawned on both Robert and me that part of our problem with each other was a generational gap. (There's eleven years between our ages.) I was drowning in jealousy and possessiveness because of Robert's promiscuous past. Robert was a child of the sixties; he grew up with sexual liberation. I was a child of the seventies; I grew up with reticence and shyness. Because of this I felt I could never trust Robert in our relationship – although I rarely said so; it only ever came out on those awful occasions when we'd arrive at a dinner party to discover that yet another of Robert's exes was present. They'd talk so freely about their relationship that I'd feel physically sick. But Phyllis made me understand that this wasn't a threat. This was a fact – a fact of the past. The past must be let go of so that the present and the future can happen. This wasn't the kind of healing I'd been expecting. But in being taken by Phyllis on this journey, that night Robert and I fell in love with each other totally for the second time. Realising I had married someone I could trust, I instantly started to feel better. The ever-present nausea started to fade away.

The work with Phyllis didn't end there. She asked that the next day I be left alone with her for the whole day and the whole night. The following morning she told me about chakras – which I'd heard of through yoga and various books on healing. I'd always had an interest in healing, so I was fascinated. My life had already changed radically, by now and I felt great trust in Phyllis. My inner turmoil was calming down all the time. Phyllis explained that a chakra is not only an energy point and a spiritual point, but also an emotional point. You have seven chakras: one in the base of the spine, the next one up in the solar plexus – a creative chakra – then one in the heart, in the throat, in the mouth, between the eyes and at the crown of the head. These all relate to your emotional life. For instance, the heart chakra relates to family, the throat chakra to voice and communication. Because of all the negativity I'd been subjected to, my chakras had started to malfunction. Some say they block, some say they actually turn off. Phyllis explained that if a chakra completely shuts down, it's preparing the body for death. This is the point when the body becomes diseased, and even though I wasn't diseased, she felt that my tampering with my body by being sterilised had triggered problems with my chakras that left me dysfunctional in a world where I really had to be on top form to survive. Also, my depression was such that my chakras couldn't give me any energy anyway. So Phyllis was going to sit with me and kick-start my chakras so the energy would flow through me.

Anyone who's had acupuncture will know about meridians. Meridians and chakras are pretty similar – they're all about energy moving through the body. If your energy is moving through the body correctly, you are healthy in mind and body. The moment Phyllis started work on me, my stomach started gurgling. I'm not talking about a polite little gurgle – it gurgled as if there was a waterfall passing through me. She asked me to lie on the floor, to keep my eyes closed and to think of anything except her. She had an assistant who sat at my feet. She said she was going to work from my feet upwards and finish at my head; then I could get up and walk around, but in the meantime I had to close my eyes and forget what was going on. Well, apart from the stomach rumbling, which had me giggling a lot, I could feel my limbs being lifted. I didn't keep my eyes closed when my right leg was lifted, because I felt it was so heavy I needed to help, but when I opened them I saw that neither Phyllis nor her helper was near me. They were in the corner of the room, talking. At that point I realised that she was more than just a marriage counsellor. There was something physical moving me around.

This went on for most of the day, as did my gurgling stomach. By the end of the session, I was experiencing something that can only be described as extreme butterflies. The only other times I have experienced this are after writing a fantastic lyric which I just know is empowered from above; or walking off stage having done a fantastic show and knowing all the energy is right – the audience and the show are in complete harmony; or with nerves – but good nerves, when I know something wonderful is going to happen, but I'm going to have to make it happen and it makes me nervous. This extraordinary feeling in the stomach, this fluttering, was happening not only in me, but in Phyllis too. With her wonderful Nashville accent, she said, 'Toyah, you and I need some whisky to calm us down.' And we sat in the twilight with New York rumbling on outside and drank whisky for an hour.

Funnily enough the alcohol had no effect on me or on Phyllis. She needed to move on to the next stage: having opened up my chakras, she now had to ask me to look inside them. This was the most surreal of the sessions. I had to imagine my chakras related to a vital organ in the body and tell her the first image that came into my head. She chose my heart first. 'Toyah,' she said, 'what do you see in your heart?' There was a mongoose. It was curled up. It was asleep. She said, 'OK, ask it to wake up.'

So I asked it to wake up. I was feeling a little bit silly during all this, but by now I really trusted Phyllis – and then, really clearly, in my head, the mongoose woke up and said, 'Tell her to fuck off.' I looked at Phyllis and said, 'You're not going to believe what the mongoose has just said.' She said, 'Tell me, Toyah.' I said, 'Phyllis, the mongoose has just lifted its head and turned to me and asked me to tell you to fuck off.' Phyllis burst out laughing. She said, 'This is good, your soul is sleeping. It's good it doesn't want to be woken up.' And so, Phyllis and I worked well into the early hours of the next day, continuing this strange form of storytelling. By my telling Phyllis about the images in my subconscious mind, she could map my soul's past.

I have never believed in reincarnation. The thought of returning here again and again fills me with horror and sickness. But what Phyllis came out with was not 'Oh, you were Cleopatra in the past' – I really wouldn't have been able to sit there and take that seriously. She mapped out my soul's persona and what it had been through. Not who it had been, but the grand total of my soul's past experience. We can all accept that we are born with genetic characteristics; what Phyllis taught me is that we are also born with characteristics of the soul, things inherited from the past. Some call it karma. And what I learned that night, from this bizarre game of storytelling, prepared me for my future, and I left New York understanding *why* – why I was who I was and why I'd experienced what I had experienced. I am eternally grateful to Phyllis.

That night we all went to bed exhausted. In the morning Phyllis left for Nashville. I gave her a huge hug and thanked her over and over again. She said, 'Just be careful on the streets of New York, will you. People will think they recognise you.' I'm not well known in New York so I took this with a pinch of salt. Robert and I continued our holiday in a state of bliss. But Phyllis was right. Every time I crossed the street, people stopped to greet me; every time a car drove past – and there are a lot in New York – they put their brakes on and said hello. Apparently when Phyllis has opened up your chakras, your inner light is so bright that people instantly think they recognise you as family. What they're really recognising is your light. It was an odd experience, walking around New York with the natives saying hello to me. That just doesn't happen in New York.

Chapter 35

I returned to England with renewed vigour. John Roseman had prepared the settlement with my ex-management, which meant that John could continue as my manager – as he does to this day. I had a new lease of creativity and energy that had to be expended. I was friends with a group called Girlschool; we decided to re-form under the name of the She-Devils and we spent the summer playing festivals in Germany, Holland and the UK. I'd become a totally different person. Nothing could hurt me. It wasn't that I was infallible, but I was no longer my own enemy. I could accept what had happened in the past and not let it hold me back from my future.

The actor Tim Pigott-Smith came to see me and asked if I'd play the female lead in *Amadeus*. It was to be a touring production for the Compass theatre company; Peter Shaffer, the writer, would be on hand for any rewrites needed. I jumped at the chance of working with Tim Pigott-Smith and also with Richard McCabe, a fantastic actor who was to play Mozart – and could play all the pieces on the piano. After a summer in the company of the She-Devils, a month of intoxication and sexual enlightenment (and by that I mean observing their sheer appetite for men), partying too hard, playing too hard, now I needed to discipline my spirit a bit. Touring *Amadeus* was exactly the right project to go into to pull focus on my career again. For Tim Pigott-Smith it was a demanding piece of theatre; for me, playing Constanza, it was above all else fun and high-spirited.

Tim asked if I would also, in the daytime, tour prisons. For this I needed to choose an appropriate story. I could have one other actor with me, so it was decided that I and an actor called

Paddy would do a performance about the life of Janis Joplin and how drug addiction destroyed her. My part of the agreement was that I'd prefer not to perform in front of anyone who had a history of child abuse, paedophilia or rape. The theatre's part of the bargain was that I'd only have to do two prison performances a week.

Amadeus was a huge success. We were on the road for three months and every performance sold out, and everywhere the reviews were glowing. The prison tour, however, was a completely different kettle of fish. One of my first dates was the Cardiff Young Offenders' Unit, where I never want to appear again. The show consisted of an hour of songs and dialogue. Admittedly I had a captive audience, but that doesn't mean a disciplined audience, and at Cardiff I couldn't hear my own voice for shouts of 'Show us your tits, come on, let's rape her.' But that was an exception. All my other prison visits were in one way or another moving experiences.

In Glasgow, for instance, the taxi driver asked to come in with me. I was quite amused by this; I didn't bother to ask him why. So I got him through security, along with the forty members of the press who were coming in to photograph the show. In most prisons, I ended up performing in the church or in the gymnasium. At the Glasgow prison I was in the chapel. The inmates loved the performance, knew all the songs and sang along; all the time, on the back row, my taxi driver was calling people from the audience over to come and talk to him. Afterwards, as he drove me back to the theatre, I asked, 'How come you knew everyone?' He said, 'Well, they're all my family. I haven't seen my cousins in weeks.' It turned out that not only his cousins were in this prison, so were his brother and his father.

In Lewes Prison I performed in an office. The prisoners were not compelled to see the show, they volunteered; at Lewes I had a small audience of about ten. All had a past of drug abuse. At the very end of the performance, we finished the story with Janis, miming, injecting herself with her last fix of heroin. When I came to this part, one of the men in the audience jumped up and shouted, 'Stop it, stop it right now.' He was incredibly upset. I stood up and said, 'I'm really sorry – are you all right?' He said, 'No, don't do it, don't do it.' He was completely involved in the message of the play. When he had calmed down, we all sat round him and he told us how he'd seen all his friends die that way and how he himself had nearly died in similar circumstances. On occasions like this it was actually really sad to leave people behind. One policy among those going into prisons to work is you never ask why people are in there. Because I had no knowledge of their crimes, I could see them as human beings.

In Belfast, where I was performing at a high-security prison for political prisoners, I didn't have to ask what the majority were in there for. Security was so tight I was strip-searched before going in and had to change into my Janis Joplin costume in front of prison officers. The performance was in the gym, where there was an audience of at least two hundred inmates. They'd all done their homework: they'd read about Janis Joplin's life and listened to her songs. After the performance, I always did a question-and-answer session; here in Belfast I listened in amazement. They didn't ask questions. They told me about the life of Janis Joplin, about her friends, her acquaintances, those who had worked with her, those who hadn't. I kept looking out over them, thinking, This is probably the most dangerous audience I will ever perform in front of and they are so bright, so witty, so engaging, they could be lawyers, politicians, doctors. This left me confused and dazed. When I collected my luggage and my clothes from security, every pocket, every turn up, every compartment had had little leaflets tucked inside saying, 'You are a sinner, you have sinned against God, change your ways.' This really shocked me, because it was only the prison officers who could have done this. I suspected that because they'd seen me play the role of Janis Joplin, they presumed I was a promiscuous drug-taking woman. I left that prison with a bad taste in my mouth.

The last prison I visited was Wakefield women's prison – the only women's prison on the tour. It was an open prison, and again I performed in the gymnasium. There was instantly an informality about the prisoners. Chairs were lined up in rows and they could sit wherever they wanted. They all sat holding hands, kissing and touching each other quite intimately throughout the show. I'd say the majority were in relationships with each other. When I was performing in the male prisons, I felt quite vulnerable, and the air was sexually charged. Here, at Wakefield, it was completely different; it felt as if I was in a kindergarten school, everyone was so affectionate with one another. In the question-and-answer session afterwards, no one really asked any questions. They all just wanted to come and touch and feel my hair and talk about clothes. They were the only audience I performed to who weren't remotely interested in Janis Joplin. I had been warned that Beverley Allott had been brought in, and she was in fact on the front row. I tried not to stare at her. The girls made me a lovely little teddy; I call it Wakefield. I promised them that one day I'd write stories about Wakefield the ever escaping teddy, and they all giggled.

Before I left, I was asked to visit the secure unit, where there was one prisoner who wasn't allowed out of her cell. In fact she was in a padded cell. I was led through many corridors into a quiet wing, where an officer unbolted a typically threatening-looking leaded door. Inside the cell was a girl who had suffered so much abuse by her own hand that she was deeply, shockingly scarred. Her forehead protruded by an inch; it was one huge callus from where she had continually banged her head against objects. Her hands and arms were covered in deep cuts. She said, 'Hello, Toyah. They wouldn't let me out to meet you.' I said, 'Hi, how are you? Are you all right?' Isn't it funny how you always ask 'Are you all right?' at the wrong moment. She said she wasn't. She was in there for good. They'd never let her out because her only ambition was to die. The reason she was locked up was because of her repeated attempts to commit suicide. I said, 'Surely you have something to live for?' And she said, no, all she wanted was out. She was bored of life and she didn't want to stay. There's not much you can say to someone like that without appearing glib or interfering. I could tell by her demeanour, the blankness in her eyes, that she really meant it. That she'd had enough. Some way or another, she was going to achieve her wish. I thought about her for a long time after, frustrated by the fact that I hadn't been able to do anything to help her, other than offer words of comfort.

After the prison tour, I had a better understanding of the word liberty and a greater feeling for not only the freedom of choice, but the responsibility of choice. All my life I had worked for fame and recognition. That was my choice, so I had to accept both the joy and the problems that fame can bring. But here I was, in my thirties, with no plans. As a teenager, I only daydreamed about what life would be like in my twenties, about what I wanted to achieve, what I wanted to see. I never planned past thirty. Suddenly, when I walked away from the last prison date, I felt surrounded by a great freedom. Freedom of choice and freedom from being compartmentalised suddenly meant more to me than anything in the world.

Life is an all-round experience. Our horizons should be broad; we should all be adventurers. These little boxes we call home are always nice to return to, but isn't it nicer setting off and exploring? Over the next few years, I deliberately didn't allow myself to rest. I went from one play to another, from one performance to another. I was more keen to learn than I had ever been in the past. I embraced being in my thirties. OK, the body was changing at a rate I wasn't particularly fond of, but though my skin was no longer as tight, my mind was getting sharper and sharper.

I packed my bags and left to live in a squat in Berlin, with a team of musicians I wanted to work with. Not speaking German wasn't a problem – communicating with sign language and broken English is always an adventure. The band used to sleep in the daylight hours and rehearse through the night. We lived off bread and cheese, which I found incredibly romantic, and on Fridays we all went down to a bar and drank raspberry beer. Everything was so clean-cut and simple. My room in the squat had just a bed, no other furniture, and a view over a dilapidated tenement. Children played everywhere. In the block I slept in there was just one toilet which all the other flats shared. And then, when we, the band – called Kiss of Reality – had written enough music, we set off in our cars and went round the country playing in universities and nightclubs.

We crossed the border to Poland to play in Warsaw. This was one adventure a little too far. It took us ten hours to drive from Berlin to Warsaw. We were carrying a lot of computer equipment, and in Poland that was gold. So we could never leave the cars unattended. When we arrived at the club we were to play, which was set in the middle of a park, we set up the equipment and took it in turns to sit by it, making sure no one ran off with all our computerised sound effects and keyboards. The music we wrote was contemporary progressive; the style was an odd mix of jazz and electronic, very popular in Europe. The local TV and radio stations treated me like a heroine and I was whisked away to do promotion. They were fascinated not only by my past, but by the fact that I was married to Mr Robert Fripp, and I was introduced everywhere as Miss Roberta Frippa – meaning 'wife of'. I found it hard to take this as a compliment and I used to correct everyone, saying, 'I'm not Roberta Frippa. I am Toyah Willcox' – at which all the women present would spontaneously burst into applause.

We'd been horrified to discover that the ticket prices for the show were the equivalent of a week's wages. We'd decided once we got to the club that we were just going to open all the exits and let everyone in for free. That's what I'd done in the punk days. I was sure it would still work. Literally seconds before we went on stage, the promoter came into our dressing room and apologetically told us he couldn't afford to pay us. We looked at each other and thought, Oh, here we go again – it's one of those gigs; but we decided to go on anyway, the people were so fantastically friendly. And the concert was exceptional, ending in encore after encore.

Eventually we were allowed to pack up our gear and prepare for the long drive back to Berlin. An amazing number of people had flown over from England to see this concert, so we were surrounded by friends. Outside, having packed up the cars, we were standing in the park, chatting and catching up with our English friends before we had to say goodbye when, I noticed fifty yards away in a clump of trees there were hundreds of teenagers gathering. It looked like two gangs meeting. At first I thought it was a friendly meeting – I could only see silhouettes in the darkness – but then I realised that both teams were pulling a man to and fro between them. When I saw a rope go around his neck, I grabbed my guitarist, David Pittaway, and said, 'David, look, they're lynching that man.' We watched horrified, not knowing what to do, until a lad from one of the gangs saw us, walked over and said, 'Are you English?' I said, 'Yes. What are you doing?' and he answered, 'Go now, go now, bad drug deal, bad drug deal. There'll be anarchy. When the police come we'll fight the police. Get out of here.'

I turned quickly and tried to tell all our English friends to move, just *move – now* – but none of them could see what was happening and they all carried on chatting happily. Eventually I had to shout at the top of my voice, 'Get the fuck out of here!' They looked at me as if I'd flipped, and I pointed to what was happening. By now the man had had a canister of tear gas burst in his face and they were winching him up by the rope. Stunned and afraid, we leapt into the cars and just drove, for another ten hours, back across the border into Berlin, finding it impossible to talk to each other. When we finally hit our beds, we slept for a whole day.

During my period in Berlin, I would hop back to England to see Robert, who in turn would hop back from New York to see me. In the summer of 1991 I landed the lead role in a film called *The Anchoress* with Christopher Eccleston, so I moved from Berlin to Belgium where it was to be filmed. Then after the filming I moved back to Britain to start my life as a presenter, which began almost by accident.

John Roseman's office phoned me up and they said, 'Oh, there's some programme called *First Night*, they want you to present the programme – you don't want to do it, do you?' I said, 'Wait a minute. What do you mean I don't want to do it? Yes, I'll do it.' And that was the beginning of a new career. Presenting was my first ever what I could call a day job. It called for a completely different discipline from the kind of work I'd done before. Most of the time I had to write my own script and be a drama critic. This writing had to happen in the moment – you'd learn it, do a piece to camera then move on. It's so different to making a film. With a film you shoot three minutes of screen time a day; with presenting you shoot anything up to two hours a day. It was a more intense experience and if anything, needed a journalistic mind – something I never had before, but I think have since acquired.

Presenting and acting are chalk and cheese. They may serve the same medium, TV, but they couldn't be further apart. What I grew to love about presenting was its speed, its unpredictability and the fact that I got to travel. I'm very nomadic by nature and I love to keep moving; I would happily flit from country to country to country for the rest of my life. Presenting was the nearest I'd come to this. It also gave me space to form a new band, which I'd tour in the evenings. Suddenly I found myself in a perfect world. I had two careers in the same day: I could write and present in the daytime and then, in the evening, vent my frustrations on stage. This situation also dealt with another problem.

For many years now, the public had perceived me as the pink-haired princess of punk. I hadn't had pink hair for many years, I was a decade older and I wanted to get on with my life. I found that growing older brought not only happiness, but also knowledge and technique and I very much wanted to show these qualities. They weren't uniquely mine – they were there in every woman who had life experience. It was time the world of the media became more age-friendly towards women. Attitudes clearly weren't going to change overnight, but by presenting, I allowed people to see me as who I was today, not yesterday. This upped my profile, and gradually, the reactions I got from the public were no longer 'Where's your pink hair, darling?' and 'Do you still sing, love?' but were more to do with the subject matter I was trying to bring into people's consciousness.

Often TV companies would approach me and say, 'What subjects would you like to do films about?' There were many things I had benefited from in my private life, but none more than homeopathy. I'd grown increasingly aware that in this age, to deal with our stress-related ills we were routinely being prescribed medication. This was all too easy and in many cases not beneficial in the long term. With homeopathy, you don't just take a pill. You have to understand how your body is working and how it responds to the stresses of modern-day life. In gaining this knowledge, you are learning how to address prevention rather than cure. In retrospect, I realised that most of my mental and physical problems in the past had been caused by stress; now, homeopathy helped me to learn to deal with stress. Stress will never go away, it's a disease of the modern world, but we can learn to ignore it, because it's not as real as we think it is. This became one of the subjects I wanted to champion. If I could get this message across even to just one person, at least I'd know I'd made that person's life a little bit better.

It's always been important to me to feel passionate about the subject matter of my work. Homeopathy doesn't work for everyone. Some people are truly ill and need conventional medicine to keep them alive. But often we can help ourselves – especially if it's simply a case of stress. However, homeopathy requires patience. It's a lifestyle rather than a quick fix. I'll give you an example of how taking time helped me.

In 1994 I was touring *Peter Pan* with Brian Blessed. We were on the road for three months, sometimes doing two shows a day. The schedule was both physically tiring and stressful. Having been born with shallow hips, I was used to a constant grumbling pain – nothing that a headache pill couldn't cure. But during the tour, the pain got worse and worse until I could no longer walk without extreme discomfort for more than about twenty yards. I started to get scared. The thought of hip replacement absolutely terrified me (and the fact that I was supposed to have had it done in my teens made me feel guilty).

I went to see the top hip specialist in the country and asked for his advice. They took X-rays, which weren't good – they showed a cyst had developed in the joint on my right side. The specialist said it wasn't a case of simple hip replacement because I lacked the socket, and what I did have had finally disintegrated meaing that I needed to take nine months off – immediately – for three major operations to rebuild a socket around the joint. I phoned Robert in floods of tears. I couldn't take nine months off. I couldn't afford it professionally or financially. So Robert took me to see his homeopath.

Initially, the homeopath could only give me ingredients to discourage inflammation, but then he gave me some whose long-term effect would be to encourage strengthening of the bone. After I had promised to stay on his recommended diet of no red meat, very little citrus fruit and no alcohol, and to keep taking his specially prepared medication, he recommended that I see an acupuncturist. Please remember here, I am naturally cynical and usually don't believe in anything until it works. I went to see my local GP, told him the problem, and asked what I could do. He happened to be an acupuncturist and started treating me that day. Within a week, the pain had gone. I'd had acupuncture before for voice loss and muscle strain but never had it worked as successfully as this. I was very lucky that my GP was so sympathetic to alternative therapies – even though in general these therapies should be complementary, working hand in hand with conventional Western medicine.

I let the hip specialist know that in no circumstances was I prepared to go ahead with the surgery, but that I would like to seek further medical advice. He referred me to a man he knew who was born with the same condition as me, Eric Askew, who was based at the Salisbury Odstock Hospital, and who told me that he too had suffered from a cyst in his bad hip joint and had refused surgery. His way of dealing with it was to realign the spine. Like him, I was born with one leg shorter than the other, so he measured up my left leg and made special insoles which I always wear in my left shoe to bring my left leg up to the same height as my right leg, therefore straightening the spine and taking the stress off my right joint. Eric also insisted that I wear silicone pads in my shoes – taking seventy per cent of the strain off my hip when I move. Within a matter of days, the pain had gone; now it's been a matter of years and I have no problem with my hip whatsoever. I can even run again. It took time to discover all this, and a lot of patience, but above all, I listened to my own body. I listened to it when it grumbled, for instance when I ate my favourite fruit, mango – if I eat it, I'm in pain the next day. Now I know that certain things will cause me physical pain, I can stop eating them rather than reach for the pain-killers. Self-knowledge is incredibly important.

My sister, who's a nurse, happens to be married to one of the most experienced medical doctors in the land. On asking him if he could find a specialist who dealt with my condition, he arranged an appointment for me at Bart's in London. All I wanted to know was what might be the consequences of growing older and not having the surgery I should have had as a teenager. Then I would make the decision as to whether to have surgery or not. There was an added complication that came with age: my knee socket, which is shallow as well, was starting to dislocate. With time and experience, I had grown used to realigning my leg on my own. (It had a habit of dislocating at the strangest times, such as in bed, or in the bath, which could be dangerous, but anyone who has suffered a dislocation knows that you deal with it quickly.)

At Bart's, I was led into a room where I met the elderly physician. He had twenty students with him. The physician had no idea who I was; when he asked if I minded standing in my underwear, the students started giggling and one of them explained to him that I was a TV presenter. I said I didn't mind at all. The physician was particularly interested because my condition is more common in males, and also because I had trained my body to deal with the misalignment. He asked me to walk up and down, all the time explaining to the students how my brain had trained my body to hold itself in a certain way. He was also fascinated by the fact that I'm very muscular, and that muscle texture was keeping the skeleton in check, especially the spine. I explained that when I was a child, my mother had made me do copious exercises to strengthen every part of me that was weak.

At the end of this medical exhibitionism, I asked him about the consequences of never having surgery. He said that in his experience it would be a miracle if I could make it to my seventies without some kind of correction. I told him that I was no longer in pain and my diet was good and I wasn't doing physical exertion that could bring the pain on. He answered, 'Well, pain is your body's way of telling you that it's had enough of something.' So the conclusion I came to was that as long as I could control the pain, I could keep the knife at bay. As I left, the physician said, as an aside, 'Please consider leaving your skeleton to Bart's, won't you.' Everyone burst out laughing.

I remember the nineties more affectionately than I do the eighties. The eighties was like surfing on a tidal wave. But the nineties had something very special. It was the first time I truly enjoyed being a woman. It was as if everything feminists had worked for in the past century was coming to fruition, and anything was possible for women. For me, age brought stability, and great confidence. But in the outside world too, wonderful things were happening. Madonna and the Spice Girls were proving that it could be a woman's world. On my level, I was managing to run three careers successfully in parallel – acting, singing and presenting. It was just a very satisfying decade. I went from play to play, from country to country, from concert to concert.

There was such diversity. One year I presented a programme about sex, which I slightly dreaded doing because I didn't want

strangers approaching me in the street with indecent proposals
– but that didn't happen. The show was humorous and funny
and that's what I experienced on the street: people having a
great laugh, talking about their private lives. The show brought
an openness which I respected in everyone I worked with. Then
I was lucky enough to move on to present a show about feminist
theology, a programme about how organised religion and its
historical documentation have marginalised women and how
wrong that has been.

Working with such a wide spectrum of subject matters has
been more rewarding than anything else in my life; in many
ways diversity keeps me sane. Another reason I am much
happier is because my attitude to work has changed. I've learned
that I need to be constantly occupied; I'm not a person to be left
to my own devices. But whereas in the beginning my work was
aimed at achieving maximum attention, now it's more of a
process of discovery that's almost sacredly private. Knowledge
has become gold. I leapt to fame with very little technical
experience. One day it was poverty and stage school, the next I
was in a place it takes many people a lifetime to reach. For me
the last decade has been about laying foundations, solid foundations, which I never had time to do in the past. I've learned
techniques that I never had to learn before, when I just used to
rely on youthful energy to get me by. But technique is a
monolithic strength to older generations. It's our weapon against
ageism, which is the next battle I'm going to fight with a passion.

Towards the end of the nineties, I was touring *The Live Bed
Show* with Joe McGann, working with Arthur Smith, the writer.
The play, about the complexities of a sexual relationship, all
took place in bed. It was nothing but a scream. Working in a
two-hander is about creating textures. You don't have an
ensemble around you; the audience have to listen to just two
voices throughout the night performance. One great thing about
doing comedy with Joe McGann is that he's six foot three and
I'm about five foot, a comical sight in itself. Joe was a generous
actor in that his comic timing is close to perfect, and I had to
learn all about that – I had only done Shakespearean comedy in
the past. It's very hard to muck up Shakespeare's timing. With
modern dialogue, Arthur Smith's dialogue, it's important that
there's some technique in place. As always with comedy, you

don't get the laugh in the same places every night. Sometimes a line that's usually guaranteed a laugh won't get any response at all – and that's to do not so much with timing as regional differences. The joy of theatre is that everywhere you go you get a completely different reaction from the audience.

It was while I was on tour with Joe McGann in Cheltenham that I found my parents' house at last. I'd heard that there was a cottage for sale in my favourite village in England, on the River Avon close to Evesham. I zoomed off from the theatre in my car, got the estate agent to let me into the house, bought it on the spot, and so achieved the main dream of the whole of my working career – to get Mum and Dad out of the city. That made the end of the nineties near perfect for me. It wasn't quite as easy or as simple as that, believe me – anyone who's tried to move their parents knows the trials and tribulations that come with doing it. But once my parents were in, I knew their future was safe.

Having finished *The Live Bed Show* I set off on my travels, working for *Holiday*, the BBC holiday programme. I was in a different country every week – a lifestyle that suited me ideally. I'd often lived out of a suitcase and had a great love for discarding things. There's no room for accumulation of possessions when you're constantly on the move. I suppose I'm addicted to airport life. I would occasionally nip back to England or Ireland when I was lucky enough to have a part in a feature film. Then I'd be off, across the world again, to make a holiday programme in, say, Malaysia. Robert and I have always been used to meeting up whenever it's convenient, wherever we are in the world, so this wasn't a problem.

By the beginning of 1999, I was feeling truly at ease with my life, which had found a balance and a reliable pattern that worked for me. At last I felt I was going to move into the new millennium knowing who, what and where I was. For the first time I had a sense of security. Who'd have thought you could hit forty and be happy, but I'd never felt better about things.

Then I got a phone call that turned everything upside down. My best friend, my neighbour, rang to say that CNN had called her direct. Why her, how they found her, who knows. They wanted to know how I felt about Jill Dando being killed. Jill and I shared an office; we were both managed by John Roseman, and were both so inundated with fan mail that we hired a secretary together. I'd seen Jill only the other week for her leaving party from the holiday programme. I said to my friend, 'I'm sorry, this isn't funny, it's a hoax, tell them to bugger off.' But my friend insisted, 'No, I think she's been hit by a car, she's been killed.' I burst into tears and I ran to the television, put on the teletext and there it was. Jill Dando had been shot. I phoned the office but everyone was in tears. No one could get any words out. Alison, who looked after both Jill and me, was inconsolable. She'd only recently spoken to Jill on her mobile and just couldn't fathom what was going on.

My heart goes out to everyone who has been affected by Jill's death. It certainly affected me very badly – so badly that Robert and I decided it was time to leave Reddish House. The parish council had made our lives difficult ever since we'd moved there, and when we put in a request to make the property more secure because of the problems with stalkers, the request was denied. In the light of Jill's death we were left no choice but to leave for more secure surroundings.

By the middle of 1999 my life had changed beyond recognition. I'd moved to Glasgow for three months to shoot *My Barmy Aunt Boomerang*, a children's drama for BBC1. That offered some stability and great friendship. Glasgow is my kind of town, full of my kind of people, and the BBC were fantastic about security. Being in Glasgow allowed me some kind of anonymity. The Glaswegians are wonderfully gregarious people, but they don't point in your face and tell you you're Toyah Willcox. They just give you a wink and walk on by.

I didn't know Jill terribly well on a personal level, but on a professional level I knew her very well. Her life was just becoming everything she wished for: she'd found her partner, Alan Farthing; they were about to be married; her work was exactly what she wanted it to be. I'd never seen her happier. It was as if the stars, the whole universe, had conspired to make her life perfect – and then someone just took it away. This profoundly troubled me. I spent the rest of the year reasoning with God as to why nothing is allowed to be perfect.

I believe one great gift we are given in life is the ability to evolve. Our spirits can evolve. We can evolve as personalities, as people. I'm certain that nothing ever really dies. Instead, we transcend into a different life experience, and every life is important in that every living thing leaves behind the consequences of its existence. So let those consequences be light, happiness and joy, because the emotional qualities those bring are what leads us closer to our God. I am pantheistic; I think everything is God. The highest form of God must be joy, because it is such a healing experience. But God has proved to me that he has both light and darkness, and in my life, many of the best lessons have come from His darkness. Pain is an extraordinary experience, whether it's physical or emotional. I now see both kinds as a gift to creativity. Both are spurs to drive us forward, not only as individuals but as a race. Dare I say, my soul is only truly alive when facing adversity. And yes, I do prefer to be comfortable and on a pedestal, admired, looked up to, but nothing really happens once you're up there. I'm only half-way through my life and I'll be damned if I'm going to lie down and let the next forty years just pass me by. I don't think I'm any different from anyone else in that.

The greatest currency anyone in middle age can offer society is their life experience.